PRAISE FOR *JEFFERSON'S WHITE HOUSE: MONTICELLO ON THE POTOMAC*

"This well-researched and colorfully written book deftly humanizes Jefferson and reveals the traits that endeared him to family and friends and disarmed potential political enemies. It is a significant contribution to Jefferson scholarship."—**John Boles, author of *Jefferson: Architect of American Liberty***

"*Jefferson's White House* vividly captures the third president's time in America's most iconic home. James B. Conroy goes into incredible architectural and aesthetic detail, highlighting not only how Jefferson understood and used these spaces to project his political and ideological beliefs, but also how visitors, dignitaries, peers, and enslaved persons experienced them firsthand. For anyone interested in Jefferson's presidency and the relationship between politics and place, this is a must-read."—**Matthew Costello, assistant director of the David M. Rubenstein National Center for White House History, White House Historical Association**

"*Jefferson's White House* is an invaluable contribution to our understanding of a controversial figure at a critical time in the new American nation's history. By focusing on the third president's ongoing efforts to transform an unfinished house into a home, James B. Conroy brings the place and the people who lived, worked, and visited there to fascinating life. His portrait of Jefferson as genial host, partisan politician, family man and friend, employer, and slave owner is sympathetic yet unsparing, making a complex character comprehensible to contemporary readers. An ambitious, enlightening, and brilliantly realized project."—**Peter S. Onuf, Thomas Jefferson Professor of History Emeritus, University of Virginia, and coauthor of *"Most Blessed of the Patriarchs": Thomas Jefferson and the Empire of the Imagination***

"*Jefferson's White House* opens the door to an amazing world. One can feel from the first pages the force of Jefferson's determination to create a truly democratic space in that elegant, unfinished house, making dinner guests fresh from the wilderness the equals of the British ambassador. The reader meets the fascinating collection of people who crowded his presidency, while Jefferson is discovered as he wished to present himself: leading the emerging American democracy, but—consistent with his hallmark of equality—also revealing his flaws. Conroy gives us a true and unvarnished portrait of this controversial man, totally at home in the lovely Irish-Palladian white palace set in the mud and muck of the bucolic capital."—**Patrick Phillips-Schrock, author of *The White House: An Illustrated Architectural History***

"James B. Conroy is a gifted writer and historian. There is something almost magical about the way he transports us back into the world of Thomas Jefferson by re-creating, through telling detail, the President's House as it was in the beginning, new and raw but elegant and worldly, as contradictory as its brilliant occupant."—**Evan Thomas, historian, journalist, and best-selling author of *First: Sandra Day O'Connor***

"In his engaging narrative, Conroy surrounds his pivotal figure, Thomas Jefferson, with the vivid characters that formed the presidential sphere from political friends, foes, and family members to the free and enslaved staff that insured the President's House functioned properly. A strength of the book is the ample number of direct quotations from this wide array of characters, evincing the research that supports this compelling story of Jefferson and his use of the presidential mansion to promote his ideas of true republicanism."—**G. S. Wilson, author of *Jefferson on Display: Attire, Etiquette, and the Art of Presentation***

JEFFERSON'S WHITE HOUSE

JEFFERSON'S WHITE HOUSE

MONTICELLO ON THE POTOMAC

James B. Conroy

ROWMAN & LITTLEFIELD
Lanham • Boulder • New York • London

Published by Rowman & Littlefield
An imprint of The Rowman & Littlefield Publishing Group, Inc.
4501 Forbes Boulevard, Suite 200, Lanham, Maryland 20706
www.rowman.com

6 Tinworth Street, London, SE11 5AL, United Kingdom

Distributed by NATIONAL BOOK NETWORK

British Library Cataloguing in Publication Information Available

Library of Congress Cataloging-in-Publication Data

Names: Conroy, James B., author.
Title: Jefferson's White House : Monticello on the Potomac / James B. Conroy.
Description: Lanham : Rowman & Littlefield, 2019. | Includes bibliographical references.
Identifiers: LCCN 2019014316 (print) | LCCN 2019015443 (ebook) | ISBN 9781538108475 (Electronic) | ISBN 9781538108468 (cloth : alk. paper)
Subjects: LCSH: Jefferson, Thomas, 1743-1826. | Jefferson, Thomas, 1743-1826—Homes and haunts—Washington (D.C.) | Presidents—United States—Biography. | White House (Washington, D.C.)—History—19th century. | Washington (D.C.)—History—19th century. | United States—Politics and government—1801-1809.
Classification: LCC E331 (ebook) | LCC E331 .C73 2019 (print) | DDC 973.4/6092 [B]—dc23
LC record available at https://lccn.loc.gov/2019014316

∞™ The paper used in this publication meets the minimum requirements of American National Standard for Information Sciences—Permanence of Paper for Printed Library Materials, ANSI/NISO Z39.48-1992.

For Mira Ling

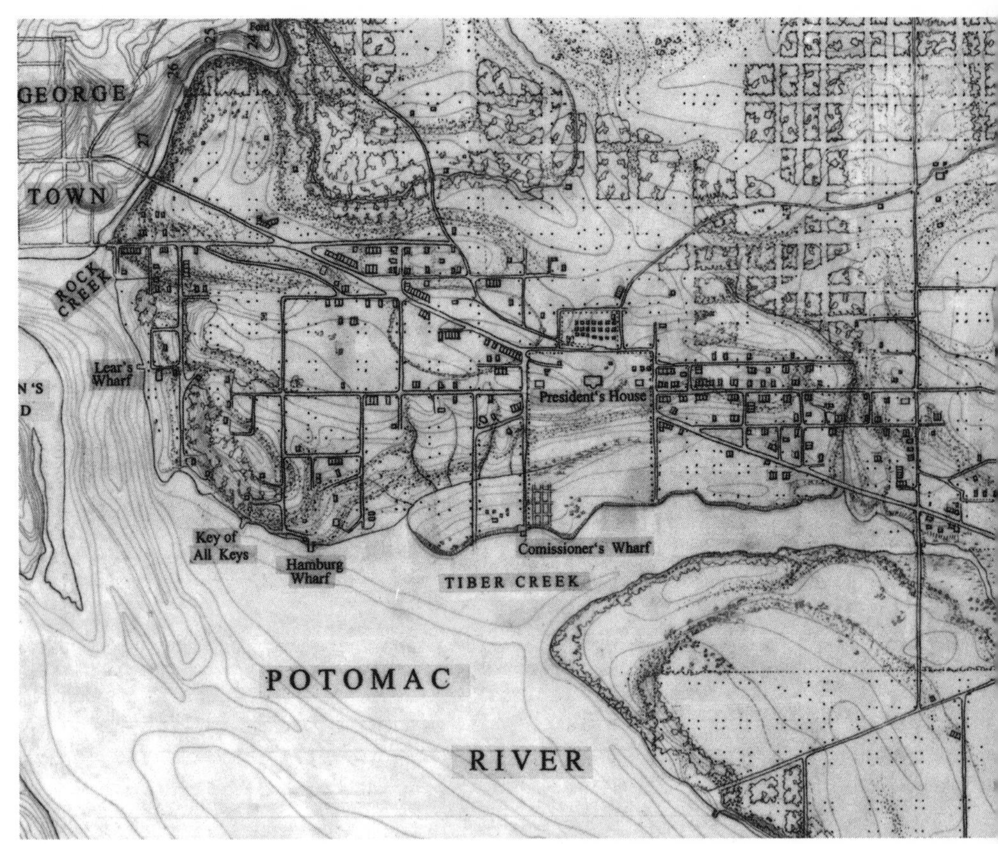

Re-created map of Washington City in 1801, with unbuilt streets shown as dots and woods covering future streets shown with trees. *Don A. Hawkins*

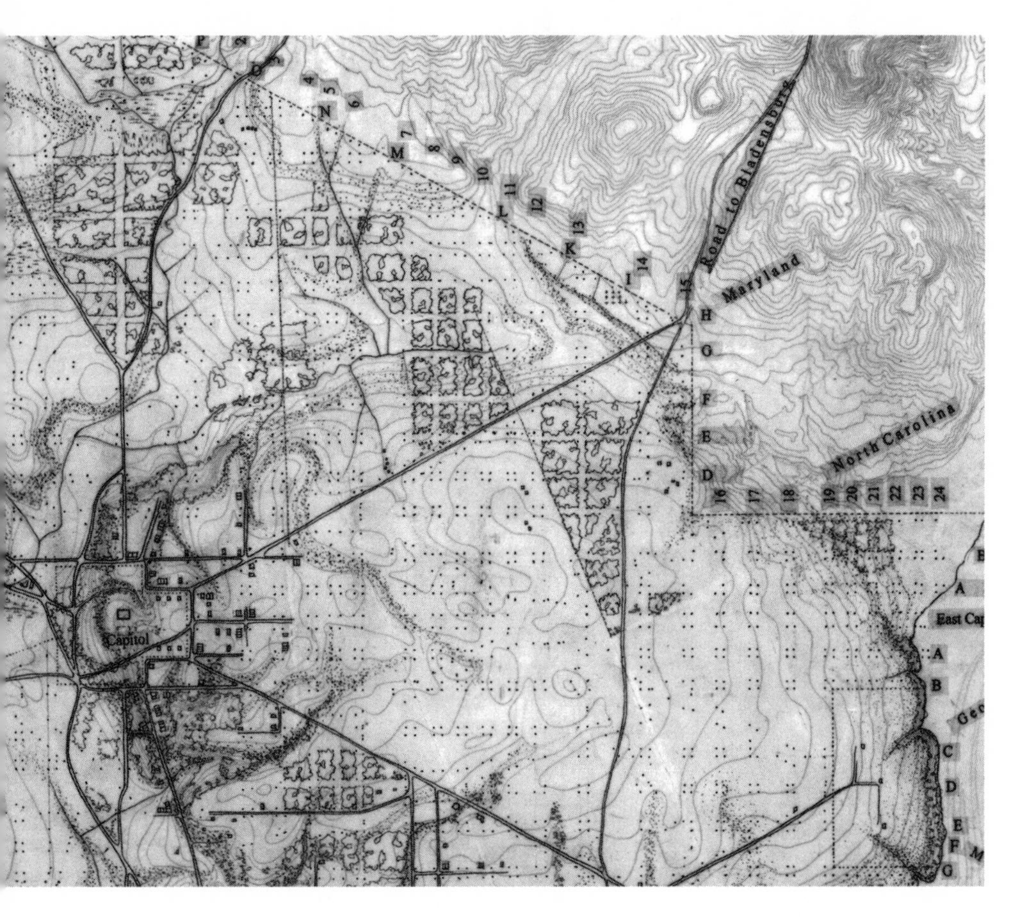
Road to Bladensburg
Maryland
North Carolina
Capitol
East Cap

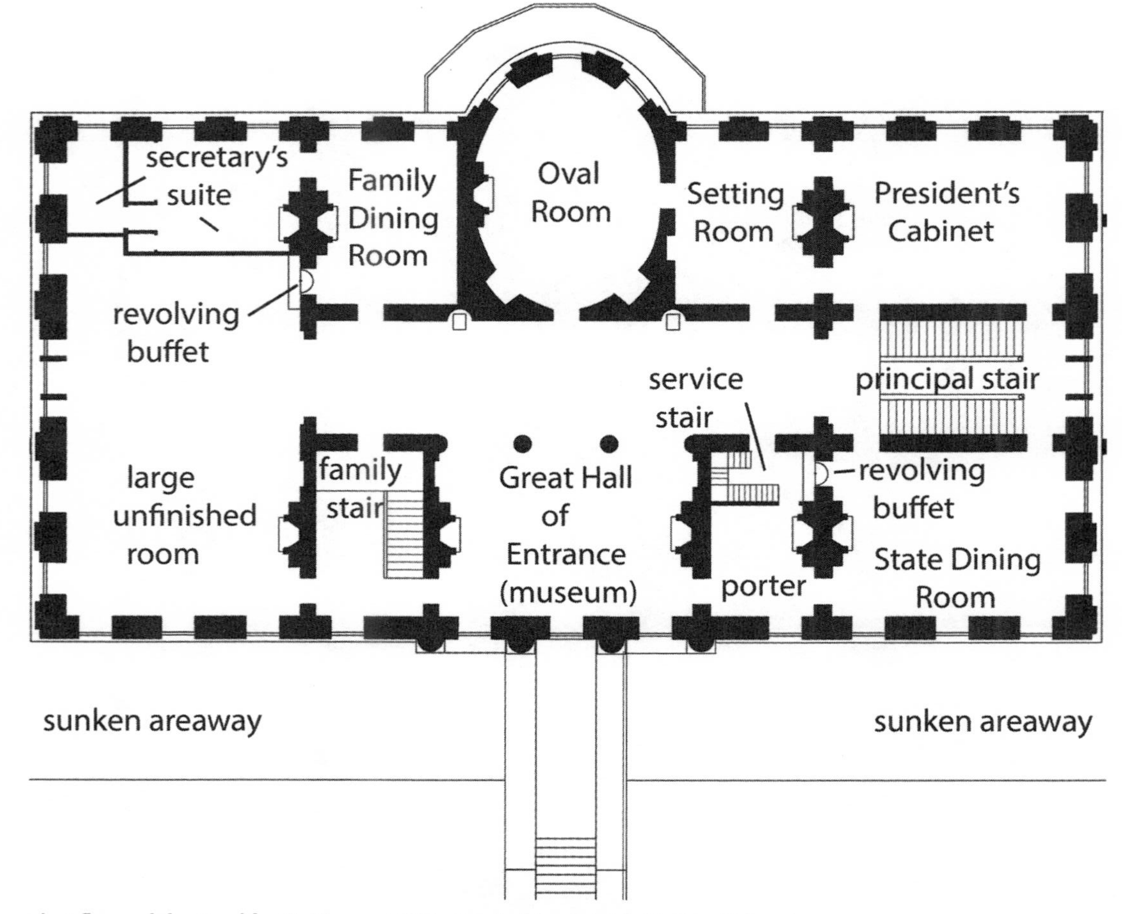

First floor of the President's House, 1808. ***Created by Patrick Phillips-Schrock***

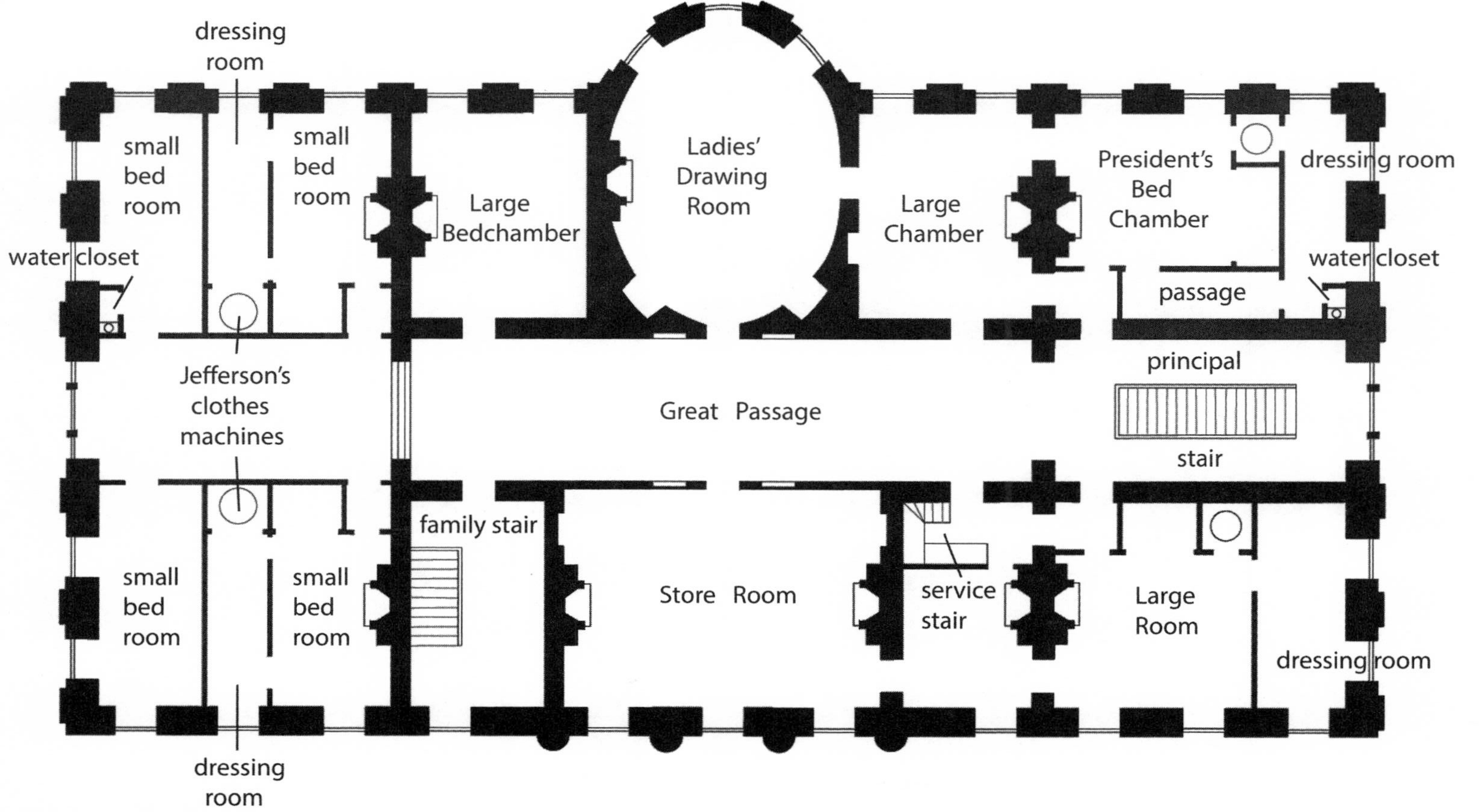

Second floor of the President's House, 1808. ***Created by Patrick Phillips-Schrock***

CONTENTS

PROLOGUE

On a cold December day in 1804, a young British diplomat, quick with a pointed thought and new to his post in America, sent a letter to his stylish mother, the daughter of an earl and a longtime guest of the Duke and Duchess of Devonshire. He was glad to let her know he was safe in Washington City, "but such a place," he wrote, "you can have no imagination of it."

Steeped in the Enlightenment at Oxford, London, Paris, and Berlin, fresh from the Kingdom of Naples, and fully unprepared for the strange Yankee capital in the woods, Augustus John Foster had just been presented at the President's House, a magnificent Georgian mansion on a frozen field of weeds enclosed by a split rail fence. The house was a work of art. A plain New Hampshire senator had called the rustic fence "unfit for a decent barnyard." A picture book village of neat homes and shops was spreading east and west of the great white house and its weeds, with little to the north but played out grain and tobacco fields and ancient, sunless woods. To the south there was nothing at all but the wide Potomac River, its tributary streams, a freshwater wharf, and a vast malarial marsh. Conceived in 1790 in a dodgy political deal and christened in 1800, the infant capital of the United States was a space chopped out of nowhere, a place, a novelist wrote, "where frogs make love in a most sonorous and exquisite strain, and bellow forth their attachments as if they were determined to make no secret of it."

The land between the President's House and the Capitol Hill was as wild as Kentucky, a travel book said, except that the soil was no good. On the ride into town on the Baltimore stage, a ten-hour trek through a forest, you passed the occasional hut and bounced and pitched for miles on a bad dirt road without catching sight of a soul. Many weary passengers got out at an open space, asked how far they were from Washington City, and were told that they were in it.

Few Americans and fewer Europeans who did not have to go there did. So poor were the roads in and out of the place that the people's representatives risked broken wheels and bones on their way to and from their posts. On the three-day expedition from Philadelphia, from which the capital had been moved in 1800, coachmen would shout to their passengers to lean left or right as they dodged rocks and pits. From many legislators' homes, the ride in a jolting stage, elbow to elbow and knee to knee with lightly bathed companions, took a week over unpaved roads and unbridged streams that cut the path in two. When a river could be crossed at all, depending on the rains, the driver lashed his horses through the current and prayed for good footing. At the Bladensburg Run on the outskirts of Washington City, a former senator was told he was lucky that the water only washed the horses' bellies. As the coachman urged them across, he pointed under the wheels to the spot where a team had drowned and consoled his wide-eyed client with a nod toward the tree where "all the passengers *but one* were saved. Whether that one was gouty or not," the senator wrote, "I did not inquire."

On the bruising ride from anywhere, the typical accommodation offered miserable food and a sketchy bed often shared with a new associate. In response to a complaint, the keeper of a Charlottesville inn defended its dirty sheets "on account of the number who had slept in them." To keep a stranger out of his bed, a Mr. Turpin falsely claimed he had the itch, an affliction spread by lice, but the man climbed in and gave Turpin the itch.

A common first impression on arrival in Washington City was a disorienting sense of oddity. The palatial President's House and the less than half-built Capitol stood on rough dirt roads with nothing much else around but striking natural beauty, piles of spoil and debris, and what Foster dismissed as "a heap of human abodes calling itself a city." The banks of the Potomac had been thick for a thousand years with sweeping drifts of wildflowers, azaleas, and fragrant wild grapes, and the view from the hills was bucolic. Through much of the so-called city ran a wandering country stream filled with perch, shad, and herring, lined by graceful sycamores with their roots intertwined on its banks "in which turtles concealed their nests." The city fathers called it the Tiber, and it widened beneath the President's House on its way to the Potomac. Hiking down houseless roads on a hot summer's walk in 1803, an English writer cooled off in the woods along the Tiber, a name too portentous to believe. When a group of black children came along to fill pitchers and pails, he asked a little boy what the stream was called. "Goose Creek," the boy replied. "Where is the Tiber?" the Englishman asked. The boy had never heard of it.

Scornful English wit was common in Washington City, but George III's thin-skinned minister to the United States, regrettably named Anthony Merry, had no sense of humor at all, and Merry called the American capital "a space of wild country, six miles square." Most of its lettered or numbered streets and crosscutting avenues named for the seventeen states existed only on maps or as stump-studded swaths through the fields. The rest, Merry said, were unspeakable in winter and dangerous anytime. Apart from the Pennsylvania Avenue, newly graveled between the Capitol and the President's House, none of the streets were paved, none of them were lit, and all of them were laced with tooth-breaking holes. After a week of heavy rain, several men caught on the flash-flooded avenue "would have gone in the river if they had not grabbed onto some tree branches near Young's house and been rescued by some horsemen."

Augustus Foster, Anthony Merry's only aide, unfailingly polite, unimpressed as a rule with Americans, and contemptuous of democracy, looked hard at Washington City with fresh foreign eyes. Just turned twenty-four, raised in Ireland on his father's estate, educated at Oxford, groomed in London by his fashionable mother, at ease since his teens in the best European society, he had chatted with the likes of Goethe, Schiller, Napoleon, and his sidewinding foreign minister, Charles Maurice de Talleyrand-Périgord, more frugally known as Talleyrand, "a shocking ugly fellow," Foster had found him to be. But the young man found himself now "a sad distance to be at from all the civilized world" with "an immense swell of sea between me and it."

For Foster's presentation to the president, he and Merry came by carriage in the cold from their K Street embassy, a barely habitable brick shell compared to what they were used to. Having safely reached the President's House, they crossed the wooden ramp to its door, sheltered by nothing at all, much less by a pillared portico, and were shown to an elegant room with a neoclassical frieze along the edge of its double height ceiling, furnished in the style of Louis XVI. The pastoral view was lovely, but for the dug up grounds and the workmen's sheds. After a little while, a door opened suddenly and Thomas Jefferson walked in.

Smiling kindly at his British guests, strikingly tall at six feet two and a half, youthfully fit at sixty-one, world famous since his early thirties, the president wore his full head of copper-gray hair loose over the ears and longish in the back, "neglected," Foster thought, at a time when younger men were cutting theirs and fastidious older men tied their queues with black silk ribbons. A hot

Sketch of Thomas Jefferson by Benjamin Latrobe, 1802.
Maryland Historical Society

revolutionary in 1776 when he drafted a screed against their king, Jefferson welcomed his envoys now with the poise of a born aristocrat in the clothes of a simple farmer on a Sunday in his pew. In this there was no surprise, for no one knew better than Merry that the president "affected to despise dress." His garments were chosen for comfort alone, insulation in a poorly heated house. Foster considered them amusing enough to record—an unremarkable blue coat; a waistcoat of rough gray wool with a dated red vest lapping underneath; old fashioned green velveteen knee britches, pearl buttoned above the calf where silver buckles should be; a tradesman's spun yarn stockings over slippers down at the heels.

He "behaved very civilly to me in general," Foster told his mother, but with no hint of ceremony. "He thrust out his hand to me, as he does to everybody, and desired me to sit down. Luckily for me I have been in Turkey and am quite at home in this primeval simplicity of manners." Whatever they thought of his politics, nearly everyone agreed with a book dealer named Whitcomb that Jefferson was invincibly likeable face-to-face. Putting his guests at ease from the moment he walked in, he spoke with a gentle voice in an animated, effortless mix of casual Virginia gentry, European chic, and dry wit. Having lived for five years in Paris, "he shrugs his shoulders when talking," Whitcomb said, "has much of the Frenchman," and he liked to chat lounging on one hip. As he chatted with the king's men now, he spoke of Samuel Chase, an instinctively waspish signer of the Declaration of Independence and a justice of the Supreme Court about to face an impeachment trial for shameless partisanship on the bench. Chase's acquaintance, the president said, was best left alone. Then he turned to the joy of bare feet. He stripped and bathed his feet several times a day, he said, "in order to keep off colds," and "expressed his wonder that feet were not as often washed as hands." Looking back when he knew the president well, Foster suspected he would have endorsed "a still greater degree of nakedness" if he could, "so fond was he of leaving nature as unconfined as possible in all her works."

Foster wrote no more of his first taste of Thomas Jefferson, but he never stopped abusing Washington City: "It is an absolute sepulcher, this hole." With a social life spoiled by the miserable roads and carriages, one of which overturned and dumped him in a gully, he was wasting life's best years, he wrote, with "absolutely nothing, not even books to be had. I shall forget almost how to be cheerful in this sink of imagination." In Foster's expert view, wit was neither spoken nor understood in Washington City, and the arts were next to unknown, fixed as the locals were on politics and money.

There were so few buildings in town that none of them had a street number or needed one. It was enough to post a notice that a house for sale on Delaware Avenue could be found near the one Mr. Carroll owned, rented to Mr. Dalton across the street from General Dearborn. In the capital of the United States, there was not so much as a public garden, a puzzling thing in a place overrun with green. Even for Jefferson, a country boy hostile to cities on paper and fond of them on foot, there was too much rudely fenced land "worn down with Indian corn." Gentlemen carried sticks to pole their way through the mud and fend off feral dogs. Foster complained about speculators who bet their money on vacant lots and left them to crack in the sun, "so that the whole place has a deserted dry appearance." After several months, he wondered how Merry and his wife bore "the horrors of a Washington residence. I admire at my own endurance of it."

Few Americans were as snide as that, except for the rare sophisticate. A simple New England senator who had never been to London saw his country's infant capital as the very sort of place he had known all his life, "a little village in the midst of the woods." It was more like four separate villages than one, and it was risky to travel between them on roads thick with mud when wet, cut by rain-carved ravines when dry. The bridges over streams were laid with loose planks, and there was no bridge at all for miles up the Potomac. Directly from Washington City, its riverfront neighbor Alexandria could only be reached by boat or ferry.

There was good snipe and partridge hunting on the slopes of the Capitol Hill, whose crest held the smallest village, just a few simple buildings, mostly brick, scattered around a construction site. The Capitol's Senate wing was not quite finished, its House wing had barely risen off the ground, and its dome existed only on paper. Both houses of Congress met in the usable wing, which reminded a Maryland farmer of "one of our Dutch barns, with an end blown down and the roof off." Some muddy-booted congressmen started the day with a bird gun and a spaniel and strolled into the chamber with their hats on their heads and their dogs at their heels. Not a single senator or congressman owned a house in Washington City, which they occupied less than four months a year. A handful rented separate lodgings, and the rest lived in boardinghouses near the Capitol, the lot of them served by "one tailor, one shoemaker, one printer, a washing woman, a grocery shop, a pamphlets and stationery shop, a small dry goods shop, and an oyster house."

Washington's second little community had grown up around the Navy Yard on the Eastern Branch of the Potomac, overlooked by "a very large but perfectly empty warehouse." Most of the navy's workforce and some officers lived there, a place known for "tippling shops and houses of rendezvous for sailors and their doxies, with a number of the lowest orders of traders."

It was fashionable to live and shop in the third, largest village, which had grown up around the President's House. Advertisements for nice new homes often noted their proximity to the grandest house in America, which was only partly habitable. A dozen years after its cornerstone was laid, just a few of its thirty-six rooms were finished. Craftsmen and unskilled laborers were always at work on the house and its grounds, painting or gilding moldings; varnishing forty-three mahogany doors; crafting ornamental plaster pediments over the doors and classical friezes along the edge of the ceilings; hauling away debris; digging and walling two wells; nailing up lathing for ceilings and walls; troweling on a skillful mix of water, plaster of Paris, sifted sand, pulverized lime, beeswax, olive oil, and hog bristles bought by the keg.

Two identical executive office buildings of elegant stone-trimmed brick stood 450 feet from either end of the President's House on attractive white stone bases rising to a tall man's height, complementing the whitewashed mansion—the Treasury Department's building to the east, the State, War, and Navy Departments tripling up in its twin to the west, where Secretary of State James Madison received foreign ministers in a commonplace room. Nothing connected the executive buildings to the President's House but footpaths worn through the weeds, with mud so thick when it rained that the superintendent of the District of Columbia thought a simple bluestone path would make a reasonably frugal accommodation for the president, his executive council—sometimes called his cabinet, English-style—and their callers.

On the other side of the rutted dirt road that passed in front of the President's House, the President's Square had been part of the mansion's grounds until Jefferson had it ceded to the city, too ostentatious for a republican front yard. Now it was a vacant lot, recently cleared of workmen's shacks, as empty as a pasture and half as neat. Rhodes Tavern and a handful of common buildings stood around its rim with unfilled blanks in between.

Not far west of the President's House on the Pennsylvania Avenue stood the Seven Buildings, a row of connected brick houses between Nineteenth and Twentieth Streets and a similar block, called the Six Buildings, between Twenty-First and Twenty-Second. The adjacency was defensive, the city having burglars but no police. Beyond them was a half mile of nothing on the way to the M Street bridge, raised for masted vessels running up and down Rock Creek past George Town, sometimes written as Georgetown and half a century older than the rest of Washington City. Abigail Adams had called it in 1800 "the very dirtyest hole I ever saw for a place of any trade or respectability of inhabitants"; but by 1804 it was known for its shops, a decent grocery where the president's staff bought his vegetables and meats, and a chance to buy a look at the odd itinerant elephant. The Catholic College of George Town, founded in 1789, overlooked the Potomac in a fine brick building on high ground. "It appears that the situation is very healthy," a man of science would soon suggest, for no student had yet died there.

Capital society, "determined rather than brilliant," was composed of the ranking local families, foreign diplomats, senior military officers, the cabinet, and the leading senators and congressmen of the day, almost all of whom left their wives at home, producing a shortage of couples and female company. During the Revolution, America's political and social paragons had generally been one and the same, gentry, by and large, similar in dress and manners and led by extraordinary men, "an assembly of demigods" Jefferson called them in 1787. Assembled in Washington City in 1804, congressmen and senators varied widely in taste and talent. A noble *émigrée* who had fled the French Revolution found society "very inferior just now!" The cabinet and most of Congress were Jefferson men, "and for the most part people of low extraction," leaving her no option but to "employ my leisure hours in reading."

For less selective folk, there were daytime visits; dinner parties followed by music, cards, or chess; afternoon teas for the ladies; evening billiards for the gentlemen; modest balls in winter; the occasional visitor from civilization; and little by way of scandal, though Vice President Aaron Burr, a small, polished man with magnetic eyes, had lately made a splash by killing Alexander Hamilton.

Early in Jefferson's presidency, two brick houses had been put up for sale "on the Pennsylvania Avenue near the President's House" with attractive parlors, fenced-in yards, walkways paved to the street, and flexible terms: "A family of slaves will be taken in part payment, or lots will be exchanged for slaves." Several slave pens thrived in the capital of American liberty, where men, women, and children were bought, sold, and stored. Slaves led in chains through the streets were a novelty for many tourists and even shamed a few.

There was not much else to see but the picturesque falls above Georgetown, two thriving garden nurseries, the jail's public whipping post and pillory, Alexandria's riverfront wharves, miles of wilderness in every direction, and the foul-smelling marsh that spread from the Potomac to the foot of the Capitol Hill to the lowlands below the President's House, spawning plagues of mosquitoes in summer and adhesive mud all year, which ran into the streets and sucked the shoes from pedestrians. And "there sits the President," a Philadelphian said, "like a pelican in the wilderness."

* * *

For a bitter minority in Congress and many outraged Americans, the President's House was enemy ground. Ten years earlier, during Washington's first term, two hostile parties had formed to contest the very nature of the United States, still thinly rooted in democracy. Broadly speaking, the elitist, strong government Federalists had a moderate wing led by John Adams and a right wing in Hamilton's orbit. Jefferson led the populist, small-government Democratic-Republicans, who typically called themselves Republicans, their original name, having added Democratic when the Federalists made it an epithet. In American political history, no fiercer fight has been waged. In the end it cost Hamilton his life. In 1794, a year after he resigned from Washington's Federalist cabinet as secretary of state, Jefferson told a friend that the government's suppressions of liberty had "come upon us a full century earlier than I expected." Four years later, he privately called the Adams administration "a reign of witches." In 1803, Senator Timothy Pickering, a hawk-faced, permanently angry Federalist from Salem, Massachusetts (aptly enough), called Jefferson "one of the worst men who ever directed the affairs of a free country," sullied by "the little wretched, contemptible principles" of liberal democracy, free thought, and social leveling.

As Jefferson sized them up, the Federalists had betrayed the Revolution to match "their darling model the English government." In essence they believed in a powerful chief executive and a dominant federal government protective of wealth, manufacturing, commerce, and cheap labor; hostility to revolutionary France; alignment with aristocratic Britain; a dread of "excessive democracy"; and a formidable army and navy, not only to repel invaders and protect foreign trade but also to keep order at home. The Federalist strongholds were New England, merchant cities elsewhere, and conservative Southern enclaves. The pillars of their support were wealthy businessmen, political and social conservatives, and influential Protestant clergy who kept their flocks in fear of God and Thomas Jefferson.

The Republicans took the opposite view on each of the foregoing points, shaped by a vision of a lean, sharply limited federal government deferential to the states, a thoroughgoing democracy, and a simple, egalitarian, agriculturally based society in which the people held power, by which they meant the white middle class. The party was strong in the South, largely led by Virginians, with strength in New York and Pennsylvania and a base composed of landowners, farmers, craftsmen, recent immigrants, and tradesmen. Jefferson was wary of commerce. "He told me more than once," Augustus Foster said, "that he wished the United States had never possessed a ship." Ironically enough, many of the party's leaders owned slaves, but at small political cost. At no time in anyone's presidency—Washington's, Adams's, or Jefferson's—had slavery been an issue on the national stage, and human rights were tightly construed. Only three states gave the vote to all adult white males; none gave it to women; and people of both genders and all races were whipped for minor crimes, as were soldiers and sailors of the armed forces of the United States.

In 1776, Jefferson had composed at the age of thirty-three the Declaration of Independence and a list of the 117 "souls in my family"—his wife and his child, his employees and their dependents, and the eighty-three men, women, and children he enslaved, most of them inherited. Their number expanded over time, and all but the old, the very young, and the ones trained in skilled occupations were compelled to hard labor. Basic food, shelter, clothing, and medical care were provided to them all, with incentives for good work, opportunities to earn small sums of cash and advance within the system, and limited freedom of movement for trusted individuals. Despite Jefferson's criteria for hiring overseers—"I love industry and abhor severity"—some of his slaves were whipped with his knowledge and consent for repeated attempts to free themselves and other intolerable crimes. They were all created equal to their fellow men and women and endowed by their Creator with certain unalienable rights, including liberty and the pursuit of happiness, which he alienated in pursuit of his own.

In the only book he wrote, *Notes on the State of Virginia*, published in 1785, he confessed "a suspicion only" that blacks were inferior to whites, a bigotry widely shared, and without the equivocation. He later wrote he hoped for its "complete refutation," for with people trapped in slavery, "opportunities for the development of their genius were not favorable and those of exercising it still less so." On views such as these, not much separated North from South. Slavery was rife in the South and not yet dead in the North. The Bostonian John Hancock and the Pennsylvanian Benjamin Franklin had owned slaves. So had Abigail Adams's father. Many Northerners still did. Abraham Lincoln's future secretary of state William Seward was growing up with them at home in New York. Far more unusually in his time and place, Jefferson had tried to chip away at slavery in Virginia's courts and legislature, and his draft of the Declaration of Independence excoriated it before his peers took the passage out. "The whole commerce between master and slave," he publicly confessed in his book, was "unremitting despotism on the one part and degrading submissions on the other. Our children see this, and learn to imitate it," corrupting master and child. "I tremble for my country when I reflect that God is just, and his justice cannot sleep forever." An explosion was inevitable, "and the Almighty has no attribute which can take side with us in such a conflict."

Having pushed against slavery in his youth, he had simply given up in middle age, and left its extirpation to the next generation, convinced that his own had a "wolf by the ear," unable to hold on or to safely let go. In the end it took two generations and a civil war. Ashamed, in his words, of the "hideous blot" of slavery, he was neither a hero nor a villain in the long, sordid tale of its "moral and political depravity," not a hero because he did nothing heroic to attack it as president, not a villain because few of his peers did better. Every Founding Father who signed the Constitution signed slavery into the system; Northern shippers and merchants made fortunes exploiting it; and millions in the North and the rest of the Western world enjoyed without a qualm the cotton, tobacco, indigo, and sugar produced by slave labor, knowing they were doing it. A few members of Congress refused to dine at the President's House because Jefferson was hard on privilege and soft on democracy, not because he owned slaves, which no one seems to have mentioned as a cause to shun his table. Slavery was not a Southern sin. Slavery was an American sin, and British, French, and Spanish. Many congressmen and senators despised it, but none had done more to attack it than he, stung as he was by the truth of the charge that a slaveholding egalitarian was neck deep in hypocrisy.

For Jefferson, the centrally important question of his time was whether the American form of government would survive, led by the will of its citizens and guided by their interests, or degenerate into oligarchy, republican in name but ruled by the rich and a thought-controlling clergy. Behind a rhetorical facade, the opposing parties' zealots shared no vision of America itself. Partisans on both sides were fighting for its soul, despite their common cause in the Revolution, now receding into history. In the snake pit of Washington City, a senator's wife feared that hatred might "eventually destroy our republican form of government."

The Federalists called Jefferson a demagogue and his Republican partisans "Democrats," intending no compliment. Some called them Jacobins, the killers of the French Revolution, half expecting guillotines on the President's Square. A Federalist senator considered Napoleon's ambassador a war criminal with "a heart devoid of morals" who showed nonetheless the "decency & politeness to which many of our Democrats are strangers." Even a North Carolina Republican reproached himself for failing to constrain democracy, which had cost him his Senate seat. "This excess of liberty will prove the ruin of our Republic," he wrote, "as it has all who preceded us." The Republicans, in turn, cast the Federalists as aspiring dictators, tools of the rich and the Crown. Both parties saw the republic at risk from the other. So intense was the partisan divide that physicians in Philadelphia were split between a Republican treatment for yellow fever practiced by Jefferson's friend Dr. Benjamin Rush and a Federalist alternative endorsed by Hamilton. Decades later, an elderly Bostonian said of her youth, "I should as soon have expected to see a cow in a drawing room as a Jacobin."

A culture war raged beside the political battle. Jefferson was a child and a hero of the French Enlightenment, the father of freedom of religion as a tenet of American life, a world-renowned egalitarian, and a brilliant man of science, free thought, progress, and invention. Much of the Federalist elite admired none of these things. To them he was a godless innovator, a redundancy for many who could see their country changing. A rising crop of new young leaders equated religion with superstition in "the spring tide of infidelity," as a Federalist called it later. Cultural conservatives called it "French Infidelity," and it shocked them. Abigail Adams worried deeply about a growing impiety in America, "an alarming corruption of manners from the highest to the lowest ranks of society," and her troubled country's fate under a president "whose only religion is benevolence."

In 1741, when witch trials were a living memory, the flame-throwing Calvinist Jonathan Edwards had preached a horrifying sermon, "Sinners in the

Hands of an Angry God," that haunted New England's dreams. Four months after Jefferson's election, Edwards's grandson Theodore Dwight gave a speech in New Haven that followed the family tradition. The country was governed by knaves who would "force mankind back into a savage state" where marriage is rooted out; "our wives and daughters are thrown into the stews [a colorful word for brothels]; our children are cast into the world from the breast and forgotten; filial piety is extinguished, and our surnames, the only mark of distinction among families, are abolished. Can the imagination paint anything more dreadful on this side of hell?" With Jefferson in the President's House, Dwight and his ilk could not.

His brilliance they saw as dangerous. Quite apart from his primary authorship of the Declaration of Independence, Virginia's groundbreaking Statute for Religious Freedom, and a reformation of its laws protecting aristocracy, no living American matched the sweep of his achievements. A chaotic mix of currencies had hobbled the national economy until he designed in 1784 a system based on decimal fractions of a Spanish coin called the dollar. Recognized worldwide as a man of science as well as political theory, he made significant contributions to archaeology, entomology, zoology, botany, navigation, vaccination, and architecture, and contrived, among other new things that survived him by more than a century, an ingenious encoding device, the United States Senate's parliamentary procedure, the first wheeled threshing machine, and the first metric system, all before he was president. Taking stock of his life six months before his swearing in, he wrote himself a note: "I have sometimes wondered whether my country is better for my having lived at all. I do not know that it is." He had been "the instrument" of many good things, "but they would have been accomplished by others."

Senator Pickering, Salem's favorite son, called him the instrument of the devil, "a Parisian revolutionary monster, prating about humanity" and "his infidel and visionary schemes." With Jefferson in mind, the Reverend Jedediah Morse of Charlestown, Massachusetts, alerted the unwary to "the insidious encroachment of innovation, that evil and beguiling spirit which is now stalking to and fro through the earth, seeking whom he may destroy." Repulsed by unconventional thought if not by thought itself, men like Morse called Jefferson a "philosopher," perhaps not a sin per se, but a cultural degradation, for philosophy connoted science, skeptical inquiry, and deductive reasoning independent of Holy Writ. Thomas Moore, a celebrity Irish poet with an acquired English accent, thought the President's House too fine for "the philosophical humility of its present possessor, who inhabits but a corner of the mansion himself, and abandons the rest to a state of uncleanly desolation, which those who are not philosophers cannot look at without regret." Senator Pickering feared the President's House had become the unmoored vessel of "the moonshine philosopher of Monticello."

And so it had. When Jefferson the revolutionary theorist became Jefferson the chief executive, the government was scarcely twelve years old, divided on the wisdom of democracy itself, marooned in a distant capital not half-built, thin on norms and tradition. Jefferson had given up on the ideologues like Hamilton and Pickering who believed in an American plutocracy protected by law, a very limited sort of democracy, an alliance with Britain just short of reunion, stringent new constraints on immigrant voting, mass deportations, the suppression of vigorous dissent and "false" criticism of the president, and an army prepared to subdue it. The High Federalists they were called. Jefferson called them the incurables. If their hatred of him subsided, he wrote, "I should become suspicious to myself."

And yet he was sure that most of the Federalists in Congress, "the federal sect of republicans," as he liked to think they were, had simply lost their way, led astray by rabid leaders bent on authoritarian rule. Just before he took office, he told a friend he devoutly hoped they still embraced the Revolution and could be wooed back into the fold. Expecting a Parisian monster as they were, a merely moderate set of reforms would settle their nerves, and fellowship in the President's House would help heal the nation. "If we can once more get social intercourse restored to its pristine harmony," Jefferson wrote, "I shall believe we have not lived in vain."

AUTHOR'S NOTE

Thomas Jefferson was a tangled up mix of contradictions, a torrid revolutionary and a temperate head of state; a passionate egalitarian who owned slaves and hated slavery; a champion of the people wary of the common man; a patrician despised by his own privileged class. Two centuries after his time, it is fashionable to attack him with modern sensibilities and ample ammunition. But accurately portrayed as a shockingly brilliant, instinctively kind, irresistibly charismatic, sometimes disappointing, unevenly admirable human being who revered his country's principles and subdued his better instincts in complicity with its sins more often than conscience allowed, he was much like our other great presidents, let alone the rest of us who are not shockingly brilliant or irresistible. Judged against his founding peers in his own time and place, his contributions were second to none and his flaws on a par with theirs. Most important, perhaps, for our own troubled time, his vision of how a president can heal a divided nation and restore its aspirations shows us what is possible.

This book is about the White House in Jefferson's time, the people who passed through it, the village in which it stood, and the roundly imperfect genius who used it to resist plutocracy when the republic was new and at risk. Less is said here about his statecraft than his character; the house he transformed from a nearly barren shell to a magnificent salon in a wide spot in the wilderness; and the men, women, and children, high and low, slave and free, who came to know him there. What they saw and heard from Thomas Jefferson as a friend, an enemy, a leader, a host, an architect, a father, a grandfather, an employer, and an owner of human beings, sheds light on him and his time and more than a bit on ours.

To help re-create the look, sound, and feel of the house and its cast more than two hundred years ago, I have let its occupants and visitors speak freely, attractively or not, without twenty-first-century correction. Dolley Madison, for example, was "Mrs. Madison" to almost everyone, never "Madison," and sometimes a "lady," who referred to Native Americans as Indians, and so it is all written here. Also served up whole, often without instantaneous rebuke, is conduct, speech, and bigotry more disturbing than dated terminology and archaic forms of address. "Facts are stubborn things," John Adams famously said, and facts speak best for themselves.

A word should be said about the title of the book. The White House was the President's House in Jefferson's time, a house of whitewashed stone. In May of 1809, two months after he left it, his secretary of war called it "the white house," which had surely bubbled up before then. *Jefferson's White House* is a stretch nonetheless, but *Jefferson's President's House* would not have rolled off the tongue and might have caused confusion.

To save them from distractions, quotations may include corrected spelling, altered punctuation or capitalization and the like, but never with a change of meaning. When original irregularities are revealing, they are quoted as is. The flow of the book is broadly chronological, with occasional diversions to cover contiguous ground. Portraits of most of its characters can be found online.

Many people who are innocent of its faults deserve thanks for their roles in this book, starting with my family, here and gone, who encouraged me to love and write history; Alice Martell, the best literary agent in New York, who pushed me into the publishing world against its better judgment; and Janice Goldklang, who made an author of me. Many thanks go to Jon Sisk, my wise and patient editor and friend; Kate Powers, his able editorial assistant; Chelsea Panin, who stepped in when Kate moved up; Lara Hahn, the book's talented production editor; April LeHoullier, its meticulous copyeditor; and many helpful librarians like Emily Levine, Carolle Morini, and Mary Warnement at the Boston Athenaeum, my stunning second home. I am grateful to Joan Brancale, who painted the cover art. Lucia Stanton, Charles Cullen, and Gaye Wilson, accomplished figures in the world of Thomas Jefferson, read parts or all of the manuscript in various drafts and saved me from several embarrassments, the rest of which are my own. Their professional colleagues Peter Onuf, at the beginning, and John Ragosta, near the end, contributed helpful thoughts. The multitalented architectural historian Patrick Phillips-Schrock guided me through the President's House from the start, consulted on the cover, added striking illustrations, and carefully parsed a draft of the text. I owe him endless thanks.

Without my wife, Lynn Conroy, none of my books would have been written. I expect she would agree with a hostess of Jefferson's time who learned from hard experience that she would sooner have a raven in her house than an author.

1

IT WAS MORE THAN I EXPECTED

On Friday, December 12, 1800, the wind was blowing snow, rain, and hail into Washington City, postponing a sale of slaves, when Jefferson learned in a boardinghouse room that South Carolina had made him president and unseated John Adams. Apart from the private parlor where he greeted his many callers and played his discordant roles as Adams's vice president and the leader of his opposition, neither of which came with an office or a staff, Jefferson lived like the other lonely men at Conrad & McMunn's, just this side of a monastery, a fellow boarder said. Having little to do after hours on the barren Capitol Hill, the congressmen and senators who inhabited such places talked politics and dealt cards. Most lived two to a room, though some had separate quarters. A congressman from Connecticut was grateful for a separate bed.

Almost every boardinghouse was confined to men of the same party, usually the same region, and sometimes the same state, keeping Federalists and Republicans safe from one another and Northerners, Southerners, and Westerners apart. A Republican from Pennsylvania said a few other boarders drank, "but the majority drink naught but politics, and by not mixing with men of different or more moderate sentiments, they inflame one another." At Conrad & McMunn's, Jefferson lived with thirty other Republicans a short stroll away from the habitable wing of the Capitol at the corner of C Street and New Jersey Avenue Southeast, a steep and exceptionally poor dirt road, but the view looking west toward the President's House captured Washington City whole, from the hills above Georgetown to "the river and the heavens."

Washington in 1800, a wealthy Delaware congressman wrote, had nothing but the name of a city and next to no diversions. "An invitation to dinner costs you a ride of 6 or 8 miles, and the state of the roads obliging you to return before night, you have just time to swallow your meat." There were scarcely more than a thousand souls in residence, many of them enslaved. Almost half of the capital's three hundred dwellings were neat brick homes, but the rest were "miserable huts." The local entrepreneurs who expected this so-called city to be magnificent in time were thought to be deranged. "No stranger can be here a day and converse with the proprietors without conceiving himself in the company of crazy people."

At Conrad & McMunn's, dignity, taste, or both kept Jefferson out of the tavern when "The Learned Pig" selected lettered and numbered cards for the amusement of his admirers. In a big room called the Ordinary, Jefferson dined on whatever was served that day. Typical boardinghouse fare included good poultry, eggs, and mutton; mediocre beef; and the occasional vegetable. His colleagues had offered him the head of the table, closest to the fire. He insisted on taking the lowest, coldest seat, a gesture of republican humility, tactical or sincere. But his humble accommodations seemed about to improve. The story got around that when Adams called him down to the President's House and confronted him in a rage—"You have put me out! You have put me out!"—Jefferson reminded him that it was Adams who had helped design the system while his friend was a diplomat in Europe, and they parted in something like peace. Then the shocking news broke that Adams was out but Jefferson might not be in.

As the system then worked, both parties had run two candidates, the winner to be president and the second-place finisher vice president. The Republicans had planned to have one elector vote only for Jefferson and not for Aaron Burr, their vice presidential pick, but no one had made it happen, a gaffe of impressive proportions leaving both men tied with seventy-three votes to Adams's sixty-five and his running mate's sixty-four. The Constitution threw the tie to the outgoing House of Representatives and its Federalist majority, soon to be displaced. Everyone knew the mandate was for Jefferson, but Burr, never famous for his scruples, was game for a deal. Abigail Adams's wry remark that the choice between Jefferson and Burr was enough to give one pause about elective government was no joke to some of her friends. The republic's first transfer of power from one hostile party to another led to talk of civil war. When a plot was hatched to put a Federalist in power, pending some future election, Jefferson asked Adams to squelch it. Should the scheme proceed, he said, it was likely to be met by force, with "incalculable consequences."

In the middle of all of this, having heard that Mrs. Adams was about to start for home, Jefferson called on her at the President's House. When he and her husband had been diplomats in Paris in the 1780s, she had treasured him as "one of the choice ones of the earth," and he had returned the compliment, even flirted with her playfully. But in more ways than one it was no easy thing to enjoy each other's company now. A packed dirt causeway crossed the long arm of marsh reaching out to the foot of the Capitol Hill, partly "corduroyed" with logs to subdue the mud. The Pennsylvania Avenue, it was called. In rain or snow a carriage could take an hour to slog through it. On Monday, February 2, 1801, Jefferson crossed it in rotten weather, almost certainly on horseback, on his way to Abigail Adams.

For more than half a mile from the Capitol, marsh and old fields were everywhere. A pleasant little spring watered giant oaks a quarter mile from the President's House; a neighbor's buckwheat field was closer still, cropped and forlorn in winter; and the elegant white mansion stood on its rough construction site like a carved ivory brooch on a dirty shirt. A travel writer warned that its grounds disgraced the country, and careless guests who crossed them in the dark risked bodily harm, for "instead of finding your way to the house you may perchance fall into a pit or stumble over a pile of rubbish" or the heartbreaking stump of an ancient tree cut down for fuel or lumber. The president's cows grazed on ground "in great confusion," a neighbor said, strewn with saw pits filled with rainwater, trash of all kinds, and junk on an architectural scale—three walk-in beehive brick kilns, sheds turned into chicken coops, a shack occupied by goats. A derelict house, once the heart of a family farm on which the mansion had been built, stood abandoned near the wreckage.

In November of 1800, Mrs. Adams had been impressed, amused, and alarmed when she moved into the mansion with the election under way that would take her husband out of it. Though every formal room was rich with architectural detail, only six were close to finished, and the servants kept a dozen fires going to ward off the cold and damp. A forest ruled by bears was an easy walk away, but firewood was scarce with no one to cut or cart it. Were it not for a lucky purchase of two hundred bushels of coal, the president and Mrs. Adams would have suffered. As it was, their bedchamber was comfortable "whilst the doors of the hall are closed." Snow melting through the roof woke Abigail up one night, and the servants "set tubs to catch the water. The ceiling is not yet dry," she wrote her son Thomas, "though more than a week since."

When Jefferson rode up to the President's House in the rain, Mrs. Adams was bracing for "this dreadful journey" home, a week or ten days on the way back to Quincy, Massachusetts, crossing 450 miles of bad winter roads. Her husband would man his post through the month that was left to him there, choking on the thought of handing it to Jefferson. Mrs. Adams wished her old friend well for the country's sake, and perhaps a bit for his, but her feelings had been hurt.

"The Vice President made me a friendly visit," she wrote Thomas the next day, "in order to take leave and wish me a good journey. It was more than I expected."

It was well within Jefferson's character to ride in filthy weather more than a mile and back just to wish Mrs. Adams farewell, but a good domestic staff was vital to his plans for the President's House and the presidency itself. An expert on houses and their furnishings, he had been on top of this one since its inception, but Mrs. Adams knew the staff. As they chatted over tea in an unfinished parlor, she offered him her thoughts about its six usable rooms and their furniture, provided he wanted to hear them. Since she mentioned it, he said, passing the house itself, he would gladly keep every servant she could recommend. It was not a large number, sad to say. Wary of all things Southern, Mrs. Adams had told an uncle that "the lower class of whites" in Washington City were "a grade below the Negroes in point of intelligence and ten below them in point of civility" and weak on punctuality. They were good at "fair promises, but he who expects performance will assuredly be disappointed."

Joseph Dougherty was an exception. A literate, Irish-born coachman in his twenties with a wife named Mary and a small herd of children, Dougherty ran the president's plain brick stable two blocks east of the mansion at Fourteenth and G with an eye for opportunity. He had surely made himself known to Mrs. Adams, and Jefferson kept him on. In time he would find the Irishman "sober, honest, diligent, & uncommonly intelligent in business," provide him a family home in the basement servants' hall, and give him room to grow. Christopher Süverman, a footman on the staff, was another commendable man, and Jefferson kept him too.

Before he said farewell, Jefferson told Mrs. Adams that nothing would please him more than a chance to help her, Mr. Adams, or their family, and she thanked him for it. He inquired about her brilliant son John, her husband's minister to Prussia, and it pleased her once again that Jefferson never saw her without asking affectionately about him. In France, the freethinking Virginian had mentored the pious boy like a son. Browsing in a Paris gallery, John had been repulsed by a "groveling, despicable, and impious" painting of the Holy Family doing peasants' chores, but an infidel was his beau ideal. "Spent the evening with Mr. Jefferson," he wrote, "whom I love to be with."

Their bond would mature when the younger man joined the United States Senate and his mentor in the President's House tried to make a Republican of him. Mrs. Adams might have guessed, had the riddle been posed, that if anyone could charm a fish out of water or an Adams out of Federalism it must be a choice one of the earth. In 1825, when John Quincy Adams was president-elect, his father would write to Jefferson about "our John" and his travails. "I call him our John," Adams wrote, because he had been Jefferson's boy almost as much as his.

* * *

Jefferson's presentation of himself as a simple republican family man was complicated by the absence of a family. The lack of a wife in particular would hobble him in the President's House, and the want of a loving confidante would be worse. In 1782, his beautiful wife Martha had died at thirty-three, leaving him crushed at thirty-nine with three young girls, one of whom died in early childhood. At his dying wife's request, it was said, he had promised her never to remarry, and he never did.

Their firstborn child, also named Martha, was twenty-eight on the eve of his presidency, the bright and likable mother of four young children. Her husband, Thomas Mann Randolph Jr., a troubled young man whose demons would haunt the President's House, had inherited a plantation soaked with debt near Monticello, a second home for the Randolphs and their children; and from Jefferson's boardinghouse room, home seemed like heaven. To Martha he confided that he felt himself in "an enemy's country." A plot to dissolve the government rather than make him president, he wrote, had weakened just enough to let him hope the public will would prevail, which would be a mixed blessing. "I long to be in the midst of the children, and have more pleasure in their little follies than in the wisdom of the wise." For nine year-old Anne, the eldest, he enclosed a little story. "Kiss them all for me and keep them in mind of me," he wrote. "Tell Ellen I am afraid she has forgotten me," an absent grandfather's classic worry.

Five-year-old Ellen was counting the weeks until his return and warning little Cornelia of the consequences. "Long is the list of misdemeanors which is to be communicated to you," their mother informed him by mail, of which the theft of two potatoes that Ellen had been saving for him "forms a weighty article." Martha was feeling cheated by his last trip to Monticello, when family time was lost to strangers. Guests had been a pleasure in their quiet country home, but the prospect of his presidency had turned them into hordes. No one could suffer more than he from loss of time with family, he replied, worn down by work and worry, "surrounded by enemies and spies." Home was love and harmony, and "the eternal presence of strangers goes very hard indeed," but everything they had striven for demanded it.

Martha had accompanied him to Paris when she was twelve, a shock for a country girl dropped into the sparkling world of Louis XVI and Marie Antoinette. A fluent conversationalist in four languages and a gifted singer and musician like her father, she was blessed with much of his brilliance and a far better business sense. People called her a feminine model of him, six feet tall "and stately-looking," with his casual air of distinction, easy smile, red hair, and fair coloring. She was not considered handsome, according to a female friend, but magnetic when she spoke. Years later, Ellen recalled her disposition with "the sunshine of heaven in it." She had always lived with her father, at or very near Monticello, except when he served in office. At ten years of age she had seen him led away almost helpless from her mother's deathbed, followed by a grief "to this day I dare not describe to myself." Martha had never left him as they walked and rode horseback for weeks. Her children were almost his, one of them later wrote, having lived with him all their lives, a loving substitute for their troubled father.

His younger daughter Mary preferred to be called Maria, a sensitive, blue-eyed, arrestingly beautiful young woman of twenty-two. Said to resemble her mother, Maria was bright, articulate, and generous, easily moved by music, and fluently multilingual, all of which her letters prove, but still not as quick or talented as her sister, much less her father, and more than a little cowed by the difference. A male family friend of Maria's age knew her older sister Martha well, but Maria spoke too rarely to reveal herself. All he really knew was her delicate face, "and that was divine." Sitting quietly in friendly company, she would look from one speaker to the next with such unassuming intelligence and exquisite beauty that the words to describe it failed him. He could hardly look away.

"My aunt," Ellen later recalled, was "singularly beautiful" but "never fond of dress or ornament." If anything, her looks embarrassed her. She was only admired "for that," she would say, because she could not be praised for better things. Clinging almost childlike to her father as a young wife and mother, she was capable of writing "my dear papa" four times in a single letter. "I feel my inability to express how much I love & revere you," she wrote in another, "but you are the first & dearest to my heart." When he sailed for Paris with Martha in 1784, Maria was only six, and he left her with loving relatives until he sent for her three years later. The Adamses were in London and took her in on her way to France, a bright, inquisitive, "lovely little girl," Mrs. Adams wrote her father, "the favorite of every creature in the house." Mr. Adams was smitten too. "In my life I never saw a more charming child." Family lore recalled her as "rather a querulous little beauty" nevertheless, whose return to Virginia at eleven upset her as much as leaving it had at nine. Martha tried to calm her when they docked at Norfolk, but Maria was inconsolable. "*Mais c'est bien différent de Paris!*"

In temperament, Maria remained vulnerable all her life. She had lost her first child in infancy and had not yet had a second. Jefferson liked her husband, John Wayles Eppes, whose inherited plantation ninety miles southeast of Monticello overlooked the Appomattox River. Nothing could please him more, he wrote Eppes from his boardinghouse room with the presidency not yet won, than to appear in their home by magic, "and sweeten some of the comfortless moments of life." Ambitious though he was, he did not enjoy the thought of solitude in the President's House, and yet, he told Maria, he meant "to see our government brought back to its republican principles, to see that kind of government firmly fixed to which my whole life has been devoted."

* * *

On February 17, the House of Representatives made Jefferson president on the thirty-sixth ballot, tipped by Delaware's only congressman, a Federalist fed up with Burr and chaos who had lately advised Hamilton that the government might not survive the "moral & political experiments to which it would be subjected in the hands of Mr. Jefferson." It was said that when the news of his election broke, old ladies in Connecticut hid their bibles in hollow trees.

Set to be inaugurated in fifteen days, Jefferson pushed ahead with an anxious search for a staff who could help him make the President's House a place to unite his friends, disarm his foes, and heal his country. With a mansion to staff in two weeks, the president-elect had no aides, no wife, and no government funds but his pay. His $25,000 salary was the richest cash income of his life, but his expenses would soak it up. The government contributed nothing to run the house. He would pay its staff himself, as well as provide their meals; their medical care; and the clothes they wore at work; the food and wine they served him and his guests; the wood, coal, and candles that lit and warmed the place; the carriages, horses, and tack in the stable; the stable hands who shoveled the stalls; and the shovels.

The challenge at the start was to find any staff at all, beginning with a world-class steward, butler, or maître d'hôtel, depending on his country of origin. Such men were scarce in Washington. Offering himself to Jefferson as "a Stuard of your family," one Patrick Sim assured the president-elect he would be "satisfyed with very Moderate Wagers." Mrs. Sim had been "in that line of life which has qualifyed her to manage a Genteel Famely," and "we have One of the best Cooks this part of the Cuntry affords, wich you can also have if you chuse."

Jefferson turned for alternatives to Philippe André Joseph de Létombe, the French consul in Philadelphia, a longtime friend and collaborator. A scant ten days before his inauguration, he wrote to Létombe in English, never confident of his written French. Having met as much difficulty "in composing my household as I shall probably find in composing an administration," he needed a professional. "You know the importance of a good maître d'hôtel in a large house & the impossibility of finding one among the natives of our country," he wrote, a judgment he may not have shared with them. Létombe would much oblige him by finding a suitable man among the many French expatriates in Philadelphia. An easygoing, steady temperament and the virtue of discretion were important qualifications, but only two were indispensable: "honesty and skill in making the dessert."

Despite his trust in the common man as a matter of Republican theory, examples in the flesh were inclined to make him wary. If Létombe could find him a maître d' it would help all the more to "fix him to some reasonable demand," or he might arrive in Washington "and, seeing my distress, take advantage of it to extort what would be unreasonable." His needs, he thought, were limited: "I have a good cook, it is pour l'office [for the domestic operation] & to take charge of the family that I am distressed," "the family" being a common term for a household's servants. In fact his distress was deeper than he thought, for he *had* no cook, and the presumption that he did would catch him up short.

He wrote on the same day to a Baltimore innkeeper, an acquaintance named William Evans, and reminded him of James Hemings, a cook at a Baltimore tavern and "my former servant." More specifically, Hemings had been his slave, inherited with many others through his late wife Martha, whose father, John Wayles, had owned them. Awkwardly enough, Wayles was Hemings's father too, which made Hemings Martha's half brother. Wayles's enslaved mistress, Betty Hemings, had given birth to his children James, James's sister Sally, and other siblings.

Jefferson had been fond of James since he paid him to capture mockingbirds when James was his eight-year-old slave. When he went to Paris in 1784, he had taken James with him and apprenticed him at nineteen to a caterer, hoping to bring him home as a master of an emerging French cuisine based on subtle sauces, stocks, and creams prepared with great precision and served in separate courses, an art that Jefferson adored and an English cookbook called "an odd jumble of trash." After Hemings trained for three years, Jefferson made him his chef and paid him a fair wage. French law entitled slaves to freedom when they set foot in France, but Hemings chose to stay with Jefferson on the strength of his promise to free him in time. After they returned to America, Hemings delighted his master's guests until 1796, when Jefferson kept his promise and Hemings chose a new life in Baltimore. His younger sister Sally, who had brought Maria to France, had returned with them as well, pregnant with Jefferson's child.

Now Jefferson reminded the innkeeper William Evans that Hemings had said he would like to be the president's cook. Would Evans tell James he would be glad to have him back as soon as possible? He felt differently about Francis Say, another "affectionate and honest servant," now a laborer in Baltimore who wanted to serve him again. Say had begun to drink a bit, Jefferson told Evans.

Fond of Say as he was, he wrote, he might have taken him back nonetheless, but could not employ his wife, a washerwoman. Influenced by "the fear of his drinking and of getting his family into distress by removing them," the president-elect went on, "I endeavored to throw cold water on his proposition." Why he could not employ Mrs. Say he did not explain. Two women would be hired as laundresses in the President's House.

Despite no intent to rehire him, Jefferson had asked a favor of Say, who wrote him back about a talk with James Hemings, "according to your desire." Hemings "was willing to serve you before any other man in the Union," Say wrote, a testament to Jefferson's treatment of his servants slave and free, but Hemings claimed to be uneasy about a staff he did not know, and "would be very much obliged to you if you would send him a few lines of engagement," setting out his wages and other terms "with your own hand writing," a plain point of pride having nothing to do with strangers.

Whatever cold water Jefferson may have dropped on Say's rehire had not been cold enough. Having spoken to Hemings as Jefferson asked, Say inquired how soon *he* would be wanted at the President's House. He had refused a good job, he wrote, in reliance on Jefferson's intentions, and "you know very well that I am a poor man." A few days later, Evans wrote to Jefferson that Hemings had said again he would only go to Washington if Jefferson wrote him personally. Evans added that he had discouraged Say's hopes, for Say liked his drink, possibly more than was good for him.

Biding his time and weighing his options, Jefferson did not reply at once to a freed slave's request for a letter from the president-elect.

2

WITH VERY DECENT RESPECT

Jefferson's inauguration, held on Wednesday, March 4, 1801, was Washington City's first, and John Adams turned his back on it. Boarding the 4:00 a.m. stage to Baltimore, he started in the dark that dreadful journey home that his wife had already endured. When the word got out that Adams was on his way to Quincy and not to his successor's celebration, remarks about manners ensued, but the outgoing president had written a courteous if not congratulatory note to Jefferson. He would leave in the stable two carriages, seven horses, and their tack. "These may not be suitable for you," Adams wrote, whether too grand or too humble he did not say, but Jefferson would save money by keeping them, "as they belong to the stud of the President's household."

A congressional committee composed only of Republicans looked sideways at the stable's contents, a dashing two-wheeled carriage described ominously in their report as an "elegant chariot," a small coach, two sets of harness—one of brass, the other of silver plate—and those seven horses, "well looking" but "chiefly advanced in years." Adams had bought it all secondhand with part of an appropriation to furnish the president's household, which did not include his stable, in the minds of indignant Republicans. Congress ordered everything sold and the proceeds spent on furniture at the incoming president's discretion. A gentleman could have taken it as a slur, and Adams apparently did. The British minister to the United States thought he shunned the inauguration over it.

The inaugural events were plain and their military movements benign, a victory for the anxious founders, Federalist and Republican, who had worried about bloodshed days before. Artillery woke up the Capitol Hill, and a small body of infantry paraded at ten on the New Jersey Avenue, the broad stretch of dirt fronting Conrad & McMunn's. Jefferson emerged at noon in his ordinary dress. Four years earlier, Adams had been inaugurated in Philadelphia in powdered hair and a pearl-colored suit, with a sword on his hip. Jefferson skipped the powder and the weapon, marks of aristocracy both, and walked past the construction site to the Capitol's north wing with a token militia escort, a few Republican congressmen, and two members of Adams's cabinet showing patriotic solidarity. Artillery roared again as they walked in.

The new Senate chamber was jammed for the inaugural address, which many Federalists expected to be frightening. Jefferson had written it carefully himself and read it in a voice so soft his nearest listeners strained to hear it. Schoolchildren would memorize it for generations, and nearly every newspaper endorsed its signature line: "We are all republicans, we are all federalists," written by hand with a lower case *r* and *f* to assure every one of his fellow citizens that the republican federal government he led transcended their divisions, and he meant to serve them all. "My object is to re-harmonize my countrymen," he soon wrote a friend, "without abandoning republican principles," failing to capitalize "republican" again.

As chief justice of the United States, Jefferson's distant cousin John Marshall swore him in, a rare Virginia Federalist whom Adams had appointed *after* his defeat, confirmed by the outgoing Senate. And so, Marshall wrote that day, "the new order of things begins" with two kinds of Republicans, "speculative theorists and absolute terrorists. With the latter I am not disposed to class Mr. Jefferson." It was the kindest thing many Federalists could bring themselves to say. With a touch of gentle wit in their mutual old age, Marshall would call his cousin the "great lama of the mountains."

Cannon boomed again, wafting acrid smoke through the crowd, as Jefferson walked back to his boardinghouse and left the President's House empty while he thought about what to do with it, fixed on distinguishing presidents from kings. Some Federalists walked over to Conrad & McMunn's with the Republicans to shake his hand, relieved by his conciliatory speech and spotting no guillotines. The reluctant Delaware Federalist who had made him president seemed surprised to write home that Jefferson had received them "with very decent respect." As the modest crowd disbursed, an Englishman went back to his hotel, finding "nothing more to detain me among the scattered buildings of the desert."

Attuned to the rhythms of the farm, Congress adjourned the next day, March 5, and went home for the planting season, not to return until after the harvest, nine months later. Most of its members were gone within days, leaving Jefferson alone.

* * *

Jefferson got a gift on Inauguration Day, a letter from Philippe Létombe, who had found in Philadelphia a perfect maître d'hôtel, an honest, even-tempered, forty-two-year-old man, comfortable in English, "skilled in all the minor chores, understanding perfectly the pantry," whose wife, as *femme d'charge*, would keep the house in impeccable order. The couple had planned to retire, for "God had blessed their labor," but the husband had served Jefferson as the Portuguese minister's maître d' and claimed to treasure the memory. A hundred guineas a year would pay them both, a trifle for what they could do. "You see, sir, there are no more difficulties in forming your household." The maître d's name was Joseph Rapin, and Jefferson was relieved to have him, but he was counting on his friends to find him a chef of modern French cuisine, a focal point of his plans, and Hemings's request for the courtesy of a letter would wait while they looked.

Jefferson turned for help to Létombe and the Spanish minister to the United States, Carlos Martinez d'Yrujo y Tacon, the Marquis de Casa Yrujo, a blue-eyed, fair skinned, elaborately clothed, fortunately married man whose engaging wife was the daughter of the governor of Pennsylvania, formerly known as Sally McKean and now as the marchioness. The capital of the United States may have moved to the wilderness, but Yrujo had not. He stayed in Philadelphia, where a marquis could be comfortable, and came to Washington when he could not avoid it. Yrujo told Jefferson it would not be easy to find a chef for the president of the United States. Two good ones had already said no, but an upper-end mediocrity could be had for $20 a month.

Better news came to Conrad & McMunn's in the person of Joseph Rapin, Jefferson's new maître d'hôtel, fresh from Philadelphia with a letter from Létombe, who had found him not one but two superb cooks. If the president would say what wages he could pay, Létombe would tap the better one and strike the best bargain he could. Jefferson was pleased with Mr. Rapin, as he thought it right to call him, and asked him if he knew the cooks Létombe had found. Rapin imagined Honoré Julien was one of them, the best cook in Philadelphia, which was saying a good deal, and Jefferson asked Létombe to snap him up. Understanding that the top Philadelphia chefs earned twenty dollars a month, he would go as high as twenty-five "rather than fail." Taking no chances, he sent Yrujo a note of thanks for seeking "a minister of the kitchen" and asked him too to persuade Julien. "You see how much I count on your friendship."

Julien was forty-two, Rapin's age exactly, earning twenty-five dollars a month in a private home with the right to sell the kitchen grease. Now he asked for thirty, but Létombe knew he had cooked for a while for President Washington for twenty-five. A bargain was struck for Julien and his wife at thirty for them both. If anything was said about grease it was not written down. Julien wished to give his current employer time to replace him, a courtesy that Létombe had applauded. Madame Julien would not follow her husband to Washington until the president was perfectly satisfied with him. As he left for Monticello, Jefferson wrote back "to rejoice" in Julien. "It places me at ease to know that I may depend on finding him here on my return."

Only then, rejoicing and at ease, did Jefferson reply to the Baltimore innkeeper William Evans, who had told him a month before that James Hemings would gladly cook for him again if only he were asked. Jefferson had seen "in the difficulties raised by James," he wrote, "an unwillingness to come here, arising wholly from some attachment he had formed at Baltimore, for I cannot suspect an indisposition toward me." But Hemings had raised no difficulties and had made his disposition clear, a willingness to serve Jefferson more than any other man, asking nothing but a letter, a test of a gentleman by a cook who had been a slave. Jefferson had concluded "at once," he told Evans, "not to urge him against inclination."

And yet he was not unkind. "I would wish James to understand that it was in acquiescence to what I supposed his own wish that I did not repeat my application, after having so long rested on the expectation of having him." It was not an ungracious note and not an honest one, and he wrote it to Evans, not Hemings, who had lost his place in the President's House to the unrequited idea that all men are created equal and endowed with a right to be asked. As for Francis Say, the president was "glad Francis remains there" in Baltimore, "as I cannot bear a servant who drinks."

* * *

By way of professional staff, Jefferson would have next to none. If anything was traditional in a government twelve years old, presidents had just a single private secretary, combining in one man, paid by the president himself, a clerk, a well-dressed courier, and a point of communication with Congress. Jefferson had no other aides and needed none.

Hamilton had written Washington's speeches and public messages, but Thomas Jefferson needed no ghostwriter. A wrist he had fractured in a fall in France, set by a poor physician, made writing a physical challenge, but he wrote his own public messages and letters, and presidents rarely gave speeches—a good thing for Jefferson, who knew he was no orator. Adams, who could not recall that the Virginian had spoken a word in the Continental Congress, had delivered some public remarks as president, sometimes in uniform with a sword on his hip, but Jefferson's two inaugural addresses, both of which he wrote himself, were his only presidential speeches. He rarely appeared in public at all. But for the occasional spotting at the races at the Washington Jockey Club's track just west of the President's House or some other public event where he made no point of himself, the only place to catch him off the back of a moving horse was at home. Most politicians want to be seen and heard. Jefferson wanted to disappear, as he thought the government should.

A staff of paid savants would not have occurred to him. Having served as a senior diplomat and Washington's secretary of state, he knew as much about foreign policy as any other American, and his own secretary of state, James Madison, one of the geniuses who founded the republic and wrote the Constitution, was steeped in it. His secretary of the Treasury, Albert Gallatin, was the sharpest fiscal strategist in America. Expertise on every other point of law, politics, or policy could be summoned from the Capitol Hill or obtained from several dozen correspondents, including the surviving Founding Fathers of Jefferson's choice. What little military advice he needed came directly from his senior officers or his secretary of war, General Henry Dearborn.

Jefferson described the unorthodox qualifications he had in mind for a private secretary in a letter to Meriwether Lewis, a twenty-six-year-old Virginian and a junior army officer, one of his crowd of distant cousins, from a family distinguished in the Revolution and colonial affairs. Lewis's plantation, ten miles from Monticello, made them neighbors as they knew the term, but Meriwether Lewis was no gentleman farmer. An athletic young man with pale blue eyes and a strong nose and chin, he had grown up an outdoorsman, the mounted master of his fields. Tutored at home and educated at a local school, he had earned a reputation as a deadeye hunter by the time he was eight years old.

Jefferson had guided the boy since he lost his father at the age of five and watched him become a rugged, introspective young man. In 1792, Jefferson had proposed to the American Philosophical Society an expedition up the Missouri River to "the Stony mountains" and the Pacific, to be risked by one man and one companion, to avoid alarming the Indians. Not yet out of his teens, Lewis had volunteered. A botanist had been chosen instead, but Jefferson's view of gentleman explorers had evolved. These Western expeditions were so hard and dangerous, he wrote, "that men of science, used to the temperature & inactivity of their closet, cannot be induced to undertake them." Meriwether Lewis, on the other hand, had served under "Mad Anthony" Wayne in the Northwest Indian War. Jefferson was looking for a private secretary now, he told Lewis, not just for help in the President's House but also for information about the army and the

Meriwether Lewis. ***Missouri Historical Society***

rugged Ohio valley. The $500 salary would barely exceed his army pay, but the job would be easier and expose him to men of influence in public affairs. Food and lodging would be provided, "as you would be one of my family."

According to a cousin, a jealous one perhaps, Cousin Meriwether "was stiff and without grace, bow-legged, awkward, and almost without flexibility," but his imaginatively spelled reply to Jefferson's offer dashed across the page: "I most cordially acquiesce," and "not a moment has been lost in making the necessary arrangements." Nothing had been needed but the president's thought that "I could be serviceable to my country, or ucefull to yourself . . . Receive I pray you Sir, the most undesembled assureances of the attachment and friendship of Your most obedient, & Very Humble Servt, Meriwether Lewis."

Lewis had not expected Jefferson's confidence in his qualifications as a president's secretary, but Jefferson had every confidence in his fitness for what he had in mind. Having no sense that the taxpayers should support his secretary, he arranged to have Lewis keep his military rank and seniority, with the public relieved from his pay.

* * *

Throughout his eight years in office, Jefferson brought just five different slaves to the President's House, never more than four of its staff of ten or twelve at any given time. "At Washington I prefer white servants," he privately wrote, "who when they misbehave can be exchanged," but the notion that he could not exchange one slave from home with another seems odd, especially since he did. More than likely, he saw risk in mixing slaves from Monticello with free white servants in the President's House, doing the same jobs, living in the same quarters, reporting to the same steward, speaking freely with one another, coming home with new ideas.

And yet, having cast two native Frenchmen in the staff's leading roles, he began the second level with John Freeman, an enslaved footman about twenty years old, a seasoned waiter with no Monticello ties, leased rather than bought from a Maryland physician. Freeman may have chosen his own aspirational name, having made a contract with his owner to buy himself gradually with the wages he earned on lease, culminating in his emancipation in 1815, a not uncommon arrangement. Jefferson paid his earnings directly to his owner, but gave him the same two dollars a month "for drink," a sort of tip often paid to domestics, that he gave to all his presidential servants, slave or free, a feature of the subtle gray-tinted zone between slavery and employment he created for enslaved men and women at the President's House. He liked and trusted John, as he called him. In time, he doubled his drink allowance and bought him outright in 1804, subject to his contractual liberation date. The bill of sale described him as if he were lightly used merchandise. "Very pleasing countenance," it said, five feet seven inches tall, "straight and well made, with two small scars on his forehead, no other perceivable marks or scars."

Freeman was bright, ambitious, and literate, earning Jefferson's high regard as his personal servant and also as a first-class waiter in the dining room, the most important room in the house for the president's political purposes, where servants were most visible to guests. Freeman wore the same livery as the other footmen, blue broadcloth coats with silver plated buttons, red collars and cuffs edged with silver lace, red waistcoats, and velvet or corduroy pantaloons, typical of what was worn in the service of Washington and Adams and America's wealthiest families but a puzzling choice for Jefferson, who liked his republican simplicity visible as well as philosophical.

Had he wished to keep slaves out of sight of his guests, embarrassed as a hypocrite would be, he would not have had Freeman serve them dinner. Having made his name as a radical egalitarian while recognizing slavery as an "abominable crime," the fraught implications of displaying it in the President's House could not have failed to occur to him. Putting Freeman in front of all comers, Northern and Southern, foreign and domestic, in eye-catching livery if the point needed emphasizing, was an active demonstration of his health, capabilities, and courteous treatment in the hybrid brand of slavery Jefferson brought to Washington City. Concealment would have implied guilt. Display dealt the card faceup. Freeman left no record of what he saw and heard in Jefferson's dining room, or what he made of it, or what he thought of its host, and what a revelation that would be.

* * *

Under Washington and Adams there was nothing so prestigious as a dinner with the president and nothing quite so tedious; but Jefferson planned to make the President's House the most attractive place in town and its table the most enjoyable. What he needed was a staff who could pull it off in a clearing in the woods where the homes with top-shelf servants could be counted on two hands and a gentleman, let alone a president, could not raid the ones worth raiding.

A Capitol Hill boardinghouse was no place to look, but he did recruit from Conrad & McMunn's a touchy white servant named Edward Maher, a first-rate footman and porter who greeted the president's visitors and waited on his guests. Edward, Jefferson called him. Edward got twelve dollars a month and his extra two for drink, two suits of clothes, and a decent room and excellent food in the servants' hall, a comfortable enough place for basement quarters reminiscent of the medieval, with plastered groin arches of brick and stone. Jefferson paid and fed his servants well, despite his recurring suspicion that workingmen took advantage of him and his kind.

He liked his second footman, Christopher Süverman, the holdover from the Adams administration, and paid him the same generous wage he gave Maher. Jack the scullion earned eight dollars a month and one for drink. Given his duties—scrubbing pots, saving fat and grease, cleaning the kitchen—and Jefferson's omission of his last name in his ledger, Jack was probably a free black man. A third footman named John Kramer earned Süverman and Maher's rate of pay and a pair of boots. Noel, the *garçon de cuisine*, Jefferson called him, added lightly skilled kitchen help and was paid like the footmen. Maria Murphy, probably a maid and Irish born, joined the staff at the scullion's wage. Jefferson had no valet. The aristocratic conceit of keeping a man to dress him, groom him, and wait at his beck and call clashed with his republican maxim, "Never allow another to do for you what you can do for yourself," a rule he interpreted loosely.

On his mountain at Monticello, nearly all of his needs were filled by the people he kept in bondage. In Washington, with no enslaved village at his feet, he engaged independent craftsmen. A prosperous tailor named Thomas Carpenter and his staff made the servants' livery, a frock for the stable groom, hip-length jackets with pantaloons for the footmen and the coachman Joseph Dougherty, and a greatcoat for the latter, with silver plated buttons and crimson facing, a mark of his trade and status. Jefferson paid for it all. For himself he chose the best fabrics, then wore them hard and kept them, to the far side of respectability or beyond. Carpenter's work for the president included "twilled fancy cord" britches, one coat of superfine black cashmere and another of blue, both with velvet collars, silk-lined sleeves, and plain steel buttons instead of silver or gilt, a modest touch in formal clothes. But much of the president's clothing was not new. Carpenter's repairs of his fraying coats and threadbare britches showed everyone who noticed, and many did, his republican commitment to frugality, simplicity, indifference to fashion, and humility, the first three of which were genuine.

* * *

Jefferson's mended clothes and undressed hair were a conscious display of republicanism and a personal preference too, but more important still for the new republic's image was the impact of brick and stone. On December 15, 1802, the *National Intelligencer*, Washington's Republican newspaper, ran an Englishman's critique of the capital's emerging architecture. It may have been Jefferson who caused its republication. Great buildings can inspire a nation, the article said. Statesmen can be as wise in a shack as in a temple, but splendor generates awe, and stirring public architecture enriches a nation's soul. To "uplift the national sentiment by national ornament" was a necessity for all countries, particularly a "young knot of provinces" whose choice of government buildings would help define its character.

No one was better suited to make that weighty choice than Thomas Jefferson, a talented amateur architect, self-taught from books, who cherished classic forms with "the approbation of thousands of years," admired innovation and craftsmanship, and encouraged new construction as a sign of American progress. His passionate love of architecture informed his belief that it mattered, that beautiful public buildings proclaiming the republic's permanence, simplicity, and classic form would inspire pride at home and respect abroad, that the Old World's architectural treasures should be honored and their influence sustained but adjusted to American tastes and reduced in cost and show.

As a guest at Monticello, it occurred to a French marquis that Jefferson might have been the first American who "consulted the Fine Arts to know how he should shelter himself from the weather." He designed or redesigned every house he ever owned and helped Madison and other rich Virginians do theirs. In Paris and Philadelphia he remodeled homes he *rented.* Having started on Monticello from scratch at twenty-four, he never stopped expanding and improving it, ordering materials and sending directions from the President's House but allowing not a nail to be driven in his absence. Halfway through his second term, he would start on Poplar Forest, his second plantation home, in Bedford County, Virginia, an octagon-shaped mansion, modest as mansions go, with features unique in the world.

His interest in architecture and decor, as opposed to his talent, was not rare among his peers. Many great men designed and furnished their homes, but no one took it more seriously, enjoyed it more thoroughly, or did it more beautifully than he, and his eye for perfect form never closed. Out riding in Paris in the 1780s with Gouverneur Morris, a fellow Founding Father and a future Federalist adversary, he led the rich New Yorker to the Bridge of Neuilly for the sheer love of beauty. It was the handsomest bridge in the world, he said. Morris had crossed it four times and never noticed.

Jefferson was comfortable with the artistic sensibilities of arches, barrel vaults, and pediments, and also with nuts and bolts—the building of ridge and gutter joists; the costs, risks, and benefits of alternative grades of rolled iron; the specific Bohemian window glass best suited for the President's House; tongue-and-groove flooring in its icehouse to keep dust out of the ice below. He was capable of reminding his surveyor of public buildings that every rib of a domed roof "will be a portion of a circle of which the radius will be determined by the span and rise of each rib," and no one saw the President's House more vividly than he as a national and international symbol of republicanism itself. He would have designed it differently—simpler, smaller, and distinctively American, which it only came to be by long association, decades after his time—but its grounds were wide open to him, none of its rooms were finished, and many were not yet rooms. Improvements and repairs were needed, modifications could be made, and he never stopped working on any of it.

So sure were some of his critics that Jefferson would dismantle the federal government that one of them predicted he would tear its very buildings down and dig out their foundations. He would have done it if he could, and raised them up again, to match the republic's simple values and enjoy the sheer fun of the thing. His admirer Margaret Bayard Smith, married to the *Intelligencer*'s editor, said he loved the "putting up and pulling down," and he started more easily than he stopped. His greatest achievement at the head of his country may have been to reverse its slide toward oligarchy and his greatest joy to advance his architectural vision. He told a friend in 1805, a "single example of chaste architecture" could guide a new city's taste, and classic style, "the delight of the world for three thousand years, costs no more than the barbarous and tawdry fancies of each individual workman, and generally not so much."

In the 1790s, when Washington was president and Jefferson was secretary of state, they had planned Washington City together. Enticed by the very idea of a rural capital, Jefferson outlined the city's building regulations before it was a city and before it had buildings and sketched in 1791 a smaller version of the grassy pedestrian mall between the President's House and the Capitol that later occupied the same site. Had it been up to him, the capital in the woods would have been a model of the republic he envisioned, elegantly simple, economically built, and planned on a human scale, with a forum of public buildings of stone-trimmed brick set on open, welcoming ground, around which a town would grow. But Washington's choice of city planners, the Frenchman Peter L'Enfant (born Pierre), a talented, impossible man, had designed a heroic city with a President's Palace that would have shamed a Borgia pope. The city, unlike its principal buildings, was laid out as L'Enfant planned.

In 1792, a prize competition was held to design the Capitol and the President's House. But for Boston's Charles Bulfinch, few American architects deserved the name, and none of them participated. All nine proposals for the President's House came from amateurs, including an anonymous design for a house of classic form, too small for a head of state, almost surely submitted by Jefferson himself, a brick homage to Andrea Palladio, the sixteenth-century architect he admired. A humbler participant named James Hoban, an Irish-born carpenter turned architect, designed in regal stone, with a touch of Irish taste, what Washington and Hamilton envisioned in a government and Jefferson abhorred, something big, grand, and English.

To choose the winning entry, Washington and the commissioners for the District of Columbia spent a day in Georgetown peering through their spectacles and making polite remarks, but the winner was no surprise. There was nothing republican about Hoban's design, even before Washington had him expand it and add garlands of carved stone. The huge eastern room was designed for entertaining on a royal scale, and the arcs at both ends of the oval drawing room were perfect for the president's weekly receptions, where gentlemen stood and bowed to him in a reverent half circle. Unconscious of the irony, the commissioners declared that "the President has approved the plan for a palace." As the mansion rose on the Burns and Peerce family farms, Republicans attacked it as unfit for any honest American, much less the people's chief servant.

By November of 1800, when the Adamses moved in, almost everyone was calling the "President's Palace" the "President's House," including the Adamses. Pompous though he was prone to be, John Adams had more than enough sense not to govern from a palace. In a teasing mood, only a few sophisticates called the mansion the "Presidoliad."

3

TRUE REPUBLICANISM

A week after Jefferson's inauguration, the *Intelligencer* shared a thought absorbed from him: The completion of the capital's public buildings should reflect the "simplicity and purity of our republican government." The President's House, thirty-six rooms of Irish-influenced Georgian architecture with neoclassical elements, was neither simple nor pure, but Jefferson could hardly decline to move into it, waste the public money that had built it, insult the sainted Washington who had blessed it, or snap the short string of continuity that linked him to his predecessors. Too far along to reconstruct and impossible to abandon, the building could be reformed.

As a student of public culture in an infant capital, Jefferson meant to use the house to reform the presidency itself, with little to constrain him. No business or cultural establishment wielded much influence in the city, such as it was. Washington had never lived there, Adams had moved in in November and moved out in March, and Congress had gone home. Jefferson had written in Paris in 1785, "I am savage enough to prefer the woods, the wilds, and the independence of Monticello to all the brilliant pleasures of this gay capital," not denying that he enjoyed them. Now he would shape the President's House in the wilds of Washington City, challenged to pull together in one place his savage preferences, his brilliant pleasures, and a tight Republican budget.

Though Adams had left for home, Jefferson stayed at Conrad & McMunn's for two weeks and began to transform the house before he moved in. Adams had found it excessive too and considered giving it up to some other public use. Washington himself had raised the idea of designing it in such a way that parts could be built at the start and others added later, based on the sensible thought that a smaller official residence could be adequate for its first few occupants but unfit for "a more distant period." No one could doubt that it needed attention now. The cavernous space at the eastern end of the house would one day be called the East Room. Only days before the inauguration, the commissioners for the District of Columbia had it swept of debris, its southern door fortified with "good strong boards," and the drainage ditch that ran from the Pennsylvania Avenue to the Tiber "cleared of the earth which has fallen into it, so as to give a free passage to the water." Congress authorized the sale and replacement of any decayed or unfit furniture, and most of the mansion's rooms had no furniture at all. Some had no floors on which to put it.

A minor federal official named Thomas Claxton had secured the house when Adams left, and put himself at Jefferson's service. In 1789, when the government was in Federalist hands, Hamilton had recommended him to Congress for whatever job might be had. His application, Hamilton wrote, would display "some literary pretension," but Claxton was a printer, which was wrecking his health, and a Federalist who "has suffered as such." Starting as a doorkeeper, he had played his cards well and snagged a higher post as agent for furnishing the President's House. Jefferson kept him on, despite the liability of Hamilton's recommendation, and kept him busy. On February 27, 1801, Claxton had taken an inventory.

The Great Hall of Entrance looked empty with nothing but a clock, two tables, two stoves, and "common carpeting." In the center of the southern half of the second floor, the oval-shaped room overlooking the river, favored with a valuable chandelier not yet unpacked, was beautifully furnished, but for a pair of mirrors too small for the room. Mrs. Adams had told her daughter, "I have no looking-glasses but dwarfs for this house; nor a twentieth part lamps enough to light it." Her husband's office down the hall was simpler, with mahogany furniture, a washstand, a costly handmade Brussels carpet, and a seemingly adequate looking glass. These were the best-appointed rooms in the house.

Well over a hundred wooden chairs were deployed about the rest of it, most of them mahogany, others of humbler woods painted black, red, or blue with gold trim. Common Windsor chairs they were called, common because they were popular. Jefferson called them "stick chairs" and ordered them by the dozen from their Philadelphia makers. Scattered here and there were several mahogany sideboards and tables, a few sofas, two easy chairs, a great deal of silver, and the occasional noteworthy carpet. The rest of the house's contents were odds and ends—whale oil lamps, "a few old chairs" in a servant's room, an "old looking glass" in the housekeeper's, "33 pair of sheets, generally good," four "beer cans," and "39 table cloths, in tolerable condition," which would not do for Jefferson's plans.

The *Philadelphia Aurora*, where Jefferson could do no wrong, told its readers how Adams had sinned. "An inventory has been taken of the furniture," its editor wrote, "observe I say the *furniture*," which revealed that the *stable's* contents had been bought with the household furnishings fund, a scandal in Republican eyes. The same Republican committee that had called the issue out added nothing to that fund. Shortly before the inauguration, a South Carolina Federalist who had demonized Jefferson for years stood up on the House floor and moved to increase it. Some thought he wished to impress the president-elect, others that he wished to impress certain ladies in the gallery, "a very reasonable suspicion," the *Aurora*'s editor thought, but "the true reason was not furnished." A Republican leader killed the idea. Mr. Jefferson, he said, did not wish "to plunge himself into extravagance" and waste the people's money "on articles which would require an extraordinary number of servants barely to keep them clean." Combined with the stable sale's proceeds, about $10,000 would be left to furnish the house, quite enough to support a Republican's fear that any more might require a raise in the president's pay to "bring him up to the style of his furniture."

* * *

Poorly engineered and poorly built, the house was decaying before it was finished, but much as Jefferson would have plunged into improvements if he could, a costly buffing up the grandest house in America, in which he would reside, would not have been a wise exception to republican frugality. Instead he reassigned its rooms to new purposes, used its furniture fund carefully, and started on its ugly grounds with picks and shovels, hired carts, and unskilled labor, all of which were cheap.

On the south side of the house, where the ground sloped down from the north, the basement was a brightly lit walkout. Along the other three sides, an "areaway" had been dug between the earth and the basement, which admitted some light and air into its other rooms, including the north-facing kitchen, and let deliverymen come and go and trash be removed unseen. To reach the house's front door, you crossed the areaway over a wooden bridge. On Jefferson's orders, hired laborers cut a bank around the areaway, covered it with fresh-cut sod, and lined it with a light wooden fence to keep people from falling in.

It was not the mansion's first excavation with a president in residence. Abigail Adams had watched from her window for days as a dozen black men moved earth from the front of the house in four horse carts. Time after time, they loaded all the carts at once, and four of them drove to a dumping ground and back as the other eight leaned on their shovels. Southern efficiency, Mrs. Adams thought. Two hearty New Englanders would accomplish as much in a day, which was not the fault of the slaves who did the digging, for "true Republicanism" drove them, "half fed, and destitute of clothing," as their idle owners watched and got paid by the day.

At next to no expense, Jefferson repurposed some of the first-floor rooms, all grandly scaled with eighteen-foot ceilings. The one he had his eye on in the southwest corner had a polished mahogany floor, an elegant fireplace, and five dramatic windows on two sides, one of them floor to ceiling, the others nearly so, all of them recessed and shuttered but undraped, admitting air and a flood of light. Like every other south-facing space in the house, the room had sweeping marsh and river views, once you looked past the torn up grounds. Adams had held his receptions there, but Jefferson made it his office, a wonderful place to work and retreat. He called it his study or his Cabinet, a word for a private chamber or museum, and there he was not disturbed.

Over time the room improved as he filled it with some of his favorite things and the eyesores outside were cleared. His mockingbird cage housed a species

Jefferson in his Cabinet with Meriwether Lewis. ***Painted by Peter Waddell, courtesy of the White House Historical Association***

he described as "a superior being in the form of a bird." Rarely fond of confining nature, he often freed "Jack" and his successors, "the delight of every hour," to hop, fly, and sing around the room and follow him through the house, trained to respond to whistles and said to display an "uncommon intelligence and affectionate disposition." There was space in the room for the long, narrow table where his executive council sat, its drawers on both sides neatly filled with his writing and drawing materials, his potting trowels and clippers, and his delicate craftsman's tools. Evidence of philosophy was everywhere—weather and scientific instruments; an elegant globe on a handsome stand; an eclectic collection of maps; many books; an adjustable writing desk with a top that locked in a choice of positions; a curiosity called a swivel chair; a cushioned leg rest with a revolving writing surface built to his specifications; potted plants on window stands—geraniums, roses, and experimental exotica; a custom-built chest for the seeds that diplomats, friends, and botanists sent him from around the world; assorted tables, drawers, and cabinets keeping each item safe in its place. There was evidence of love as well, in the English artist Richard Cosway's sketch of his stunning wife, Jefferson's *amie de coeur* in Paris.

"Passing as I do the active hours of my life in my study," Jefferson wrote, "I have found it essential to bring all the implements I use there within the narrowest compass possible, and in no case to lose a single inch of space which can be made to hold any thing. Hence every thing is placed within my reach without getting out of my chair." In his Cabinet he wrote and worked and fed "a canine appetite for reading."

The privilege of admission was rarely granted to anyone but his executive council, his secretary, and a few close friends, one of whom kept a souvenir with a note on the envelope that preserved it: "A geranium leaf stolen from Mr. Jefferson's cabinet on the 4th of July 1804." The room was no less sacred than his study at Monticello, where Margaret Bayard Smith was told with pointed mock solemnity that the president alone opened its door. Little Ellen was proud to bring him messages there. One of her sisters said, "We would not speak out of a whisper" in its vicinity.

An interior door from his Cabinet led to another splendid south-facing room, beautifully furnished and finished over time, where he welcomed those of his callers who never reached the inner sanctum. Like many of his fellow Americans, Jefferson set rather than sat, and he called this his Setting Room. It would one day be called the Red Room. Adams had used it as an overblown breakfast room. Like all of the first-floor rooms, it was accessible through the hall running lengthwise through the house, but Jefferson used the interior doors to his Cabinet to move privately between the two spaces, an office suite of sorts.

The Setting Room led through another interior door to the striking drawing room in the center of the south side of the house. Jefferson called it the circular room or the Oval Room, a fashionable shape of the 1790s. Future residents would call it the Blue Room, the best room in the house, and Adams had wasted it as a vestibule. The front door had not been used in his short time in residence. People had gone around the back to get in, climbed a steep set of stairs to the wooden balcony that opened into the Oval Room, and merely passed through it on their way to other rooms. Switching the entrance from south to north, Jefferson had a path cleared from the road to the north door, which opened into the Great Hall of Entrance. The back stairs were pried away, leaving the balcony enclosed by a balustrade, and the Oval Room became the highlight of the house, as Hoban had intended. Claxton's inventory found it "vastly deficient in furniture," which Jefferson enjoyed fixing.

To say that the house needed work would not say enough. Nearly half of its rooms, most of them upstairs, were nothing but studded shells lacking finished floors, walls, ceilings, or all three. The formal staircase at the western end of the hall had yet to be built. The only routes to the second floor were the simple family stairs to the east of the Great Hall of Entrance and the twisting servants' stairs tucked out of sight in the porter's lodge beside the front door. Abigail Adams had loved her upstairs river view, watching boats pass under sail, and Jefferson surely did too. He took the Adamses' stately bedchamber in the southwest corner, the warmest spot in a cold house.

Warmth was a matter of degree. On a frigid winter's day, Jefferson had written at Conrad & McMunn's, "I have often wondered that any human being should live in a cold country who can find room in a warm one," and the President's House was no improvement. Its fireplaces, almost more attractive than useful, burned Virginia-mined coal and scarce cords of wood, but the grates were inefficient, the draw was poor, the ceilings were high, and the windows leaked. There was nothing odd in this. It was hard to keep any home warm. On a cold day in January, a prosperous Washington diarist "froze in the house last night." Jefferson wore a fur-lined wolf-skin cloak on winter days in the President's House, where cold was the ordinary thing, most chillingly of all in the privy out back, ten feet wide and four deep with a three-hole bench that made for less waiting and a chance to socialize.

Jefferson condemned it immediately and ordered indoor plumbing, a wonder he had first seen in Paris and no one had seen in Washington. The commissioners had learned, probably from him, that a Philadelphia merchant sold water closets "cleansed constantly by a pipe throwing water through them at command from a reservoir above," and asked an agent to inspect and price them. Two were ordered for upstairs use, the water to be thrown from attic cisterns filled with rain. The servants would keep their privies. By the middle of 1802, every functional bedroom had a white ceramic washbasin, pitcher, and chamber pot. Bottles and pots designed to be heated in the fireplaces provided hot water en suite.

An admirer of porticos, Jefferson had given Monticello two, front and back, and drew them on all four sides of his rejected design for the President's House, but Hoban's winning design had none. The mansion's northern face was flat, excepting a barely protruding row of engaged Ionic columns. On the southern side of the house, the stacked oval rooms on the first and second floors made a stylish bow in the middle, but the absence of an overhanging roof made the balcony unusable on hot days and the Oval Room hardly cooler. With no poetry at all, Jefferson called the even hotter oval-shaped room above it "the circular room upstairs." The Adamses had called it the Ladies' Drawing Room.

Having conducted a walk-through inspection during the fortnight after his inauguration, Jefferson moved in on Thursday, March 19, 1801, and was not as pleased as he might have been. On the following day, the commissioners wrote to a contractor like remodelers through the ages: "We are sorry to be obliged to complain of the want of attention shown to our earnest desire to have the work completed for the president's accommodation. He returned yesterday and is put to the greatest inconvenience not having any necessary." Having relied on the contractor's pledge that the installation of the water closets was his first priority, "we find that it is not begun and yet other jobs of the most trivial nature have been undertaken since the work was engaged. We beg you to say whether you mean to execute the work immediately or not."

The commissioners asked their man in Philadelphia to find them a bell hanger (Washington had none), and a dozen bells and pulls were soon ready to summon the servants. A dozen were more than enough, fewer than twelve rooms being habitable. Pending Meriwether Lewis's arrival, the president had no office help at all, and the chief State Department clerk carried his messages. A makeshift bedroom and office suite was rigged for Lewis, reputedly using sailcloth and studs, in the south-facing quarter of the future East Room, a vast storage space with rough plank floors and unplastered walls. Variously called the Grand Audience Chamber or the Public Audience Room, it had no settled name and no audiences. With the pith of a Weymouth Yankee, a nephew of Mrs. Adams called it "the large room at the east end of the house."

After dark, flickering firelight and atmospheric candles lit the President's House. High glare whale oil table lamps shed brighter light for reading, writing, and other close work. In time, Jefferson would order to his precise specifications lacquered and gilded brass lamps with faintly green glass cylinders, the equivalent, by his reckoning, of six or eight candles. The staff broke them out at dusk from the porter's lodge and the housekeeper's room in the basement, set them up where they would be used, and cleaned and stored them in the morning. In the first several years, the house had no mantel lamps at all. As particular about them as he was about everything else, the commander in chief took the time to make drawings of the look and style he wanted, sent them to the best Philadelphia lamp merchant, and asked that they be tracked down or made "exactly to my fancy."

Cut glass chandeliers lit the two oval rooms on the first and second floors, raised and lowered with tethered counterweights to change, ignite, and extinguish the candles. At dusk, the footmen lit the silver candelabras on the president's dinner tables, casting his guests in a flattering light. In the corridors and halls, wall-mounted lanterns held one or two candles each, dim cones of illumination. Candles were expensive, and the stubs were saved for remolding. Abigail Adams had found that lighting all the rooms "from the kitchen to parlors and chambers is a tax indeed."

After less than two weeks in the President's House, Jefferson wrote to Lewis. He would leave for Monticello for a month to make moving arrangements and had hoped for Lewis's arrival in time to come along, but Rapin would provide for him. Lewis reached Washington only hours after Jefferson left. "I have taken up my lodgings in the President's House," he wrote back, "where I feel myself much pleased." Rapin and the others had been kind, and Lewis had brought a young soldier as his servant. Rapin was glad to tell Jefferson by mail that Lewis was an early riser and would have his Cabinet in order at six when he came downstairs.

* * *

Jefferson selected at Monticello a wagonload of things for the President's House and hired a carter to carry them up in May, when the roads would be dry enough to risk. Other bits and pieces would make their way to Washington City in Davy Hern's wagon over time. A trusted, enslaved wagoner, Hern made the kidney-bouncing trip several times a year, hauling assorted goods north and a mixed load back, bantam chickens for a granddaughter, thorn bushes for fencing, hundreds of unusual acorns and peach stones and a new strain of corn received as gifts at the President's House and sent home for planting.

On April 18, Jefferson wrote Rapin that he expected to start back to Washington on the twenty-fifth, health and weather permitting. Two gentlemen would come with him "who will possibly take beds with us," implying guestrooms with ceilings and floors. He was eager to meet his new chef, Honore Julien, and try him, perhaps, on his travel companions. "I hope I shall find Julien with you, and every thing mounted for the entertainment of company." He barely knew Rapin but closed with warm regards to make him feel at home. "Accept assurances of my friendly attachment."

A week of intermittent rain delayed him, enough to make the roads and rivers more challenging than usual on a trip that required four days, three nights, and a constant risk of misfortune. Jefferson typically rode horseback and sometimes arranged to be met at a wayside inn by a servant with a light open carriage, but unless another gentleman was headed in the same direction and tagged along for company, his only escort through miles of dense woods was the enslaved John Freeman, who usually went along as a riding valet. The president described one such trip as "the hottest journey I ever went through in my life & the most distressing to my horses. A thunder shower caught us in an uninhabited road" where the rain fell in sheets for an hour and a half. "In five minutes from the beginning every drop that fell pierced to the skin."

He carefully counseled guests who risked the trip. There were three routes to Monticello, a journey of 120 miles, not counting "a thousand meanders round the mud holes." The one he preferred crossed eight streams or rivers, five with no bridge or ferry. You waded your horse across, dodging holes and slippery rocks when you could. After several days of rain, the mud could be deep the whole way. Even in dry weather, Jefferson wrote, the roads "begin to be difficult to find" near Orange Courthouse, and no unrested horse alive could pull a carriage "without everlasting balking" on the hills near Bull Run. There were three overnight stops at a choice of fourteen inns. Four were pretty good, nine were so-so, Brown's was perfectly awful, and "cold victuals on the road will be better than any thing which any of the country taverns will give you."

With the president out of the house, Rapin unleashed the staff on its dust and dirt. He took down the curtains to be washed, had Lewis's man do the windows, and struck a bargain with a team of plasterers bound for Monticello to clean and whitewash five suites of rooms for five dollars each; but trouble had started downstairs just a month into Jefferson's term. Servants were common in Washington, but liveried servants were not, and their peers were known to mock them. Whether Edward Maher, fresh from Conrad & McMunn's, liked his livery or not, the same regalia Freeman wore in the dining room, cleaning was beneath him. Three days after Jefferson left, Rapin let him know that Edward had shown up just once, and only for his dinner. Mr. McMunn had come by to see the house and said Edward was not pleased that Jefferson had hired a Negro before him. Rapin heard Edward mutter he would not wear the same livery as a Negro.

"Of Edward I know very little," Jefferson replied, "as he has been but a short time in my service." Time would tell if he was fit for it, but "the Negro whom he thinks so little of is a most valuable servant." The president said nothing about truancy, but the implication was clear that Edward would wear the livery Freeman wore or Edward, unlike Freeman, was free to leave.

* * *

Jefferson returned on April 29 to complete his moving in and his first rearrangements of the mansion and its grounds. Among many payments made for workmen's services, a contractor received $19.50 for laborers' shoes in part payment for their hire. Mrs. Adams's nephew Judge William Cranch was pleased despite himself by what Jefferson was said to be doing with the place. "I have not yet made him a visit of respect," he told a brother Federalist, but "if these household improvements are the prototype of his political improvements, we shall have no cause of complaint." Some of their brethren complained nonetheless. Mocking the man of the people, the *Washington Federalist* said he had taken up residence in "the great stone house, big enough for two emperors, one pope and the grand lama in the bargain." Secretary of State Madison, Secretary of the Treasury Gallatin, and their families would be moving in too, the satirist wrote, paying rent to the Treasury. "That is republican and economical."

The Gallatins had rented a house on the Capitol Hill, but the Madisons and Mrs. Madison's younger sister, Anna Payne, had indeed moved in with Jefferson while they looked for a place of their own. In the vicious brawls to come, Federalist rumors would spread that the president and Dolley Madison had disgraced themselves unspeakably, choreographed by her husband, while they all lived together in the President's House.

The Madisons soon were gone, and the missing residents of the great white house were not the pope or the grand lama but the president's family. He was lonely under pressure in toxic times, and he sent his younger daughter an unspoken plea for a visit with a not so subtle touch of guilt: "An immense accumulation of business, my dear Maria, has prevented my writing to you since my arrival in this place," but he missed her every hour of every day. A worthy social group made life agreeable in Washington, he wrote, and it would cheer him, and them, to have his daughters come; "but this desire, however deeply felt by me," must yield to their husbands' "private concerns." At the same sitting, he made the same case to Martha. With the Madisons gone, "Captain Lewis and myself are like two mice in a church. It would be the greatest comfort imaginable" to have a daughter there, but their families came first. Mrs. Madison's presence had let him have the local ladies to dinner, but Mrs. Madison having left, the women would feel awkward "in the present construction of our family."

Poor as a church mouse will be, Lewis, at least, was happy in the president's family. Jefferson assured his son-in-law Randolph that he too was settling in, and tempted him and Martha to see for themselves. "We find in this a very agreeable country residence," he wrote. "Good society, and enough of it, and free from the noise, the heat, the stench, and the bustle of a close built town."

He was working on a better-built town. On his orders, the commissioners started grading the Pennsylvania Avenue and laying down a road from the President's Square to a broken brick path by the Tiber. He paid five dollars for a year's access to a new commercial lending library that advertised itself at "the first door west of the President's Square" and failed before the year was out, but a shop soon opened touting "beautiful editions" of *The Vicar of Wakefield* and *Saltzman's Gymnastics, or A Demonstration of the utility of Athletic Exercises in the Education of Youth.* One of the president's health care providers advertised too. "T. Bruff, Dentist and inventor and patentee of the perpendicular extracting instruments," assured the public that "to cleanse the teeth is one thing, and to restore them to their natural elegance with perfect safety and without pain is another."

4

MEN OF 1776

The Madisons had moved to 1333 F Street, a short stroll away from the President's House and a hub of capital society in the hands of Dolley Madison. Together with the other members of Jefferson's executive council and their wives, they made up the central cast of his plan to make the President's House a graceful, welcoming place.

Called the father of the Constitution in his own time, Madison was the son of the leading squire of Orange County, Virginia, a day's ride northeast of Monticello. Educated at Princeton's College of New Jersey, he was fifty years old in 1801, eight years younger than Jefferson, who had befriended him in 1776 and admired him ever since. A national figure and a founder of the Republican Party second only to Jefferson himself, Madison was the obvious choice for secretary of state. Despite his capacious mind, "Little Jemmy Madison" was unlikely to draw a crowd by the look of him, uncommonly short and slight, with a deep widow's peak and all the apparent zest of a dying man. A visiting Scottish barrister put his finger on it: "He had altogether the air of a country schoolmaster in mourning for one of his pupils who he had whipped to death." The young British diplomat Augustus Foster found him even better informed than Jefferson, but older than his years, in vintage powdered hair worn long in an old-fashioned queue. Even a protégé called him taciturn, stiff, and preoccupied in general society. Always dressed in black, he draped himself literally in frugality. An enslaved servant said he "never had but one suit at a time."

He made a poor first impression on Frances Few, a teenage niece of Mrs. Gallatin's introduced to him before dinner at the President's House: "Quite devoid of dignity in his appearance," he bowed very low with his eyes on the floor.

"His dress is not a bit smarter than Mr. Jefferson's. His skin looks like parchment." But everything changed when the undertaker turned into a humorist. As soon as you got to know him, Miss Few soon found, you saw "nothing but what pleases you," a gently smiling man with expressive, penetrating eyes. John Quincy Adams's wife Louisa, a pitiless Federalist critic, found him downright playful, a happy blend of intellect and wit with a knack for "the simple expression of the passing thought," the first brilliant man she had ever met without a hint of pedantry. A younger man later recalled that when the ladies left the gentlemen to their after-dinner chat, the author of the Bill of Rights told stories of a kind that were now, "in the improvement of manners, happily excluded from good society."

While her husband surprised the president's guests one by one at dinner, Dolley Madison's vivacious sense of fun put the room in the palm of her hand. "The Foreign Ministers were at her feet," Louisa Adams said, "and the world seemed to bow before her." Mrs. Adams called her "rather masculine in personal dimensions," unlike "her little man," but the equally caustic Frances Few admired her majestic height. Miss Few thought her "fond of admiration," finery without taste, and a bit of affectation, but her company was a pleasure and her instincts acute. "There is something very fascinating about her, yet I do not think it possible to know what her real opinions are." Jefferson adored her.

Albert Gallatin, his forty-year-old secretary of the Treasury, well born and highly educated in Switzerland, had emigrated from Geneva to Pennsylvania in 1780 and built the first glass factory west of the Alleghenies. In three spectacular terms in the House he had risen to lead its Republicans in his thirties, the master of their minimal tax and spending policies and Jefferson's fiscal expert in his wrestling match with Hamilton. A portrait painter described Gallatin as tall and thin, with coarse dark hair, a "yellow complexion, long nose, hideous mouth & teeth, but a black, intelligent & piercing eye." He spoke better English than most upper-class Americans, with a French Swiss accent that Federalists used against him. The well-traveled Louisa Adams found him one of the most charming, gifted people she had met "in any country. This was a mind of the highest order, blended with a brilliant wit and keen observation," quick to take your measure. "Shrewd, subtle, and penetrating, there were few who could cope with him," and thoughtful people stayed on guard, "as subtlety is a dangerous characteristic." With a mind so deft he owned the conversation before you knew he did, he startled Joseph Story, an important future justice of the Supreme Court who consulted him on business. The issue was obscure, but Gallatin knew it cold and took it apart. Despite his guileless face and open mind, his "deep, piercing eyes convince you at a single glance of his resources."

Hannah Nicholson Gallatin, a bold, gregarious figure from a leading Republican family in New York with insights as sharp as her husband's, had been schooled at her father's table by the likes of Aaron Burr and Thomas Paine. Louisa Adams did not know her well, and cheerfully explained why. "Eccentric in her dress, singular and unattractive, there was nothing to lure to her society, either in manner or appearance." Others thought her stylish. Her husband didn't care either way. "Her person is far less attractive than either her mind or her heart," he told a friend when he married her, "and yet I do not wish her to have any other than that which she has got." Her other credentials were sound. She was bright and well informed, "perfectly simple and unaffected, she loves me and she is a pretty good democrat."

The other three executive council members seemed inconsequential in the shadow of Jefferson, Madison, and Gallatin, but they were capable, good men and they rounded out the core of Jefferson's circle.

Secretary of War Henry Dearborn, a lightly educated, well-respected veteran of the Revolution from New Hampshire who had fought under Benedict Arnold before he turned his coat, had served in Congress with Madison and Gallatin, representing the District of Maine. Now he had little to manage but Indian affairs and a miniature standing army. Gallatin sized him up as "a man of strong sense, what is called a man of business. He is not, I believe, a scholar; but I think he will make the best Secretary of War we have as yet had." Looking down her Federalist nose, Louisa Adams had Dearborn pegged as a "kind family man a little puffed up by the station into which he had popped."

His still kinder wife's simplicity did not quite save her from Louisa. "The poor old lady was for ever pining over the chickens and cows that she had left in Maine," Mrs. Adams later recalled, abandoned in the wake of her husband's call to service. Still and all, Dorcas Dearborn was a goodhearted, "true specimen of Yankee housewifery," who "mourned for the loss of her occupation of cheese maker almost with tears of sorrow." The president liked the Dearborns, "plain & excellent people," he called them, entirely "without ceremony," qualifications he valued highly. He invited them to Monticello and made careful arrangements to ease their trip's discomforts.

Attorney General Levi Lincoln, a smiling model of old-school courtesy, *was* a scholar, recognized as such in the legal community. The eldest executive council member at fifty-two, six years younger than Jefferson, Lincoln was a Harvard graduate from the bucket-making coastal town of Hingham, Massachusetts, who could not have known of his common ancestry with a president not yet born. After practicing law on Martha's Vineyard, he had only recently been elected to Congress from his adopted home in Worcester County. Another plain New

Englander, Lincoln had published in the Boston press a series of unsigned "Farmer's Letters" critical of President Adams. Federalists smirked when they called him "the Worcester Farmer," but Gallatin saw the truth in it. "He has never, I should think from his manners, been out of his own state." Gallatin was a cold-blooded judge, and Gallatin judged Dearborn and Lincoln well. "Both are men of 1776, sound and decided Republicans."

Robert Smith, the cordial secretary of the navy, was a wealthy Baltimore merchant's son and another graduate of Princeton's College of New Jersey. The only executive council member who had never been in Congress, Smith knew little about the service he led and had been a common soldier in the Revolution before he was commissioned, a commendable thing but a weak qualification to head the navy. Three better-prepared men had turned the job down, but Smith was a leader of the admiralty bar and popular among the navy's officer corps, heavy with Federalists though it was. Some of the gentry found him surprisingly well mannered for a man whose family wealth had been earned in trade, and Frances Few guessed he would be good looking "if he was not disfigured by his nose," but he struck her as a silly man, "excessively fond of parade and show, and though his origin was low, very low," he boasted of his family and his furniture.

His sweet-faced wife got away with a review as strong as Miss Few ever gave: "rather inanimate" with a hint of the melancholic, but still surprisingly handsome though knocking on forty's door. She was "much devoted to dress," but she chose it with good taste. Louisa Adams thought more of her than that. A "perfect lady" she was, affable and attractive, an aristocrat at a glance, and yet "not a general favorite. Why? Because she was always correct, therefore said to be cold."

* * *

On May 13, 1801, Gallatin's arrival from Pennsylvania completed the Jefferson administration's assembly none too soon, for the bey of Tripoli declared war on the United States the day after that, having heard that the Adams administration had assigned him less protection money than it paid the ruler of Algiers, a competitor in the piracy industry. Composed of the president, the attorney general, and the department heads—the secretaries of state, the treasury, war, and the navy—Jefferson's executive council was an exceptionally close circle. Only Gallatin, who managed more than half the federal employees in Washington, had any junior officers or professional staff. Madison had no subordinate specialists in foreign affairs, and Dearborn and Smith had no military aides, just a few clerks and a messenger each. Attorney General Lincoln did not even have a building to house a Justice Department, which was just as well, since he had no

Justice Department. He had no help at all, not even a government desk. Jefferson himself had his presidential staff of one in the person of Meriwether Lewis.

The president left minutiae to his cabinet but never took his eye off their portfolios. After months of trial and error, he reverted to Washington's scheme. They could see him whenever they thought it was worth his time, and they passed him every substantive letter they got, simply for his information if no reply was needed, accompanied by a draft if it was. Any complications were reserved for the next meeting. "A very little experience," the president told Gallatin, would establish what he should see, and "the bundle of" Gallatin's mail "would hardly be worth sending to me." The system kept him abreast of every issue worth noticing and let him pass judgment on every one, a demanding but not impossible task. The federal government did next to nothing, and its tiny Washington workforce totaled 130 men, too many for Jefferson, who was "hunting out and abolishing multitudes of useless offices."

Firm as he was in control, he understood the risks of one-man rule. When the government was formed, he told a French admirer, "we had many doubts on this question, and many leanings toward a supreme executive council." It was only by chance that the Washington administration experimented with a single leader while revolutionary France tried a directorate. The founders watched the two plans play out "with an interest and anxiety proportioned to the importance of a choice between them." In the end, the French fell into dictatorship from a fatal mass of equal jealousies. Consensus comes, Jefferson wrote, when a president who leads his executive council with respect for their wisdom and information "brings their views to one center."

Consensus, for him, was crucial. It satisfied his need for harmony, showed the world a united front, and gave him limited shelter from blame for failure. Having learned that they differed on a point of fiscal policy, Jefferson sent a messenger to Gallatin with Madison's written thoughts and asked him to consider them closely. He hoped they could reach the same view. If not, he would decide the point reluctantly. Even then he would only set governing principles and let the comptroller apply them. After his administration had passed into history, it pleased him to say "we were one family."

When the family met around his Cabinet table, he jotted down their thoughts as they spoke. Washington had convened his executive council regularly, but Jefferson thought group discussions of issues that concerned just one or two of them were a waste of time. They met often in the first few weeks but less after that, almost always to face a crisis or something involving Indian tribes or the European powers, which involved them all. Jefferson sometimes asked them to do him the favor of meeting and "add that of dining with him." When war with

Britain seemed imminent in 1807, they could have met every day, which would have kept them from anything else, having no empowered subordinates. Instead he encouraged them to see him whenever they wanted, and if Gallatin came at dinnertime, sparing himself the ride home and back from the Capitol Hill, "you will always find a plate & a sincere welcome."

Except for Attorney General Lincoln, who had nowhere to hang his hat, their offices in the executive buildings were only a few muddy steps from the president's. When he wanted to see one of them, he usually sent a messenger to invite them to his office and occasionally walked over to theirs. Even in a crisis, a note to his homeless attorney general set a calm and casual mood: "As soon as Mr. Gallatin comes to his office I have desired him to walk with me to Mr. Madison's office to consult on an important & pressing subject. Can you meet us there & amuse yourself till Mr. Gallatin comes, the moment of which I am not able to fix." Open as he was to conversation, he preferred writing. He traded notes with Gallatin almost daily and with Madison hardly less, which promoted orderly thinking, saved his time and theirs, and kept them "most strictly in the spirit of the constitution," meaning that the choice was his and not the group's. Courteous as a man could be, the president was in charge.

When a big issue reached his desk, he told his cabinet in writing and asked for written opinions. Lacking easy copies, bundles of documents wrapped in red tape passed slowly from one department head to the next. Their memoranda to the president were respectful and sometimes ornate in the manner of the day, but Jefferson neither wanted nor received obsequious deference. His advisors gave him candid, even sharp advice in writing that might have been inhibited face-to-face. Having considered it all, he often wrote his thoughts out too, to synthesize theirs and test his own, as putting quill to paper will do. In a crisis, the process accelerated, followed by a cabinet meeting to which an out-of-town member might be summoned to come "without a moment's avoidable delay," which sometimes took days.

Perhaps most important to Jefferson, his system minimized conflict, which he avoided in every phase of his life. Consulting department heads individually, he never had to take a stand against any of them as he nudged them to coalesce, and no one had to back down from a fight or even know he was in one. For Jefferson, sharp differences were not merely awkward but distressing. Years after the fact, he recalled with unhealed pain his misery in the Washington administration when "Hamilton & myself were daily pitted in the cabinet like two cocks."

The Adams administration too had endured its ugly scenes. Accurately or not, Jefferson had heard that Adams had been known to overrule his executive council while "dashing & trampling his wig on the floor." No wigs would be flipped in the Jefferson administration. The odd jolt of tension was inevitable, notably between Gallatin, who did not believe in a standing navy, and Smith, who led one, but Jefferson said his cabinet scarcely ever failed to reason things out. In fact he claimed there was never an "unpleasant thought or word," a communion too pure to be believed. A perfect control of temper through eight years of stress was unlikely among powerful men, and the absence of an unchristian thought impossible, not to mention unknowable; but in 1817, John Quincy Adams confirmed the general idea: "Mr. Jefferson alone of our four Presidents has had the good fortune of a Cabinet harmonizing with each other, and with him, through the whole period of his Administration."

Jefferson never issued a public statement without a written critique from every cabinet officer, beginning with his secretary of state. A note to Madison with a draft of his annual message to Congress was typical: "Will you be so good as to give this a severe correction both as to stile & matter, & as early a one as you can, because there remains little enough time to submit it to our brethren successively, to have copies made, etc." Madison's replies tended to be gentle but direct. Gallatin's were thrown back hard in blunt Swiss style. When Jefferson asked him to spend his first available moments on one such critique, wishing him health and happiness, Gallatin gave writing lessons to the author of the Declaration of Independence: "It would be better" to use the active voice instead of the passive; in place of a general term, "I would prefer" a specific one; and so on. He added as a sort of reminder a "hope that your Administration will afford but few materials to historians," for "the things you want to be done are very few."

Like any confident writer blessed with a confident editor, Jefferson went back for more. His draft of his second inaugural address said the Louisiana Purchase would probably pay quickly for itself. Gallatin thought it was "rather going too far in saying that such event is probable; it is barely possible." As Jefferson had it, the bigger the country got, the less "local passions" would shake it. Gallatin didn't think so: "Is not this doubtful and too generally expressed?" A request for ship repairs should be dropped. Too much was said already about ships at the Navy Yard "rotting in the Eastern Branch, as if the waters of that creek had a peculiarly corrosive quality." Gallatin was of the view that partial credit to God was unseemly: "I do not like limiting the quantum of thankfulness to the Supreme Being."

The other cabinet members were uncomfortable editors of Jefferson's work. Attorney General Lincoln would suggest only one slight change in a draft if "obliged to maintain an exception to any part of it." Secretary of the Navy Smith gently questioned a reference to people "burthened with families" and elderly relatives: "Ought it to be said that a family is a burthen?" His uneasiness with "disappearance" was not as helpful: "Is there such a word?" Indeed there was, and Jefferson had not invented it, unlike the ones he had, including "counter-offer," "Anglophobia," and "monotonously," having found a need for them all.

* * *

Despite a workload that made him regret the impossibility of answering most of his mail, Jefferson found time to choose and position furniture, a productive way to relax. Margaret Bayard Smith, a fallen away Federalist, thought his choices could be questioned for simplicity, putting comfort ahead of fashion, but never for taste. His love of beauty ran to fine French furniture on its way out of style. In Louis XVI's Paris, he had collected, au courant, the best new sofas and chairs, perfectly crafted in red, blue, and crimson silk, patterned velvet, and morocco leather with carved mahogany frames trimmed in gold leaf and white paint. In 1790 he had it shipped home by the crate, the most spectacular collection of modern furniture in America. Some of it surely reached the President's House, carefully packed at Monticello and carted north by Davy Hern. The official furniture buyer, Thomas Claxton, bought more in Philadelphia and may have picked up bargains at the Georgetown auctions.

Following instructions to put the Oval Room's furnishings first on his shopping list, Claxton proposed a fine Brussels carpet, four candelabras, and no less than three dozen black-and-gold-painted stick chairs to accommodate receptions. Low-priced curtains for the upstairs windows would look as good from the ground as the costlier kind, but a spyglass was "much wanting for the convenience of the house." What needed convenient spying Claxton did not say, but the outside help would be a fair guess, or perhaps only boats under graceful sail on the Potomac. As additions to Claxton's shopping list, Rapin's needs were plain—brass candlesticks, more whale oil lamps, three "common beds for servants," and a cast-iron kettle.

5

NOTIONS OF EQUALITY

In 1788, Jefferson had written a letter of contrition from Paris to the new French minister to the United States, who had tripped into controversy in New York, the first American capital, over the formal presentation of his credentials. The issue was how "persons less respectable in point of rank" would be distinguished from their superiors at the ceremony. Every country set its own diplomatic protocols and assigned foreign envoys their respective social stations. Jefferson saw no good reason for any of these things, least of all in a country born free and clear of them. If *any* diplomatic precedence were needed, he wrote tongue in cheek, it should be based on something in nature, like the age of the persons concerned. Even height would be better than rank.

Having started what he called "The Revolution of 1800" to save the Revolution of 1776, he knew it would take time to subdue inherited privilege. He could push "the great machine of society" only so far, he told a friend, and "no more good must be attempted than the nation can bear." In a four-year term, he could only hope to build some fences around constitutional rights, check the growth of federal power, stop the waste of public money, "drive away the vultures" who feasted on it, "and improve some little on old routines." The fence building and vulture scattering would take years, but the regal protocols that Washington had established and Adams had sustained could be dropped overnight, and Jefferson dropped them.

Washington had been a tall, aloof, even regal man, the most heroic figure in the history of the American people. Sworn in as their first president in 1789, every move he made set a precedent for what a president should do and be, and many people raised under a king were prepared to treat him as one, encouraged by Hamilton and other accused monarchists. As children "we were educated in royalism," Jefferson wrote, "no wonder if some of us retain that idolatry still." He admired Washington's character and shared most of his principles but thought him poorly served by his advisors, not least in matters of form. In 1793, disenchanted as secretary of state, Jefferson had reminded Madison of an observation he had made when he came back from Paris, that the sycophants in Washington's orbit "had wound up the ceremonials of the government to a pitch of stateliness" no successor could maintain, that even Washington could not sustain it, and the newspaper ridicule pained him. Naked he would have been revered, but "the rags of royalty" diminished him in a country that despised kings.

Soon after Washington's inauguration, Hamilton had advised him that public "notions of equality" would not permit "too immense" a gap between him and the people, but the dignity of his office demanded isolation, short of provoking "extensive disgust or discontent." To make himself accessible (a regrettable necessity), he should hold a weekly levee, choreographed like London's rituals of the same name where privileged men and no women paid homage to George III. There he would chat "cursorily on indifferent subjects" with the proper sort of men and bar the other kind. As a rule, only senior federal office holders should be invited to dinner, where the president should never linger. Cabinet members, foreign ministers, and senators should have access to him like "peers of the realm," but only to discuss public affairs. Lacking the powers of advice and consent, congressmen should be excluded. "On the whole," Hamilton wrote, "I think the discrimination will be proper & may be hazarded."

Locked in combat with Hamilton every day, Jefferson told the purist revolutionary Thomas Paine "we have a sect preaching up and panting after an English constitution of king, lords, and commons, and whose heads are itching for crowns, coronets, and mitres." Happily, he said, the people would not have it. But when he became president nine years later, some powerful heads still itched, and some Republicans feared betrayal. On April 20, 1801, Nathaniel Macon, a Republican congressman from North Carolina, sent the new president a short list of expectations sounding more like demands. "Suffer me to say to you that the people expect that levees will be done away." The people expected too that he would give his annual message to Congress in writing, not in a speech (the king gave speeches to Parliament) and that the navy, the diplomatic establishment, and federal spending would be cut. Jefferson's reply was just as plain. "Levees are done away," he wrote, he would only address Congress in writing, the navy and the diplomatic corps would be trimmed, and the army subjected to "a chaste reformation." As for spending, "We shall push you to the uttermost in economizing."

President Washington had been treated with extravagant deference, an arguably necessary sign of respect for the infant presidency. Stepping into the great man's shoes, Adams had felt a need for regal pomp, and merely eased it back. Jefferson wanted none of it. Confident in his status from birth, the most celebrated American on earth, the paramount Founding Father now that Washington and Franklin were dead, he had nothing to prove but his loyalty to the Revolution, which required no pomp at all.

The colonial tradition of observing the king's birthday had been converted in Washington's time to a celebration of his. When the Washington's Birthday Ball continued into the Adams administration, Jefferson squinted hard at it. "This is at least very indelicate," he wrote Madison, but the best that could be done was to think of it as revering the general, not the president. Adams was miffed too, but his own birthday was celebrated on Boston Common. Washington's birthday survived as a secular saint's day in the Jefferson administration, but when the city fathers asked him to date his own, he politely declined. The only civic anniversary Americans should celebrate was the Fourth of July, he said, an honor not to be shared with any individual, implying, perhaps, that it might be shared with him if modesty did not forbid.

Republican form did not exclude the old-school manners that Jefferson had absorbed like air. For him and his social peers, courtesy was more like breathing than breeding. His grandson Thomas Jefferson Randolph, Martha's son, sometimes perhaps called Jeff and impossible to refer to otherwise without awkwardness or confusion, recalled in later life the colonial Virginia civility that made his grandfather instinctively "courteous and considerate to all persons." By this he meant all persons. As the two of them were out riding one day, a black man gave them a bow that the president returned and his grandson ignored. Jeff never forgot his quiet reprimand. Would he let a slave be more a gentleman than he?

In a formal age, Jefferson's informality was a matter of degree. Even in private, he addressed old friends as Mr. Jones and Mrs. Smith, but manners were not to be confused with pomposity, especially in Virginia, where gentlemen were notoriously short on form and fashion, and "'Virginia carelessness' was almost a proverb." John Adams's observation that in Virginia "all geese are swans" took a perfect shot at their pride, not their feathers. Looking back decades later, his descendant Henry Adams wrote that poor, gifted men like Patrick Henry who led the Virginia bar were "welcomed into a landed aristocracy simple in tastes and genial in temper." An American etiquette book said that "ceremony is the superstition of good breeding," and Jefferson despised superstition. The people, he wrote, were for republican principles, simplicity, economy, religious and political freedom, and republican forms, plain, unpretentious, only lightly deferential to position.

His nonchalant dress in the President's House was not an act put on for show but a comfort put on for him. Who would not want to work in soft clothes and relax his guests in a house that could turn them rigid? But the unpretentious image was no accident. Proficient at dressing for effect, he had polished himself to a pretty high gloss in Paris and Philadelphia, advised his daughter Martha in her youth to arrange herself "without a pin amiss," and modeled himself as a simple republican in the President's House. Still and all, the policy was sincere, the habit was in his roots, and he dressed for sheer comfort for the rest of his life, long after it mattered politically.

Even so, in a country new to Republican presidents, many people had no idea of Thomas Jefferson as their servant as opposed to their king, a point they proved in their letters to him, all of which he read and kept on file, at least in the beginning. "I Cannot well express my Self to you Sir," a woman wrote, "as I am not acquainted with such importance. If the dictates of my letter are wrong I hope your lordship will excuse me." A veteran of the Battle of Bennington had no sense of entitlement to his ear. "When an unknown individual shall attempt to rise from obscurity," he wrote, "and address the greatest Character in the Nation, the natural enquiry will be: From whence comes this audacity?" A simple Virginian's letter began with the salutation "Great Monark."

Even if Jefferson had not despised the obsequious pomp and royal festoons his predecessors had draped on the presidency, and he did, he could not have left them there. The Republicans had made a living attacking class-based formalities, even in daily life. "Etiquette! Confound the word," a party leader wrote in 1800, "it ought not to be admitted into an American dictionary." Madison said the removal of the capital from a city to a village favored a relaxed protocol, and Jefferson relaxed it immediately. Washington and Adams had bowed to their callers, getting deeper bows in return. Steeped in the patrician tradition since he learned how to stand, Jefferson bowed to everyone he met, high and low, then proceeded to shake hands, the plain American habit Europeans found common. "They are very civil," the London-bred Augustus Foster said of his hosts, but oddly mannered. "It is the custom on introduction to shake hands familiarly & on returning home to shake again & your hands are pretty well shaken before the end of the day." And so it would be in the President's House.

Presidential dinners were another point of departure. Washington had made a solemn sacrament of them, and Pennsylvania's senator William Maclay, a hard-bitten Jeffersonian and a veteran of the French and Indian War, had barely gotten through one. Scarcely a word was said until the table was cleared. Then

Augustus John Foster, painted by Christian Albrecht Jensen, 1825. ***Crown copyright and permission of the UK Government Art Collection***

the president proposed a ponderous toast, mentioning each guest by name, followed by formal salutations that Maclay found excruciating. "Indeed, I had liked to have been thrown out." After the ladies retired, the president told the gentlemen a tidy little story about a clergyman who lost his wig, which drew a ritual laugh, followed by a dead calm. Washington broke the stillness with a banal remark, fell silent, tapped absently with a fork on the edge of the table, and led the men upstairs for coffee, a treat Maclay declined. "I took my hat and came home."

Though not as numb as Washington, his successor was no charmer. Adams shared the general's self-regard but lacked his charisma, an unfortunate combination that left him unfit for the same heroic role. Hamilton called him "vanity without bounds." Maclay found him "wrapped up, I suppose, in the contemplation of his own importance" and thought he should have been a tailor, "so full of small attentions is he, and so well qualified does he seem to adjust the etiquette of loops and buttons." His social events were not as austere as Washington's but no outbursts of merriment either. According to the *Aurora*'s Republican editor, William Duane, a dinner with President Adams blended sullenness and pomp, and the chief occupation of the guests, too dull for conversation, "too stiff for hilarity, too numerous for recreation," was their deference to "the principal personage."

After twelve years of this, Jefferson held no formal state dinners at all. Under Washington and Adams, an evening at the President's House had been an ordeal. For Republicans and Federalists alike, a dinner with Thomas Jefferson was a ritual-free pleasure involving superb food and wine and delightful, uninhibited company.

Following Hamilton's advice, Washington's weekly levees had been staged like state funerals. A Republican called them "fixed days to gaze upon him." In theory they were open to any man. In practice, most men lacked the polish, clothes, and nerve to try the door. Every Tuesday afternoon at three, Washington struck a pose in formal dress with a cocked hat in his hand and a sword on his hip, while a procession of stiffly clothed men bowed low to "His Excellency" one by one. When each had taken his place in a deferential arc, the president passed among them speaking six or eight meaningless words to every lucky man. No hands were offered and no conversation indulged. On Friday evenings, "Lady Washington" presided over mixed gender levees, seated on a raised platform. His Excellency attended as a private gentleman but was scarcely more approachable for that. Congressman Gallatin privately mocked "our most gracious queen."

President Adams and Lady Adams held levees too. Jefferson killed them outright from the start, which disappointed some ladies and gentlemen who did not take it lying down. After he moved in, they showed up at the President's House en masse in formal dress at 3:00 on levee day. When Jefferson returned from his afternoon ride, he grasped the plot immediately and cheerfully passed among them, booted, spurred, and muddy, delighted to find them all come together by chance. The intriguers never tried again.

Jefferson replaced weekly levees with an open door, swamped though he sometimes was by a "mass of public calls." Any man or woman of any class in any clothes could see him any morning, barring some unusual demand on his time. Hamilton's college roommate said the president "observes no ceremony—often sees company in an undress, . . . always accessible to, and very familiar with, the sovereign people," a term of mock solemnity in the Federalist world. Many men and women of Jefferson's class were convinced he was playing a part for the groundlings, a populist sham he could not take seriously. "Anybody might introduce at the President's," Augustus Foster wrote, "where every blackguard might go, and at one time the dirtier the better received," which suggests a more selective admissions policy evolving over time. As Jefferson's mornings filled up with the common man and woman, they appealed to him more in principle than in person. According to Margaret Bayard Smith, he took down the bars that had kept them out but was not beneath discouraging them. His demeanor toward certain callers struck a tone of "restraining dignity," she wrote, "which repressed undue familiarity and prevented the intrusion of promiscuous or undesired visitants." Senators and the like were free to stop by as promiscuously as they pleased, and left their cards when he was busy.

But his critics were wrong to accuse him of a cynical show for political effect. His open door set the tone he thought crucial to democracy and kept him informed. Having toured rural France under Louis XVI, he encouraged the Marquis de Lafayette to do what he had done, to go among his people alone, simply dressed, if he hoped to understand their lives and desperate needs. "You must be absolutely incognito, you must ferret the people out of their hovels as I have done, look into their kettles, eat their bread, loll on their beds under pretense of resting yourself, but in fact to find if they are soft." A surreptitious tour of plebian America would have been unseemly even if it were practical, but riding alone among the people unrecognized, reading all of his mail, and chatting with whomever came to see him was the next best thing. Any caller might tell him something useful. A New England minister said he had asked President Adams to contribute to a college in Tennessee, and Adams had replied that Northern men had no cause to support Southern institutions, for the Union was sure to dissolve. Whether Jefferson believed it or not, he wrote it down.

Congressmen and senators brought constituents and guests. In 1803, Secretary of the Navy Smith presented a seventeen-year-old midshipman named Oliver Hazard Perry and four other officers fresh from the Mediterranean on the frigate *John Adams*. But unendorsed callers were freely admitted too. When the president was busy with someone else, they might leave a message with the porter. A woman who "waits at your outer door" sent in a note asking to see him "once only," or to hand in a petition "if you will not permit her in your presence." She prayed for her husband's release from debtors' prison and his creditors to "trust to his future amendment." Her husband was a kind man, she wrote, who "never misused or abused her in his life, that she knows of." People like her were seen and heard by President Jefferson, if not always pleased with the results.

To some intruders he seemed to enjoy the intrusion. A Scottish mapmaker named Melish asked friends to introduce him and was told "Mr. Jefferson was a man of no ceremony," and Melish could simply show up. When he did, he was led to the Setting Room, and Jefferson came in from his Cabinet. He offered the Scotsman a chair and started a friendly chat as if he had nothing to do. Where had Melish entered the country? New York, he replied, which he thought would be America's great port. Jefferson predicted Norfolk, though a "putrid effluvia" arose from its stagnant pools and lifted disease up the mountains. Melish said the swamp below the Capitol Hill did the same, which Jefferson confirmed. Looking out his window, he had often seen fog rise and settle on the hill, "and the inhabitants coming out of their warm rooms breathed this cold contaminated vapor," which carried a pestilence in it.

Despite Hamilton's advice to seal himself off in splendid isolation, Washington had sometimes been accessible to "respectable" citizens with letters of introduction, and so had Adams. Jefferson required no such letters, but when people handed him notes from the likes of Lafayette it could not have hurt. John C. Calhoun, having "finished his education at Yale College," brought a letter of reference in 1805. An obscure inventor named Eli Whitney did the same. An intrepid old man carried his letter all the way from Ohio, written by a settler who introduced him as "a very worthy Indian," a Shawnee who wished to see the president and "the great council of the white people" and "has behaved with propriety as far as I can learn (the time of war excepted)."

For the first time ever, the president of the United States was accessible to literally anyone. A newspaper agent who brought him a bill was only turned away, Jefferson later explained, because he was deep in business. A destitute black man came to say he had lost his only coat to one of the servants, who had falsely accused him of taking it from the President's House. Jefferson called for the coat, took a quick look, and gave it back to the poor man. It resembled his servants' coats, he said, but was not trimmed in livery like theirs.

His Setting Room was a magnet for gentlemen of science, a place to spread their wares as well as their ideas. He told an English historian that his countrymen had barely entered the race of science, but would soon begin "on the high ground prepared by their transatlantic brethren from the days of Homer," and he meant to give them a push. When "an Italian Physio-mechanic" presented himself as a glassblower of scientific instruments who "executes ingenious things in that line," Jefferson asked a fellow member of the American Philosophical Society to commend him "to some of the chemical gentlemen." A Massachusetts inventor named Pillsbury brought him an example of the first practical corn-shelling machine, and he ordered one. Over the years, he picked up the odd little gadget for the President's House himself, including a $13 "refrigerator," a cedar tub in a tin box covered with rabbit skin and cloth, contrived to carry butter to the Georgetown market from its inventor's farm.

* * *

As Jefferson began to build a plainer presidency, he made an unlikely friend. Edward Thornton, the king's bachelor envoy to the United States in 1801, was thirty-five years old with the third-class rank of chargé d'affaires, which some Americans took as a slight, as if London thought them unworthy of a full-scale ambassador. Knowing that Thornton and his government despised republicanism, Jefferson welcomed him cordially to the President's House.

Despite his Cambridge education and conservative politics, Thornton was no aristocrat but the third son of an innkeeper who had climbed above his class through a run of good luck and learned to look down on it. He struck a colleague's wife as quiet, sensible, and well-informed, showing no sign of brilliance but "well educated and full of information, which he details slowly from a natural impediment in his speech." After a good many years in America, he had taken a dislike to its Anglophobic citizens, their "barbarous dialect," and their curious love of liberty, not least "the liberty of talking in bad English." Apart from polished speech, he did not expect much more from Thomas Jefferson. As secretary of state, Thornton recalled, Jefferson had presented him to President Washington "in the plainest ordinary dress," and "both then and afterwards appeared to make a republican virtue of it," which Thornton did not.

When the Republican tide hit the Federalists in 1800, Thornton reported to Lord Grenville, the king's foreign minister, as if breaking the news of a death. "I am sorry to have to observe to your lordship," he wrote, that "a decided majority in favour of the new order of things" was likely in the House, and much of "the sound part of the Senate" would be lost as well. By and large, the "Jacobin candidates" had prevailed. But Thornton was encouraged by his chats with the Jacobin in chief. Jefferson said his government would be as cordial toward Britain as his predecessor's. His supporters had portrayed him otherwise out of politics, and His Majesty's government was too just to credit the "newspaper trash" that cast him as its enemy and "a creature of France." He might have had an interest in *republican* France, but not in Napoleon, and Thornton was glad to hear it.

Thornton called often at the President's House, and reported to his superiors Jefferson's contempt for Napoleon's love of adulation. But after several such chats, Thornton saw what he first expected, and informed Lord Hawkesbury, the new foreign minister, accordingly. Jefferson was careful to display to the people "a republican simplicity of manners" and refuse the smallest distinction, receiving everyone who approached him out of business or curiosity "with a most perfect disregard to ceremony both in his dress and manners." For Thornton, this was hypocrisy. In the 1790s, when his party endorsed the French Revolution and "the wild doctrines of equality grafted upon it," Jefferson had attacked the regal forms he himself had taught General Washington (so Thornton's Federalist friends had said), and now he could not bring them back, "for the public voice was never perhaps louder against them than at present." None "of this leveling spirit discovers itself in the interior of his house," Thornton went on, "which is far better arranged than in the time of Mr. Adams." There was now less ceremony and ostentation in the President's House but no sacrifice of luxury.

Only part of this was fair. Jefferson loved beauty and a splendid table, and he brought them to the President's House without apology, but he never confused republicanism with monasticism or condemned a gracious presidency as opposed to a regal one. Form reflected substance. It mattered what signs a president displayed, whether the "leveling spirit" Thornton mocked, or a rule of privileged access and a culture of aristocracy. "There would be little in these trifles worthy of Your Lordship's attention," Thornton told Lord Hawkesbury, "were it not for the doctrine connected with them, and were they not attended to with a minuteness and an affectation" designed to make a point "too palpable" to miss. Jefferson's style might not be worth His Lordship's attention, but social leveling in the English-speaking world was.

Despite his Tory fear of republican ideas, Thornton assured Lord Hawkesbury that Jefferson gave him "every possible mark of deference and attention" and spoke with him freely and warmly. He invited him to dinner and chess at the President's House, and later to Monticello, where the younger man guessed that only in Virginia would wealthy folk live in "an unfinished house till it is falling around their ears." Though Thornton's dispatches stuck needles in Jefferson's eye, they suggest nonetheless that he liked him, as his enemies often did. Thornton took him, in time, for what he was, as sincere in his love of liberty as his love of haute cuisine.

A year into his presidency, Jefferson told Tadeusz Kosciuszko, the Polish military engineer who had fortified the Revolution, "we have suppressed all those public forms & ceremonies which tended to familiarize the public eye to the harbingers of another form of government." With the people nearly united in republicanism, the impotent Federalist venting would soon be confined to captive newspapers, "chimneys to carry off noxious vapors & smoke." Two years later, he proudly wrote anonymously in the *Aurora* that his administration had "buried levees, birthdays, royal parades, and the arrogation of precedence in society by certain self-styled friends of order" who were "truly friends of privileged order."

Federalists saw it differently. In 1811, after all three men had retired, John Adams answered a letter from Benjamin Rush, a fellow signer of the Declaration who hoped to make an old man's peace between Adams and Jefferson. Adams replied that there had never been a war. His disagreements with the Virginian had been respectful, their stylistic differences "miserable frivolities," and Jefferson and Rush should blush for making something of them. "I held levees once a week," Adams wrote, "that all my time might not be wasted by idle visits. Jefferson's whole eight years was a levee. I dined a large company once or twice a week. Jefferson dined a dozen every day. Jefferson and Rush were for liberty and straight hair. I thought curled hair was as republican as straight." He had nothing to say to Jefferson but to wish him "an easy journey to Heaven when he goes," which he hoped would be delayed as long as his life was agreeable.

Jefferson would have enjoyed the Yankee wit and denied the proposition. His view of his predecessors' protocols as dangerously monarchist was well founded. At a formative time in the republic's history, they promoted an elitist culture and an authoritarian trend that had peaked in the Adams administration in the Alien and Sedition Acts, which suppressed the immigrant vote and made published disrespect for the president a crime. Kingly style made a president seem like a king, and Jefferson tore it up.

* * *

Jefferson always rose before dawn and soaked his feet in cold water. He typically worked until nine; received callers before an early afternoon ride on a splendid Virginia horse named Wildair, succeeded in time by Jacobin, equally well bred and sardonically named; came back to greet his guests at 3:30 for a 4:00 dinner; returned to his desk at six or seven; and went to bed at ten. The best part, for him, was on horseback. Knowing health demanded exercise, he rode out from the President's House between two and four o'clock every decent afternoon year-round, usually alone, sometimes with his secretary, never with a retinue, often humming or singing softly to himself. Riding was a dignified, gentlemanly, republican activity, a respected skill requiring subtle athleticism, done well. Riding alone through nature, Jefferson wrote, "renews the pleasurable sensation that we are still in society with the beings and the things around us."

President Washington had rolled through Philadelphia like George III in a fabulous cream-colored carriage drawn by four white horses with a liveried servant on the coachman's box. He held himself out in "a very kingly style," Thornton told London at the time, using secretaries as postilions who stood with their horses' bridles in their hands until Washington boarded his coach, then rode before his carriage. A socialite thought it notable eight years later that President Adams had cut back to a simpler four-horse carriage and a single mounted servant.

Jefferson wanted no coach at all. He walked or rode horseback alone in ordinary clothes, a rarity in a privileged Virginian, a Massachusetts congressman said. A New Hampshire senator called it a "singularity" and perhaps an affectation, but whatever it was, "the appearance ill accords with the dignity of the Chief of a great nation." When a gentlemen rode, an escort rode a deferential length behind, deterring risks and annoyances accepted by lesser men and silently announcing a figure entitled to respect. Jefferson had followed the form as secretary of state but not as president. For the French ambassador, his going about town *sans domestiques* was a lapse of dignity, but he enjoyed it and wished to be seen doing so. As he rode past his neighbors alone, stopping at the homes of friends to admire their grandchildren and their gardens or share a cup of tea, he looked like a farmer on a fine horse. Many ordinary folk had no idea who he was. Like a fairy-tale king in disguise, he could chat with the villagers unrecognized, sometimes about nothing and sometimes about current affairs and public men, an anecdotal form of polling.

Augustus Foster found it possible to ride for hours within the city limits without encountering a soul "to disturb one's meditations," and Jefferson's meditations preserved his equilibrium. In January 1802, he wrote that "seven hours of close business in the forepart of the day and four in the evening leave little time for exercise or relaxation," but he took the little he could. He envied men who had "the sole property in their own time," and his rides in the woods were a reward he seldom denied himself, finding refuge "in every bud that opens, in every breath that blows around me," in the freedom to think or go blank, "owing account to myself alone of my hours & actions." In full command of his mount, he was spotted standing straight in the stirrups plucking acorns from a tree, sure to fall if the horse moved a hoof and as perfectly relaxed, his observer thought, as if reaching for a book in his library.

He varied his destinations with no risk of monotony, Rock Creek for its beauty and unusual botany; the F Street shops, where he hitched his own horse and ripped a nail off a finger in the process; the marine barracks for a chat with the troops (there were only about a dozen, enough to provoke Gallatin, who wanted *none* in the capital); the commercial market gardens, where he gave their owners seeds and reserved the first produce of their fields; the quiet woods and empty hills that enticed him to dismount and climb rocks or wade a marsh to snip an intriguing plant; the two commercial nursery gardens, Theophilus Holt's by the Eastern Branch and Thomas Main's by Georgetown's Little Falls. Everywhere he went, he exchanged information and cuttings. After his ride, he would open the cage in his Cabinet, whistle to his mockingbird to hop upstairs at his heels, and lie on his couch to rest with an hour's serenade.

* * *

Anniversary celebrations of the Declaration of Independence could do no harm to its author. His supporters made a point of the connection, and Federalists began to shun the holiday. On July 4, 1801, Jefferson held his first Independence Day reception at the President's House and started a tradition with about a hundred celebrants, including what the *Intelligencer*'s editor Samuel Harrison Smith privately described as "most of the respectable citizens and strangers of distinction." Inclusive Republican theory notwithstanding, "respectable" and "distinction" were meaningful words. The reception was open, theoretically, but no one coaxed the lower classes in.

To kick the day off, smartly uniformed militia paraded before the house, stepping around a freshly dug well. The party began at noon in the Oval Room, where a copy of the eccentric celebrity artist Gilbert Stuart's full-length portrait of President Washington offered his hand to his fellow Americans, entirely out of character.

The first to arrive found Jefferson in a seated circle of Chickamauga Cherokee chiefs who had fought as British allies in the Revolution. Unlike other factions of their tribe, the Chickamauga Cherokee had rejected assimilation and moved to a place their descendants would call Alabama, near the Catawba tribe. Hoping to discourage random Indian delegations, Jefferson had declined an official meeting with their warrior chief named The Glass, also known less elusively as Catawba Killer.

Jefferson led the crowd to the big State Dining Room in the northwest corner of the house and mingled with them there. On its three massive sideboards (one "elegant," two "common"), stood silver bowls of punch, a selection of good wines, and a choice of sinful cakes, arranged under the eye of Monsieur Rapin. People sipped, laughed, and nibbled their way through the sideboards, stood around in clusters and chatted over the din, took seats in the painted stick chairs, juggled their plates and glasses, fanned off the heat, and enjoyed the bloom of the wines. Partway through the festivities, music drifted in through the open windows as the scarlet-coated Marine Band, "The President's Own," paraded toward the house playing Jefferson's March on instruments of music while performing military drills. Escorted by his cabinet and the diplomatic corps, the president walked out to watch on the high wooden steps to the door, followed by the crowd, tall and easy to spot, unstylishly bareheaded, his hair disarranged by the breeze. In the hall that bisected the house, the band played patriotic tunes until two.

Neither Washington nor Adams had held such a festive event. Jefferson had shown the people how to celebrate like republicans without a hint of the crown. For seven more Independence Days, other heroes of the Revolution would come to the President's House, reminding the young of what their fathers and grandfathers had given them.

6

GRUMBLE WHO WILL

Jefferson respected physicians and distrusted their art. When a bowel disorder followed him into the President's House, Dr. Rush prescribed a blistering of the wrists and ankles to stimulate the sympathy between the skin and the intestines. Wearing muslin shirts might help, and if all else failed, mercury taken with opium or rubbed on the skin almost always made a "permanent cure." Permanent it may have been had Jefferson tried it.

From the marsh below the President's House, mosquitoes rose in clouds in the hot, wet summers, with unsuspected consequences. Men of science debunked the myth that the capital was unhealthy. It was well known that marshes exuded fever-breeding gaseous miasmas, but a marsh was a marsh wherever you went, and people got sick in summer from exposure to sunshine on sand. Jefferson knew nonetheless that the tidewater region where Washington City sat was unusually lethal in summer. On a hot day in 1800, just home from the President's House, a physician and a friend had helped a poor sick man, prostrate under a tree, whom no one would take in for fear of the yellow fever. They got him out of the heat and into the president's stable, "very ill." A neighbor's lovely daughter, five years old, "was well on Friday and dead on Sunday night." When Louisa Adams came down with the yellow fever on her way to Washington, the doctor made her stretch out her arm as far as she could before he would feel her pulse, and would not look at her throat.

And then there was the weather. "Hot! Hot! Hot!" an Englishman wrote home, "and I am not aware that much alleviation has been derived from being assured by our neighbors that the season has been upon the whole a remarkably mild one." Trapped in Washington in summer "I swear occasionally," he wrote, "you women cannot conceive the comfort of swearing."

Jefferson called August and September the capital's sickly months, avoided them literally like the plague, and spent them on his mountaintop, whose cooler, drier air he compared to Washington City's like the climate of another country. It was too much to ask "a person from the mountains to pass the two bilious months on the tidewaters," he wrote, "and nothing should induce me to do it." He was not entirely sure what caused the deadly miasma; but whatever it was, he left for Monticello at the end of July 1801 for the first of his "executive recesses."

They were annual working vacations. Jefferson liked to think of them as reserved for his own affairs, but the country's never stopped, and were harder to address without his secretary, his files, and his department heads. A letter from Gallatin that "must have slept a week somewhere" was not unique, but the postmaster general had the president's mail brought to Monticello every Tuesday and Friday on a three-day run—two days by the mail stage to Fredericksburg, on horseback the rest of the way—which kept him in touch with his cabinet. In 1806 he hired "an express," a young man to bring messages to his secretaries of war and the navy on horseback at speed. Food and lodging for man and beast were provided at the President's House. By 1807, Jefferson's mail came to Monticello every day, and visitors reached the foot of his mountain on the weekly stage, to be met by a servant in a coach.

Federalists objected to the first of these breaks, which he thought his health demanded. Washington had gone home every year for two months and Adams for eight, and restoring the norm to two should provoke no grumbling, "but grumble who will, I will never pass those months on tide water." If he lost any sleep over the ditchdiggers, craftsmen, and foremen at work on his projects in the capital, he did not record it. But for everyone in the President's House, slave and free and all their families, he provided the costly year-round services of his personal physician, including smallpox vaccinations, medicines and ointments, twice-daily visits to a sick servant, and treating Julien's kitchen burns.

* * *

Pleased as Jefferson was with Monsieur and Madame Rapin, they had decided by June of 1801 to return to Philadelphia after only three months as maître d' and *femme d'charge* of the President's House, for reasons they did not share, but Rapin volunteered to stay until he was replaced. Philippe de Létombe, who had found him in Philadelphia, recruited one Charles Schroeder there, a former maître d' to the French minister to the United States, but Schroeder and his wife wanted almost half again as much as the Rapins were paid. Jefferson told Létombe that Schroeder "must reduce himself" to a hundred guineas and be told it was "a fixed sum beyond which no pretensions will carry me. I have had to do the same with my other servants, who finding that I am fixed, now stay contentedly & gladly." Again a firm hand applied to the common man.

As Jefferson prepared to return to Monticello, Létombe found Étienne Lemaire, a Paris-trained maître d' who would serve him for thirty dollars a month. Jefferson sent Rapin "express to Philadelphia" to dispel his fellow Frenchman's doubts, "if he has any," and propose to deliver the house to him while the president was on his mountain. As Jefferson had foreseen, Lemaire drove a harder bargain when he realized he was wanted and by whom. In addition to his pay, he told Rapin, he understood he would get two suits of clothes a year. "I told him that he had been ill informed," Rapin advised Jefferson, but his laundry would be free. Lemaire took the job and a private room on the sunny walkout side of the servants' hall. In a gracious note to Rapin, Jefferson said he was glad to have Lemaire; "still this does not suppress my regret at losing you," having enjoyed "the most perfect satisfaction" with the Rapins. As a parting favor, he asked Rapin to impress upon Lemaire that "while I wish to have every thing good in its kind, and handsome in stile, I am a great enemy to waste and useless extravagance and see them with real pain." The key word here was "useless," for useful extravagance would advance his public agenda after Congress returned to be wooed at his table.

A considerate man with a paunch who kept the house orderly, happy, and secure, Lemaire supervised the domestic staff, presided over dinner, and hired free black women by the day to clean the chimneys and the privies and care for the servants' children. As Margaret Bayard Smith could see, he "understood his business to perfection, having served in some of the first families abroad." Working closely with Julien, Lemaire trained the kitchen and dining room staffs and did most of the shopping in Georgetown and the Washington City market from a three-wheeled horse drawn cart, occasionally joined by the president of the United States, who knew a ripe melon when he saw one. On Fridays Lemaire bought meat and fowl for the Protestants and the Deists and the best available fish for the Catholics.

Lemaire paid the household bills, and the prodigious sum of ten thousand dollars a year, more or less, passed through his clever hands. Jefferson's sharp-eyed daughter Martha suspected that some of it stuck. Lemaire was "a portly, well-mannered Frenchman," she later recalled, "of whose honesty his master had a higher opinion than the world at large, and who I fancy made a small fortune in his employ. But he was civil, and a useful man, and merited reward."

In fact he was kind and generous, and if he rewarded himself illicitly, he outfoxed his meticulous employer. Lemaire kept daily track of the mansion's expenses in a log loosely spelled in French and nearly free of grammar, which Jefferson reviewed every week, converting into dollars and cents the Virginia pounds, shillings, and pence Lemaire spent, summing them up once a month in his own punctilious ledger and handing Lemaire a bank draft to cover them. In characteristic style, Jefferson combed the numbers into all sorts of tabulations, including the average sum he spent on dinner guests, per person, separately for when Congress was in and when it was out, and also for his servants' meals when he was in Washington and when he was at Monticello, suspicious of the latter.

During one of his absences in the bilious months, Lemaire wrote to him in French that he had taken the liberty of sending help to the family of "Joseph, the poor gardener," who had died of a fever. "You did right," Jefferson replied in English. His Monticello overseer Edmund Bacon, summoned to Washington several times, was struck by Lemaire's decency as much as his competence. He was smart, Bacon thought, "as much of a gentleman in his appearance as any man," and his kindness to the staff was returned. In September of 1802, Jefferson's business agent, John Barnes, let him know that Lemaire had come down with a "foul Stomack" and a high fever and, "like most patients," was "fretful & fearful," as every feverish patient had cause to be. Jefferson's physician Dr. Gantt attended him constantly, at the president's expense, and Julien, "who is quite the good nurse—sets by him day & night."

In the following August, another bilious month, Lemaire was down with a fever again and wrote to Monticello seeking three weeks leave. "I beg you Sir, if this is possible, I would be infinitely obliged. If you have the slightest objection, however, I will stay. . . . All the family here is well, as is your bird, which continues to be charming." Jefferson promptly agreed and let Lemaire know his job was safe: "Be assured of my attachment to you." A year after that, the Frenchman's health rose again to a presidential concern: "I hope you will keep yourself still for the benefit of your leg," Jefferson wrote, since "nothing but rest & time will restore it."

Kind and likable as Lemaire was, Jefferson's worldlier guests may have found him a touch underdone for a presidential maître d', starting with his weak command of his native tongue, but Jefferson found his abysmal French entertaining instead of disqualifying. In 1803, Jefferson sent Maria some of Lemaire's French recipes. The spelling, he wrote, "will be puzzling and amusing." His English cannot have been better, but amusing it surely was, and Jefferson valued skill more than polish. He liked the "good humor, industry, sobriety & economy" he found in Étienne Lemaire, who kept the keys to the President's House until they left it together.

* * *

Jefferson planned to enclose and improve fewer than nine of the sixty acres L'Enfant had laid out for the president's grounds, an estate that would have flattered the royal House of Bourbon and embarrassed the republican house of Jefferson. In the summer of 1801 there were no real grounds at all. On the day before Jefferson left for Monticello, one Richard Forrest, Esq., was engaged to enclose the President's House. The budget allowed for nothing grand, just an honest split rail fence "of good, sound white oak," six rails high on eight-foot posts planted two feet in the ground, the sort that kept goats out of gardens. It would stretch more than half a mile around and be done in two months, before the president returned. The fence, once built, was "a very rude pale," said the poet Thomas Moore, "through which a common rustic stile introduced visitors," one of whom recorded the sight of "his Excellency's stockings and shirts" hung out to dry on its rails with a maid's blue petticoat.

With Jefferson gone until October, the heroic task of clearing the grounds by hand began under his orders. In the blanket of humid heat that smothers a Washington summer, sweating men, slave and free, moved a dozen workmen's shacks off the grounds, ripped storage sheds apart, tore brick kilns down, carted away debris, and dumped it who knows where, all in the bilious months. The demolition of the presidential privy, unsightly in Jefferson's eyes, unremarkable in others', would wait until the end of 1803 for want of tin pipes for the water closets. The last of the brick kilns would stand in the front yard until the spring of 1807.

The interior work continued while the president was away, sparing him the saws, shouts, and hammers; the reek of paint and plaster; and the comings and goings of scaffolds, ladders, and carts. Thomas Claxton chose an attractive Brussels carpet for Jefferson's bedroom, and an enclosure was built for its water closet. Carpenters, painters, and plasterers improved the Oval Room. Its chandelier and drapes went up, its carpet went down, and Claxton told the president "it looks well indeed, considering that all its furniture is common," but the sofas were still with the upholsterer, "who is deliberate with all his work." Claxton promised to put everything in order "as soon as the different mechanics are out of the house."

After Jefferson was done with it, a labor of love that lasted years, the Oval Room would be anything but common, with paneled wainscoting, decorated overdoor pediments, and classical friezes along the edge of the double height ceiling. The five tall windows facing the river were glazed with translucent glass, and the matching five alcoves across the room paned in mirrors and finished in sash, all ten of them draped with toile de Jouy curtains. In a decorator's faux pas, four informal mahogany sofas upholstered in black and stuffed with horsehair made an unholy alliance with two dozen gilded Louis XVI chairs, very rare in America and slightly out of style, delicately done in blue silk, foreshadowing the Blue Room that the Oval Room would be.

In late September the commissioners sent anxious notes to contractors, imploring one of them to deliver the fan lights for the demilune windows Jefferson wanted up before his return, the other to ship on the first boat from Alexandria a long ignored order for twelve panes of glass to finish them, "as the President is expected in a few days, and we wish to have the workmen out." On September 30, after four trying days on the road, he returned to a house in disarray. Whether the windows were up or not, the Oval Room was unfinished, its contractual completion date out of reach. The split rail fence, supposed to be done by now, would expand for two more months, double the bargained-for time. The decorative caps for thirty-two doors would not even be ordered until November; the walls, or rather the studs, of the full-length room at the house's eastern end were still not lathed for plaster, and neither were most of the bedchambers, or the anticipated site of the main staircase. All of that work and more would go on for months before Jefferson's eyes and ears. After decades of cohabiting with builders, anything else would have surprised him.

Worse news reached him soon. James Hemings, the Paris-trained chef he had lost for the staff of the President's House for lack of a nice little note, had cooked for him at Monticello during the summer. How this was arranged will never be known, but Jefferson paid him twenty dollars a month with room and board. Julien got thirty at the President's House but was hired away from Philadelphia at the same wage, and free men and women earned rural compensation at Monticello. In early October, after Jefferson left for Washington, having no open place for a cook at the President's House, Hemings returned to Baltimore and took his own life. The president made inquiries, but could not reconstruct what he called "the tragical end of James Hemings."

* * *

When Jefferson returned to his desk, its drifts of unread paper included an unpaid expense account that Rapin had left before he went home to Philadelphia. No one could have quit the president of the United States after a few months of service and received a more considerate note than Jefferson wrote to Rapin, which speaks well of both men. Lemaire was excelling in Rapin's place, "and I am in hopes that we shall be perfectly satisfied with each other." Rapin's expense account was "perfectly right & just" and about to be paid in full. His service and integrity had been exemplary, and whatever circumstances obliged him to leave, "if they were for your benefit it will be a consolation, as I shall be happy always to hear of your success in life."

On October 19, with a chill in the air, Claxton wrote the president from Philadelphia, falling all over himself with excuses and "great mortification." There was no chance of getting good fireplace grates in time for winter. He had ordered them in June from one of the city's best craftsmen, who had suddenly turned unreliable. Having promised the grates half a dozen times, he had not produced a single one. Claxton thought he could find some crude ones in Washington to get them through the winter. Carefully installed, "they may appear tolerably decent," a pretty low bar for the President's House and a president who noticed. Jefferson's reply could not have been more forgiving, to the point of seeing nothing to forgive. Regarding "your disappointment as to the grates," he wrote, as if Claxton alone were disappointed, "common cheap ones" would do for one winter, and proper ones could be ordered from England. Claxton could buy a kitchen grate as he thought best. "Accept my best wishes and esteem." We can almost hear Claxton exhale.

A notice in the *Intelligencer* solicited interest in a brick house that fall, but despite its prestigious location, "North front of the President's House," with two parlors and four bedrooms, "convenient to the public offices," there were no takers, and when Jefferson came down from his mountain, the local eyesores may have looked sorer. On October 13, he sat with the commissioners and their maps and directed them to finish the two great avenues, the Pennsylvania Avenue, which stretched from Rock Creek past the President's House to the Capitol, and the New Jersey Avenue's run up the Capitol Hill. To "finish" meant to tear out the scattered brush, pull out the occasional stump, and smooth out the dirt, which was all that republican economy allowed.

A few weeks later, the commissioners ordered the sale and removal of the shacks on the President's Square, home to several poor families. The buyers would pay a punishing ten-dollar weekly surcharge until the ugly things were gone. They were auctioned on the square at Rhodes Tavern the next spring, with their occupants allowed to stay as long as four months before the buyers jacked them up and hauled them away. Also auctioned off, wasting nothing, were odds and ends from the house's construction on the order of one iron kettle, two cartwheels, and a barrel of tar.

The ramshackle sheds at the open-air market on the President's Square, jammed with peddlers' carts once a week on market day, were soon gone too, to the benefit of the view from the State Dining Room. The dislocated vendors set up shop at the new Centre Market between Seventh and Ninth on the Pennsylvania Avenue, built by James Hoban, the designer of the President's House. As the vegetable men picked their spots and arranged their goods, Washington's first public streetlight went up on the New Jersey Avenue bridge, another was hung from a tree where the Pennsylvania Avenue reached the Capitol, and a third by the M Street bridge, all of them whale oil fueled.

* * *

Though Lemaire tried to keep them downstairs, some of the servants' frictions, factions, and feuds found their way to the president, shedding light on him as an employer, and therefore as a man, and exposing the inner house.

Jefferson later said he employed Joseph Dougherty "rather as a riding agent than as the head of my stable," a subtle distinction that omitted his sharp eyes and ears in the servants' hall. An ambitious young man, Dougherty had come from Londonderry in the North of Ireland, surely with a formidable accent sometimes lapsing into dialect. He was one of the president's favorites, bright with "all the glow of affection and enthusiasm peculiar to his nation," said Margaret Bayard Smith, who stooped to credit him with "a degree of elevation and refinement of feelings and views seldom or ever found in his class."

In April of 1802, as Jefferson paid for himself and three friends to marvel at coal gas Thermo Lamps, a "New Mode of Obtaining Light" in a new house on the Pennsylvania Avenue, Dougherty addressed him in writing. What he had to say was "more than I Can do when face to face so I beg leave to do it in this manner so as it may be correct." Apparently, "Mr. Lamaire" had asked Dougherty's wife, Mary, a housemaid in the family, to count the linens. "She Don't wish to refuse it," Dougherty wrote, "but she is not willing to do it on the account she knows the number will be far short of what it should be." The theft should have been "prohibited." By whom he did not say, but Lemaire was the sole prohibitor. Dougherty had known "there was pilferers in the House," but "it was kept from me as much as possible."

When Mary was sick, Dougherty said, Betsy Süverman, Christopher Süverman the footman's wife, had gone into Mary's room and taken a five-dollar note when she thought her victim was sleeping. When confronted she proclaimed her innocence "with an oath." No one had told Dougherty, including Mary, until the linen count. Christopher kept his room locked, and who knew what was in it? Dougherty had said nothing, thinking that Mr. Lemaire would handle it, but "he is two easy a man for Betsy & Christopher," and "Christopher being my old fellow servant," would it not be "a hard circumstance to be the first in the House to hurt his character." (Harder still, since Christopher had gone nearly blind and was now in Philadelphia with Rapin.) Dougherty asked that his name not be mentioned and added a touch of mystery. "There is something as yet of more Importance that I Dont wish to Let you know untill I try to investigate the truth." Wherever his investigation went, it did not hurt Christopher in Jefferson's eyes. He commended him years later as an honest man.

Two weeks after that, other troubles reached the president at Monticello. The footman John Kramer had left, Dougherty wrote, "on account of his new wife's ignominious behavior," implying by omission that Jefferson knew the particulars or could guess. Dougherty was not pleased that Edward Maher had been rehired to take his place. "If he is continued sir, you may rest assured that his stay wont be more than two or three months. Moreover you know Sir that he is a verry disagreeable Man in a family although he is a good servant." Maher, the footman who did not do windows and balked at wearing the same livery as a slave, had quit in the fall. "Sir," his resignation letter read, "as you Cant a ford me more weages I must See and beter Myself. I am sorrey to leave you. Edward Maher." Jefferson gave him a full month's pay for his self-inflicted pain and made a note in his ledger: "He goes away." Now he had come back.

In a separate letter to the president, unaware of Dougherty's, Lemaire broke the news in French, more kindly than Dougherty had done in English, that John Kramer had gone, and "left his new wife since they could not live together." Now there was no one to help Captain Lewis's man, Abraham Golden, with the cleaning, but Edward Maher was available for rehire, contrite about quitting (especially, perhaps, since his new employer had moved away), and had promised to make the president glad to take him back. Lemaire did not add that he had already given Edward the job.

Jefferson replied immediately. He was not sorry to lose John, who had his good qualities but was "awkward & ignorant." Nor was he keen on Edward, whose porter's rank set his nose too high: "I think it better not to take Edward. He is a very capable servant, but stands too much on etiquette. I like servants who will do every thing they are wanted to do." Edward was fickle too, having "served all the masters in the world" for six months. Mr. Rapin should be asked to find in Philadelphia a "sober, diligent and good humored" porter who would keep the Setting Room, the Cabinet, and the Oval Room in order, leaving the dining rooms to John Freeman.

Rapin came through at once. Lewis stopped to see him in Philadelphia, where they spoke about John Kramer's "stupid action" and Christopher Süverman's disability. Rapin had proposed to replace them both with a valet named Duval. Duval's last employer had given him sixteen dollars a month and his old clothes. He would probably ask the president for eighteen, "perhaps a little less if laundry were included." Rapin did not say whether Duval was Jefferson's size. Süverman was staying with Rapin while a Philadelphia doctor, a specialist procured by Jefferson's physician Dr. Gantt, tried to save his better eye. Perhaps "this poor unfortunate will have to go to the hospital or the poor house," but if his sight could be partly restored, he might find work as a doorman "with a recommendation from your excellency."

Jefferson wrote Lemaire that the more he thought about Edward Maher, the more he did not want him back. Even John Kramer had more to commend him, illiteracy included, for whenever the president left his Cabinet, he had reason to believe that Edward read the papers on his table, "and it was impossible for me to lock them up every time I stepped out of the room. It was therefore a recommendation of Kramer to me that he could not read writing."

"I let Edward go," Lemaire replied, tacitly admitting that he had rehired him to begin with, and replaced him with an "intelligent and very clean" footman named William Fitzjames, who stayed for years, cleaning and scrubbing in workman's clothes, putting on livery when he kept the door. Rapin's recommendation of Duval the valet did not please Lemaire, who took a rare shot at them both. Regarding Duval, "I beg you to take my word for it that he is not the man you need." It was surprising that Mr. Rapin had not mentioned him to Lemaire, "since he does not know the valet as I do." Duval spoke no English, which would not be an issue were it not for "other defects. I will tell you the rest when you return."

Jefferson dropped the curtain on this comedy of manners in a letter to Rapin, thanking him for recommending Duval and finding a silver lining in his rejection by Lemaire: "Some difficulty" might have come from his expectation of eighteen dollars a month. The other servants got fourteen, and an expectation of a raise "might have been accommodated." He would send Christopher Süverman some money, and hoped he would regain his sight. If not, he could find better work in Philadelphia than in "this place," and his wife was able bodied. The Süvermans were dropped from the payroll the next day. Three days after that, having given Christopher a month's pay in advance, which he never earned, and ten dollars "in charity" in the fall, Jefferson sent him an additional twenty, another ten a month later, and thirty more the following year. All told he gave Süverman six months' pay, apart from the cost of his expert medical care. Throughout his presidency, Jefferson's account books are riddled with endless entries, large and small, labeled "charity."

Dougherty could be charitable too, and had taken a liking to his subordinate, "Stable Jack" Shorter, a slave leased from his master. During Jefferson's 1803 spring interlude, Dougherty sent him a note. "The family is all well and live tranquil Sir," he wrote, and Shorter's master proposed to sell him to the president, subject to his right to freedom in 1810 under an old master's will. Dougherty plainly hoped that Jefferson would agree. But the president had not seen the last of his servants' disputes. In May of 1803, a brother of Sally Houseman, a washerwoman at the President's House, wrote to tell him she had been ill used by her colleague Abraham Golden, more specifically, "knocked prostrate on the floor, and that without any assault from her side." Her brother did not wish the president to "reap satisfaction," but merely to preserve "peace and tranquility, without which it is impossible to live consoled," Jefferson's sentiments exactly.

In July of 1804, the president was told no damage had been done, but "malcontents" on the construction crews at the President's House and the Capitol had gone "riotously parading about the streets" and been dismissed. Some were Irish, some American, "some free blacks & slaves" (as opposed to Americans). Some of the Irish shovel men had begged forgiveness, including in particular one "poor, ignorant, inoffensive creature." All of them had invoked "their numerous, helpless, and almost starving families," a hint at the cause of their discontent. Jefferson took them back, excluding the ones who were "active and insolent on the late occasion," hungry families or not.

As the free white servants and poorly paid laborers jockeyed in and out of position, the *Intelligencer* published alternatives. "FOR SALE," one notice read. "An excellent Blacksmith, together with his wife and three likely children, to wit, two boys, 10 and 8 years of age, and a girl four." The wife washed and ironed, but if $1,400 was too much to pay for a family of five, "a negro woman about 21 years old" could be had for less, "a good cook and a complete house servant in every other respect—also a large, well formed horse that goes well in a carriage and pleasant under the saddle."

In 1773, Jefferson had bought an enslaved cook named Ursula and her two children and believed her breast milk may have saved little Martha's life. Perhaps at Ursula's request, he later bought her husband George Granger, who refused to betray his master's whereabouts to Benedict Arnold's British troops when they came for him during the Revolution. Jefferson later made Granger his only enslaved overseer. In the fall of 1801, thinking of his retirement and the risks of engaging free cooks, he brought to the President's House a granddaughter of the Grangers, also named Ursula, for Julien and Lemaire to train, seeing something special in her, apart from his respect for the Grangers. Some but not all of his thoughts about uprooting slaves involved those "as could be persuaded to it," and Ursula may have been asked rather than compelled to come and rise within the limits of her enslavement. Having never been away from home, she found herself suddenly in a city, more or less, in the grandest house in America, supervised by men, however kind, whose English must have puzzled her. She was fourteen years old. Perhaps unknown to Jefferson but probably not to Ursula, who may already have married Wormley Hughes, a twenty-year-old gardener and hostler at Monticello, she was pregnant.

James Hemings, a free man, had passed up a job at the President's House for want of a letter. Ursula Granger may have been glad to be there, but she had no right to say no. Working among white and free black servants, she earned two dollars a month "for drink," two more than her master was obliged to pay, but his white servants earned eight to fourteen, all told, with a right to leave at will, as some of them did.

* * *

On October 26, 1801, Jefferson wrote his younger daughter Maria a theme on loneliness in the President's House, where his visitors buzzed around his power. "I have here company enough," he wrote, "part of which is very friendly, part well enough disposed, part secretly hostile, and a constant succession of strangers. But this only serves to get rid of life, not to enjoy it." True happiness was found only in love of family, and he felt it when he was alone, "beyond what can be imagined."

Loneliness, soon enough, was the least of his worries. On November 6, Maria wrote him a letter she had hoped not to send. The "hooping cough" was wracking her infant son Francis, so violently that it turned his little face black. It had killed her two-year-old sister Lucy in 1784 when Maria was six. Francis had been suffering for eleven days, and Maria's optimism could not have cheered his grandfather: "my hopes are great" for his survival.

At about the same time, a servant brought Jefferson two letters from Monticello, one from his daughter Martha, the other from his granddaughter Ellen. "How do you do my dear Grand papa," the five-year-old began. "I thank you for the picture you sent me. I hope you will bring me some books." Her sisters had the hooping cough, she wrote, and "the children made such a noise I could not write well. Make haste & come home to see us." The letter from her mother was terrifying. There was fear, Martha wrote, that Ellen and her sister Cornelia had worms, which would probably kill them both if the parasites could not be destroyed. Little Virginia was choking with the hooping cough as though strangling, and Martha herself had been ill from lack of sleep. Jefferson must have opened her next letter with dread. Maria's baby Francis was "in a very precarious state of being," and Ellen had a shockingly violent cough, though the crisis may have passed. "My God what moment for a parent." Her husband was no help. "The agonies of Mr. Randolph's mind" left her struggling as "nurse to my children and comforter to their Father."

What a moment for Thomas Jefferson, alone in the President's House in the gloom of late November. To his ultimate relief, all of the children lived.

7

CHIEFLY OF THE SNEERING KIND

Jefferson wore spectacles to read and write, starting with half-sized lenses he could peer over and progressing in 1807 to "Dr. Franklin's plan of half glasses of different focal distances," which he ordered to his specifications with silver frames. Given the piles of paper that crossed his desk, he needed them.

One sort of mail came from office seekers, most of them unqualified, like the "class of swaggering sycophants" who showed up in person and offended "distinguished and well-bred people," one distinguished, well-bred person said. "I need not tell you I am poor," a Quincy, Massachusetts, man's letter began. "If I were not I should be spared the disagreeable feelings I experience in commencing a beggar." He hoped John Quincy Adams might endorse him for an officer's commission. "Not that I have any acquaintance of him, but he being a resident in Quincy has probably heard of me." George Meade, a supporter whose unborn grandson would make his name at Gettysburg, had a friend who had been removed from office and another on the block. Something should be done, and while he was thinking about it, any highly paid office "I would not refuse myself."

Jefferson rarely answered such letters, on the theory that the successful applicant had his answer in the result, and so did "the unsuccessful multitude." To explain himself would consume all his time, and "into what controversies would it lead me?" For every post he filled, he wrote, he made a hundred enemies and one ingrate. Nothing like a perquisite, the duty to make appointments was a burden, and yet, "like the office of hangman, it must be executed by someone."

Aware since the Revolution that historians would read every word he wrote for centuries, that even careless scribbles would be kept and saved forever like notes to posterity in a bottle, he composed some letters meticulously, and some he dashed off in one go, denying himself revisions he did not have time to make. An instinctively graceful writer, he was capable of drafting grocery lists with charm, and much of what he wrote on an ordinary day mixed the memorable with the mundane, sometimes irregularly spelled in an age of optional spelling. At a single sitting, he was capable of inviting three different guests to come to dinner at "Sun Set," "sun-set," and "sun:set."

Forty years of correspondence with coal brokers, tobacco farmers, granddaughters learning to read, and the leading philosophers of the Western world had made him a fluid letter writer. As president, he often wrote five or six a day, many of them weighty and long, folded and sealed with wafers and addressed on the obverse side. No presidential letterhead existed. Always using the finest materials, bought at his own expense, Jefferson ordered from the Republican editor and stationer William Duane the best woven English stationery and "fine vellum hot pressed letter paper" by the ream; Irish wafers by the pound; thick and thin inks by the vial, quart, and gill; dozens of premium Middleton pencils; hundreds of invitations and imported Dutch quills and "best quills No. 4"; one glass inkstand; two Wedgwood inkstands; a marble note presser; and lengths of red tape for binding documents. When he wished to send papers he did not want creased, he rolled them on wooden dowels. Since paper was expensive, he generally used a modest 9" × 6" sheet and advised his friend Charles Willson Peale that "if one has to write the punctilious correspondent who might consider his dignity implicated in the size of the paper on which he is addressed," a 12" × 9½" sheet "leaves a good margin."

In his first seven years in the President's House, he wrote with goose quill pens as he always had, common pens, he called them, common since antiquity, but not for their convenience. They required constant dipping and a sharp penknife to reshape the point and trim the feather as the tip wore down, which led him to pens made of wood or glass. In February of 1804, Peale sent him a pen he had made of steel, perhaps the first in America, hoping to make a fortune leaving feathers to the geese. Quills were troublesome, Peale reminded him, and costly too. But fond of clever tools though he was, Jefferson liked his quills, having done pretty well with them. He did not give them up until March of 1808, when half a dozen of Peregrine Williamson's slit metal pens converted him, though they wore out fast.

He had written and kept tedious summaries of every meaningful letter he wrote until 1785 when he saw in a Paris shop a desktop copy press invented by James Watt, the Scottish steam engine prodigy, and paid its hefty price. He would have spent ten times as much, he told Madison, to have had it since the

Stamp Act. To operate it, you laid a thin sheet of moistened paper over a letter written in ink, cranked it through a set of rollers, and peeled off a blurry copy. In 1786, Jefferson designed a portable model and had it made in London to his ingenious specifications, a test of British craftsmanship involving little brass rollers and springs. He loved it at first sight and took it to the President's House, but early in his presidency, his purchasing agent Thomas Claxton brought back from Philadelphia a more highly evolved model. A terrific innovation, Jefferson found it to be. It worked with a screw and lever like a miniature printing press and struck off as many copies as you liked.

In addition to copying by machine every significant letter he sent, Jefferson filed with his own hand every significant one he received, often jotting a note on its face. With a constant view toward history, lacking confidence that his files were safe, and knowing that the executive departments kept the official records, he gave the appropriate department a copy of every letter he sent and received. Taking time to influence history, not just preserve it, he arranged them in the order in which he wanted historians to study them. Given that he made almost no public speeches at all, the care he took with his archives shows far more concern about his place in history than his image in his own time.

In an 1801 letter to Virginia's governor James Monroe, Jefferson made it clear that in matters reserved to the states he would write to the governors as Washington had, on an "absolutely equal" basis, and paused to add convincingly, "if it be possible to be certainly conscious of any thing, I am conscious of feeling no difference between writing to the highest or lowest being on earth." His letters to ordinary beings prove him right, showing empathy and respect, no condescension, and hardly less care than he gave to the world's great minds. He wrote 116 letters in his own hand in his first month in office, many of them long and several of them moving.

The emotion comes through in some personal notes he sent in his first weeks in the President's House to each surviving signer of the Declaration of Independence, a sentimental courtesy to his brother revolutionaries. To Samuel Adams, one of the oldest at seventy-eight, he cast his inaugural address as "a letter to you, my very dear and ancient friend." He had asked himself as he wrote it, he said, "is this exactly in the spirit of the patriarch of liberty, Samuel Adams? Is it as he would express it? Will he approve of it?" It would have been a glorious day for the republic had Adams been called to be president, "but give us your counsel, my friend, and give us your blessing," for "I shall ever bear you the most affectionate veneration and respect."

With a stiff shot of anger and no hint of reverence, he wrote a different kind of letter on the same day, probably at the same sitting, to Elbridge Gerry, another

Massachusetts signer but a fellow arch Republican a year younger than he. From New York through the South, he wrote, the people had rejected Federalism, but New England had "drunk deeper of the delusion," and powerful men were "prostituted there to toll us back to the times when we burnt witches," the old swipe at Massachusetts. Gerry's people would rise to republicanism again, and Gerry would lead them. Despite "the howlings of the ravenous crew from whose jaws they are escaping," a restoration of "harmony and social love" among all Americans was "almost the first object of my heart, & one to which I would sacrifice everything but principle."

In the Declaration of Independence, Jefferson had accused George III, famously and furiously, of almost every regal crime imaginable. A trace of irony may have crossed his mind as he wrote him several times as president, beginning with the ritual salutation to heads of state, "Great and Good Friend," and closing with the standard blessing: "I pray God to have your Majesty in his safe and holy keeping."

Tardy with replies to his mail, he justly blamed his burdens. In the summer of 1804, he apologized for putting aside no less than ten of an old friend's letters over a three-year stretch. "So constant is the pressure of business that there is never a moment, scarcely, that something of public importance is not waiting for me. I have therefore, on a principle of conscience, thought it my duty to withdraw almost entirely from all private correspondence." It was not quite true, but close enough for a friend. In 1805, even his fourteen-year-old granddaughter Anne tried to shame him: "I wrote to my Dear Grand papa last post but I suppose he did not receive my letter or he certainly would have answered it. In my last letter I mentioned the changing my name to Anastasia but you did not say whether you approved it."

He resolved to resist corresponding with scientific gentlemen at all, denying himself "the pleasure of mathematical & other speculations which are not immediately connected with my duty." Even so, he experimented at the President's House on a silk rug's conduction of heat, interested in the warming qualities of fabrics used in clothing, agreed to turn a "machine" brought to him there in a carriage, and sinned by answering mail from men of science more often than his conscience liked. In 1804 he replied within days to an amateur astronomer who sent him the longitude and latitude of the President's House, and a letter's passing reference to a mill moved by none of the known means was too much to resist. When told of a claim of proof that stones fell from the sky, he replied that he neither believed nor disbelieved it, for "chemistry is too much in its infancy to satisfy us." It reminded him of a friend incapable of an untruth who claimed to have seen a rain of fish. "How he could be deceived in such a fact was as difficult for me to account for as how the fact should happen," which led him to defer an opinion "till new rains of fish should take place to confirm it."

In 1802, a literally mad scientist, later said by his lawyer to suffer "mental wildness and incapacity," wrote in detail to the president. Properly adjusted, the madman wrote, a steam engine could drive a carriage or a plow. Jefferson quickly replied. His duties demanded the whole of his time, "and more than the whole, if more there could be," but the leisure to study the idea "would be peculiarly agreeable to me." Recent work on the power of steam would produce "a great change in the situation of man," steam-driven carriages not excluded. "No law of nature forbids us to hope this," and "that you may succeed in it, I sincerely wish."

The law entitled him to send official letters postage-free, a privilege he exercised scrupulously, buying stamps for private mail. Citizens' letters to *him* could be sent free too, and he got close to two thousand in his first year in office, not counting what his department heads sent almost daily. No one screened any part of it and, remarkably enough, Jefferson seems to have skimmed it all, at least in the beginning, no matter how trivial, though the writing often ranged from the illegible to the incredible. With his own hand, he endorsed every item with its date of receipt, sometimes adding a note, not excepting the work of "beggars," as he classified more than a few.

Some unfortunate citizens seeking help positioned themselves as entrepreneurs. A Maryland man sent five copies of Jefferson's inaugural address and suggested a five-dollar payment, "as the goddess of fortune has not been over liberal in bestowing her gifts upon me." A man who had once repaired clocks at Monticello, now "Verging into the Deepest Vale of Misfortune & Distress Brought on by a Variety of the Cruel Vissitudes of Life," offered a "Very ancient" diamond ring for whatever price "your Excellency in your wisdom shall think fit to give."

Many good people asked for charity, having nowhere else to go. "Sir," a letter sent from Baltimore began, "a poor and distressed girl now addresses you. I give you no title, fearing to expose my ignorance an least I should offend you by thinking it would be pleasing." She asked for a little help for her ruined father. "This day I have entered my seventeen year, and I must meet my father with a smile for he little nows how I have spent the Morning." An educated Annapolis woman, desperate from "the irreparable loss of $340," reached out "from the very ashes of despair." Others tried a breezy approach. "I dare say you will be much surprised at receiving a letter from one you have not the least acquaintance with upon-earth," a Washingtonian began. "And much more so when you hear the subject . . . the lone of a little money to carry me to Baltimore." Another plea for help was impatient: "this Sur is the Secont that I have Sant to your honor and I hope Sur that I shant have a Cashon to Sand No mor." All of these Jefferson endorsed as received but not as answered. He could not support every pauper or even start. Churchmen often asked him to help fund a new meetinghouse. He was obliged to deny all such requests from beyond his home county, he told a Rhode Islander, for so many came in that "no resources I can command could answer them."

Many voters were displeased with him and less respectful than they might have been. A Republican wasted no words: "That you are a damned Scoundrel is the opinion of your former friend but present enemy." Calmer citizens sent him advice, much if not all of which he read. Knowing that the annual plague of yellow fever ended with the first frost, a thoughtful citizen proposed moving victims into icehouses. Implying that the idea intrigued him, Jefferson filed it under "yellow fever," instead of "lunacy," as he sometimes did with others. Early in his presidency, he forwarded to the secretary of war with a generously open mind an anonymous letter, "chiefly of the sneering kind," that included a good idea. Some of his mail must have given him a laugh. An English seaman named William Jefferson had an older brother Thomas who had vanished forty years earlier. "Hearing your Name in the Papirs a little while back," the sailor wrote, it would give him "Infinite Pleasure to hear by a line that a Brother was Still in being."

Unbalanced men and women called out to him through the mails. One inquired "wether I shall be a Member of Congress or not." Another sent word of "an endeavorment of killing me mystically by electricity or magnetism." A letter from a man who took arsenic daily, "inspired by God Almighty" in Maryville, Tennessee, said "the United States will all be ruined if they do not desist from such wicked practices," which he did not specify. "Should you hang me that will close the scan of my unfortunate life." Even this Jefferson filed with a notation: "Madman." Threats were not uncommon. A Philadelphian applied for a diplomatic post in France (specifically not in "the barren quarters of Barbarry"), for otherwise he must "preyh in the streets." His appointment, he said, was "the most advisable thing you can possibly think of, and that immediately. Other wise, you must most assuredly hear from me or mine in language different from this."

Presents of all kinds came regularly through the mail. A dictionary sent from New Haven by one Noah Webster arrived with a request for "such encouragement as you may think it deserves," which Jefferson gave to its author if no one else. The motives behind most gifts were "honorable to me, and gratifying," he explained to one man, and he would accept a pamphlet, a book, or a curiosity worth a sum "below suspicion. But things of sensible value, however innocently offered in the first examples, may grow at length into abuse, for which I wish not to furnish a precedent." He returned "a very elegant ivory staff" with "the same thankfulness as if accepted."

8

A FRENCH WAY OF COOKING THEM

Meticulous in all he did, Jefferson had crafted his first inaugural address to define his presidency. It included no careless remarks. Among other domestic peace offerings, it foreshadowed his intent to make dinner at the President's House an evening of bonhomie, a refuge from division, a reminder of old endearments. "Let us restore to social intercourse," he said, "that harmony and affection without which liberty, and even life itself, are but dreary things."

Jefferson made it possible with the gift of conversation and a knack for putting his guests at ease regardless of background, rank, or politics. An American in Paris had described him in the 1780s as an affable man "of infinite information" and engaging conversation enhanced by a command of delicate French cuisine, classic Virginia fare served simply on the Seine, and fine European wines. His friend François Alexandre Frédéric, duc de la Rochefoucauld-Liancourt, a fugitive from the guillotine who had known a sophisticate or two, found Jefferson's conversation "of the most agreeable kind," softened rather than blunted by a certain reserve, with knowledge inferior to none and a contagious joy in sharing it.

Many genteel families hosted parties without dinner known as "drawing rooms" for the formal parlors in which they were held. Washington and Adams had held them, but Jefferson never did. The form was unknown in Virginia, and he associated it with European aristocracy and politically influential women, approving of neither. No one but close friends ever called on him at night. Card parties were popular, but no cards were dealt in the President's House. Jefferson "knew not one card from another." To him they smacked of a gambling set of drunken Virginia gentry who affected a devil-may-care dissipation, which he despised. He did like chess, once referred to Mrs. Madison's sister affectionately as "the chess heroine," and sometimes invited men, one at a time, to dinner and a game. Relatively casual dinner parties were his only other form of entertaining, but there was nothing casual about their bridge-building intent.

There was also nothing casual about their cost. An English expatriate thought the president's $25,000 salary "may enable him to ask a friend to dine with him *pic nic*, but will not qualify him to impress a foreign ambassador with much veneration for the first executive office of America." The Englishman did not know his man. Jefferson would spend what it took to set the best table in town, though far from indifferent to its costs. He ordered its large-scale provisions personally and recorded every cent he spent and how many guests he could serve with every crate of tea and every cask of wine. Keeping track of the price of every ham, bean, and apple, he calculated the average cost of each of thirty-four meals served at the President's House during the week of October 4–10, 1801, at precisely $1.43, a considerable sum.

There was never any question of the government covering any of it, and the personal liability should have terrified him. Despite his meticulous accounts, he sailed too close to the wind and lost track of unbilled expenses. The costs he incurred in the President's House exceeded $16,000 the first year, including $2,797.38 for wine, and his combined spending at Washington and Monticello approximated $33,000—over $4,000 more than his total income from all sources. "My funds here," he wrote in 1807, "are always more than exhausted at the end of a session of Congress," but he thought his lower costs when Congress adjourned would save him, an ignorance based on estimates kept in his head.

Having made his guests happy for decades, he had two Parisian accomplices in the President's House, Lemaire, his maître d'hôtel, and Julien, applauded as a master chef, said Margaret Bayard Smith, "even by those accustomed to the best tables." Far from Paris and Philadelphia, the Frenchmen met their challenge on barely civilized ground from whatever could be plucked from local farms, fields, and streams, ordinary fare made extraordinary.

Jefferson loved vegetables and kept a chart of the first and last appearances of his favorites in the market. You could find on a good day in Georgetown choice ingredients like Havana chocolate, Jamaica sugar, Holland gin, Massachusetts cranberries, Madeira wine, nutmeg, mace, cinnamon, cloves, almonds, raisins, the occasional pineapple, even oranges in January, and the local woods and waterways were full of fish and game. Delicious little perch ran through the Tiber in the spring in shoals so thick you could shoot in their general direction and "get a good dish full," Augustus Foster said, "for as many will leap on shore from fright as can be killed with the shot." Schools of flipping shad were scooped up in nets at the Potomac's little falls, where two-hundred-pound sturgeon were caught by hook and line for their delicate taste and caviar. Hunters shot partridge and snipe on both sides of the Pennsylvania Avenue. In winter, migrating canvasback ducks, a delicacy Jefferson prized, were hunted from boats on the Potomac. Local farmers carried the morning's milk, cream, and eggs to his door, and a baker named Peter Miller delivered a dozen loaves of fresh bread a day.

Jefferson's favorite foods, as he recorded them, included basted suckling pig; oysters pulled fresh from Chesapeake Bay, marinated or baked in a pie; string beans with herbs; slashed veal "with stuffing in the slashes, roasted with clear gravy"; spit-roasted duck, boned, stuffed, and fricasseed; and rabbit stewed with bacon and small onions "in claret or white wine. Red wine is the best." For dessert, one happy guest told his wife, Lemaire appeared with "innumerable" delights most Americans had never heard of, delectable French confections of the sort the president described as "pastries of puff paste, in various shapes, garnished with jelly, gooseberries or apples," "custard glazed with a hot poker," "small meringues with cream," "quaking jellies," and "frangipane (a sort of custard made with milk, sugar, eggs, a thickening agent, and pulverized almonds)."

Every one of these things could be served on an ordinary evening at the President's House, every dinner a holiday feast. On one unexceptional occasion, the meal progressed through soup, mutton chops, loin of veal, poultry with oyster sauce, sausages, assorted vegetables and pickles, stewed apples, "jelly cake of a different sort," oranges, raisins, and prunes, four kinds of nuts, cheese, and buttered crackers. A succession of Madeira, Baccarella, Hermitage, and Neboulle wines were served in temperate pours. On the next evening, not counting the wines, there was soup, mutton, beefsteaks, fish, poultry, potatoes, rice, a spinach and egg dish, pickles, salad, and a "second course nearly the same as yesterday." On the evening after that came soup, tart à la Boullie, partridges served with sausages and cabbage ("a French way of cooking them"), turkey, Virginia ham and bacon, potatoes, beans, olives, pickles, and salad, "a kind of custard with a floating cream on it," apples, oranges, nuts, and more. Even the president's critics were pleased, despite the inevitable miss. In 1807, someone forced the season before it was ready. A plate of strawberries "scarcely eatable" was served in May, cherries "not eatable" in June.

Simply put, Jefferson was America's chief gourmet, a condition for which his countrymen had no word. "He was never a great eater," a close observer said, "but what he did eat he wanted to be very choice." There were only two meals in the President's House, an early breakfast and an early dinner, often followed before bed by a light snack with tea, but Jefferson made them count. Excited in his travels by European cuisine, he had taken careful notes and sent home from Italy and France a near shipload of curiosities, including eighty-six crates of copper pots and pans; exotic kitchen implements and supplies like a Neapolitan macaroni mold and several Dutch waffle irons, unheard of in America; one case of raisins, two of macaroni; and 680 bottles of wine.

In Paris he wrote recipes down in French, slipping into his native tongue when the new one failed him. On the issue of salad dressing he was capable of rapture and experimented with tropical sesame seed oil at the President's House with childlike excitement: "This is among the most valuable acquisitions our country has ever made. It yields an oil equal to the finest olive oil," an exotic treat in itself. He tried it at several dinner parties, "having a dish of salad dressed with that and another with olive oil, and nobody could distinguish them." He delighted his guests, and sometimes disconcerted them, with other delicacies they had never tasted, like Dijon mustard, Parmesan cheese (which arrived packed in lead), anchovies, figs, vanilla, "Italian paste (macaroni)," and the irresistible French treat introduced to a grateful nation as "potatoes fried without their jackets, cut in small slices and served with various sauces."

And yet he did not abandon the foods of his youth. For foreign guests, a British statesman wrote, "such native luxuries as soft crab and cakes made of Indian corn opened a new field to the curious appetite." Julien paired turnip greens and black-eyed peas with pâté de foie gras, and a discerning appreciation for Virginia fare shows up in an order Jefferson sent to Richmond. He needed "fine hams for table use" in Washington, not the big ones, "but rather small hams, which are generally finer grained, sweeter, & better for the table, if well fatted & cured." Planters produced the best results, he wrote, and sold them in small parcels. He wanted two or three hundred "hams, not shoulders, of the best kind & best cured," shipped "as they are procured, for I am entirely unprovided for present use." In the spring of 1805 and again in 1806, nine dozen Virginia hams made their way to the President's House in three barrels drained of rum.

Yet Jefferson knew his limits. He may have influenced the occasional menu, but the kitchen was Julien's. Years later, an enslaved Monticello man told an interviewer that his master always had at least eight dishes at dinner, "if nobody at table but himself," and as many as thirty- two with guests, but he "never went into the kitchen except to wind up the clock."

* * *

Just beneath the front door, facing the sunken areaway, Julien and his assistants plied their trade in the huge, stone vaulted kitchen in the basement whose windows of blue-tinted English glass admitted a little light on a bright day. The President's dinner guests crossed the wooden bridge over the areaway, greeted

The President's House seen from the west, 1802. Note the icehouse near the center. ***Created by Patrick Phillips-Schrock, based on documentary evidence***

by the racket of large-scale cooking. Poor ventilation, it was said, "perfumes the whole house with the steam and smells of the victuals."

Two enormous brick hearths commanded the kitchen, vestiges of the 1790s. President Adams's staff had worked with iron pots and pans over open flames, a technique resistant to nuance and hazardous to the help. It would not do for Jefferson and Julien. Au courant cuisine demanded adjustable heat in sensitive, coal-fired stoves and dutch ovens, a proper pastry oven, and copper saucepans, pots, and skillets, all of which Jefferson supplied in time. His polymath friend Charles Willson Peale informed him that copper pots and pans were unhealthy unless tinned, and American stoneware stew pans were unsafe. Exposed to intense heat, they broke as if shot with a pistol, but English stoneware would stand the fire. Such was the level of kitchenware managed personally by the commander in chief. On his orders, blacksmiths fitted one of the fireplaces with an iron range, something new in America, with spits to turn roasts and a crane to lift heavy pots and swing them in and out of full or partial heat. In 1804, Henry Foxhall's Georgetown foundry produced European-style, charcoal-heated, cast-iron stew holes encased in brick with iron grills for the President's House.

* * *

If Jefferson's culinary expertise was rare among his countrymen, his mastery of wines was unique. Urban sophisticates and plantation grandees enjoyed their glass of wine, but their subordinates had no experience with it, and did not care to acquire any. America was a cider-, beer-, and whiskey-drinking place with a dash of Caribbean rum, and vintners were as scarce as Hindus; but whiskey was easy to distill, a handy way to change crops into cash or amusement. Wine was foreign, and foreign was bad.

Nothing was more popular, Jefferson wrote, "than fine Hughes' crab cyder" distilled from Virginia crabapples, and he ordered ten barrels for the presidential cellar, but wine was his drink of choice and he served no liquor at all. He was fond of a touch of glow to ease conversation, and nothing pleased him more than enjoying his guests "after dinner, sitting at our wine," but an enslaved man at Monticello who knew him well never saw him "disguised in drink," and he used his table and tariffs to fight drunkenness. By serving delicious wines to congressmen and senators influential in their communities, he hoped not only to please them but also to spread a taste for something softer than whiskey and loosen its grip on their constituents. A lower duty on imported wines, he told Gallatin, "would wonderfully enlarge the field of those who use wine, to the expulsion of whiskey," for "a great gain to the treasury, and to the sobriety of our country."

In wines as in politics, he was careful nonetheless not to take his country where it was not yet ready to go. In 1805, an enterprising vintner brought him two new Kentucky wines to try on his guests. Jefferson served them cautiously to the family alone, and gave them as much praise as he honorably could. They were "capable of being good," but "no wine on earth was ever drinkable the spring after it was made." Eager as he was to promote American wines, he decided against introducing Kentucky's to his guests. Persons unaware of "the undrinkable state of green wines, even of the best kinds, cannot make the just allowance & would therefore condemn them in the lump."

Even wine was not safe from politics, one of the lesser effects of the wars, alliances, and interdictions that Britain and the wine-producing countries moved in and out of almost constantly. Before the Revolution, the mother country's trade had shaped American tastes. Britain shipped Madeira, ports, and other heavy Iberian wines to the colonies from its Spanish and Portuguese allies, and Jefferson enjoyed them in Virginia, but he and other bon vivants were nearly ignorant of the lighter, subtler wines produced by the French enemy. Champagne was unknown in America. In the 1780s, Jefferson's exposure to France and Italy changed his tastes and his country's, and for him words like "dry," "hard," "soft," "brisk," and "silky" acquired new meaning. Educating himself literally from the ground up, he dressed in the simplest clothes (no sacrifice), went into the fields to interview the peasants who cultivated the grapes and the coopers who made the barrels, and befriended the great wine merchants. He came home an expert, and more than a few of his founding brothers relied on him to choose their wines and place their orders for labels like Moët et Chandon and Veuve Clicquot.

Fine wines were a key to his entertainments at the President's House, and he spent much precious time choosing his stock, negotiating its price, seeing it properly stored, aged, "broached," and served, and planning its replenishment. It came from Europe by sea in the temperate seasons, and even then at a risk enlarged by wars and pirates. In 1807, he feared that an overdue shipment from "the vineyards of the ancient Jesuits" had been "intercepted by the lawless rovers of the ocean." To be sure his wine bills were paid, he used banknotes torn in half, sent by separate mail, based on hard experience with "the infidelities of the post office." Some of his letters had been opened and published by men who "twisted and tormented" their contents, which, "like the words of holy writ, are made to mean every thing but what they were intended to mean."

All told, Jefferson served thirty-seven imported wines at the President's House and a few from the Ohio valley. Iberian wines showed up often, for most Americans preferred them. It was said that the president served French wines to British diplomats to tweak them, and was disappointed by their gratitude. Depending on their origin and characteristics and the volume he could use, he imported and stored his wines in long tapered barrels called pipes, holding well over a hundred gallons each, or in smaller casks and kegs, or in sturdily crated bottles ordered by the dozen or the hundred.

Jefferson served his guests in Washington an astonishing quantity of imported wines, including, among many more, 249 bottles of Sauternes; 270 bottles of claret; 276 bottles of rich Hungarian varieties; 833 bottles of Montepulciano; a thirty-gallon cask of a dark peasant red from Rota, Spain; a tierce (sixty gallons) of Malaga, vintage 1775; and no less than eight pipes (eight hundred gallons) of alcoholic Brazilian Madeira, the most popular wine in America. In 1805, he discovered pale rosés. Spotting in a white Arruda "a reddish tinge sufficiently distinguishable to the eye," he assumed it was a flaw. In 1802, thanks to the Spanish minister's courtesy in giving up half his stock, he startled his guests with a hundred bottles of champagne. Seeing how they embraced it, he ordered another 860 bottles over time. By 1803, leading Washingtonians were enjoying champagne at home. *Vin ordinaire* came from Philadelphia, but the American consul in Bordeaux had great wines shipped directly to the President's House.

If the number of wines Jefferson served was abundant, he never encouraged anyone to drink past a sociable repose. A wine merchant was pleased to see his guests indulge "to the digestive point and no further." The occasional beverage enthusiast must have tottered away from his table, but the old English custom of endless toasts was banned. The French, the president said approvingly, did not ruin their meals "by transforming themselves into brutes," and Washington's remark in 1788 that American gentlemen no longer "forced drinks on their guests or made it a point of honor to send them home drunk" was premature. At a banquet on the Capitol Hill in 1804, some dignitaries drank enough toasts to leave without their hats. Toasts were so often proposed to the health of friends and politicians that "healths" became their synonym. When partisan toasts were offered, people either drank to their heroes or sat on their hands, a sure way to expose their opinions and their tempers.

Jefferson would not allow it. "The Health Law," as he called his rule, put three constraints on dinner conversation at the President's House and only three: "no healths, no politics, no restraint," all of them keys to his eight-year campaign to make the capital of the United States a civil, harmonious place.

* * *

Jefferson took his meals and gave most of his dinners in the Family Dining Room, the bright, south-facing space, later called the Green Room, between the Oval Room and the huge storage room to the east. Adams had furnished it with what Jefferson described as an "elegant side board with pedestals & urn knife cases," a large and a small table, three candelabras, thirteen black-and-gold stick chairs, a looking glass, two lacquered metal racks to warm plates in slots by the fire, and a colorful Brussels carpet that Jefferson moved elsewhere in order to display the "very handsome floor," a particular compliment from a veteran of Versailles. Over time, he added a third plate warmer, a third table, and two glass cases displaying hundreds of pieces of silver when they were not being used or polished. The fashionable chintz curtains, floral prints on a light cotton background, came from India.

Closely guiding Thomas Claxton's acquisitions as his purchasing agent, Jefferson spent more time on household goods than might have been expected as he fought off threats to democracy. It is hard to say which was more remarkable, his opinionated interests in so base a thing as grease-free dining room floors, so elevated a thing as the latest evolution of drawing room music, so innovative a thing as woven metal window screens, his expertise in all three, or the thought he gave to their influence on the President's House and its visitors.

He wanted two wire screens for his Setting Room windows to keep out "candle flies and bugs in the evening which abound here in most uncommon quantities." With typical precision, he specified the size of the holes in the mesh and a particular Philadelphia craftsman. Five years would pass before screens were installed in his bedroom and "the room we dine in every day." He had Claxton order green painted canvas floorcloths, a washable form of protection rolled out under the dinner table before meals and rolled up again after, but Claxton sent him samples of mats custom made in China in red-and-white straw from a floor plan sent with the order. Very chic, Claxton thought they were, preferred by "the genteelest people," and cheaper than the English-made kind. No one liked the American. Jefferson thought they were beautiful but would "fur up" with grease and wear out in the rolling and unrolling, and the English goods were overpriced. The cheap American kind would do, genteel people notwithstanding. Claxton proposed, if the president did not object, to have a pianist choose a fortepiano, but the president did object. A fortepiano would be "perfectly proper," but necessities left nothing in the budget for such a thing, and the latest instrument of music might be preferable if they did; a "claviole" it was called. On a cheerful note, Jefferson sent the news that "our workman on the blinds goes well. He reforms a window a day."

At least some of Jefferson's dinner tables were round or nearly so, not only to prevent a seat at the head or the foot from implying rank, but also, as Margaret Bayard Smith observed, to promote conversation that straight lines prevent. Everyone could see everyone else "and feel the animating influence of looks as well as of words. Let any dinner giver try the experiment and he will certainly be convinced of this fact." Durable green baize covers protected the tables, spread with white linen cloths and napkins before meals and removed after dessert to show off the mahogany instead of stained linen, which helped provide employment at seven dollars a month for the washerwomen, Sarah Houseman, and Biddy Boyle, the lowest-paid domestics not enslaved. Extra washers were brought in as needed at forty-five cents a day.

Jefferson's bigger, more elaborate dinners, closer to official events than private affairs, were served in the State Dining Room in the northwest corner, which was bigger than the Family Dining Room, with a set of massive sideboards. Its tall, rotating dumbwaiter snugly built into the doorway to the adjoining porter's lodge was a memorable use of mahogany. Unseen servants carried food up from the basement stairs into the porter's lodge, loaded it into the dumbwaiter's circular shelves, and spun it around into the dining room, one course at a time, at the touch of a spring-loaded lever. Dirty dishes put back on the shelves were whirled around in reverse, a process "so contrived," a delighted guest said, that "all appeared or disappeared at once." A similar crowd-pleasing marvel was probably installed in the Family Dining Room.

A Virginian named William Tatham tried to turn a dinner into an opportunity. Tatham was full of ideas, Jefferson wrote, but rarely "well-digested," though thoughts "susceptible of improvement sometimes escape him." When Jefferson mentioned whimsically after dinner one evening that he wished someone would invent a device to pass decanters around his table, Tatham proposed to build one. If the result did not please the president, "I will bear the loss." If it did, "the public shall pay a reasonable expense." No reply survives.

* * *

For Margaret Bayard Smith, the annual adjournment of Congress was "the most dismal day of the year; such a breaking up; such a scattering abroad" left the locals bereft in "the now desert city." For Jefferson, all was "business, hurry, interruption" on that last hectic day, but the eight-month congressional hiatus of 1801, which began on Inauguration Day, gave his French accomplices time to train a staff before the nomads returned. In the meantime they would practice on the cabinet, the half dozen diplomats from Britain, France, and Denmark (Sweden and the Batavian Republic would send envoys later), and what Mrs. Smith called, in less than republican style, "the respectable citizens of Washington, Georgetown, and Alexandria."

Working his way through that cast, some more discerning than others, Jefferson invited a dozen or more to dine about three times a week, entertained them with the gracious hospitality in which he had been raised, and often came to the table as he did to nearly everything else, at least as casually dressed as a gentleman could dare to be. A young lawyer put it simply: "He is accused of being very slovenly in his dress, and to be sure he is not very particular in that respect, but however he may neglect his person, he takes good care of his table. No man in America keeps a better." Mrs. Smith declared the defective idea that never had there been a plainer man than he and the undeniable truth that never had a president given such dinners. At Jefferson's table, "republican simplicity was united to Epicurean delicacy," a mix he enjoyed and meant to use on Congress, friend and foe alike, to bond with the Republicans, back the Federalists off from personal hostility, and put them in his social circle if not in his camp.

The shift to informality reversed twelve years of precedent, but trying once again to settle Federalist nerves rather than poke them, he made no point of it. Instead he underplayed it, inviting his guests as a private gentleman rather than as president, taking a bit of wind out of complaints about demeaning the office. In the Washington and Adams administrations, invitations had been sent by "The President of the United States." Now "Th. Jefferson" asked the favor of your company. Most of his invitations, "billets" they were called, consisted of printed cards with spaces left for names, dates, and times, filled in by Meriwether Lewis. If he knew a guest well, the president might write by hand a casual note like the one inviting Samuel and Margaret Smith and "any friends who may be with them" to dinner, or a friendly congressman to dine *en petite comité* (in a small group).

Transportation to a presidential dinner was generally manageable. You could stable a horse around town, rent one, or use the public coaches lined up for hire where people were prone to need them. Hacks, they were called, often beat up and smelling of stale cigars. When a Virginia protégé planned a stay in Georgetown with a friend, Jefferson urged him to board his servant at the President's House and "take a hack & come here generally at the hour of dinner." With luck, you could hail one in the street, but you might be marooned in Georgetown with no hack in sight and walk three miles to the President's House "in a broiling sun in a suit of black cloth."

To entertain women, whether brought by men or other women (an unescorted lady was unthinkable), a hostess was required, and Jefferson's lack of a wife or a resident daughter was an issue. Early on, Dolley Madison was his hostess while the Madisons and her sister, Anna Payne, stayed with him, but he could have no women to dinner after they left, unless he found substitutes. He wrote them a note on the day they moved out: "Th. Jefferson was much disappointed at breakfast this morning, not having till then known of the departure of Mr. & Mrs. Madison & Miss Payne. He hopes they will come and dine with him today with the Miss Butlers, who were assured they would meet them here, and tomorrow with Mrs. Gallatin and Mrs. Mason." It took him just a week to ask again, and it may not have been mere grace that moved him to tell Gallatin it "will be conferring a real favor on Th. J" if both Gallatins dined with him every night until they set up house. In the long run, cabinet wives filled in ad hoc.

The arrangements seldom varied. The guests arrived at 3:30 and were shown to the Oval Room for casual conversation. As the house's décor improved, the banter may have started with compliments. Having worked with the enslaved footman John Freeman to prepare the table, Lemaire the maître d' entered the Oval Room at four in old-school knee-length britches, waistcoat, and jacket, and announced dinner in a charming French accent. In Washington's and Adams's time, the president had led the highest-ranking lady to the table first, and the rest of the guests had followed, the ladies' escorts having been assigned in hierarchical order. Jefferson showed his company to the dining room willy-nilly and insisted on being last through the door.

Washington's and Adams's secretaries had drawn up seating charts based on rank, assigned the gentlemen to hand specific ladies into dinner, and prearranged the order in which they would be served, when they would start and stop eating, who would give which toasts first, and almost every other detail but digestion. Jefferson's guests came to the table with whomever they pleased and sat wherever they liked. *Pêle-mêle* the disorder was called, a "tumble" in playful French, an arrangement accepted in Europe in certain situations. In Jefferson's house it was *pêle-mêle* in every situation. His guests took the chairs they got to first. They were free to sit next to him if they were quick enough, take the view instead, warm themselves close to the fire, or grab a seat by a fetching guest. Madison explained it clinically as "a voluntary distribution of the company according to taste, health, or comfort." Occasionally, the president sat someone beside him because he wanted to, not because of rank or station.

Deployed around the table in their livery, the footmen met everyone's needs before they knew they had them, prompted if necessary by Lemaire, who struck a dignified pose. In France, Jefferson had assumed the staff were spies, bribed by the police or some enemy, or simply inclined to repeat whatever they heard, "mutilated and misconstrued." For him these "mute but not inattentive listeners" were security risks, yet another suspicion of the common man, this one fully justified. To mitigate the risk and create an informal atmosphere, he added five rolling mahogany dumbwaiters to the Family Dining Room, one large and four small, something like tall, wheeled end tables with tiered, open shelves. In Paris, where he discovered them, dumbwaiters were just that, serving food and lacking speech. After his guests were seated, the footmen wheeled the large dumbwaiter next to him, set the four smaller ones around the table, loaded the food into the dumbwaiters next to serving forks and spoons, added dishes taken from the racked metal plate warmers by the fire, and set out the evening's wines, the whites in decanters packed with ice, the reds left to breathe. And then the servants left.

Working from the big dumbwaiter, Jefferson passed cold meats and salads down the table, filled his neighbors' plates from silver bowls and covered dishes, and poured their wine while the guests beside the smaller dumbwaiters gamely did the same. Summoned by the pull of a bell cord, the servants returned to serve a second or third hot course and change the plates, the usual thing in wealthy French homes and a rarity in the United States. A relative who had traveled abroad said Jefferson's was the only table in America where he "would dare ask for a clean plate." Family-style dining produced a sense of ease, and everyone spoke freely without fear of repetition by the dumbwaiters if not by each other. A gentleman fresh from Europe was speaking barely audibly when Jefferson said there was no need. "You see we are alone, and our walls have no ears."

By way of a grand finale, Lemaire presented the dessert, a treat for all five senses, counting the oohs and aahs. In the Adams administration, the women had left the table after dinner to gather in the Ladies' Drawing Room (Jefferson's "circular room upstairs"), and the gentlemen had bowed them out, then talked and emptied bottles. Never keen on drunken camaraderie, Jefferson led his male and female guests back to the Oval Room for tea and coffee, a practice that "preserved temperance," Mrs. Smith observed, and produced "a most refined" enjoyment. What the gentlemen thought must have varied.

All in all, a cornucopia of exquisite food and the world's great wines produced a memorable experience in America's grandest home, capped by a leisurely chat with Thomas Jefferson. He and his guests often ate, talked, and amused one another by candlelight well into the night. Mrs. Smith watched him lead the discussion many times, fluent in every subject, keeping a dozen guests engaged in the same banter, untying "little knots" of conversation, noticing who was silent or nearly so, understanding in some mysterious way what the wallflowers could add and how to help them bloom. Before dessert was served, every dull man or woman at the table was "a personage of considerable importance."

When Jefferson made his own remarks, often well into the evening, his charm was as natural as a bird's. Augustus Foster found him "visionary" in conversation, a man who "loved to dream eyes open, or, as the Germans say, *zu schwärmen*, and it must be owned that America is the paradise for *Schwärmers*, futurity there offering a wide frame for all that the imagination can put into it." A scholarly Republican considered the president deeper "in human nature and human learning than almost the whole tribe of his opponents and revilers," but even this some revilers begrudged him. Senator Pickering, the Salem-bred Federalist zealot, begrudged him everything. "Without any pretensions to literature myself," Pickering told a friend, he found Jefferson's range superficial. Having read so many books, he was fluent in most subjects "without being profound in any."

His speech was soft and gentle, even musical, drawing his listeners in like a quiet violin. An off-the-cuff remark could stay with you for good, and a thought about the weather could be poetry. Out riding one day with winter in the air, he stopped at the Smiths' little cottage in the woods and spoke of Monticello. "You can form no idea of a snowstorm," he said. To see one "in all its grandeur you should stand at my back door. There we see its progress, rising over the distant Allegany, come sweeping and roaring on, mountain after mountain, till it reaches us," its windblown sleet "pelting against the window," defeated by a cheering fire in the hearth "and the comforts of a beloved family."

"It is a charming thing to be loved by everybody," he told his grandchildren, "and the way to obtain it is never to quarrel or be angry with any body and to tell a story." An English actor who came to dinner twice said the president "fixed your attention the instant he spoke," not with the weight of his office or the brilliance of his mind but with effortless finesse. His philosophical remarks were as plain as a Quaker's, the actor said, and his thoughts on human nature delivered in the form of anecdotes laced with self-deprecation. He often recalled his encounters with ordinary folk whose provincial accents, inadvertently apt malapropisms, and unexpected insights had touched, entertained, or enlightened him.

As one such story was told, improving in the telling, a farmer fresh from Connecticut rode up and trotted beside him on his afternoon ride, educating himself about the capital and the country "contagious" to it. "This Thomas Jefferson," the farmer asked, had he seen him? He admitted he knew him well. The farmer was intrigued. "They tell me he never goes out, but he's got clothes on his back that would sell for a plantation." Jefferson said the president dressed no better than he. As the President's House came into view, the man asked who lived there and was told. "If that sight doesn't come over a man like a suspension of the works of nature," he said. "A house as big as Noah's Ark must have 30 rooms at the smallest." Who could want more than six? "I ha'nt got more than *four*."

The president's recollections of the Revolution, now known to many Americans "only from the cold page of history," as he told Thomas Paine, could be spellbinding. In 1824, when Jefferson was eighty-one, his dinner recollections of those perilous times enthralled the up-and-coming congressman Daniel Webster. Fifteen years had passed since Jefferson's presidency, but old men tell old tales, and the stories Webster heard at Monticello had surely been told repeatedly at the President's House.

In the Continental Congress, Jefferson told his guests, no one showed more wisdom or zeal than Samuel Adams. "But he could not speak. He had a hesitating, grunting manner." His cousin "John Adams was our Colossus on the floor. He was not graceful, nor elegant, nor remarkably fluent, but he came out occasionally with a power of thought and expression that moved us from our seats." And then there was a fellow Virginian. As a boy of about fifteen on his way to the College of William and Mary, Jefferson had stopped to see friends in Henrico County, and "there I first saw and became acquainted with Patrick Henry."

Seven years older than he, dead since 1799, Patrick Henry had been his nemesis. Among other sour lines that the president may have quoted at dinner, his rival told incensed Virginians that "Thomas Jefferson came home from France so Frenchified that he abjured his native victuals," an attack to be laughed away, but some of the others hurt. As governor of Virginia during the Revolution, unprotected by any guard and moved by the reasonable thought that neither his capture nor his death would serve his country, Jefferson had fled from Monticello to a rugged place called Carter's Mountain minutes ahead of 250 British cavalry who had brought a set of irons. Henry, who had fled from them too, started a legislative investigation that devastated Jefferson personally and wounded him politically. He was ultimately cleared and thanked, but a label his enemies relished and enjoyed repeating, "The Coward of Carter's Mountain," did not warm him up to Patrick Henry.

As the president recalled at dinner, Henry had been a barkeeper and had married very young and started some business that failed. When he and Jefferson clashed in the colonial legislature at Williamsburg, his ignorance had been shocking. "He was a man of very little knowledge of any sort," Jefferson said. "He read nothing and had no books." His biographer later claimed he reread Plutarch every year, but Jefferson thought it was nonsense. He was certainly no wordsmith. "He wrote almost nothing. He *could not* write." His accent was vulgar, and "I have often been astonished at his command of proper language. How he obtained the knowledge of it I could never find out, as he read so little" and rarely spoke with educated men. Jefferson saw him angry once or twice, "and his anger was terrible. Those who witnessed it were not disposed to arouse it again." He behaved well enough in good company and seemed to understand its proprieties, "but in his *heart* he preferred low society," hunting in the woods with overseers "and people of that description," camping out for a fortnight "without a change of raiment."

Every bit of that having been said, every bit of it was forgotten when Patrick Henry stood up and spoke in the House of Burgesses. His oratory, Jefferson said, was a force of nature akin to a hurricane, and the only thing you could do when you found yourself a victim in its path was to "pray for his imminent death." His eloquence was unique, "if indeed it could be called eloquence, for it was impressive and sublime beyond what can be imagined." After he had spoken, it was hard to recall what he had said, but while he held the floor he drove a nail through every point. His attack on "*my* opinion," Jefferson told his guests, was so effective that *he* was "delighted and moved" and could not say why. "I have asked myself when he ceased, 'What the Devil has he said,' and could never answer the enquiry."

Had their most gifted speaker not led them through the Revolution, Jefferson said, perhaps with a Frenchified shrug, the other Virginians may have managed, but he left them all behind. He didn't read anything, he didn't know anything, and "it is not easy to say what we would have done without Patrick Henry."

9

UNFINISHED PERSONS

The Seventh Congress of the United States convened on December 7, 1801, just enough of its members having rattled into town to make a quorum of exhausted men bedraggled by the punishing roads. The House would now meet in a temporary pile of mortared brick, promptly dubbed "the Oven" for its shape and its suffocating air. When its walls began to buckle they were buttressed with leaning beams that its occupants hoped might keep it off their heads. A covered wooden passage connected it to the Senate.

It was the first of Jefferson's eight consecutive winters wooing Congress in the President's House. He called them his annual campaigns when the term was purely military. The other times of year were "blessed interims." Tests of courage though he found them to be, his campaigns were less like wars than seductions, a courting of wary Federalists and a charming of willing Republicans over candlelit dinners, heady wine, and flirtatious conversation.

Yet another retraction of royalist form preceded his first campaign. In New York and Philadelphia, Presidents Washington and Adams had done their annual duty to report on the state of the Union by riding past cheering crowds in a regal coach and addressing Congress in person, much as the king opened Parliament. After the move to Washington City in 1800, Adams had been driven

The Capitol in 1802. ***Architect of the Capitol***

up the Pennsylvania Avenue to speak in the half-built Senate chamber, and Congress had returned the favor, descending on the President's House in a fleet of hacks driven down from Baltimore, led by the sergeant at arms clopping through the mud on horseback with his mace. What may have looked grand in London looked ridiculous in Washington City. More important, it looked like monarchy.

Jefferson dropped it. Lewis brought his messages to Congress in writing, and its members were spared a trip down the Capitol Hill. Preferring writing to oration as the president did, his replacement of a speech with a memorandum matched his talents, saved his time, kept his profile low, and blew away a whiff of the Crown. Edward Thornton, the king's man in Washington, confessed to Lord Hawkesbury that the abandoned tradition bore "a considerable resemblance to the practice of the British monarchy," but what Jefferson cast as humility Thornton condemned as "a studied and disdainful pride." The public liked pomp, Thornton wrote, which appealed to "the natural vanity of the Americans," and Jefferson's scheme to demean himself did not.

Washington Irving had a character say of Jefferson, "he is rather declining in popularity, having given great offense of wearing red breeches and tying his horse to a post," but the president's constitutional status left him room to diminish himself without demeaning his office. His $25,000 salary more than quadrupled any other federal officer's, he was privileged not only to live in the country's grandest house, but also to finish it with public funds, and a tradition borrowed from the crowned heads of Europe exempted him from returning social calls. He gladly took advantage of all these kingly privileges, the salary because he needed it, the house because he loved the putting up and pulling down, the one-sided invitations because they spared him from people he did not want to see and time he did not want to spend. In London in 1786, endless full dress calls on the nobility had maddened him. Now he made no such calls, and dropped in on friends on his afternoon rides when it pleased him. Who could ask for more?

In every other way—personal, social, even grammatical—he underplayed his status without dishonoring it. The comfortable horse, clothes, and dining were no hardship for him, they matched his sense of what a republican president should be, and they cost him not a shred of his power. In letters to anyone but family, he often referred to himself in the third person and never as president. Asking Dolley Madison to choose gifts for his granddaughters, he suggested that "Mrs. Madison knows better how to please the respective parties than Th. Jefferson does." The intent was the opposite of narcissism, to avoid the self-referential egoism he had been brought up to see in the first person singular. The President's House was "this place."

* * *

Eight months into his presidency, Jefferson said he spent between twelve and thirteen hours a day at his desk, leaving no more than four for riding, meals, and a touch of relaxation, the rest for visitors and sleep. When Congress convened he was more pressured still: "My occupations are now so incessant that I cannot command a moment for my friends." Whenever Congress was in, he felt like closing his open door, "closely confined by the run of visits" as he was, mostly from people who wanted something. Only his early morning time and his nights were uninterrupted.

As a motive for having a dozen politicians to dinner several times a week, pleasure can be ruled out. When Martha complained about rural entertaining, he replied from Washington City, sick of greeting guests without joy. "But there is no remedy. The character of those we receive is very different from the loungers who infest the houses of the wealthy in general," and the "revolting conduct" of dropping them "would undo the whole labor of our lives. It is a valuable circumstance that it is only through a particular portion of the year that these inconveniences arise." In 1804 he wrote Martha as Congress was about to convene: "I dread it, on account of the fatigues of the table in such a round of company, which I consider as the most serious trials I undergo." If only he could "turn it over to younger hands and to be myself but a guest at the table, and free to leave it as others are." He missed the family always, but especially at meals and in the evenings, when he had his chance to "unbend." An hour with Martha and the children was "worth an age passed here."

Entertaining earnest Republicans was work. Hosting High Federalists was pain. As secretary of state, he had vented his frustration to Madison as he fought aspiring oligarchs all day, then sacrificed his leisure to dine with them, odious men "of whose hatred I am conscious" even in conviviality. He soldiered on in the President's House nonetheless, not just polite to his enemies but alluring more often than not.

Intending no humor, Mrs. Smith said his dinner parties were small, "seldom, if ever, exceeding fourteen," with no one invited "promiscuously" to such a tight circle. When Congress was out of town, he chose his mix of guests with care. When Congress was in, his choices were fussier still, and seldom politically diverse. With rare exceptions, he invited only Federalists or Republicans to the same table, not only to avoid discomfort, conflict averse as he was, but also because his goals for the parties diverged. The Republicans he hoped to bond with him and each other. The Federalists he hoped to disarm, not expecting to convert them on the spot but to soften them up. Some of them had literally demonized him, few had ever met him, and many left his table surprised to find he might not be Satan incarnate.

His first goal was simply to know them. Having presided over the Senate as vice president, he knew every returning senator, but few of the 107 members of the House. In January of 1801, after he defeated Adams but before the House broke his tie with Burr and made him president, he was seated next to Mrs. Adams at a dinner at the President's House, a gracious gesture under the circumstances. Several congressmen shared her table's linen cloth and silver candelabras.

"Pray," Jefferson asked Mrs. Adams, "who is that gentleman who sits next but one to the president?"

"That is Mr. Waln of Pennsylvania."

"I never saw him to know him before. Pray, who is next?"

"That is Mr. Holmes. Surely you know him, he is a Democrat." If Jefferson had known anyone in the House it should have been Mr. Holmes, a young Virginian and a fellow graduate of the College of William and Mary.

"No, I do not," he said.

"I know nearly all the gentlemen of both houses," Mrs. Adams said, "a few violent Democrats excepted, who have excluded themselves from our table."

"I do not know one in twenty," he replied. "They complain and say that I will not take my hat off to them when I pass them, but I cannot help it. I have no means of knowing them. I never see them but at your table."

"Do you never go into the House of Representatives?"

"No. I cannot," he said, for some Federalists would insult him for the fun of it.

"I cannot answer for them," Mrs. Adams replied; hostile Democrats had kept her from the House "by the same consideration. Party spirit is much alike upon both sides of the question."

Jefferson would ban it from his own presidential table, but as people do in times of politics as unarmed war, his friends and enemies saw two different men when they looked at him. Republicans saw a hero saving the Revolution. Many Federalists saw a demagogue, insincere in his declarations of self-evident truths. Catharine Mitchill was a New York Republican senator's wife, and "the thoughts of meeting so great a man as Thomas Jefferson" gave her literal palpitations, thrilled to be led into dinner in his hand and seated by his side, dazzled by the "very clever fellow" she had hoped he would be. The Federalist Louisa Adams saw him differently. "The House of the President is considered the House of the People," she wrote, much like a public accommodation, except that in a tavern "your money buys respect and convenience," for Jefferson gave the commoners neither. She thought a bankrupt debtor was the closer analogy, for no partial payment of faked esteem would satisfy the mob.

As president, Jefferson never went to Congress, which etiquette forbade, except for informal tours of the Capitol's construction, sporadic attendance at Sunday church services in the House chamber, signing bills on adjournment day, and his second inauguration. Congress came to *him*, individually and in small groups, for politics, business, courtesy, or dinner. Neither Washington nor Adams had hosted congressional dinners. Jefferson invented the form. When Congress was in session, he invited its members three times a week, a dozen or so at a time, until nearly all had come, some more than once. In 1804 he started keeping lists, to be sure he neither missed nor overexposed anyone unintentionally. He could not have apologized more profusely to a Rhode Island Republican he had overlooked.

Dinner with the president was a prize. Apart from the prestige, there was almost no alternative for fine dining and ambience, the three foreign embassies excepted. Few local families even knew it when they saw it, and fewer still had the houses or staff to offer it to their guests. Society "was always in some degree like that of a bathing place," the British diplomat Augustus Foster wrote, a lot of strangers in a strange place where no one knew who was respectable, for "no man is thrown out of society here from the badness of his character." For the boardinghouse dwellers on the Capitol Hill, invitations to the President's House were a necessity, "unless they chose to live like bears, brutalized and stupified."

Later in the century, the capital in Jefferson's time was compared to a frontier settlement where a single hotel was the only place to socialize and "the White House was the hotel." There were no eating clubs, and the closest things to a restaurant were a few dreary oyster houses and taverns. Congressmen and senators had nowhere to go for a good night out but the gambling halls, even less respectable places of amusement, the drawing rooms and tables of the scarce wealthy families who would have them, and what Foster dismissed as a "miserable little rope-dancing theater" where acrobats and the like performed a few blocks east of the President's House at the corner of Eleventh and C. Jefferson went at least once, buying one-dollar tickets for himself and his secretary. Across the river, no easy place to reach, the Alexandria Theatre produced a play in 1802, followed by Mr. Sully, who "will perform his unparalleled feats in Ground & Lofty Tumbling," followed by a song, followed by *The Jew & Doctor*, the Jew played by Mr. Bernard. The scarcity of higher amusements can be measured by the Supreme Court's gallery as a cure for "the dullness of the place."

Some members of Congress, appalled by Washington City's amenities, tried to move the capital to an actual city, but as Foster told the tale, the Virginians kept it close to home, backed by a Republican majority of "rough and unfashioned persons, to whom it is of consequence to be in a place where they are attended to more than they would be in a large city." Jefferson attended them well. Congress typically adjourned at 3:00, their boardinghouses fed them at 3:30, and the president usually asked them to come to dinner at that hour, or "whenever the House shall rise." Sometimes he urged one or two to come early for a private conference or to linger after the others left, or drop by after dinner. Presidential invitations were not command performances, and regrets were not uncommon, most of them sent without intending offense.

Jefferson snubbed just a handful of passionate Federalists. It took talent to make his blacklist, and some of the militants he did invite turned him down, intending nothing *but* offense. Out of respect for the office, Boston's congressman Josiah Quincy called on the president exactly once, almost visibly holding his nose, and declined to taste his boeuf bourguignon or sip his pinot noir. "I came to Washington with an abhorrence of Jefferson's political character," Quincy privately explained, and declined several invitations, which, combined with certain remarks in the House, "made Mr. Jefferson to understand that I had no wish for their renewal." Democracy, the Bostonian said in print, unconnected to his shunning of the president's dinners, was "an Indian word, signifying 'a great tobacco planter who had herds of black slaves.'"

A South Carolina Republican let the president down more gently and explained himself. He had thought of President Adams's dinners as decoys set out to lure Congress, to put them in the president's debt, and he could not accept now what he turned down then. Jefferson thanked him for his candor. He was right to decline what made him uncomfortable, and "no one has a right to complain," but the president gave an explanation in return: "I cultivate personal intercourse with the members of the legislature that we may know one another." A few pleasant hours over dinner produced harmony, trust, and "opportunities of little explanations" that cleared away jealousies and suspicions and let him take the nation's pulse.

The South Carolinian's instincts were sound nonetheless. It was hard to say no to a president who welcomed you to his home, fed you with his own hand, poured you his wine, and flattered you with his friendship. Not every Federalist was lost on every issue, and Republicans on the verge of opposition on a given point were heard to admit they were silenced by a dinner.

* * *

Jefferson's French cuisine was a revelation to almost everyone. In France he had charmed the locals with exotica like buttered and salted corn on the cob plucked from his Parisian garden, and he enjoyed the sport in reverse in Washington

City. A plain New England senator who dined with Napoleon's ambassador was not reluctant to admit to himself "I do not relish French cookery," but the president's table delighted most of his guests. Ice cream was not unusual in some American homes, but baked ice cream was. After dinner at the President's House, a sophisticated woman from New York marveled about "ice cream enclosed in a cover of warm paste, which gives it the appearance of having just been taken from the oven."

The typical American diet was high in pork and starch and dangerously low in vegetables. Almost every poor farmer grew potatoes and corn, kept pigs left to root in the woods, and relished the occasional cabbage. Hoecake, a fried cornmeal dish, and hominy, kernels of corn boiled with lime, lye, or ash, were staples in the South. At a decent Washington hotel, Northern guests got used to hominy at breakfast, lunch, and supper served with biscuits, bread, and hoecake. But for the elites in a handful of cities, even the most fortunate of Jefferson's countrymen served their guests salted meats and common vegetables spiced with boiling water. Many families ate nothing green at all. One prosperous Virginia host announced before dinner, "Gentlemen, bread is our only vegetable."

Good tableware and good manners were even scarcer than steak or spinach. The poorest Americans ate with their knives and fingers directly from the pan. It took a middle-class income to buy spoons, plates, and cups, and only wealthy homes had forks and glassware. Whether fine dining appealed to them or not, some Republicans were innocent of the manners that went with it. Not long after Jefferson's time, the British ambassador was chatting with a dinner guest when he heard his wife say quickly, "My dear Mrs. S, what *can* you be doing?" Elbow deep in the salad bowl, Mrs. S explained herself happily. "Only rollicking for an onion, my lady." Having met and entertained many members of Congress, the ambassador found some of them respectable, but the men of the frontier states showed up "in perfect costume" for the role. "They may be capable of making the very best laws, but I should not want to meet them in a lone place."

For the first time ever, Jefferson gave them all a place at the president's table. The seating was *pêle-mêle*, and politics were off limits. Most senators and many congressmen were worldly men who accepted his invitations like a drowning sailor grabs a rope. Delaware's gentleman congressman James Asheton Bayard wrote a fellow Wilmington lawyer, "I cannot express too strongly my desire to leave this place. Washington is tolerable for a few days but detestable for a winter residence." He wrote again after his friend succeeded him: "Four months almost killed me, and how you continue to survive six or seven I do not know." Dinner at the President's House eased the pain, but some of Jefferson's congressional guests had scant exposure to gentility.

A contemporary book of etiquette described what Jefferson would have seen at his table when Congress was in session: "Ashamed and confused, the awkward man sits in his chair bolt upright," while his beautifully mannered companion is "used to good company" and carries himself at ease. The well-bred man does "not eat awkwardly or dirtily, or sit when others stand," or declare that the guest beside him is "a blockhead and not worth hearing." The uncouth man plunges "up to the knuckles in soup and grease," sticks his elbow in his neighbor's plate, "eats with his knife to the manifest danger of his mouth," blows his nose after picking it clean, "looks in his handkerchief," and "crams his hands first in his bosom and next into his breaches."

In America, Augustus Foster observed, manners "are not a prevailing feature in the great mass of society, being, except in the large towns, rather despised as a mark of effeminacy by the majority." At the British minister's table, an unimpressed member of Congress declared his host's Rhine wine inferior to Kentucky cider, which he proved by spitting it out. Even well-mannered men from rural constituencies were often out of their depth. Amazed by a fortepiano in a Washington City parlor, two elderly senators searched under, around, and through it in search of the music. "Dear me," one said, "what a parcel of wires." The magnificent President's House and its haute cuisine must have struck them dumb.

Even patrician guests brought a regional menu of manners to the President's House. Privileged Southern men had always been more relaxed than their stiff New England cousins, and by Jefferson's time they had slid into the risqué when the ladies left the room. "All the gentlemen of that generation had fallen into this sort of talk," a younger man later said, picked up from pro-American elements of London society, "where a foulness of conversation had been propagated." New Englanders were shocked by the louche Virginians and disbelieved what they saw from barbarous Tennessee. The president of Yale College "looked upon whist as an unhappy dissipation and upon the theater as immoral," Henry Adams later wrote. "He had no occasion to condemn horseracing, for no racecourse was to be found in New England." Things loosened up as you went south and west. In the parlors of Philadelphia, women of high station were capable of indelicate remarks that made ingénues raise their fans to their giggling faces. A tourist in the Ohio valley was advised that a respectable place of entertainment could be distinguished from the other kind by "observing in the landlord a possession or an absence of ears."

Many leading Republicans were Southern gentry, "Gentleman Jacobins" more refined than any Federalist. "The dirty set," Foster found, were generally Northerners of Dutch or German extraction. When a Southerner was unclean it was usually "to appear democratical, but not often from taste, as was the case with some of the others." Maybe five members of Congress looked like gentlemen to Foster, including John Randolph of Roanoke, an undersized viper of a Republican congressman. Exquisitely eccentric, the peculiar lord and master of Bizarre, his Virginia tobacco plantation, Randolph was in his early thirties and could have been mistaken for a twelve-year-old boy, "the strangest-looking demagogue you ever set eyes on," Foster said, an opinion Gilbert Stuart confirmed in paint. The rest of the House did "well indeed if they look like farmers, but most seem apothecaries and attorneys." Foster sometimes had Republicans to dinner but was careful about the Irish, "who would have desired no better sport than to shoot at Randolph." When a Federalist congressman *was* shot and nearly killed in a duel with a Republican for whom Jefferson's son-in-law Eppes served as second, Louisa Adams called the wounded man "a shining light" lost on a "horde of half savages." Foster was amused to find among the Republicans a butcher, a printer, and a hangman. The latter, a former sheriff, was proud to have hanged his felons himself, Foster wrote, pleased "to save a dollar and make his son drive the cart." In fairness, he "was by no means an ill-meaning or uncivil person, tho' not particularly agreeable."

Familiar with all of these cultures, the president made their envoys to Washington City feel welcome. The Jeffersonian senator Thomas Worthington of the frontier state of Ohio found the friendly entertainment at the President's House just what he had hoped it would be, and Jefferson too, "plain in his dress and acting the true part of the first citizen of the Republick." Worthington was no woodsman, but for rougher hewn men the experience was educational. After a time or two at the President's House, congressmen who hunted possum debated the weaknesses of crème brûlée. Republican simplicity was dead, a satirist later wrote, "stuck to death with four-prong'd forks."

Jefferson had been stuck with satirists for years. Jumping on his speculation in 1785 that wooly mammoths might still be grazing on the far Western plains, a reasonable conjecture, no white man knowing what was there, Federalists mocked him as "The Mammoth of Democracy," prompting nimble Republicans to make mammoths a sort of mascot. The battle was one of class, fought with passion. In 1801, two Pennsylvania butchers sent the hindquarter of a calf to the President's House, "The Mammoth Veal," they called it. Jefferson replied that their gift was too far gone for the table but beautiful nonetheless and told friends it encouraged his hopes that workingmen were shaking off the fear of republicanism that the privileged orders spread.

Behind the Federalist satire was rage mixed with fear. For the first time in the country's brief history, populists controlled the presidency and the House and had fallen just short in the Senate. A year after Jefferson's inauguration,

Gouverneur Morris, who had written the preamble to the Constitution, grumbled to Hamilton about the harm "His Majesty the People" had done to the Union, having written two decades earlier that "We the People" had formed it. For Morris and his sort, Jefferson was an old friend and a great man brought low by the great unwashed. With just a two-vote majority in the Senate, Morris wrote, "we cannot expect that it should be a dignified body," but it kept some *semblance* of dignity. At "headquarters there is such an abandonment of Manner and such a Pruriency of conversation as would reduce even Greatness to the Level of Vulgarity." Many Federalists had started a revolution in 1775 based on principles they mocked in 1801. All but a few of the founders had left the stage, and greatness had skipped a generation. The names of less than a handful of men in Congress would outlive their times, one of whom was Morris, and the Revolution of 1800 appalled him.

* * *

A freshman congressman at sixty years of age, the Reverend Manasseh Cutler of Essex County, Massachusetts, the very shrine of Federalism, was a well-fed, pleasant-looking man with thinning hair and a ruddy face. Yale educated, medically and legally trained, a botanist who dabbled in astronomy, and a record-breaking mountaineer, Reverend Cutler had watched the British limp into Boston from Lexington and Concord, served as a chaplain in the Revolution, and led the establishment of the Northwest Territory. But despite his broad experience, he was taken by surprise when he arrived in December of 1801 in Washington City, the den of Republican iniquity. The setting was "much more delightful than I expected to find it," the Northerner wrote his daughter. The air was fresh and remarkably mild, and the President's House "superb, well proportioned and pleasantly situated." He was happy with his lodgings too. In a row of attached brick buildings on the Capitol Hill, the boardinghouse room he shared with a fellow Massachusetts man had a scenic view, and in the evenings the landlord's daughter sang at the fortepiano, a relief from "the harangues of the Hall in the day." Cutler liked his fellow boarders, every one a Federalist. "An unbecoming word is never uttered, and the most perfect harmony and friendliness pervades the family."

Jefferson's crowd he saw as the wreck of the nation. The congressman lived in a tragic time "when the best of all governments is crumbling to ruin." He might not be believed, he wrote, if he described what the Democrats would do in pursuit of the multitude. "May kind Heaven interpose, as in time past, in the hour of extremity." Oddly nonetheless, some of the Jeffersonians showed him every courtesy, and the Speaker was "as honest a man as a Democrat can be." Stranger still, Jefferson himself was the picture of civility. He had senators and congressmen to dinner "and what is strange (if anything done here can be strange)," he never mixed Federalists with Republicans. Cutler was soon invited with seven other Federalists who, perhaps to their surprise, found the aroma of French cuisine in the President's House and no reek of sulfur. They were "handsomely received and entertained" and responded in kind, and the dinner was superb.

On a cold day in February, Cutler dined again with other Federalists at the President's House and found the infernal Jefferson as likable as before. They discussed Dr. Jenner's work on smallpox, which put them on common ground. When dinner was served, the congressman enjoyed imported fruits in the dead of winter, a tasty beef and rice soup, turkey, mutton and loin of veal no doubt prepared in the French style, Virginia ham, fried eggs, and a round of beef, boiled to make the soup, browned in a dutch oven, and served with gravy. What threw him was "a pie called a Macaronie, which appeared to be a rich crust" filled with strings of onion, "very strong, and not agreeable." Meriwether Lewis let him know it was Italian, and there were no onions in it, just flour and butter and a Mediterranean sauce, none of which tempted Reverend Cutler. The desserts he liked much better, ice cream with a thin, crumbled crust; something like a pudding, but "very porous and light with a delicious cream sauce"; and "many other jimcracks." In the end the New England Federalists enjoyed a cup of tea with the Parisian monster. A messenger soon brought Cutler a gracious note from the President's House and the loan of a book on smallpox, which he read and returned with thanks.

Three weeks later, Congress repealed the Judiciary Act of 1801, which the Adams administration had contrived to expand the courts and pack them with Federalists only hours before Jefferson took power. Cutler was sure that "our happy Constitution" had died, born in 1789 "and expired, after suffering extreme convulsions, on the 3d of March, 1802, in the evening, aged just 13 years." And yet, from talk around the boardinghouse fire, Cutler began to see that Jefferson was inviting more Federalists to dinner than Republicans, and courting them. "His dress has been quite decent" (faint praise, to be sure), and he seemed to "exert himself in sociability."

On one occasion, four Connecticut Federalists refused their invitations in "pretty plain terms," having noticed that Jefferson had snubbed their fiercest colleagues. They asked Cutler to stay home too, but he came without them. "Invitations to dine are mere compliments," the congressman wrote his son, "which every gentleman has an undoubted right to exercise as he pleases." Every man at the table knew why four of their peers were missing, and the conversation sputtered awkwardly until it occurred to Cutler to mention his trip to France, after which he and Jefferson prattled on "with scarcely a word from any other person, till we had finished with our ice cream," but once the wine passed freely, "all their tongues began to be in motion," and the rest of the evening went "tolerably agreeably." By the time he next returned, Cutler had turned blasé and barely mentioned his evening with "his Democratic Majesty" in his diary: "Dinner handsome, not elegant."

10

MEAN AND LITTLE PASSIONS

In January of 1802, Congressman Samuel Latham Mitchill of New York, one of Jefferson's several physician friends and the Senate's leading philosopher, told his wife that "New Year's Day was a time of great parade in the city of Washington." Stepping out in good clothes on a sunlit, springlike morning let everyone "exhibit," and the place to see and be seen was the President's House. In upper-crust Manhattan, wealthy people called on each other on New Year's Day. In democratic Washington, "every body crowded to Mr. Jefferson's," where the gentry joined the public, "all mixed in the same room without the possibility of ceremony."

Adams had hosted a public reception on the first day of 1801, the opening of the social season, and Jefferson followed suit. Before the public came in, the diplomatic corps, draped with sashes, swords, and gold braid, savored ice cream, Madeira, and light conversation with Jefferson and his soberly dressed cabinet in the State Dining Room. The Spanish minister, the Marquis de Casa Yrujo, and his pretty American wife were ready to leave, Yrujo wrote, when they glimpsed through a window "a rolling ball of burnished gold, carried with swiftness through the air by two gilt wings. Our anxiety increased the nearer it approached" until it stopped at the president's door and disgorged, "weighted with gold lace," the French minister, Louis-André Pichon, a shoemaker's son, and his entourage. The glittering wings turned out to be footmen with gilded skirts and fancy swords. The "natives," the Marquis said, "stared and rubbed their eyes to be convinced 'twas no fairy dream."

Then the president's doors were thrown open to the world, and any respectable citizen could wander in and enjoy his cakes and wines, take him by the hand, and look him in the eye. Louisa Adams thought that most people, alluding to her privileged circle, "disapprove of this sort of company, but with all my supposed aristocratic tastes I think it is a privilege due to the People to permit them to see their President in his house once a year," to pay their respects to him "and their homage to the Nation." But Jefferson's open house gave them too good a time. "Order should be observed and decorum required, and then the privilege would be esteemed."

After a modest military parade, the troops were dismissed and the officers invited in. Here was *some* sign of rank and privilege. Everyone who was anyone had dressed for the occasion, but the editor of Hamilton's favorite paper, the *New York Evening Post*, noticed Jefferson's leather-stringed common shoes, associated with him since the 1790s. Buckles were "superfluous and anti-republican," the editor sniffed, "especially when a man has strings." In their bright scarlet uniforms, the Marine Band played "Jefferson and Liberty" without offending his humility. Some diplomats and department heads brought their families, and so did others with families to bring, military officers in deep blue, gilt-trimmed, high-necked jackets, government clerks, and locals in their Sunday clothes. The children gawked at the Miami and Pottawatomie chiefs wearing native dress and paint, in town for talks with the president, among them the famous Little Turtle, Five Medals, He Who Sits Quietly, and other veterans of battles with U.S. troops, some of which they had won.

Poor whites were not barred, but as James Fenimore Cooper would condescend to say two administrations later, the "poorer and laboring classes" would "of course" not be comfortable at a President's House affair and "consequently stay away." It would never occur to a black man or woman to come. At the other end of the social scale, some Federalists stayed home too, refusing to legitimize the president. But Manasseh Cutler and some others came down for the sake of civility in a convoy of hired coaches. Cutler had to admit they were "tolerably received," though disgusted by the novel entertainment provided by the elder John Leland, a forty-seven-year-old self-taught Baptist preacher long known to Jefferson as a champion of religious liberty.

On the night before the reception, Leland had hauled to the President's House on a six-horse wagon a cheese as big as a millstone, a 1,238-pound gift from the western Massachusetts village of Cheshire and its nine hundred cows, "not one of them a Federalist." Nearly every soul in Cheshire was a Republican and a Baptist, reviled in both capacities by the surrounding Congregational clergy, the Federalist politicians who ran the state, and the partisan press. Embracing a hostile headline that mocked them and their gift, the villagers called it "The Mammoth Cheese."

Before Leland hauled it south, they had carted it around in a common man's parade that the *Stockbridge Western Star* called "a ludicrous procession in honor of a cheesen God." As Leland and the cheese made their way to Washington City by sled, boat, and wagon, the word of their coming preceded them, and Leland preached democracy to cheering crowds. The Mammoth Preacher, the hostile press called him, and he made the cheese famous on its way, adding cheese jokes to mammoth jokes in the arsenal of Federalist wit. An often-quoted line in Jefferson's inaugural address had condemned "taking bread from the mouths of labor." Now it was said he should fill them with cheese. Alert to a shift of mood in Massachusetts, Jefferson saw republicanism in the cheese "in a state where it has been under heavy persecution." When Leland brought it into the President's House on New Year's Eve, Jefferson had a stand built to display it in the vast eastern storage room.

At the height of the next day's reception, he gathered the crowd, announced that the Mammoth Cheese was in the Mammoth Room, and encouraged a tour, led in line by the Mammoth Preacher. Cheesen theater. "The parade was ludicrous enough," the Connecticut Federalist John Cotton Smith wrote a friend, "but what is there appertaining to the left-legged ruler of this ill-fated country that is not ludicrous?" Leland's home state congressman Manasseh Cutler was righteous in his anger. "Leland the cheese monger," Cutler wrote a friend, the "poor, ignorant, illiterate, clownish preacher," had brought "this monument of human weakness and folly to its place of destination."

Leland handed the president a cringe-inducing "Ode to the Mammoth Cheese" ("no traitor to his country's cause" would ever "have a bite of thee between his jaws"), and read a passionate speech. God had raised Thomas Jefferson up to save republicanism and "baffle the arts of Aristocracy," and honest freeborn farmers had produced the Mammoth Cheese without a single slave. If Jefferson winced and Cutler smirked, neither expression was recorded, but the president told the crowd it was one of the happiest moments of his life, for the cheese was a model of the people's skills and their fidelity to equal rights. Lemaire cut slices of the reddish-yellow giant, served with fresh baked bread, as Jefferson introduced Leland one by one to his friends. A few days later, tapping his own pocket and honoring his policy of declining costly gifts, he quietly gave Leland a $200 donation for the cheese, much in excess of its worth, whatever you thought of its taste. "It is said to be good," Gallatin told his wife. "I found it detestable."

On the morning after the cheese, eight leading Federalists made a pilgrimage to Mount Vernon, where Martha Washington gave them breakfast and stoked their fears. Thomas Jefferson was "one of the most detestable of mankind," Lady

Washington said, his election one of the great misfortunes in American history. Cotton Smith was moved when she walked them through the grounds. "I felt myself on enchanted ground." Stealing away from the others, the congressman walked alone down a winding gravel path and stood at Washington's tomb, watching the rolling gray Potomac, thinking of the leader in the grave and the leader in the President's House. "Was it unmanly to weep?"

The Mammoth Cheese stayed in the Mammoth Room for more than a year, getting riper by the day in a death of a thousand cuts. Some said what was left was dumped in the Potomac in 1803, not a moment too soon, others that the last fragrant morsel was nibbled on the first day of 1804.

* * *

The first child born in the President's House was born into slavery. In March of 1802, Ursula Granger, the teenage cook Jefferson had brought pregnant from Monticello, gave birth to a boy, and Jefferson paid for her lying-in. Minor pediatric ills were treated with home remedies, but a doctor was summoned in April and again in May, and sickness put a strain on the president's two kitchens. When Monticello's cook, the enslaved Peter Hemings, James's younger brother, fell ill in June, Jefferson told Martha he hoped for a quick recovery, "or I know not what we should do, as it is next to impossible to send Ursula & her child home & bring them back again." The child, it seems, was chronically ill. Lemaire called him "Asnet," perhaps an approximation of what Ursula had named him. On August 17, Lemaire sent the president a report that began with a broken pump and ended with two lines that show Jefferson knew the baby's name and imply by their brevity that he had known his condition: "Sir, the poor little child Asnet died on the 14th of this month, but I assure you that the good Lord rendered a great service to him and to his mother, since he would have been infirm all his life." Asnet's father, in Virginia, probably never saw his son.

For reasons that can only be guessed, Ursula was done with Washington City, voluntarily or not, and was sent back to Monticello, her time to be split between the kitchen and the fields. When Jefferson returned to the President's House in the fall, Edith Fossett, a fifteen-year-old girl enslaved at Monticello and married to an enslaved blacksmith named Joseph Fossett, took her place. Described in later life as "a woman of brown complexion," five feet two inches tall, Edy Fossett had been a baby minder for Harriet Hemings, the infant daughter born to Sally Hemings in 1801, almost surely Jefferson's child. A bright and talented cook, Edy stayed and learned in Julien's kitchen for six and a half years, the rest of Jefferson's presidency. She too had left her family at Monticello and was left behind in Washington when Jefferson went home to enjoy his. On January 28, 1803, a few months after she arrived, the president paid a doctor five dollars to attend her "in childbed" in the servant's hall. The baby, named James, survived but his father missed his birth.

* * *

Early in 1802, Jefferson reminded his daughters how much they would enjoy Washington, and pressed it in the spring. Eager for release from Virginia, his younger daughter Maria had saved a little money to spend in Washington. Martha, her older sister, was less enthused, wary about a "return to the world from which I have been so long secluded, and for which my habits render me in every way unfit," but she agreed to come too, and bring the older children. Jefferson had just returned to the President's House from Monticello without incident, "other than being twice taken in soaking rains," and he sent her a review of every inn, including its distance from home. If she liked, John Freeman, his enslaved footman, would meet her partway with fresh horses and a second carriage for the children. Two weeks later, the children had the measles, and the trip was postponed. Their grandfather was sorry, he wrote, "not only from my disappointment here, but also from what they are to suffer," and the servants were disappointed too.

On September 1, 1802, the Federalist *Richmond Recorder* told the world what Albemarle County had been buzzing about since 1789: "The man *whom it delighteth the people to honor*" had been keeping a slave concubine for years. "By this wench Sally our president has several children," and the "AFRICAN VENUS is said to officiate as housekeeper at Monticello." For weeks the ugly storm blew across the Federalist press, mixing fiction with more than enough fact, and never quite blew away. At Monticello when the story broke, Jefferson made no public comment then or later. No one knew what he told his family, but the scandal gave his daughters a push to stand by him in the President's House, literally and figuratively, and plans for a family trip were made.

Safely back in Washington but sore all over with a ringing in his ears, which he chalked up to passing through fog, Jefferson sent his daughters travel tips, and Martha wrote back to ask Mrs. Madison to order wigs from Philadelphia in "the color of the hair enclosed and of the most fashionable shapes." With no ladies' maids in the President's House, the wigs would spare Martha and Maria from dressing their own hair, "a business in which neither of us are adepts." No hair was enclosed, and Mrs. Madison trusted her own judgment. Jefferson wrote back that Martha should bring Peter Hemings's muffins recipe with her, proving that Julien was human. "My cook here cannot succeed at all in them, and they are a great luxury to me."

On November 5, Maria wrote again, sorry that she could not leave sooner, that "the visit will be scarcely worth making for so short a time." A month-and-a-half stay was nothing by Virginia standards. It would be just "a flying visit," Martha wrote in a letter of her own, and she would only bring Jeff, her ten-year-old boy. They planned to return in December, probably in bad weather, and she would not "risk such a journey with a carriage full of small children." In time she relented and brought Anne and Ellen too, having surely been cajoled, and left her two youngest with their nurses. Just turned six, Ellen adored her grandfather. When asked where he was in 1798 while he served as vice president, she would point to his picture on the mantel. Maria's one-year-old boy was too young for the trip.

On Wednesday, November 17, Captain Lewis rode out to Strode's wayside inn in Culpepper County with four rented horses, a rented carriage, and a rented driver. There he relieved Maria's husband Mr. Eppes as the family's escort. They reached the President's House on Sunday, having traveled five days instead of the usual four. Their six-week stay gave Jefferson time to enjoy them, pretend to wave off their awe at his elevated state, and enjoy some relief from its burdens. Maria and the children may have been more thrilled to see him in the President's House than he was, but Martha was dangerously ill with a lung infection. On doctor's orders, she expected to proceed to Bermuda for its climate, but with odd good luck she recovered overnight and stayed.

At Monticello, said Margaret Bayard Smith, the children behaved so well at the table "you would not know, if you did not see them, that a child was present." Perhaps it was the same in Washington, but they may have spent more time with their grandfather upstairs than down. Maria loved their happy times in "the little room" where he always sat, surely meaning the study adjoining his bedroom—no first floor room was little—but she fretted about "the unsafe and solitary manner in which you sleep upstairs" without a servant in shouting range. Few gentlemen took such risks, never mind a head of state in an unguarded house exposed to a thousand enemies, some less stable than others.

Washington was not Philadelphia, let alone Paris, which Martha and Maria had absorbed *avant le déluge*, but it was growing. While they were in town, the Union Tavern & Washington Hotel opened its doors, "first house east of the President's," with a sidewalk to the Pennsylvania Avenue, thirty well-furnished rooms, a commodious Coffee Room, and an upstairs meeting space "with a pleasant view of the Potomac and the surrounding country." Fifteen houses, three stories high, had gone up on the avenue in the past seven months alone. But Congress was out of town when the family arrived, and their coming woke the capital up. Their father showed off his daughters at a cascade of dinners, feeding the curiosity of the observers and the observed. Soon after Congress reconvened in December, Manasseh Cutler found it odd that he and other Federalists were the first to be invited, but he brought the kind of gift the president accepted, bits of wadding for ladies' cloaks and mattress stuffing produced by a Beverly, Massachusetts, factory, a sign of American progress. Jefferson was engagingly social and proud of his daughters, who "appeared well-accomplished women" to Cutler. It was not too much to say they were "very delicate and tolerably handsome."

The New Year's Day reception of 1803, "a festal day in high style at the President's House," Cutler wrote, was staged in the Oval Room, "which seemed to be improved as a levee room," crowded with chattering cabinet officers, colorful foreign diplomats, the president's liveried staff, and an ecumenical mix of Federalists and Republicans being civil. Cutler found the conversation lively among sitting or standing groups broken up in little clusters, with plates of cake, cups of punch, and glasses of Jefferson's wine being managed by upright guests or balanced on seated knees. A good many women were there, Martha and Maria, Mrs. Madison and her sister, the French minister's wife, a few congressional wives, "some very elderly ladies," and a woman in a stylish white turban.

The president went up to Cutler and his Federalist friends and told him over the din that his wadding was still on the table where he had left it, to be shown off to guests, which could not have done Jefferson harm with the congressman or his companions. Cutler just happened to have more of the bed ticking in his pocketbook, and the ladies suggested new uses for it, stuffing bed quilts, "weather coats," and more. On Cutler's way out, he passed the great eastern room, thought of the Mammoth Cheese, and asked a liveried servant if it was still there. Indeed it was, and he went in to take a look. It was not a tempting sight. The president had just remarked that sixty pounds had been cut from its middle "in consequence of the puffing up and symptoms of decay."

Martha's life at Monticello had made her an able hostess, and Margaret Bayard Smith, six years her junior, admired her. In a private letter, Mrs. Smith called Mrs. Randolph "rather homely, a delicate likeness of her father," as if it looked better on him than her, but more interesting than her sister and "one of the most lovely women I have ever met." She positively beamed with a smart benevolence and a manner so frank and affectionate "you know her at once, and feel perfectly at your ease with her." For Louisa Adams, no lenient judge, Mrs. Randolph was a likable woman who merited respect. After dinner one evening, she regaled Mrs. Smith in the Oval Room for two hours with a soliloquy on her children and her husband, in a show of "that rare but charming egotism" that can rivet an indulgent companion to someone else's vanity. "I could have listened to her for two hours longer, but coffee and the gentlemen entered and we were interrupted."

Little Ellen was a charmer too, without the self-absorption. "Extravagantly fond of poetry" at the soft age of six, she listened with apt expressions changing on her face as Mrs. Smith recited "The Hermit," Oliver Goldsmith's poem of gentle solitude, "her eyes fixed on mine and her arms clasped close around me." Her aunt Maria made a different mark, visibly ill at ease in a sea of important guests, despite her conversation-stopping beauty, but Mrs. Smith found her engaging, relaxed, and revealing when they spoke alone.

Short of excitement since they came back from Paris in 1789, Martha and Maria enjoyed an onslaught of parties and receptions, none of them at the President's House. Anne was a year too young for society at fifteen, but her mother saw her off to a ball under the wing of a motherly friend. A month into their visit, Mrs. Smith understood she should host no entertainments for Martha and Maria, "of which they assured me they were heartily tired." Falling naturally into line with the president's social leveling, his daughters declined any special deference and made and received morning calls in his dashing chariot, tucked away new for more than a year and used for the first time for its intended purpose, drawn by splendid Virginia bays driven by Joseph Dougherty, posing on its box in his fancy coat. Jefferson had ordered the coach built in Philadelphia and had his name withheld until its price was fixed, preferring to give his money "to some greater object of charity than the workman generally is."

After dinner at the President's House, when the guests had gone home and candles had been lit against the winter night, Jefferson and his daughters, and perhaps the older children, laughed or vented together according to the day's events, bonding as they had when Martha and Maria were girls and their father had the leisure time. The relief it gave the president cannot be oversold. He may have played his violin, not as well as he did when he practiced every day and gave Jeff his earliest memory, of "my grandfather's playing on the violin and his grandchildren dancing around him, in which he delighted."

* * *

As Congress convened in December of 1802 with the president's family in town, a new rustic senator rumbled into town on the Baltimore stage after more than a week on the way from Epping, New Hampshire, a farming and lumbering village

Senator William Plumer. ***Library of Congress***

of fewer than two thousand souls that offered its sober residents "few temptations to idleness or immorality." Senator William Plumer, the very model of a moderate Federalist, saw a good deal of both on the Capitol Hill. Like most of his freshman peers, he had hardly been more than a day's ride from his family. "I was much affected" on leaving them, he wrote, but the mild Washington winter agreed with him, and so did Frost & Quinn's, his serviceable boardinghouse. "None of the lodgers are noisy. Each is sober. All are Federalists."

A tall, dark, sensible man of forty-three, Plumer was blessed with an open mind; a temperate disposition; an attractive, principled wife; five young children; thick black hair; and kind black eyes, "bright and beautiful," Mrs. Plumer said they were, the lights of "a manly face." Before they sent him to Washington with a healthy New England dread of Thomas Jefferson, his colleagues had made him Speaker of New Hampshire's House of Representatives and president of its Senate. His careful handwriting made "no attempt at ornament and no unnecessary flourish," and his speech was fair and thoughtful, "not elegant or scholar-like," but "never low or vulgar."

Guided by a father "prompt to notice any impropriety in his children," Plumer had grown up in Epping, where no one was very rich, no one was very poor, and nearly everyone worked his own land. He was hoeing a field at sixteen when he heard the thud of cannon fifty miles off on Bunker Hill, but poor health kept him out of the war. He was schooled only three months a year, for his father valued money more highly than learning and kept only two books in the house, the Bible and *The Morals of Epictetus*, a man who prized discipline. William walked miles to borrow books he knew nothing about from men he had never met. His teacher said the boy should be groomed for Harvard, but his father was sure he had wit enough already. Religion ruled in Epping, and infidelity was suppressed with authority, not reason. A few eccentric Quakers excepted, everyone belonged to the Congregational church, whose tax-supported minister reminded parents at children's funerals that Adam had sinned quite enough to condemn them, and infants "who could not discern their right hand from their left" burned in hell with the rest of the damned.

Epping's Congregational monopoly ended when a Baptist preacher arrived in the religious revival of 1779 and converted Plumer, who became a traveling revivalist too until doubts seeped in, which a peer advised him to dispel through faith instead of thought: "Resist the Devil and he will flee from thee." Satisfied that thought was no crime, Plumer went back to his farm to pursue what seemed to him "the religion of reason and nature," a Deist conviction shared with Jefferson that a benevolent God set the universe in motion but did not intervene. He studied law in his twenties, and his neighbors sent him to the legislature despite his apostasy. One of his speeches helped kill a bill to punish blasphemy with a white-hot iron pushed through the sinner's tongue, which failed only narrowly, but his politics were thoroughly Federalist. At a time of sharp division about the nature of government itself, the more serious threat for him was "not tyranny in the head but anarchy in the limbs." Subject at every step to "the severe check of reason" over emotion and exposed to nothing much by way of aristocracy, Plumer was polite, even cordial to Republicans, whom he saw as fellow patriots and men of goodwill.

Many Federalists, Jefferson said, condemned whatever he did because he did it, and "pretend that even chance never throws us on a right measure," but most of the ones who knew him "give a credit to my intentions which they may deny to my understanding." William Plumer came to know him at his table.

* * *

The day after Plumer reached Washington, he was introduced at the President's House, the grandest work of human hands he had ever seen, accompanied by a few Republicans as new to it as he. They had waited for a while in a splendid room when a tall, smiling man in a worn brown coat and old-fashioned clothes walked in. As others had and would, Plumer took him for a servant gone to seed and was startled twice, not only to be told this was Thomas Jefferson but also to find that he liked him, a cordial, unpretentious man.

Plumer's mood changed when a still more disheveled character walked in and was introduced as Thomas Paine, disorder in the flesh, the British-born author of *Common Sense*, *The Rights of Man*, and *The Age of Reason*, which the *Evening Post* had lately called "too blasphemous to meet the public eye." Fond of his own English voice, Paine plopped himself down at the president's side like an oaf at a tavern bar and started talking. Two Washington taverns, in fact, had refused to seat him. A proficient drunk with matching social graces, a bloodshot nose, and piercing black eyes, the untamed revolutionary had a rugged red face, "much hackneyed in the service of the world," a Republican said. Religious liberal though he was, Plumer was appalled that even Jefferson would have "that infamous blasphemer" in the presence of his grandchildren, let alone take him in for a two-week stay as he shocked the capital of democracy with democratic ideas. In public, the *Port Folio* wondered whether "the greatest infidel on earth" was a fit companion for the president of the United States. In private, Manasseh Cutler charged Jefferson with bogus piety for taking his daughters to public services while he harbored an atheist in the President's House.

Jefferson admired Paine, brilliantly militant and fearless as he was, and knowing the price of his visit, didn't care enough to avoid it. Perhaps he even relished it. A leading Republican senator had hosted Paine too, but Plumer noticed neither man asked Federalists to dine with him. "In this they show their prudence."

Plumer had his first presidential dinner at a table manned by Federalists and confided to his diary his disapproval of Jefferson's politically segregated guest lists. If men of all persuasions came together at the President's House, they would have to be civil, get to know each other, and learn to respect their adversaries, for the more good men associate, "the better they think of each other, notwithstanding their differences of opinion." The dinner was superb nonetheless, the fruits and sweetmeats in particular, the president's company was a pleasure, and Plumer had never enjoyed such wine, "particularly the champagne, which was indeed delicious." But likable as Jefferson was, the senator kept his bearings. "I wish his French politics were as good as his French wines."

At Plumer's Epping law office, "the little knot of village politicians" enjoyed his letters, which his twenty-year-old clerk, Daniel Webster, read eagerly. Customs differed in the House and Senate, Plumer wrote. Congressmen sat with their hats on their heads and took them off when they spoke. Senators kept their toppers in their hands. For a man without a party, Aaron Burr presided smoothly over the Senate. His fellow Republicans distrusted him, having watched him as the House picked a president, poised to snatch Jefferson's prize like a crow in a tree. But cunning as he was, Plumer wrote, he would struggle "to inspire confidence or esteem. His arts have alarmed the fears and awakened the jealousies of the President."

* * *

On December 28, Martha's husband came to Washington to bring the family home and break the president's heart. They all stayed a few days into January before Jefferson helped them board the Georgetown ferry and rode along a few miles into Virginia, sizing up the roads and fretting. When Maria assured him by mail that they were safely home she confessed it had been a "disastrous journey." The pain of seeing him turn back alone had made her heart ache, she wrote, and the costs he had borne for their visit worried her. For him it had been a joy. "You did not here indulge yourselves as much as I wished," he wrote her older sister, "and nothing prevented my supplying your backwardness but my total ignorance in articles which might suit you," but their parting had been hard. "I felt my solitude too upon your departure, very severely," the kind a grandparent feels when the family goes home and the house goes suddenly quiet.

He presumed Lemaire's recipe for "*panne-quaiques*" pleased Martha as much as the misspelled French and half-learned English amused her. "Edy has a son and is doing well," he added, a sign of their mutual interest in Edith Fossett, the apprentice cook enslaved at the President's House, her newborn child, and their health. It was known by this time, midway through Jefferson's first term, that a Republican tide in the midterm elections of 1802 had swept the Federalists out of power in the Senate and put both of his sons-in-law in the Republican-controlled House as Virginia congressmen. When Congress convened in March of 1803, they moved into the President's House, leaving their families at home, and joined him at his table most evenings, with or without guests, a joy that would curdle in time.

Jefferson had encouraged his daughters to marry within the family, as Virginia gentry often did—there were only so many suitable matches to go around—and Martha's husband, Thomas Mann Randolph Jr., was her cousin. Jefferson had mentored him in his youth, and called him "a man of science, sense, virtue, and competence; in whom indeed I have nothing more to wish," careful words of scant affection. He and Martha had a simple, comfortable house at Edgehill, his inherited plantation, but lived more often than not across the river at Monticello on the charity of her father, for Randolph was caught in a vortex of debt, most of it inherited, but mortifying nonetheless, and mortification did not suit him. In 1858, a writer who had interviewed his children called him "impetuous and imperious in temper" and "eloquent in conversation when he chose to be." Thomas Randolph was a troubled man.

Educated at William and Mary and the University of Edinburgh, he claimed descent from Pocahontas and had much in common with the president. Tall, strong, and athletic with an air of distinction, he was cultured, bright, and polished, more generous to failing relatives than he could afford to be, bound to agriculture by birth more than choice, a gifted musician and singer, and Virginia's leading botanist, but everyone around him coped with darkness. To her sorrow, what his wife described with palpable distaste as "the Randolph temperament" was jealous, melancholic, irritable, and inclined to "mean and little passions," inflamed in his case by insecurity and financial embarrassment. In 1794 he had suffered a mental breakdown.

His son recalled him bitterly in old age. "My education was neglected," Jeff said, for "my father, himself educated at Edinburgh, was too prodigal to others to retain any thing for himself or his family. I was sent irregularly to inferior schools but never to college." Randolph showed little interest in his children, who turned to their grandfather for male love and guidance. In her own old age, Jeff's sister Ellen called their father cold, austere, "morose, irritable, and suspicious," none of which was plain when he married their mother. "The defects of temper & the growth of evil passions which subsequently made his family miserable & destroyed the esteem of his friends were the baneful development of other, later, wretched years," some of them in the President's House.

He had suffered a humiliating defeat in a run for the Virginia House of Delegates, despite his famous connection, and the seat he won in Congress in 1802 irresponsibly increased the burdens he was already struggling to bear. Without consulting Jefferson first, he had run against a man who had helped make him president, and had won only narrowly, another embarrassment for all concerned. In midcampaign, Randolph told his father-in-law that his welcome into the family had filled him with gratitude spoiled by "something like shame," for he felt himself so different from that splendid mix "as to look like something extraneous, fallen in by accident" to spoil the batch. At ease with his peers, he wrote, he felt among the Jeffersons like an empty-headed bird among swans.

Jefferson's younger daughter had made a better match. In 1797, Maria married John Wayles Eppes, a cousin on both sides. She had known him all her life. In contrast to Martha's, Maria's marriage gave her father "inexpressible pleasure," convinced, he told Maria, that Eppes possessed "every quality necessary to make you happy and to make us all happy." He had studied law at William and Mary and the University of Pennsylvania but never practiced. Instead he managed Eppington, his family plantation a hundred miles southeast of Monticello, where he and Maria spent their summers, making a full house with the Randolphs, the children, and the president. Jefferson's overseer called Eppes a handsome man, "a great favorite with everybody." Another Jefferson protégé, Eppes had lived with him in Philadelphia in his teens, copying Madison's precious notes of the Constitutional Convention. Martha's children called him Uncle Jack, "a gay, good-natured, laughing man," Ellen later recalled, "inferior perhaps to my father in talent & cultivation," but much happier and far more enjoyable. With a fine eye for horses, Eppes chose many for the president.

As live-in guests at the President's House, his sons-in-law's free meals and lodgings were noticeably better than boardinghouse fare, let alone the heady mix of statesmen; diplomats; men of science, art, and literature; accomplished women; generals; admirals; explorers; and Indian chiefs with whom they shared his table. Jefferson called them "Tom" and "Jack" before their marriages, "Mr. Randolph" and "Mr. Eppes" thereafter, even among family. The closing line of a letter to Martha was typical: "Present my best esteem to Mr. Randolph, abundance of soft things to the children, and warmest affections to yourself." He was inclined to be jovial with Mr. Eppes and correct with Mr. Randolph, who noticed, of course, to no one's good.

11

BY NO MEANS DANGEROUS

Raised on the Virginia frontier within sight of Indian country, Jefferson had been pulled toward the West since his childhood. In his first inaugural address, he envisioned "a rising nation, spread over a wide and fruitful land" beyond any living American's reach; but the Mississippi was its current western boundary, and the huge swath of territory on the other side belonged to France, a potential staging ground for a Napoleonic invasion of the United States and a barrier to its expansion stretching halfway to the Pacific. Louisiana it was called.

In the winter of 1803, Lewis brought up to the Capitol Hill a secret proposal to send a band of explorers northwest up the Missouri River. Several weeks later, Jefferson wrote friends, indiscreetly at best, that Congress had secretly approved a search for a river route "into the Western ocean" and Captain Lewis, his secretary, would lead it. Lewis spent endless hours in the president's Cabinet discussing the laughable range of navigational, geographic, and scientific knowledge any hope of success would demand. Knowing the expedition could not stay secret, Jefferson asked the European ministers to instruct their countries' Western officers to pass the explorers through their territories and assist them. Early in March, after Jefferson briefed him, the British chargé Edward Thornton told London that his host hoped to distinguish his presidency with great discoveries "entirely of a scientific nature," a deceptively bent hook that Thornton swallowed. To lead this scholarly mission, the Englishman wrote, the president had chosen "his Secretary, Captain Meriwether Lewis, a person in the vigour of his age, of a hardy constitution, and already acquainted with the manners of the Indians by his residence in the Western Settlements." Thornton gave Lewis a passport.

Six days later, on March 15, Lewis left for western Virginia and Pennsylvania to buy equipment and the latest rifled muskets, assemble a traveling reference library, and be tutored in geology, botany, ethnology, astronomy, and navigation by the president's Philadelphia friends. The qualifications that could not be learned gave Jefferson no pause. In two years as his private secretary, Lewis had shown "undaunted courage" and a "firmness and perseverance of purpose, which nothing but impossibilities could divert." He had also shown a tendency toward "depressions of mind," which the president should have taken seriously.

To replace him, Jefferson recruited Lewis Harvie, another son of an old Virginia friend, reading law in Georgetown. "Some object in the Western country," he told the young man, would occupy Lewis for a year or two, and his secretary's tasks were no hardship. He wrote his own letters and copied them in a press, and most of the secretary's job came to helping with company, delivering messages to Congress, and giving "explanations" to some of its members and other dignitaries. There was little enough to do that Harvie's afternoons and evenings would be free. Beyond room and board, there was $600 a year for clothes and pocket money, a horse, and a servant, unless he preferred that his own should join the family. Harvie having threatened to shoot two editors whose attacks on Jefferson upset him, his hot reputation contrasted with his cool reply. Time for "other avocations" would be good, he wrote, for a full-time devotion to his duties "would diminish the pleasure I should take in giving them a strict attention." Jefferson was fine with a part-time aide, the only one he had.

In a playful chat at the President's House, Jefferson soon suggested to Thornton that the British might grab French colonies in a war against Napoleon, and Thornton asked "half laughingly" how Jefferson would like it if Britain took the Floridas and New Orleans and offered them to him. Jefferson said they would one day be "an indispensible necessity to the United States." Neither man knew that Britain had just declared war on France, and everything would change.

Lewis returned to Washington in mid-June and sent a letter to the feral Indiana Territory addressed to William Clark, his former superior officer, asking him to join the expedition. Clark's prompt acceptance took a month and a half to come back. Few Americans knew more about the West than Jefferson did, and Jefferson knew next to nothing. Lewis and Clark would make a heroic start, he wrote, and "those who come after us" will "fill up the canvas we begin." Expecting grave danger from Indians, Jefferson instructed Lewis to take no needless chances with his men. "We value our citizens too much to offer them to probable destruction" ("probable" was Gallatin's contribution, expanding Lewis's discretion). More than kindness was involved in this. "In the loss of yourselves," Jefferson wrote, "we should lose also the information you will have acquired."

To avoid total failure should he die, Lewis must name a successor. A few days later, the young man wrote his mother that he was taking a western trip "by no means dangerous" and could not be any safer if he stayed in Washington.

On the evening of July 3, the day before Lewis headed west, the president read a letter from his agents in Europe. They had bought not just New Orleans, as he had hoped they could, but the whole Louisiana Territory, at a bargain price. Had a playwright timed it so, Jefferson's sheer delight would have been laughed off the stage. At the next day's July Fourth reception, he told the cheering crowd from the mansion's front steps that their country would soon double in size and absorb the crucial mouth of the Mississippi. Not the least of his joys, the purchase of Louisiana would kill the existential threat of Napoleonic armies on the border. There were signs of excitement at the President's House. When Dougherty packed Lewis's saddle he forgot to include the bridle, and Lewis left his wallet and his dagger.

Jefferson must have wondered if he would ever see Lewis again. He would wonder for three and a half years. On July 15, Lewis wrote a letter from Pittsburgh that took ten days to reach the President's House. His next note came from Wheeling, seventeen days away. The one from Cincinnati reporting mammoth bone finds took three weeks to arrive. After that his letters traveled for months until they stopped coming.

* * *

Benjamin Henry Latrobe was a talented architect and a difficult man, pleased with himself to the point of generosity and not so much with others, especially in his own line of work. Jefferson's perceptive friend, the remarkable artist Charles Willson Peale, captured Latrobe on canvas, a man in early middle age in a smartly tailored dark green coat with a fashionable high-backed collar; a high, intelligent forehead; businesslike wire-rimmed spectacles perched on a head of curly dark hair; and a long, humorless face with the shadow of a beard, trying to look approachable and failing.

Cosmopolitan from birth, born in England in 1764 of an Irish father and an American mother, Latrobe had studied with a London architect who taught him the new "plain style" of classical architecture, true to ancient forms but lightly decorated. Devoted to his profession, he had mastered the art of design and the skills of a structural engineer and developed his own distinguished theory of domestic architecture. After limited success in Britain, he left in his early thirties for America, where the need was great and the competition thin. Practicing in Richmond in 1796 and then in Philadelphia, he designed important buildings

Benjamin Latrobe, painted by Charles Willson Peale, ca. 1804. ***White House Collection, courtesy of the White House Historical Association***

and almost surely met Vice President Jefferson in the old capital, an astutely inquisitive amateur drawn to the rare professional.

On November 2, 1802, Jefferson asked Latrobe to come to Washington to design a dry dock to his specifications, which were far more sophisticated than Latrobe may have thought they would be. Three weeks later, the architect went to dinner at the President's House and was taken with him. Jefferson's daughters were there, with the Madisons, a Carter of the Virginia Carters, and Dr. William Thornton, one of Jefferson's polymath friends, a native of the British West

Indies who dabbled in architecture, not to be confused with the British chargé Edward Thornton. The dinner was superb, Latrobe wrote his wife, particularly the venison in the French style and the dessert "profuse and extremely elegant." When Carter asked Martha to have a glass of wine with him, she drank to his health, and her father let her know she had broken the Health Law. She was not familiar with it, she said, it must have been enacted before she arrived. No heavy drinker, Latrobe approved of the president's ban on toasts and enjoyed his explanation of the law. For the first time in his life, he had only one glass of wine at a dinner party, "and though I sat by the President, he did not invite me to drink another."

Madison led the conversation, improved for most of the guests by all three of the available intoxicants, Jefferson's sherry, a delicious champagne, and a rare Spanish wine. The eclectic combination of soft Virginia drawls, Levi Lincoln's New England twang, and whatever was left of Latrobe's North of England speech and Dr. Thornton's Caribbean English gave the evening a multicultural touch. The president said little, Latrobe told his wife, and filled the plates himself, "with great ease and grace for a philosopher," but he broke into animated speech when the servants removed the cloth and produced an array of "knick-knacks" to be nibbled. "There is a degree of ease in Mr. Jefferson's company that every one seems to feel and to enjoy."

At about five o'clock, the ladies withdrew to the softly lit Oval Room and its tea table, the gentlemen soon followed, and the spirited conversation never lagged until seven. Rarely had Latrobe enjoyed "so elegant a mental treat," an engaging mix of architecture, literature, agriculture, "wit, and a little business." It was a charmed and charming circle he had joined.

Latrobe's next presidential dinner was in all male company, and a good deal looser for that. Every guest was a man of science, and Meriwether Lewis, who joined almost every Jeffersonian dinner, introduced them "in so slovenly a way," Latrobe later griped, that he did not catch all their names, but the lively discussion over wine ranged from immigration, to modern culture, to the properties of light. When the subject turned to languages, "the President became very entertaining" as he gave them a taste of Benjamin Franklin's abysmal French and described in comic detail a multinational party at Franklin's home in Paris where Jefferson, Franklin, and John Jay were speaking the local language with uneven results. After his son arrived and kissed every lady in turn, Franklin had asked Mrs. Jay why she blushed. An American who meant to suggest it was because he had kissed her last ("dernier") said he kissed her derrière.

In the winter of 1803, three days after Congress appropriated $50,000 for public works to be spent at the president's discretion, Jefferson made Latrobe surveyor of public buildings, reporting to him, a post he had created to complete and improve the Capitol and the President's House. So began the creative marriage of Latrobe's professional skills and Jefferson's amateur vision. Reluctantly, the president let his architect keep his Wilmington, Delaware, home and his private Philadelphia practice, making short trips to Washington City. He could hardly do otherwise; the job paid only $1,700 a year. To manage things day to day, Latrobe appointed John Lenthall, a skillful builder and hands-on supervisor, as clerk of the works.

Jefferson had picked Latrobe over James Hoban, the unlikely winner of the contest to design the President's House whom Latrobe called "the Irish carpenter," one of many competitors whose work he despised without making him a blood enemy, which he promptly made of William Thornton, "an English physician," Henry Adams later wrote, "who in the course of two weeks' study at the Philadelphia library gained enough knowledge of architecture to draw incorrectly an exterior elevation" and win the contest to design the Capitol. Unable to find a competent native-born American to rescue Dr. Thornton from his incapacity to build it, Jefferson chose Latrobe, who concluded that "the doctor was born under a musical planet, for all his rooms fall naturally into the shape of fiddles, tambourines, & mandolins, one or two into that of a harp."

Thornton loathed Latrobe in return for mocking and improving his plans. An eagle of Latrobe's design, carved in stone in the House chamber, was so flat, Thornton told the *Intelligencer*'s readers, surely including the president, "that country people mistake it for the skin of an owl such as they nail on their barn doors." Quite apart from his abysmal taste, Thornton wrote, Latrobe's reports to Congress as he desecrated the Capitol were riddled with mistakes and salted with lies. In search of an honest man, Diogenes "would never have blown out his candle on meeting Mr. Latrobe."

With the Capitol less than half-built and the President's House threatening to fall down, Jefferson spent too much time refereeing Latrobe's brawls with Thornton. Neither Jefferson nor Latrobe liked either building, but Latrobe's reviews were more colorful. General Washington gave his countrymen liberty "but was wholly ignorant of art," Latrobe wrote accurately enough. "It is therefore not to be wondered that the design of a physician, who was very ignorant of architecture, was adopted for the Capitol and of a carpenter for the President's house," which Latrobe assessed as "a mutilated copy of a badly designed building near Dublin" in an ornamented style out of fashion before it was built. Nor was Latrobe overawed by Congress. When the Senate passed an ill-fated bill to cede the President's House to the legislative branch and move Jefferson to some "suitable house, to be rented, bought, or built," it occurred to Latrobe that if

Congress evicted the president, the House of Representatives should be stuffed "into the room formerly inhabited by the Mammoth Cheese," just the right place for that "maggot-breeding assembly."

* * *

Though Jefferson would have made the President's House simpler, it was literally set in stone, and he finished it in its genre, softened by the modern plain style he and Latrobe preferred. Looking through the lens of the Enlightenment, Jefferson wished to make the mansion, like Monticello, an elevating place of classic beauty, an improving source of pride for the nation and confidence in its future. Sharing with Latrobe in the republic's formative phase the honor and frustration of finishing both of its signature buildings, saving them from poor design and inferior work, Jefferson gave close attention to the President's House but a higher priority to the Capitol, where he thought the republican experiment would play out. Fortunately, he and Latrobe shared three goals—to finish both buildings as frugally as possible, to make them as functional as possible, and to craft them as beautifully as possible, in simple, classic form.

Yet they bickered "tooth and nail," Latrobe confessed, pushing each other creatively as partnered artists do. In one of many spats, Jefferson informed Latrobe that Italian cupolas are "one of the degeneracies of modern architecture" and vetoed his plan to stick one on the Capitol. "It is with real pain I oppose myself to your passion," he wrote, "and that in a matter of taste, I differ from a professor in his own art," but he bore the pain and kept differing. Giving as good as he got, Latrobe challenged Jefferson time and again in sharp but gentlemanly terms and expressed himself snidely to others about the president's suspicion of the modern. "He is an excellent architect out of books, by the bye," Latrobe wrote his brother, but he favored Queen Elizabeth's taste. Having failed to persuade him to scrap the design Dr. Thornton had drawn for the Capitol and Washington had approved, Latrobe complained to Lenthall that "once erected, the absurdity can never be recalled, and the public will learn that one president was blockhead enough to adopt a plan which another was fool enough to retain."

Jefferson's jabs were more skillful than that, and aimed at Latrobe straight up instead of behind his back. During one of the architect's long absences, Jefferson wrote him "mortified" by the work behind schedule at the Capitol. "The gutters of this house also await you, and in the mean time are constantly pouring floods of water into it." Chasing a longtime dream, Jefferson pushed for gorgeous skylights for the Capitol dome, but Latrobe ruled them out, convinced that they would leak. "I cannot express to you the regret I feel," Jefferson replied. "I had hoped that art had resources for that."

For the first several years, not much was done with the President's House but to keep it from coming apart. Its heavy slate roof let rainwater in, gutters made of lead failed to carry it away, and the dead weight of both had been pushing the walls apart until Latrobe pulled them back with tie rods attached to the timbers. The roof was replaced with lighter rolled iron in a zigzag design encased in flat sheets, which Jefferson invented from scratch. Even Latrobe was impressed. A well was dug to replace the polluted brook that supplied the mansion's water, and a drain was enlarged to carry rainwater to the Tiber. The two new water closets Jefferson had ordered, one for his dressing room, the other for a bedchamber, had never worked well and required scarce new parts. The house's defective pipes, he told Latrobe, were rotting it at the water closets, and the water that flushed them was siphoned improperly from the cistern in the attic. The walls remained standing, but in 1803 the Mammoth Room's ceiling gave way, providentially with no one in it.

Keeping watch on the capital's other buildings, Jefferson ordered work stopped "instantly" on a house going up on F Street that violated the building code. Under his direction, almost a third of 1803's $50,000 public building appropriation was spent not on the Capitol or the President's House but the Pennsylvania Avenue, which he saw as a tangible link between the executive and legislative branches. Following his design, the avenue was divided into three lanes, a wide, graveled road for horses and carriages in the center with drainage ditches and footpaths on both sides. Four rows of poplars defined the three lanes, narrowing the view between the Capitol and the President's House and focusing it on them. Modeled on the Parisian boulevards Jefferson admired, the avenue stayed muddy in rain and pitted when dry nonetheless. The Royal George, a long-bodied four-horse stage, "either rattled with members of Congress from Georgetown in a halo of dust, or pitched, like a ship in a seaway among the holes and ruts."

At the President's House, Jefferson and Latrobe scrapped Hoban's plans to build a grand staircase in the "Imperial" style—a wide flight of stairs facing the hall and running up to a landing where narrower flights on both sides would double back to the second floor. With Latrobe's rare endorsement, Jefferson chose the opposite design. Two modest flights of stairs, one on each side with their backs to the hall, reached a landing where a broad run of steps ran the rest of the way. The result was an open view from one end of the house to the other, and the unobtrusive stairs visible from the hall made the upstairs rooms seem private, as Jefferson wished them to be.

Unable to coexist with a basement too warm for wine, Jefferson built an icehouse that doubled as a wine cellar. Steps from the mansion's western door, a sixteen-foot pit was dug, wider at the bottom than the top, lined with bricks topped with multisided wooden walls, barred windows, and a turret roof. It was larger than the usual thing, for unusual quantities of wine. On cold winter days, workmen earned their pay cutting big cakes of ice with spades from a little pond below the house, loading them into carts, and filling the pit, above which the wine chilled for months on a wooden platform.

* * *

In 1803, Charles Willson Peale succumbed to an addiction that promptly spread to Latrobe, who quickly hooked the president. An English acquaintance of Peale's had put a new twist on an old device, two pens attached to arms joined by pivots that copied a letter as you wrote it, a polygraph, the Englishman called it, from the Greek for multiple writing. Peale spent years perfecting it with Jefferson's nearly obsessive collaboration. Having hoped it would make him rich, Peale came to see it as "a dear bought whistle" for the time and money it consumed, invoking Franklin's tale about a boy who gave too much for his toy.

Latrobe foretold to Peale "that in a little time the polygraph must find its way into the study of every man who writes letters & can scrape $60 together." Jefferson was such a man, and in 1804, Latrobe loaned him his polygraph, suspecting he would like it. The president could not have been more intrigued. Here was a complicated tool that recorded every word he wrote as he wrote it, trusted no human copyist with his secrets, and challenged him to refine it. Like any lover of new technology, he simply had to have it. Suddenly, the copy press he had prized, model year 1801, was "a very poor thing in comparison with it," and the screw-pressed copies he had cherished, done in two minutes instead of no time at all, were "hardly ever legible."

In March of 1804, Peale sent him a polygraph more advanced than Latrobe's, insisted it fell far short of what it could be, and asked him to "make every objection you can after you have had a trial," for only perseverance could perfect it. For the rest of his stay in the President's House, despite the demands on his time, Jefferson spent uncounted hours in his Cabinet applying his hand-cut tools to polygraphs of every size and configuration, desktops and laptops too, adjusting every socket, spring, arm, drawer, inkwell, pivot, and screw, inch by meticulous inch, in a long-distance collaboration with Peale, a puzzle-loving tinkerer's dream. Despite his zest for progress, he could not abandon his quills for Peale's modern steel nib pens, but in a stream of fastidious letters to the

Reproduction of a Jeffersonian polygraph machine, made by William Spawn. ***Smithsonian Institution***

multitalented Philadelphian, he described his tinkering with his polygraph in minute detail, drew intricate configurations in the margins, and commissioned new examples for new purposes. In 1805, he sent a desktop model back to Peale "to have the machinery reformed to the new manner" for his secretary, had Claxton buy it with public funds, and asked Peale to apply what he had paid for it to the new portable he ordered for his private use.

Jefferson gave polygraphs to friends and colleagues and diplomats serving abroad, to erase the risk of foreign clerks copying sensitive papers. On the theory that gifts to kings should be rare and "the produce of our own country," he had Peale make three works of art in the form of polygraphs for the bey of Tunis, the bey's foreign minister, and his ambassador to America. They had to work perfectly, Jefferson wrote, "entirely mounted in silver" instead of brass, and crafted in fine mahogany. As for size, "the Moors write on a small folio paper, at least all the letters I have seen from them have been on such paper."

Given his rule on gifts, he told Peale he was "sometimes placed in an embarrassing dilemma" by declining thoughtful presents. "In these cases I resort to counter-presents. Your polygraph, from its rarity and utility, offers a handsome instrument of retribution to certain characters." Deployed on the Barbary Coast, Commodore Edward Preble had sent him a cask of wine. Calculating that Peale's finest polygraphs roughly matched its price, Jefferson ordered one custom made of fine wood and silver and sent it to the commodore with thanks for his gift and his service, confident that he would "take time to learn what will save time," and enjoy "a portable secretary." He explained to James Bowdoin, a special envoy to Spain, what a polygraph was, and got carried away. "I think it is the finest invention of the present age, and so much superior to the copying machine that the latter will never be continued a day by any one who tries the polygraph." He had Peale make one for Bowdoin and used it himself in the President's House to be sure it was perfect before it was shipped.

And yet he considered alternatives. In 1807, he tried a Stylograph, based on a thin sheet of paper blackened on both sides, "perhaps with coal," he thought, since "they call it carbonated paper." Carbon had nothing to do with it. The paper was soaked in printer's ink and dried to a black silk finish, which required delicate handling and airtight storage. To use the Stylograph, Jefferson told Peale, you laid the carbonated paper between a bottom sheet of stationery and a top sheet of "peculiar" paper, then clipped the three sheets to a polished metal tablet and wrote with a pointed glass stylus, impressing a letter on the stationery and a copy on the peculiar paper or several copies at once, made in layers. The procedure was unpleasant, he told Peale, and he still used the polygraph when he needed just one copy, as he almost always did. He disliked the feel of "a hard point on a hard surface," and the ink-soaked paper was "so fetid that one could not stay in a room where there was much of it. I could not, therefore, live without the polygraph." He could not endure a fetid Cabinet, as Peale was no doubt glad to hear.

Despite the support of the president of the United States and Peale's promotions calling it suitable even for "the feeblest female hand," the polygraph, unlike carbon paper, was too finicky and expensive to survive and dropped off the market into history.

* * *

On October 21, 1803, John Quincy Adams was sworn in as a United States senator. Even before he went home, the thirty-six-year-old Federalist left his card at the President's House, finding Jefferson not in. John Adams's eldest son was a rare exception to Jefferson's rule of entertaining Federalists and Republicans separately. Having mentored him in his youth, the president knew his brilliance and sensed in him a candidate for conversion, an independent thinker fed up with politics as war and dissent from party orthodoxy as treason, a politician in need of a home. His anonymous publication in 1802 of a less than respectful ballad about Jefferson and a woman named Sally may not have been known to the president, but a year *before* the Massachusetts legislature made him a senator, Adams had written a friend that Federalism was dead and as likely to be resurrected as "a carcass seven years in its grave."

John Quincy Adams, still and all, was no easy man to beguile. Senator Plumer once survived a coach ride home to New Hampshire cheek by jowl with him, and the week that passed before Adams got out in Boston may have seemed like a month. His memories of Europe were interesting. "He is a man of much information," Plumer told his diary, but "too formal" and "tenacious of his opinions," with a manner "too stiff & unyielding," a remarkable observation in a formal, stiff, unyielding time, all the more so in New England, the land of the stiff and unyielding.

On November 7, 1803, Adams dined at the President's House with his wife Louisa and a dozen other guests, many if not all of them Republicans, a status more obnoxious to Mrs. Adams than to her husband. Louisa Catherine Adams was a prim young woman at least as tenacious as he, with curly auburn hair, a knack for observation, and a whiplash wit. Born rich in London in 1775 of an American father and an English mother, Mrs. Adams was a well-read Tory and a conscientious snob who would live to have her grandchildren call her "the Madam." She was pleased to see capital society led by the thin-lipped Federalist families who "had not yet clothed themselves in the buffoonery of the modern democracy." When a lady let her know at a party in her drawing room that a coachman had been standing beside her with his whip in his hand and could have spoiled her dress, Mrs. Adams approached "this personage" and asked him what he was doing there. He had brought a wealthy gentleman, he said, who had been a coachman himself, and he had a right to come too. What a distressing country it was, Mrs. Adams wrote, where one's station was always on the way up or down.

The President's House she conceded was worth seeing, but Jefferson had driven her father-in-law from the place. "The ruling demagogue of the hour," she called him, and she expected no less as she watched him at dinner, seeing what she wanted to see. Everything about him was aristocratic, she thought, "except his person, which was ungainly, ugly, and common," and his "excessively inelegant" style. What was left of the aristocratic she did not say. At first he said little, with "a sort of peering restlessness about him," which Louisa took as discomfort at being watched more closely than he liked, but he proved to be an excellent host, a master of the art of drawing people out, surprising her with grace. Mrs. Adams was pleased to see that he filled the plates himself, that his butler and liveried servants looked smart, that the meal was authentically French and the wine and plate were choice. The acidic John Randolph of Roanoke and Bizarre dropped in after dinner with the Speaker of the House and displayed his venomous style "in an attack which he made upon the wine."

12

THIS WILL BE THE CAUSE OF WAR

After too many trying years in America, Britain's middle-class chargé d'affaires encouraged the Foreign Office to replace him with an aristocrat. Having gotten on well with Jefferson and the other local gentry, less so with the commonality, Edward Thornton was convinced that it would flatter the Americans' vanity, their most conspicuous trait, to send them a titled diplomat. A full-blown, noble ambassador, born to his place in the world, amused and not provoked by the "wild notions of liberty" that had turned them against the Crown, could entertain them with his wealth and awe them with his nobility without fear of debasing himself by consorting with commoners, and no one was more common than the Americans. Good advice that should have been taken.

Toward the end of 1803, London sent instead a perfectly ordinary bureaucrat with a fragile sense of dignity and no sense of humor. His Britannic Majesty's envoy extraordinary and minister plenipotentiary to the United States of America was not Lord Anthony Merry or even Sir Anthony Merry but the dull civil servant Mr. Anthony Merry, the son of a bankrupt wine merchant. Small and slight of stature, earnestly hospitable at home and wooden as an oar in public, Mr. Merry, ironically enough, was only dimly aware that mirth existed. Despite his prestigious post, a young Washington hostess would soon tell a friend that he passed "quite unnoticed" through society, "plain in his appearance and called rather inferior in understanding." Other British diplomats called him Toujours Gai, which had entertained Napoleon when Merry served grimly on the staff of Lord General Cornwallis's peace mission to France. "Mr. Merry lives with us," Cornwallis wrote home, "but although he is by no means an inefficient man in business and has good qualities, he does not conduce much to our amusement."

Fresh from the proverbially stiff court of Spain, Merry and his wife made the six-week Atlantic crossing on the British warship *Phaeton*, exposed all the way to the anti-American rants of the Royal Navy's officers. Elizabeth Merry would play a leading role in the coming altercations, described by female contemporaries as a large, talkative, "rather masculine" woman, "easy without being graceful," a person of middling origins trying hopelessly to conceal them, a bright, capable woman in a world run by men. Her late first husband had left her a comfortable merchant's fortune and a house that had a name, and her new husband's station had boosted the role of position in her sense of the scheme of things.

Rufus King, the American minister to London under Washington and Adams, hoped that Mr. Merry would be comfortable in Washington, or "his reports will be shaded with the discontents he may himself feel," a prescient observation. In November of 1803, the Merrys disembarked in Norfolk, Virginia, with half a dozen servants and so many carts of baggage that the port officials suspected contraband. While they waited for a ship to Washington, they lived with the British counsel, another Jefferson hater. The social climbing Irish poet Thomas Moore had made the crossing with them, and Norfolk did not impress him. There was "nothing to be seen in the streets but dogs and negroes," and "poor Mrs. Merry" was treated in this "comical place" without the deference due her station. Adding injury to insult, the mosquitoes "bit her into a fever."

After too long a stay in Norfolk, the Merrys fought their way up Chesapeake Bay to Alexandria for six hard days, due to "winds, tides, and ignorant navigators," according to Mrs. Merry, followed by a frigid ride in a shocking coach over shocking roads. Mrs. Merry laughed derisively all the way to a Georgetown inn that provided pathetic lodgings and served an inedible meal. As her husband kept repeating that the capital of the United States was a thousand times worse than the worst parts of Spain, Mrs. Merry kept her chin up in a letter to Moore. "A few days will, I hope, place us in some hovel of our own," she wrote, but first she would have to "exhibit" at the Capitol. "The Capitol—good heavens, what profanation!! Here is a creek, too—a dirty arm of the river, which they have dignified by calling it the Tiber. What patience one need have with ignorance and self-conceit."

On November 29, accompanied by the secretary of state, Merry presented to Jefferson his credentials from the king. His predecessor had warned him to expect something less than Spain's elaborate ceremony, but nothing short of the formal ritual that Washington and Adams had staged for an audience of rigid dignitaries. Tipped by no one, British or American, to relax the formalities, Merry showed up at the President's House "bespeckled with the spangles of our gaudish Court dress," his secretary Augustus Foster later said—silver buckles on his shoes, black silk stockings, tight white knee britches silver buckled at the knees, a deep blue coat trimmed in black velvet and roped with gold braid, a sword on his hip, and a plumed hat in his hand, like a comic opera lord about to be hit with a pie. Nearly three years later, Merry was still incensed when he told the Boston Federalist Josiah Quincy what happened next. Quincy called it "studied incivility."

As Madison walked Merry into the Oval Room, he seemed surprised to find it empty and led His Majesty's envoy back into the hall toward the president's Cabinet. They were walking past the staircase into the room when a seedy-looking older man started out from the other side. Merry backed out instinctively for this servant who had slipped down the ladder of his trade until Madison introduced him as the president of the United States. Making a quick recovery, Merry straightened his back and began a little speech until Jefferson cut it short and asked him to come in and sit down, a gallant gesture in Merry's world. In his next dispatch to London, Merry shared the news that the president was no friend of "the present ruler in France," and barely mentioned his casual style. He "received me in his usual Morning Attire," Merry wrote, "contrary to the Ceremony observed by his Predecessors." The dispatch said nothing about a snub. Privately, Merry told friends that the president had greeted him in loose hair and clothing "indicative of utter slovenliness and indifference to appearances," but it seems to have taken time and a little help to be offended instead of merely appalled, a subtle distinction to be sure. Federalists surely told him that Jefferson had contrived the whole thing for the mob, knowing it would make the rounds, and make the rounds it did.

Rufus King knew his eccentric aristocrats, Jefferson included, and King considered the incident a faux pas but not quite an act of war. Merry took it harder, egged on by Federalist friends. The president had greeted him not "merely in an undress," he told Josiah Quincy retrospectively, but in a "state of negligence actually studied," a slap in the face, not to him personally but to his sovereign. The slippers, the old clothes, even the backup into the hall had been staged, he said, and the story expanded over time. Congressman Samuel Taggart, a Massachusetts Federalist, passed the news to a fellow pastor: "It is whispered that the British Ambassador is not at all charmed by his Democratic Majesty," having called "in the robes of his office" at the President's House, where "our exalted chief magistrate received him in his gown and slippers." Some "add his nightcap," but Taggart supposed that was a stretch. The tale became a legend in the Foreign Office. A diplomat was told seventeen years after the fact that Jefferson concealed his common abilities by contriving common manners and "revolutionary principles," and received the king's minister "in his dressing gown, seated on a sofa, catching a slipper after tossing it up on the point of his foot," an impressively agile insult to the Crown.

Well aware of the diplomatic norms, Jefferson surely meant to send London a message with his casual clothes and manner: His government was no enemy, but it was no poor imitation of the Crown's; it was American and it was Republican, large *R* and small. But nothing could be gained from disrespect. If Jefferson had meant, quite unwisely, to snub the king of England, the insult would not have been subtle, and Merry would have reported it that day. He detested the British aristocracy and everything it stood for, an opinion not improved by his exposure to the breed in London, where men half as capable as he had treated him like a yokel, and George III had literally turned his back on him and Adams; but Thornton, Merry's predecessor, had informed the Foreign Office of Jefferson's courtesy as well as his wardrobe, and his treatment of Merry does not look like contempt, discounting the nightcap, the dressing gown, and the acrobatic foot.

There was nothing new or exclusively Anglophobic in Jefferson's informality, which Thornton had literally underscored in dispatches. Among other shocking things, the president had delivered his messages to Congress "by his secretary!" Nor was Merry singled out for a threadbare greeting. The king of Denmark's envoy, welcomed in the same way, had presented his credentials a month before Merry did and enjoyed it. "The president received me in a simple, open, and friendly manner," Peter Pedersen told Copenhagen, "that never fails to give one intimacy and confidence and seldom fails to win hearts." An hour's chat with Jefferson, slippers and all, "gave me the most favorable idea about his excellent intellect and wide, comprehensive knowledge." But Madison had warned the Dane that the president "keeps no etiquette," and Merry had *not* been warned. To drop diplomatic form from opulent to ungroomed was too far to fall in any case. Madison could have done better, and Jefferson could have worn shoes.

* * *

Merry's mood did not improve when he learned he was expected to make the first social calls on cabinet officers before they would call on him, a reversal of Federalist form that he saw as a new indignity. But all of this was mere foreshadowing. The heavy hammer dropped on the evening of December 2, when the Merrys came to their first presidential dinner expecting an intimate affair in their honor and found a large company paying no special notice to them. Louis-André Pichon, Napoleon's envoy to the United States, was a provocative choice of guests. France was at war with Britain, and to mix warring diplomats was not done.

Madison later explained that "a liberal oblivion of all hostile relations" should prevail at the President's House, which Merry dismissed as too much philosophy.

Days before the dinner, knowing the uproar his presence would cause, Pichon had come to Jefferson to say he would be in Baltimore, but was pressed to return and explicitly to bring his wife. Louisa Adams had found in Madame Pichon the very image of sociability. "Pretty, graceful, accomplished, with sweet manners," she was utterly unaffected, "altogether a most attractive creature," and Charles Willson Peale, perhaps the finest portraitist in America, admired her amateur painting. She would make quite a contrast with Mrs. Merry. Pichon told Talleyrand he could not resist the invitation, for "apart from the reason of respect due to the President, I had that of witnessing what might happen."

Before dinner was served, the Merrys simmered in the Oval Room with the president, the Pichons, and several guests who were not their enemies, and absorbed a second blow when Jefferson escorted Dolley Madison, the evening's hostess, to the table. He always handed his hostesses into dinner, but custom called for choosing Mrs. Merry, who was left to Madison's hand. If Jefferson and Madison had planned a deliberate slight, Mrs. Madison would have been told, but she whispered to the president, "Take Mrs. Merry," a good idea ignored. The marchioness Yrujo, the Spanish minister's wife, was overheard to assess the consequences. "This will be the cause of war."

Keeping the action going, Jefferson sat Mrs. Madison at his right, Mrs. Merry's rightful place. Mr. Merry made his way alone "towards the neighborhood of the President," but before he could sit beside the marchioness, high ranking as she was, not to mention lovely, a quick-stepping congressman got there first, leaving the king's minister on his own. For the rest of the evening, Yrujo told Madrid, Jefferson paid an obvious "and, in my opinion, studied" attention to him and the marchioness, to the clear neglect of the Merrys, whose resentment needed no description. So stunning were these things that the Merrys did not know what to do and gamely went along. By way of earnest small talk, Merry remarked to a congressman that the crawfish in the Potomac were a delicacy in Europe. His companion replied that "necessity," thank God, "has not yet driven the Americans to eat such vermin."

Merry called for his carriage the moment the table was cleared, and the sputtering on the way home can be imagined, yet he soon wrote Lord Hawkesbury that the Americans were diminishing *all* of the resident diplomats, to raise their own importance, not to denigrate Britain specifically. But that very evening, as if to show them otherwise, the Merrys were kicked again. The secretary of state was expected to entertain them, and against his better judgment, he could not contradict the president's form. Madison too invited Pichon to his dinner party and led Mrs. Gallatin to the table instead of Mrs. Merry, whose husband was left to walk her in like a tanner at a fish fry. Better prepared than he had been the first time, he marched her defiantly to the head of the table, where Mrs. Gallatin offered her place by their host, which Mrs. Merry took without a flinch. Now the Merrys perceived that the Americans had insulted them twice. "Yet Virginia gentlemen did not intentionally mortify their guests," Henry Adams wrote years later. They intended nothing worse than the breaking of regal molds on their own republican soil, a thing to be accepted, even welcomed, they thought, for the ease of all concerned. In this they were mistaken.

Yrujo reported the affair to Madrid as an international incident, and Merry wrote a letter to a friend in London that almost burned through the page. The shameful list of insults seemed calculated, not attributable to ignorance or awkwardness, "though God knows a great deal of both" was common in this place. Foreign ministers and their ladies had to shift for themselves in favor of cabinet members' wives, "a Set of Beings as little without the Manners as without the Appearance of Gentlewomen."

The Merrys' accommodations did not cheer them up. After a wretched month at their Georgetown inn, Merry rented the sort of "hovel of our own" that Mrs. Merry had expected, two attached brick houses on K Street, "on the common which is meant to become in time the city of Washington." Mere shells they seemed to him, without so much as a pump or a picture on a wall, not even bells to summon servants. Such was life in Washington City, so fraught with "misery in every respect" that decent *food* was hard to find in this "perfectly savage" place. Trying to make amends for his disastrous formal dinner, Madison invited the Merrys to a social one, but the first "had spoilt the broth at the next," he told James Monroe, now America's ambassador to Britain. Merry came, but not Mrs. Merry, though the date had been set with her. To put a sharper point on it, she declined invitations to three other cabinet members' homes while her husband agreed to come to an all-male dinner and did not show up.

The whole thing exploded in the drawing rooms of Washington City. The Yrujos allied themselves with the Merrys, and both couples let it be known they would boycott the President's House until *pêle-mêle* was dropped and rank given deference, which Jefferson refused to do. Pichon shared the American view that Yrujo, "vanity personified," had no right to complain, having cheerfully accepted *pêle-mêle* for going on three years, grabbing the best spot at everyone's table; but no one was more jealous of privilege than the Marquis of Casa d'Yrujo, and Pichon told Paris that Yrujo fanned resentment in the tiny diplomatic community and fumed about the pain his former friend Jefferson had inflicted on him.

Many Federalists were sure no principle was involved in Jefferson's casual forms but the courting of his ill-bred base and its homespun leaders like the Speaker of the House Nathaniel Macon, who chuckled at the thought of the Marquis d'Yrujo playing games with "this new-fangled doctrine of rank" in a place where neither "the people nor their form of government acknowledge any." Augustus Foster thought the especially vulgar Democrats "took their cue from the style adopted at the Great House," hurting Mrs. Merry with remarks about her diamonds and stepping on her gown at parties. She came home in tears more than once, Foster said, tormented by Republican men and women too, "a spying, inquisitive, vulgar, and most ignorant race," he was moved to tell his mother. Worst of all were the highborn "ratters" who had left the Federalists for sheer political gain and affected to be boors to impress their new low friends.

Foster understood and even shared Jefferson's view that presidents should not mimic kings, but skipping mere decorum in the house of "the chief magistrate of a great and cultivated nation" was something else again. Jefferson had watched Parisian society "give place to a disgusting democracy" and had seen the damage done. Higher bred than either of his predecessors, he should have made his home more gracious than theirs, not less, but was pushed the other way by philosophy, popularity, and vanity, all of them perverse. More than simply inciting "a newspaper-taught rabble" for political gain, Foster thought the aristocratic man of the people enjoyed the paradox. He *liked* to mortify other wellborn men who neither flattered nor embraced him, and he chose to run counter to General Washington because he could not run parallel to him. Steeped from birth in courtesy, he and Madison had decided to be rude. They were gentleman born and bred, ashamed of behaving coarsely and incapable of doing it well.

There was plainly some truth in this, but not much. Probably right about the cringe, Foster was wrong about the insincerity. Jefferson was wildly popular with most of the electorate, and a little pomp, let alone a fresh shirt, would have done him no harm, or not enough to notice. He truly despised what inherited aristocracy stood for, and he tore down its trappings in the President's House convinced that the republic was at stake. Writing Madison from Louis XVI's Paris in 1787, he had called the European model "a government of wolves over sheep" and still believed it, unlike some former revolutionaries who liked the look of wolves.

On December 23, Senator and Mrs. Adams once again joined a table of Republicans at the President's House. No notice was taken of Christmas there, or scarcely anywhere else in America, whose people disapproved of revelry. The company included the plain Republican senator Robert Wright of Maryland, who had served as a private in the Revolution, an odd sort of duck, Louisa Adams found him to be, and Jefferson's secretary of the navy Robert Smith and his wife, a lady of the highest stripe. Mrs. Adams was glad to say that among the wealthy Smiths, "democracy was imperial."

* * *

Nothing good was coming of the Merry imbroglio, and Madison asked Ambassador Monroe to douse any fires in London. Writing openly rather than in code, knowing English eyes might read it before Monroe did, Madison cast the brouhaha as "a foolish circumstance of etiquette" that could have no sane effect on Anglo-American relations, which were cordial and would remain so. The British Foreign Office agreed. Merry's huffy dispatches reported the offenses against his dignity, his wife's, and the king's, and requested instructions. His superiors never bothered to reply. Lord Hawkesbury told an American that his government's relations with the United States were not vulnerable to "trivial circumstances." An expatriate Washington socialite told friends that Merry was the news of the day nonetheless. "Tommy Jeff and his party don't care for him." The "most ridiculous scene" at the Madisons' had "made a huge uproar—as much as if a treaty had been broken!" and the Merrys had been showing off a lifestyle that did not make Jefferson happy, fixed as he was on equality and frugality in his urge to please the mob.

Merry's depth in "diplomatic superstition, truly extraordinary in this age and in this country," exasperated Madison, but he blamed Mrs. Merry more, as Jefferson did, fairly or not. Things were getting tense with the mother country. British warships had started taking British-born seamen from American vessels to man the war against Napoleon, disturbing businesslike relations, and Madison told Monroe no "foolish circumstance of etiquette" should make it worse. Remedial steps were taken. On December 26, having spoken with Mrs. Merry about her extraordinary work in botany at his now regretted dinner, Jefferson sent her a packet of seeds of the Venus flytrap, "so much celebrated as holding the middle ground between the animal & vegetable orders," the first examples he had been able to get after six years of trying, and "the half of what he received."

Mrs. Merry sent immediately a gracious note of thanks and did not show up at the New Year's Day reception. Nor did the Marchioness d'Yrujo. Their husbands attended de rigueur in their official capacities, and Yrujo made a point of saying the marchioness was well. Few Federalists came, and Senator Adams went alone, Louisa having no urgent wish to join "an unruly crowd of indiscriminate persons from every class, peculiarly annoying to the Corps

Diplomatique, whose fine clothing, carriages, etc. become the gaze of the curious vulgar." To the vulgarians themselves, Mrs. Adams thought "Tom Jefferson as the founder of democracy was obliged patiently to submit" and let the people amuse themselves at the cost of his substantial expense and annoyance. In this she was perfectly right.

Jefferson told his colleagues that Merry was as reasonable a man as the British could have sent, unlucky to be associated with a person of the opposite sort. Madison had counseled Merry to take no offense from casual forms, that equality was the very soul of American society, "that no man here would come to a dinner where he was to be marked with inferiority to any other." Jefferson thought Merry could be reclaimed but his wife had inspired a dislike "among all classes which one would have thought impossible in so short a time." It was not only Jefferson who loathed her, and not only men. Elizabeth Merry and Dolley Madison might have pulled knives on each other had they carried them, and the English-born Louisa Adams had both of the Merrys pegged. Mr. Merry was a kind, inelegant man whose principal function at his parties was to keep the waiters circulating and officiate "in the disposal of the cakes." His wife, "a very showy woman of vulgar extraction, suddenly raised to wealth and station," had congressmen fetch and carry at her dinners and told Mrs. Adams's English mother she was serving piles of *hog meat*, for the Americans had to have it on every occasion. She was said to have started her career as a Norfolk barmaid, but that was "perhaps scandal."

In search of a way to stop what was out of control, Madison sought advice, hat in hand, from veterans of the Washington administration, embarrassed, he said, to bother them with trifles. In reply, Senator Pickering, the reincarnation of a Salem witch judge, one of President Washington's secretaries of war, said the old forms should be restored out of courtesy. "Our humble Republicans," he wrote a friend, "are in a <u>hobble</u> with the British minister & his lady," taking "malignant pleasure in overturning whatever bears the stamp of Washington." For twelve good years, Americans behaved like gentlemen, but "our present modest rulers have reversed all this." Jefferson had received Merry as "he receives his democratic scullions, whom he is ready, at all hours, to admit to his presence." Madison wrote to Rufus King, the last Federalist minister to Britain, "mortified" to raise a subject unworthy of either man's time. He and Jefferson wished to substitute *pêle-mêle* for "ceremonious clogs" but not to fall short of other nations in civility. What were London's rules? Hearing what he wished to hear, Madison took King's complex reply to suggest that Merry had little cause to complain.

Yrujo told Madison he should publish a protocol that everyone could know and follow, and Madison brought the idea to Jefferson. "You can judge of his distaste," Madison told Monroe, but he needed a way out. The idea was tried on Senator Adams, who had diplomatic experience and a wife who liked the idea. *She* must seem cold to Americans, Mrs. Adams thought, but her fear of ignoring some courtesy she did not understand made her cautious. European courts gave instructions in writing, but there were no rules in a republic "where all are monarchs," and that caused harm. The story got around that the Danish minister had presented himself to the president and chatted on and on to the point of a painful silence until the poor man rose, rubbed his forehead, and made his parting bow. He told another diplomat he feared he had made some error, sitting so long with the president without being dismissed, and was told with a laugh that Jefferson sat politely with foreign ministers until *they* decided to go.

The cabinet met at length and reasoned to the view that orderly social norms were not counterrevolutionary. Jefferson composed in his own hand a set of "Cannons of Etiquette to Be Observed by the Executive," misspelling "canons" as "cannons," to be seen by a sharp-eyed historian two centuries later as an entertaining slip. Half a dozen of them amounted to a snit avoidance mechanism, prescribing who would call on whom first, depending on their public offices, not their noble titles, for people in a republic were distinguished not by birth but by the honors they earned. The other canons governed social events, based on the idea that "a perfect equality exists between the persons composing the company, whether foreign or domestic, titled or untitled, in or out of office." *Pêle-mêle* survived. In the President's House, regardless of rank or station, no Americans, foreign ministers, *or their families* were entitled to anything but a chair. Jefferson saved only one monarchical privilege for himself: the president received visits but did not return them.

The canons were explained to Merry and Yrujo, who thought they came too late. Trying to salvage Merry, Madison played the colonist in the wilderness. Americans, he said, liked to seat themselves at dinner "with as little rule as around a fire," which must have sounded right to Merry but not exculpatory. Madison could see he was hurt, and not just because Mrs. Merry was. Still fearing "what complexion this nonsense may wear" in London, Madison described their talk to Monroe, "nauseous as such a subject is." Merry had recalled every sling and arrow he and Mrs. Merry had suffered, "some of which had never been dreamed of." On his first trip to the President's House, he had come in ceremonial dress and found his host in morning clothes, not even in the formal attire one wore in the afternoon. Madison explained that American gentlemen made no such change of dress, and Jefferson had received the Danish minister in the same way. Mr. Pedersen, Merry replied, was of the third rank, and he was of the second, a very different thing. And so it had gone from there.

Madison said every country was entitled to its own etiquette, even the king observed "the pêle mêle" at levees, and Jefferson gave no state dinners. Every dinner at the President's House was informal, in proof of which wives were invited. Elaborate distinctions of rank did real harm in Europe, and "it was not to be expected that we should willingly enter into such a labyrinth." He understood, Madison said, how Merry could have felt wronged, but malicious intent was disproved twice—by America's national interest in avoiding offense to Britain and its leaders' respect for a good man. Merry was unconvinced. "I blush at having put so much trash on paper," Madison wrote. He thought well of Merry and would have liked him better still had he not diminished himself with all of this, though allowances should be made for "extraneous influences," a reference to Mrs. Merry.

Merry's pretensions were ridiculed in London, Monroe replied. Reasonable people there agreed that governments made their own social rules and foreigners followed them. But another American in London thought the rudeness in Washington City, combined with its contemptible amenities, led Englishmen "to view the seat of our philosophic empire, if not the philosophers themselves, with great disgust." In the partisan American press, the president was praised or ripped according to the publication. The *Gazette of the United States* told its horrified Federalist readers that at Jefferson's infamous dinner, *every* cabinet member's wife had been led in first, leaving the Merrys "to view the procession as it passed." In this affair and more, "our polite philosopher" had disgraced himself out of "pride, whim, weakness, and malignant revenge" on Britain. "What can be Mr. Jefferson's motives for these outrageous insults?" In a plain Republican reply, the *Aurora* explained that "the stupid etiquette of the English monarchy is not pursued in a republic."

On January 23, a blizzard lashed the President's House and Jefferson vented his anger to a veteran of the infamous dinner. Despite every effort to calm them, the Merrys were insisting on precedence at private dinners, "for of public dinners we have none," and "we say to them no." Equality was the bedrock of America, and if any group was equal, it ought to be friends at dinner. Let "the diplomatic gentry" ban themselves from his table. "Nobody shall be above you, nor you above anybody, pêle-mêle is our law," for the alternative was antirepublican. The error he confessed was in taking his hostesses invariably into dinner, which he had done for three years without provoking jealousy, a sign of gratitude, not rank, until Mrs. Merry made it such. "I have from that moment changed it." Now he took the hand of the nearest lady, and his hostesses were the first to approve. "I have ever considered diplomacy as the pest of the peace of the world, as the workshop in which nearly all the wars of Europe are manufactured." He had closed half the missions abroad "and was nearly ripe to do so by the other half." The people would be pleased if he did, and so would he.

He wrote to Martha the same day. As much as he had wished his daughters were with him when the etiquette war broke out, "I rejoice you were not here. The brunt of the battle" had fallen on the cabinet and their ladies, and Martha and Maria would have been pummeled too, only "butchered the more bloody" to cause him more pain.

Hoping to cool things down, he asked Madison to inquire whether Merry would come to dinner informally. Alone. Madison sent a go-between "to feel his pulse," and inferred that he would. On February 9, Merry was invited to dine with the president and a few friends. He replied that he was booked but would have come anyway if not for the new set of canons, which, "on account of its serious nature" he could not accept without instructions from London or a formal assurance that he would be shown the traditional distinctions. Madison sent the president's regrets about "the points of form which will deprive him of the pleasure of Mr. Merry's company at dinner on Monday next."

Jefferson and Madison dined with Pichon and made their displeasure with Merry known, which could not have displeased the French minister. "I shall be highly honored," Jefferson told him, "when the King of England is good enough to let Mr. Merry come and eat my soup." There had been no need to educate Merry about *pêle-mêle* when he arrived, Madison said. "Things of that sort announce themselves" (an accurate, tone-deaf observation), and nothing could be more foolish than "to measure the importance of one's mission by the side or end of the table he occupied."

Pointedly, Mrs. Merry filled the void that Jefferson had left when levees were dropped at the President's House. She hosted one a week, adding music, cards, and dancing, Federalist friends having told her how to poke him. When the Merrys and Yrujos gave dinners, Mr. Merry and the marquis led their wives to the table ornately, leaving cabinet members' wives on their own. Mrs. Merry accepted an invitation to a party at the Madisons', spreading hope that she had softened, but found her clothier and his wife at the same affair and never risked the indignity again. When the president sent her dinner invitations she turned up her nose and he sent no more.

Two months into the feud, Pichon told Paris "Washington society is turned upside down," for all the women had turned on Mrs. Merry, which overstated the case but correctly gauged the wind. Having taken a neutral stance, Pichon thought the president could have handled the whole thing better, but the Merrys and the Yrujos had the worst of it, and the Federalists made "a burlesque of the facts." In an unsigned column in the *Aurora*, Jefferson attacked a snickering *Washington Federalist* piece headed "Etiquette of the Court of the US." Jefferson's anonymous rebuttal started with the thought that "a great deal of unfounded stuff" should be set right. First of all, there had *been* no court of the United States since the Republican inauguration "buried levees, birthdays, royal parades, and the arrogation of precedence in society by certain self-styled friends of order, but truly friends of privileged orders." The pretensions of "would-be Nobles" had been "buried in the grave of federalism on the same 4th of March." In America, hosts seated first whomever was "next the door," and diplomats did their duty when they saw that no slight was meant.

The etiquette war of 1804 muddied all of its combatants, and Merry's grudge caused harm. Until he was recalled in the summer of 1806, conspirators of all kinds, from New England secessionists to Aaron Burr, found a sympathetic ear in him, though not in London. Mrs. Merry never went to the President's House again, and her husband only came on official occasions. "In dress, conversation, and demeanor," Merry told Federalist friends, the president studied the mob with "the arts of a low demagogue" merely to hold his base.

13

TREASURES OF INFORMATION

Prince Jerome Bonaparte, Napoleon's younger brother, was said to have ruined more than one young woman in Europe before he came to Baltimore in 1803 and fell for Elizabeth Patterson, a rich merchant's rule-breaking daughter. For ample good cause, her parents forbade the marriage until she threatened to elope. Rosalie Stier Calvert, a Belgian-born Washington doyenne, said Jerome "commands no respect. People insult him at every opportunity," and it pleased Augustus Foster to say he was "rather smaller than Napoleon." By every measure but unearned rank, Miss Patterson was Jerome's superior, "a most extraordinary girl," Mrs. Calvert thought, "given to reading Godwin on the rights of women, etc., in short, a modern philosophe." A delicately beautiful young woman with a rosebud mouth and ringlets of auburn hair falling into her sultry eyes, Miss Patterson believed and proved that "Nature never intended me for obscurity."

The Bonapartes were married on Christmas Eve 1803 and enjoyed a glamorous honeymoon that took them to the President's House in January. Madame Bonaparte having dressed in the latest fashion, hardly anyone noticed the prince. Parisian couture, avidly followed in certain sectors of the American upper class, had turned to the classical Greek for a deeply low-cut, form-clinging dress in a translucent fabric barely there, paired with frugal underclothing. For the New Englander Abigail Adams, the very thought of a Greek dress was "an outrage upon all decency." For Elizabeth Bonaparte, *à la grecque* was a perfect match, and society thought so too. When Secretary of the Navy Smith gave a ball for the Bonapartes at home, the most coveted ticket in town, Mrs. Merry graciously suspended her boycott of the Jeffersonians, richly gowned and looped in diamonds, only to be ignored when Madame Bonaparte appeared in "a mere suspicion of a dress." Her entrance threw the party into confusion, and "no one dared to look at her but by stealth." Several old-school ladies took a single glance and left. A gentleman remarked that every stich on her body could be put into his pocket, and no doubt gave it thought.

"Madame Eve has made a great noise here," Margaret Bayard Smith told her sister. Men sprained their necks and boys mobbed her carriage "to see what I hope will not often be seen in this country, an almost naked woman." Benjamin Latrobe, one of the world's great prigs, said Elizabeth Bonaparte had "scandalized the lovers of drapery and disgusted the admirers even of the naked figure." The dissolute portraitist Gilbert Stuart, who was not disgusted, painted her in his Washington studio, gracing a single canvas with three separate views, as if he could not decide on one. To advertise his skills, Stuart kept the painting on display for more than a year before he let it go. Decades later, Louisa Adams called its subject a virgin in the Muslim paradise with humdrum Washington at her feet. "She was beautiful and she was followed," Mrs. Adams said; "balls, suppers, and parties were the consequence, and we lived in a perpetual round of dissipation." Among other things, the celebrity of the hour inspired timeless art, lascivious poetry, and a dinner at the President's House.

Jefferson could hardly avoid inviting the glamorous Bonapartes, which risked graver consequences than the Merrys' tweaked pride. Napoleon was furious about Jerome's unauthorized marriage, a waste of a dynastic match, and Jefferson had no strategic reason to endorse it, especially with the purchase of Louisiana not yet closed. And yet he could not be seen letting Paris veto his guest lists. On top of that, the secretary of the navy and his brother, Senator Samuel Smith, were Madame Bonaparte's cousins. It would not be wise or even gentlemanly to snub their kin.

The president instructed his ambassador in Paris to explain the marriage to Talleyrand as a fait accompli that he had no power to annul, and gave the Bonapartes their dinner. The French minister's presence lent him cover but the Merrys were provoked yet again, not only by the very fact of his celebrating a couple named Bonaparte but also by his keen attention to the bride, far more sharply focused than his attentions to Mrs. Merry. Still fuming over his failure to honor Mrs. Merry at dinner, the Merrys were stunned to hear he had taken the hand of a libertine and seated *her* by his side, *à la grecque* and all. This time their pique was unfair. For bravely volunteering to dine with Madame Eve in the service of his country, Jefferson cannot be blamed.

* * *

Lewis Harvie had lasted barely a year as Jefferson's secretary when he left to practice law in March of 1804. The president's letterpress proved its worth when he sent William Burwell, a bright young man from an influential Virginia family, an offer letter almost identical to Harvie's, successfully asking Burwell to take his place.

Burwell joined the family as Jefferson was suffering the "inexpressible anxiety" that came with the news that his lovely young daughter Maria was in danger following childbirth. After Congress adjourned in late March, he left immediately for Monticello, where Maria died on April 17. She was twenty-five years old. Her newborn daughter lived. Her little son Francis was two. Ellen Randolph, her niece, was seven. "One morning I heard that my aunt was dying," Ellen wrote half a century later. She crept to Maria's door, heard her breathing short and hard, and ran away. "I have a distinct recollection of confusion and dismay in the household," she wrote, and a maid saying Mrs. Eppes was dead. "Late in the afternoon I was taken to the death chamber. The body was covered with a white cloth, over which had been strewed a profusion of flowers."

John Freeman, the enslaved footman leased at the President's House, had met Melinda Colbert, Maria's maid, on a trip to Monticello with Jefferson the year before. He was there when Maria died, and every slave knew that anything could happen when she lost her mistress. On the following day, a poor choice of timing, Freeman wrote a letter to Maria's stricken father. He hoped to marry Melinda, he wrote, and feared Maria's death would make them miserable "unless you will be so good as to keep us both," an implicit request to buy Melinda from Mr. Eppes, give her work at the President's House, and buy Freeman from his owner, to be sure of keeping them together. If Jefferson replied, his answer was not recorded.

In July, Eppes wrote to tell him the children were well, a fine bay horse had come on the market, and Freeman had asked for Melinda's hand. "If you are disposed to indulge John by having his wife near him," Eppes wrote, he would give her up "in exchange for anything else of the same value." Jefferson was not so disposed, and replied that he had too many slaves "in idleness" already. It was now that he remarked that in Washington he preferred white servants, who could be dismissed. As for indulging John and Melinda, John "knew he was not to expect her society but when he should be at Monticello, and then subject to the casualty of her being there or not." The horse he would take at a good price. He bought Freeman a few days later, quieting some but not all of his fears.

CHAPTER 13

* * *

In Charles Willson Peale's evocative portrait, a confident young man with casual dark hair disarranged au courant looks sideways from the canvas with penetrating blue eyes and a tangible intellect. He was small, Burwell said, palpably athletic, thirty-four years old, and eloquent in four languages. Notwithstanding his nobility and his international status as a fearless explorer and a celebrated man of science, he held himself out with the unaffected manner of an ordinary gentleman. Among other peculiar thoughts, the brilliant Prussian Baron Alexander von Humboldt had published in 1800 the notion that human activity could induce climate change.

On his way home to Europe after five years in Latin America, he had stopped in Philadelphia to meet its intelligentsia and asked to be introduced in Washington. Jefferson, he said, had inspired him since his childhood. Having seen the majestic Andes, he wrote Madison, he wished to enjoy the spectacle of a free people blessed with a beautiful destiny. He arrived in the capital on June 1 with Charles Willson Peale, two other scholarly Philadelphians, and his traveling companions in New Spain, a French botanist and an erudite Ecuadorian don. The baron and his "train of philosophers" brought "an intellectual festival" to town. When Peale came from Stelle's Hotel on the Capitol Hill to tell Jefferson the train had arrived, the president suggested they move to the City Tavern, a block away at Fifteenth and F, unable as he was to shelter five guests in distinguished style.

After three years of Jefferson and Latrobe's putting up and pulling down, Peale found the mansion stunning and the adjoining federal buildings "not destitute of beauty," but when the philosophers approached the house, "for palace I cannot call it," said the baron's young companion Don Carlos Montufar, the don was confused by the absence of a military guard or anyone else for that matter. Finding no one to open the door, they rang the bell and were taken aback when a servant let them in, not only out of livery but plainly dressed, and led them to a room simply furnished by baronial standards, "where an elderly gentleman of still plainer appearance" received them. Like many guests of lower rank, Don Carlos, a grandson of the viceroy of Peru, could scarcely believe this was the president of the United States. More than that, "He shook hands with us!" and plunged into conversation as an equal. "How astonishing!" was the don's reaction, not unlike the Merrys, but curiously pleased.

Humboldt, the president told Burwell, was the greatest man of science he had ever met, which was saying a good deal. For the next two weeks, the baron made his way respectfully through the diplomats, intellectuals, and hostesses in Washington's drawing rooms and won Dolley Madison's heart with his beautifully

Baron von Humboldt, painted by Charles Willson Peale in 1805. ***Copyright and permission of the College of Physicians of Philadelphia***

mannered travelogues and his admiration for her country. All the ladies were in love with him, Mrs. Madison wrote, despite his "want of personal charms," a curious remark, seconded by Margaret Bayard Smith.

Handsome or not, the baron was utterly "domesticated in the President's Family," said Mrs. Smith, instructed to drop in at will at any hour. Jefferson soaked him up and accepted Peale's gift of his silhouette, one of many Peale distributed in Washington. The president tried some of his own philosophical thoughts on Humboldt, including a method for finding longitude without a timepiece for Lewis to use in the wilderness. Humboldt broke the news that another clever mind had invented it independently, which Jefferson took as a compliment, perhaps with a touch of disappointment. They talked about everything but slavery, which Humboldt hated and discussed alone with Madison, sparing Jefferson the embarrassment.

On a hot Monday evening, Jefferson hosted a dinner for Humboldt, Peale, and their party. Peale had brought him a new portable polygraph, having fixed the rattles that had jolted loose on the stage, and Jefferson said he would recommend it to other public officers if he found it efficient, which delighted its maker. Peale was pleased as well that not a single toast was given and not a word said of politics. The gentlemen entertained each other with animated talk of science, the manners of different nations, and recent inventions making life more convenient, to which several of them, including the host, had contributed.

Humboldt drew a parade of literati to the President's House and sat down for hours, day after day, with Jefferson and Gallatin, drenched in humid heat, surrounded by his maps and notes, teaching the riveted Americans in rapid-fire "German, French, Spanish and English all together." Every foot of what he had seen in Mexico, Texas, Nuevo Mexico, and Nueva California was terra incognita to his hosts and a target of American expansion kept secret by the Spanish for that reason. Jefferson was dazzled by the baron and his "treasures of information" and grateful for his leave to have copies made of some of his notes and his map of New Spain. For Gallatin, the Prussian's tour de force was an "intellectual treat" but not an endearing one. "I am not apt to be easily pleased," he wrote his wife—as if she did not know—and he found Humboldt's cocky brilliance irritating, as cocky, brilliant men do.

Mrs. Smith's impression that Humboldt's "enlightened mind has already made him an American" was too generous. At breakfast one morning, Jefferson walked into the dining room with a newspaper, handed it to the baron, and showed him vicious articles that abused him. How was this possible, the Prussian embodiment of the Enlightenment asked. Why was the editor not in jail? Jefferson said the press was full of such things, and his administration had never been more popular. Humboldt, he said, should give the paper to a museum, to show the Europeans how little harm a free press could do, a truth of which the president needed reminding. Jefferson subscribed in the President's House to almost all the leading newspapers, friend and foe alike, dozens from all over the country, and kept clippings pro and con, though they often made him crazy. No happier with the press than any other president, he bought from a Republican journalist his previously read copies of the *New York Evening Post*, wishing to know what Federalist scripture said but considering it "a matter of conscience of not contributing" to its support. He had written Elbridge Gerry that "the printers can never leave us to a state of perfect rest and union of opinion. They would be no longer useful, and would have to go to the plough."

While dining at the Madisons' with Humboldt, Peale broke the gold plate that secured his false teeth. Dashing off to borrow tools from a local gunsmith, he riveted a repair and was back in half an hour. Before he left Washington, his nimble fingers made a waterproof seal from a bit of oiled silk for Jefferson's water pipe, his Chinese "hooker pipe," Peale called it, which he liked to smoke with Indians in a ritual of peace.

At Humboldt's second dinner at the President's House, the officer who commanded the frigate *Constellation* improved the conversation. Peale had no interest in the lingering over wine, of which he disapproved, and left as soon as he could, "without appearing too singular." Some cabinet members joined the president at a third dinner for Humboldt and his friends before he left for home, his conviction confirmed in "the genius of Mr. Jefferson."

14

HIGHLY EMBELLISHED WITH INDIAN FINERY

Jefferson had been drawn to Indians since his boyhood on the frontier. Gallatin took issue with a line in a draft of his second inaugural address that mentioned their virtues. "They have but a few," Gallatin opined, "I think very few." The president thought otherwise. His address showed a deep respect for their culture and the justice of their wish to be let alone. And yet he understood that their way of life was doomed and believed they shared his country's interests more than they knew. Their absorption into white American society, he thought, a "termination of their history most happy for themselves," as he chillingly called it, would make them healthier and prosperous, and those who would not assimilate must be pushed further west until the end caught up with them. Despite his admiration for the qualities Gallatin belittled, he was capable of offering a friend a position as a broker of trade with "entirely humanized" tribes.

Before Lewis left to join Clark, Jefferson had instructed him to invite to Washington under escort any influential chiefs he encountered, not only to get to know them and learn, but also to impress them with the benefits of trade and the hazards of war with a nation so powerful as the United States. The *Intelligencer* reprinted an Englishman's observation: "An embassy from the savages of the interior" should be received in an imposing place, for "the prospect of what is greater than ourselves induces ambition in a friend and obeisance in a foe." There was nothing new in this. For just such reasons, Indian delegations had been invited to white men's towns for a century and a half. Washington and Adams had welcomed them, but no Indians of the Great Plains had ever been east of Saint Louis, and Jefferson's success with Eastern tribal contacts had been mixed.

In 1801, two Chickasaws from the Deep South with a weak grasp of English appeared unannounced before the secretary of war and asked to see the president. Dearborn got them a room and told them he would bring them to Jefferson after they rested. Misunderstanding, they went to the President's House and were told he was not in. This too they misconstrued, and went home angry, leaving Dearborn to send them a message that Jefferson was "mortified at the manner of their going off." The larger delegation that followed, also unannounced, got muskets, trade goods, and an audience with the president, but had plainly expected more.

An old friend of Lewis's wrote him from Fort Wayne on behalf of Little Turtle, a Miami chief famous for his victories over American troops, a war-ending loss at the Battle of the Fallen Timbers, and a treaty signed in Philadelphia. He wished to see the president, and John Adams had called him "a remarkable man." He arrived in January of 1802 with other Miami and Potawatomi leaders and met with Jefferson and Dearborn in the President's House. Invoking "the Great Spirit who made us both," Little Turtle was sure that Congress, "the Great Council of the 16 fires," would not continue to withhold the payments they owed their red brothers, or continue to permit white settlements on their lands, or continue to condone the trade in liquor, "this fatal poison, which keeps them poor." Jefferson gave his assurances. A year later, he welcomed a delegation of Delaware and Miami leaders from the Indiana Territory, led by Owl, a Miami chief, who also protested liquor sales, and neighboring tribes selling white men lands they did not own. Promising them relief, Jefferson proposed mutual good neighborhood, open communications, and the debatable proposition that farming and grazing would serve their people better than "hunting wild beasts."

There were other such encounters, dwarfed by the arrival at the President's House of a dozen mounted Osage warriors in tribal paint, attended by two boys, the first tangible manifestation of the Lewis and Clark expedition. Convinced by the explorers to make the dangerous trek to Washington, they reached it on June 11, 1804, nearly a year after Lewis left, led by their great chief White Hair, guided by Pierre Chouteau, a Saint Louis fur trader. They produced a sensation, almost like tourists from Mars. On the day they arrived, Jefferson spent four dollars on a pair of moccasins. Fond as he was of slippers, did he greet his visitors in them?

The Osage were athletic, muscular men, six feet tall or more, with their heads plucked clean to the crown and an upright crest of hair, stiffened and dyed red, running down the backs of their heads into silver-cased queues that ended in long black locks, sometimes braided or draped with feathers and rattlesnake tails. Long, heavy earrings of silver, stone, and shell stretched their multipierced ears. The boys, not yet privileged to pluck their heads or adorn their ears, wore their hair long with bangs.

On the following day, Jefferson greeted them briefly at the President's House, taken aback by the "most gigantic men we have seen." The great tribes of the West, he told Secretary of the Navy Smith, were the Osage south of the Missouri and the Sioux to the north. "With these two powerful nations we must stand well, because in their quarter we are miserably weak." Friendship, trade, and bluff must offset weakness, starting with their reception. "We shall endeavor to impress them strongly, not only with our justice & liberality, but with our power," and send them on to Philadelphia and New York to be awed again. The French artist Charles Saint-Mémin drew their profiles with a shadow-tracing device and colored them in with pastels, the first European images of Western American Indians, which must have astonished them. They impressed their hosts in turn with detailed maps of their lands drawn in chalk on floors.

Having seen just weeks before only rooms made of sod or hides, they gathered in the President's House, probably in the splendid Oval Room, showing no concern and thinking God knows what. Jefferson had admired Indian oratory since he heard a Cherokee chief in his youth at William and Mary: "The moon was in full splendor," he recalled, "and to her he seemed to address himself in his prayers." He "filled me with awe and veneration, altho' I did not understand a word." Now he addressed the Osage with a feel for the native eloquence he had heard and admired for years, delivering through an interpreter in his soft, gentle voice a speech he had carefully prepared.

"My friends and children," he called them, an Enlightenment trope that cast native peoples as innocents needing parenting—progress, it was thought, over the sheer brutality of the past. He thanked them for their difficult journey across his country and the confidence it showed in the friendship and honor of the United States. He wept, he said, over the graves of their people killed by other tribes. "No voice can awake the dead," but the Osage were safe on this side of the Mississippi, and "we hope it will not be long before our voice will be heard and our arm respected" on the other side. In poetic native style, he linked his people to theirs. "It is so long since our forefathers came from beyond the great water that we have lost the memory of it, and seem to grow out of this land, as you have done. . . . We are all now of one family, born in the same land, and bound to live as brothers; and the strangers from beyond the great water are gone from among us." He had "sent a beloved man, Captain Lewis, one of my own household," to know them and invite them east. One of his people would go to live with them now, to learn their ways and needs and what they wanted in trade for their furs, and he hoped they would see the great

A visiting chief of the Little Osage Tribe received by Jefferson at the President's House, drawn by Charles Saint-Mémin. ***National Archives***

coastal cities under their fathers' care and protection. "And may the Great Spirit look down upon us and cover us with the mantle of his love."

The president took his own hurried notes as White Hair replied through his Canadian interpreter: "very content with speech . . . long since he wished to have a great chief . . . petty Frenchmen" would no longer give his villages bad counsel. In a tantalizing scribbled fragment, Jefferson garbled what White Hair said about slaves: "I have long since be sold as negroes are sold. I hope that is done." After the exchange of speeches, a crowd of ladies and gentlemen joined Jefferson and members of his cabinet on the front lawn of the President's House, such as it was, to watch the young Osage men dance in a blend of cultures to the music of the Marine Band. Seated together, the president and White Hair looked on in quiet dignity.

Since Washington's day, "chief coats" had been given to Indian dignitaries, deep blue, high-necked, wide-lapelled, brass-buttoned American Army officers' tunics with buff or scarlet facings and gilded epaulettes, many of them second-hand. Augustus Foster said they made warrior chiefs look like coachmen, a snide remark with the sting of truth, for the dignified men who wore them did not understand the indignity. White Hair got an elaborate general's coat, a top hat, and an American flag. He and Dog Soldier and Traveling Rain got silver "peace medals" the size of a man's palm—numismatic works of art introduced in the Washington and Adams administrations, now beautifully redesigned. On one side was Jefferson's profile, encircled by his name and title. On the other was a peace pipe laid over a tomahawk, the motto "Peace and Friendship," and two clasped hands, one coming out of a soldier's cuff, the other on a bare wrist with an American eagle bracelet. A former secretary of war turned wistful when someone told him Jefferson had designed it. "Would to God that he had confined his revolutionary genius to things of no greater importance."

A few days later, not much interested in sharing Jefferson's news of contact with the people of the West, the Federalist *Port Folio* published a satirical "fragment of a journal," said to have been found near the Potomac. "Left Sally," an early morning entry began, "must seem industrious, though nothing to do." At noon, "ordered my horse—never ride with a servant—looks proud—mob doesn't like it—must gull the boobies." Later in the day, the diarist shared jokes on the New Testament with Tom Paine.

* * *

On November 5, 1804, having shot Hamilton dead not four months before, Aaron Burr chaired the Senate with a show of nonchalance on the session's first day. Many Federalists shunned him, but Burr was as blithe as a breeze. It was surely the first time, Senator Plumer wrote his son, "(God grant it may be the last) that ever a man indicted for murder presided in the American Senate. We are indeed fallen on evil times. . . . The high office of President is filled by an infidel; that of Vice-President by a murderer." Plumer's opinion of Jefferson and his crowd had dropped a peg or two. Never doubting that Hamilton's death would please them, he had wondered if they would show it "by caressing his murderer. Those doubts are now dispelled." Plumer only nodded to Burr when they passed, but Jefferson was said to have him over more than ever, and Plumer was appalled that Madison, Hamilton's friend and collaborator in the making of the Constitution, welcomed his killer into his carriage. If Plumer had seen a Republican's letter to Jefferson about Burr, he might not have been surprised: "Was it such a crime to kill General Hamilton that he must never be forgiven?"

Yet Plumer considered wisdom no monopoly. His Federalist peers would not associate with Republicans, and vice versa, but Plumer called on Republicans, avoided sensitive points, and learned. Some Federalists found Jefferson so odious that they thought it a disgrace to set foot in his house, considering him the head of a faction, not the president of all the people. Plumer disagreed. He would visit him courteously and dine with him when asked. "He is President, and we must acknowledge him such." A respectful call at the President's House was a ceremony, not an endorsement. Plumer wanted to get to know him and discover what he was thinking, "for he is naturally communicative."

The senator called at the President's House with some fellow New Englanders on a Saturday morning in November and found him unusually presentable. His coat was worn down to a threadbare shine, but his old-fashioned scarlet vest, corduroy knee britches, and white cotton hose were in good order, and his hair was cut and powdered. Reform had its limits nonetheless. His linen stock was soiled and his slippers old. His conversation was surprisingly vapid, quite unlike his usual banter, until it turned to racing, which he thoroughly enjoyed, as Virginians did and Puritans did not. Spirited mounts and reckless riders from Maryland and Virginia raced at Georgetown every November, drawing three or four thousand spectators, "black, white, and yellow; of all conditions," the Massachusetts Federalist Manasseh Cutler wrote, "from the President of the United States to the beggar in his rags," and the mix disgusted Cutler as much as the gambling. But Jefferson teased his New England guests that racing was less corrosive than playing whist or dice like the Bostonians. A fellow could be ruined by the turn of a single card or a desperate roll of the dice, but "it requires several races to sweep a man's property, and that gives time for reflection." Last year, he went on, the Senate adjourned for the races on the pretext of a wall needing mending. What would they come up with now? Plumer's boarding housemate Senator James Hillhouse, a humorless New Haven Federalist, replied to the president's jest with a nasty poke in the eye. Perhaps they could adjourn to fit the chamber for Judge Chase's impeachment trial, he said, a hotly partisan proceeding incited by their host.

Plumer's diary recorded his own embarrassment. "The President hung his head. Silence ensued. The state of the weather became the topic of conversation. Tarried about half an hour." Unlike Hillhouse, Plumer respected his hosts and his presidents, particularly incensed about Yrujo's insults to Jefferson, delivered "in his own doors."

On the following Thursday, Plumer noticed the Senate's clock had been moved up half an hour for race day, and most of the "Democrats" were fidgety. Burr took his chair at 11:00 "by the Senate clock," suggested the absence of a quorum, and adjourned. Plumer had no complaint, for "the less business is done by Congress the better it will be for the Union. I have never attended the horse races."

* * *

On November 23, 1804, Napoleon's new minister to the United States, General Louis Marie Turreau, presented his credentials at the President's House in a diplomatic tunic laden with gold that made Merry's look drab. Having infamously terrorized villagers and killed women and children in an uprising he had crushed in western France, the general was rather proud of it. Plumer would come to know him as "a man of little learning & slender talent . . . a ferocious disposition, and brutal manners," and Turreau had Jefferson pegged for the opposite character: "There is something voluptuous in meaning well." Both men were right.

On the evening of Turreau's presentation, Senator Adams took his mother-in-law and his sisters-in-law to dine at the President's House, the only member of Congress at the table and probably the only Federalist. Jefferson spoke of Turreau: "They must get him down to a plain frock coat, or the boys in the streets will run after him as a sight." As the conversation turned to France, the president showed his guests a French book on parrots with beautiful hand-colored plates and chatted with Adams about the French *in* French. Adams was intrigued by a shift in his view of their revolution: "How contrary to all expectation" it had gone! "Who could have thought such a shaking would come to this?" The French should depose Bonaparte, restore their democratic constitution of 1789, and "call back the Old Family," an odd thing for a revolutionary to say eleven years after the old family's leading heads had been removed beyond recall.

As Adams told his diary, Jefferson said French and Spanish should be taught to all our young men. Spanish was so easy he had learned it in nineteen days on a fast ship to Europe with *Don Quixote* and a Spanish grammar. "But Mr. Jefferson," Adams wrote, "tells large stories." He had said at another dinner that a vintner in Marseilles offered to duplicate whatever fine wine you liked with a mix of vin ordinaire at "6 or 8 sous the bottle," and no connoisseur could tell it from the real thing. "You can never be in this man's company," Adams wrote, "without something of the marvelous, like these stories." It was not a compliment, at least not entirely.

Jefferson had built a reputation for telling tall tales at dinner, or tales of above average height. The Federalist congressman Samuel Taggart of Massachusetts, "corpulent and slow of movement," enjoyed the president's wines one evening, though a slice of the Mammoth Cheese "was wretched enough." Promoting the wonders of the West, Jefferson had spoken at an earlier dinner of a mountain of salt to be mined on the Missouri River, and samples had been put on the table, "but I find the salt mountain has got to be a plain," Taggart wrote, ready to be raked and bagged, "and instead of being on the Missouri it is situated on the Arkansas River several hundred miles further south." The toxic Senator Pickering enjoyed the same scene. Despite their overlapping politics, Louisa Adams was no friend. Pickering despised her husband and her father-in-law too. *Most* people, Mrs. Adams wrote, found him nothing less than repellent, but at dinner that chilly evening, Pickering had chatted with the president about raising apples and pears and promised to lend him a book on the subject before he disclosed the miraculous salt. The Indians, Jefferson said, kept the site holy as "the sacred plain," where tribes at war for generations mingled in perfect safety. After they scraped the salt it was back the next morning two inches thick. When Pickering inquired whether the salt kept rising if no one harvested it, Jefferson seemed not to have thought of that. Faced with pointed questions, Taggart wrote, "His Excellency seemed to be rather pushed, and frankly confessed his ignorance of the particulars." Pickering told the story for days.

A few weeks later, Senator Plumer noticed it was "Th. Jefferson," not "the President of the United States" who invited him to dine. Plumer thought it meant something but was not sure what, and he asked Virginia's senator William Branch Giles, Jefferson's friend, to explain. Jefferson entertained as a private gentleman, Giles said, for as president he would have to invite every member of Congress, and he did not want the gentlemen who abused him. Plumer knew some uninvited men who publicly "*reasoned*" against Jefferson's ideas, even made them ridiculous, but that was manly conduct, and Jefferson's exclusion of his critics suppressed debate. "It discovers a littleness of mind unworthy of the President of the United States," who should act as if he did not know what people said about him.

Plumer came to dine with the president in exclusively Federalist company nonetheless on the day after Napoleon crowned himself emperor, unbeknownst to the table, and found his grooming further improved. Gone were the tatty slippers, the dated red vest, the corduroy knee britches, and the elderly stains. He was clothed in respectable black, with clean white linen, powdered hair, and actual shoes; but nothing much else had changed. The dinner was sublime, with very good wines, including two Hungarians, the richer of which, the president said in dubious taste, he had paid "a *guinea a bottle*" to get. Bottled water from the Mississippi was a conversation piece, and again an aging remnant of the Mammoth Cheese, "very far from being good." The president carved, served, and poured like anyone's amiable father, but under the skin he was not himself, adding little to the conversation.

He had written to Martha that day, the lonely man in the crowd, saying Congress had little to do and complained of boredom. There were very few ladies in residence, with half a dozen diplomats and their wives out of town, a doleful list in which he included even Mrs. Merry. "The theatre fails too for want of actors." Martha was lucky to need none of these things, poor substitutes for the joy of his grandchildren. "Being this moment called off, I must here conclude with my kisses to all the dear children, and my tenderest & unalterable love to you."

Reviewing the president's annual message, Plumer recalled that it had promised mountains of salt in Louisiana the year before, but now "amuses us with lead mines," going silent on salt. It was "baits like these" that pleased the gullible and distracted them from "the immense debt we owe for that country." At $15 million, the price for controlling the Mississippi top to bottom, nearly doubling the country's size, and denying Napoleon a place from which to attack it was under three cents an acre. John Quincy Adams supported it, a lonely stand among Federalists.

* * *

By December of 1804, it was clear that the Republicans had won overwhelming control of Congress and Jefferson had been reelected with every electoral vote but Connecticut's, Delaware's, and two of Maryland's. Even Massachusetts had fallen, and Jefferson wrote a Republican veteran of the fight at Lexington and Concord to congratulate him wryly on his state's return to the Union. The Federalists were spent as a national political force and would never recover. Soon after the returns were in, the president started putting up architecture and pulling it down energetically, with no one to tell him no, and his architect, Benjamin Latrobe, started "rendering the President's House habitable."

First came unglamorous needs. Every big house needed service and storage spaces—"offices" they were called, "menial offices," Latrobe called them—and the President's House lacked offices "of the first necessity." On this he and Jefferson agreed, but not on the solution. The stable was two blocks away, and the mansion lacked a smokehouse, henhouse, laundry, abundant servants' quarters, a reasonable number of privies, and proper storage for coal, wood, equipment, and tools. Rather than litter the grounds with outbuildings, Jefferson designed, as he had for Monticello, two long white wings spreading from the house at both ends. Hoban had anticipated something of the kind, but Jefferson conceived his own design and made his own meticulous drawings, a relaxing labor of love premised on his cherished Andrea Palladio's sixteenth-century innovation of simple one- or two-story wings, beautiful on the outside, functional on the inside, with separate bays configured for each use, invisible to everyone but staff. Latrobe was not fond of wings or Palladio either.

The grounds dropped north to south, and Jefferson planned the wings to be built into the slope. Looking from the north, only the tops of the structures would be visible, and their high, north-facing windows. On the south side of the slope, the wings would be revealed as colonnaded passageways supported by white-painted Tuscan columns matching the whitewashed house. Washerwomen, gardeners, and stable boys would come and go between the bays, their interiors concealed behind louvered French doors.

In addition to their workaday roles, the wings would connect the east and west executive buildings to the house and give it a pleasing base. Their flat roofs, slightly pitched to run off rain, would double as stone-paved walkways from the mansion's first floor to the executive buildings' second, accounting for the sloping ground, hiding Jefferson's corrugated iron roofs underneath. He expected the wings' construction to start at both ends and expand as Congress funded it. The wings were unlikely to reach the house's adjoining buildings until after his time, one of many examples of his vision for posterity.

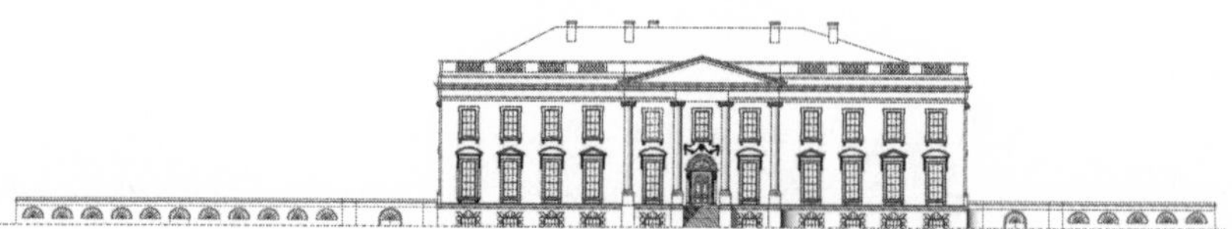

North view of the President's House, 1808. ***Created by Patrick Phillips-Schrock based on documentary evidence***

Having admired the wings in Palladio's books and living examples in France, and learned from their construction at Monticello, Jefferson drew them in fine detail, to the height, width, and depth of the bricks and mortar, enjoying every inch, working with the world's best drawing tools on red-gridded graph paper made for carpet weavers, a trick a French architect had taught him. In the western wing would be a wine cellar, firewood storage with coal underneath, a coach house, a saddle room, two eighteen-foot-wide servants' rooms, and two servants' necessaries, male and female, constructed, as Latrobe anticipated, "to prevent their being a nuisance." In the eastern wing would go a third servants' room, a necessary for family and guests, the henhouse, the stable, and the smokehouse, where meats would be salted, smoked, and suspended.

Free from unlovely outbuildings, the grounds could be groomed as a public park in front and a presidential retreat in back. Fond of the people in the abstract, often less so face-to-face, and valuing privacy highly, Jefferson also saw his wings as a functional barrier, with built-in lodges for guards, dividing the northern, public grounds from the private, river view gardens and walks. A dense screen of trees to be planted between the house and the road would also benefit future presidents, if not their constituents.

Palladio would have loved it. Latrobe did not. By April of 1805, Jefferson was pressing his architect to produce working drawings from his graphs. On May 2, Latrobe explained to Gallatin that "neither my taste nor my reason" matched the president's love of wings, and the two-pronged ordeal of subduing his better judgment while fitting the design to the topography had been "damned hard work." He complained about Jefferson more sharply still to his foreman John Lenthall: "I am sorry that I am cramped in this design by his prejudices in favor of the old French books, out of which he fishes everything." Colonnaded wings were "exactly consistent with Hoban's pile—a litter of pigs worthy of the great sow it surrounds, and of the wild Irish boar the father of her." Fond of Jefferson nonetheless, Latrobe had decided to "humor him."

In one of life's painful slips, Latrobe sent the letter not to Lenthall but to Jefferson, who returned it with a note "on his honor" (a suspiciously strong

South view of the President's House, 1808. ***Created by Patrick Phillips-Schrock based on documentary evidence***

assurance) that he had not read a word after he saw it was addressed to Mr. Lenthall. Contrite in his relief, Latrobe exhaled to Lenthall that the president could have safely read it all, "even to the litter of pigs." He was "one of the best-hearted men that ever came out of the hand of nature," but "he thinks, writes, and acts differently from others," and was therefore abused. Quite apart from his exemplary politics, his candor, kindness, and learning were second to none, with nothing to fault but "a few oddities of appearance and of conduct which are perfectly innocent and probably very right."

Latrobe had struck a different pose a few hours earlier, unaware that his remarks about pigs and old books had gone astray. With a letter to the president, sent from his Delaware home, he enclosed two sheets of drawings of the wings that upset their careful design. It would be hard to align the rooftop terraces with the executive buildings, he wrote, and horses on their way in and out of the built-in stables would soil the colonnade and make "a very unpleasant interruption to the walk." A very careful coachman might drive between the columns, but the inevitable scrapes would damage them, and the wing would "become the resort of all the disagreeable people who loiter about a stable." Instead, Latrobe had added big rectangular structures to the center of both wings, a garden pavilion on the west and a stable and coach house on the east, with an arch that coaches and riders could pass through comfortably, a hidden hayloft overhead, and two flanking pedestrian gates, in addition to other disruptions of the president's plans.

Jefferson's blunt reply was a rarity for him. He concurred on the stables, curtly, and clarified who was boss. Some parts of Latrobe's propositions were approved, some were not, and some were dubious, he wrote. They would discuss them, "*vivâ voce*, when you come here," which Latrobe would do "without delay, be it for however short a time." But "I want a coach house immediately," and the challenge of joining the rooftop terraces to the executive buildings was a "difficulty of the art which will be worthy of you to conquer." Conquer it Latrobe did, but it was not the last time he would have cause to wonder if Jefferson had read or been told after all about the litter of pigs and the fishing out of old French books. In 1807, the president asked him to return such a book. "I expect to find some good designs in that."

Work began on the wings in 1805. Breezeways were built first, where both wings met the house, providing controllable access from the northern to the southern grounds. The icehouse built in 1801 was incorporated into the western wing. At the point where the eastern wing would eventually join the Treasury Department's building, a fireproof vault was built at the latter's western end. Jefferson hovered over the smallest details of construction, like the floor of the stable, to be dug three feet deep and filled with "small clean gravel of the beach of the Potomac." Microscopic interventions such as these reignited Latrobe, time having passed since his near death experience with the misdirected letter. The architect instructed Lenthall not to grapple with the precision of the president's instructions on the size of the coal cellar and the adjoining privy. It mattered not "whether there be a foot or two more or less for coals or dung, provided there be room enough."

The wings spread slowly east and west, their colonnades lined with elegant benches crafted by Peter Lenox, the house carpenter, and stopped in 1807 when the money ran out. The eastern wing had reached the point of eleven bays, not halfway to its destination, its western twin had just five, and only parts of the colonnade had been built. The partly built wings had room for stables, storage, privies, smoked and salted meat, and minor offices, but not for all the house's needs. Worse, Latrobe's archway at the center of the eastern wing collapsed in December of 1806, its mortar having been applied after the weather turned cold and its supports knocked away too soon. The public embarrassment and the ruins left for years helped clip the wings short.

* * *

On January 11, 1805, Senator Adams and his wife Louisa dined with the president in company. Aaron Burr was there, soon to be a former vice president, Jefferson having replaced him on the winning ticket of 1804 with New York's governor George Clinton. But Burr's fatal victory over Hamilton neither barred him from polite company nor was likely to be mentioned in it, and he oiled his way into the good graces of Mrs. Adams, no easy Federalist mark. "I was pleased with him," she wrote years later, "in spite of myself." Jefferson was not pleased with him and never trusted him, but, keeping his enemy close, he continued to have Burr at the President's House even after he knew he was conniving with Merry. Jefferson seemed distracted at dinner that evening, but Adams found his "itch" for fabulous tales "unabated." The weather was painfully cold, which prompted him to say he had seen the temperature drop twenty degrees below zero *in Paris*, and not on a freakish day. "For six weeks together it stood thereabouts," never once approaching zero, which he emphatically reminded his guests was "*fifty degrees* below the freezing point."

"He knows better than all this," Adams assured his diary. "Fahrenheit's thermometer never since Mr. Jefferson existed was at twenty degrees below zero in Paris," or twenty degrees *above* for six weeks running. "Nor is Fahrenheit's zero fifty degrees below the freezing point—but he loves to excite wonder." The senator did not consider the possibility that he loved to excite the senator, to pull his humorless leg, which Jefferson seemed to enjoy.

Mrs. Adams admired everything at Jefferson's table but the penny-pinching heat. Had he given them a decent fire on a bone-chilling day "we might have fancied ourselves in Europe." When the company retired to the Oval Room in the French manner, women and men together, the temperature actually dropped. The coal so barely flickered in the grate that a guest amused Mrs. Adams with the thought of spitting it out. "Shaking with cold," she clenched her teeth to avoid a chatter, but instead of calling a servant to stoke the fire, Jefferson drew his own chair "gallantly" near it "and seemed impatiently to await our exit, which was sadly delayed by the neglect of the hackney coachman." The ferocious General Turreau dropped by and launched himself into an eccentric dance, galloping backward and forward across the room, an excuse to keep warm, Mrs. Adams thought, masked as entertainment. There was little about Napoleon's ambassador that was *not* eccentric. Among a selection of scandals, it was said that Turreau had been composing a dispatch to Paris when his persecuted wife "came by him with a smoothing iron," which provoked retaliation. "She cried murder, the children & servants came in crying," and the secretary of legation drowned out the noise playing "furiously on the French horn."

Charles Willson Peale and his talented son picked that bitter spell of winter to return to Washington City, Charles to tempt Congress with his polygraphs, and twenty-five-year-old Rembrandt Peale to paint his second brilliant portrait of the president. Charles found no buyers for his machines. Many congressmen were impressed, he thought, but too cold to think about convenience in this wilderness clearing, "a dear and miserable hole except to some public officers and a few tavern keepers." Peale liked the winter stockings Jefferson wore in the President's House, rabbit fur spun with cotton, made for warmth, not show, but Jefferson disapproved of the cold. "The Canadian glows with delight in his sleigh & snow," he wrote in the drafty house, "the very idea of which gives me the shivers." Then again, America's climate bested Europe's. "It is our cloudless sky which has eradicated from our constitutions all disposition to hang ourselves, which we might otherwise have inherited from our English ancestors."

In this "dreadful spell of weather" he let Martha know her three-year-old nephew Francis, living in the mansion with his father, Maria's widower Mr. Eppes, was in great health and spirits, though in need of a bit more polish after playing with the servants' children. "He wants only a society which could rub off what he contracts from the gross companions with whom he of necessity associates," Jefferson wrote. "He is a charming boy." His cousin Ellen wrote their grandfather a few years later and inquired about the rubbing off: "Does he curse as much as he used to do formerly?"

With the hard ground layered in snow, Rembrandt Peale painted Jefferson at the President's House in three sittings, looking confident and mildly amused, fresh off his smashing reelection in a bright red jacket and his barbarous, fur-collared wolf-skin cloak, his hair grown long, hanging loose over his ears. The warm winter cloak had a story of its own, given in admiration by a Russian tsar to Catherine the Great's freed captive, Tadeusz Kosciuszko, a Polish revolutionary, who gave it to Jefferson. The elder Peale had found his winter expedition to Washington from Philadelphia by coach as dangerous as crossing the Atlantic in summer, and decided to wait for good weather to risk his return, "as I think myself of some little consequence to my family."

While the Peales were in town, Jefferson's secretary William Burwell took a leave to serve in the Virginia legislature, grateful for the president's "uniform benevolence" and relieved temporarily by Isaac Coles, yet another Virginian in his twenties. Coles was better off than his secretarial predecessors—"one of my wealthy neighbors" Jefferson called him, "a most worthy, intelligent & well informed young man"—a handsome cousin of Dolley Madison's and Patrick Henry's, highly ranked among the most eligible young men in town.

* * *

Early in February 1805, the moderate Federalist Senator Plumer found himself uncomfortable with Washington's birthday. In the city that bore his name, the celebration of his birth was an excuse for a Federalist rally, a Federalist ball, a Federalist banquet, Federalist toasts, and the boom of Federalist cannon. Unseemly was what it was. Before the 1805 edition, Plumer tried to convince his friends that it stiffened party politics, an outright evil, and they ought to call it off. Remarkably enough, they did.

Later that frigid winter, Jefferson found time to perfect his design of an efficient new blade for the business end of a plow, using self-taught Newtonian calculus, guiding a craftsman through two models in the President's House. In this he took great pride. There was nothing so common, he wrote, "as to see men value themselves most for what they know least about." The result was an award-winning contribution to agriculture at home and abroad.

On March 4, Washington City's first inaugural parade proceeded up the poplar-lined Pennsylvania Avenue from the President's House to the Capitol, composed of the Marine Band, uniformed militia, members of Congress, and "citizens and strangers of distinction." As many as twelve hundred spectators wished Jefferson well, lining what looked like an actual street with more than a few houses if not the Parisian boulevard on which he had modeled it. Shunning any carriage at all, the president rode horseback, attended by his secretary and a groom, twice as much escort as he liked. To Augustus Foster he seemed in high spirits, dressed respectably in black.

After his inaugural address, again hard to hear beyond the first few rows, "he received levee" at the President's House. The crowds at these public events had grown larger and dramatically less exclusive over time. Four months later, on the Fourth of July, Dolley Madison would speak of sitting in the Oval Room, "amusing myself with the mob." Augustus Foster watched a "very mixed company" swarm into the inaugural reception, "some lolling about on couches in dirty shoes." Almost unbelievably, "even Negro servants" helped themselves to the president's wine. A procession of Irish laborers and other "low persons" came down the Pennsylvania Avenue to the mansion, and "the jingling of a few pipes and drums finished the day. There was nothing dignified in the whole affair."

Jefferson took a moment to write a note to Ellen, enclosing some poems, encouraging her collection and saying not a word about his honors. "I am called off by company," he wrote, "therefore god bless you, my dear child, kiss your Mama and sisters for me, and tell them I shall be with them in about a week from this time."

* * *

On April 7, 1805, Ludwig van Beethoven conducted in Vienna the first performance of his *Eroica* symphony, and Meriwether Lewis sent a messenger to Saint Louis with a letter to Jefferson from a winter encampment with the Mandans, a "brave, humane, and hospitable" people in a part of the world later known as North Dakota. Enclosed was a list of artifacts—animal, mineral, and vegetable—on their way back to Washington City; a map of the expedition's progress; and the journal of Captain Clark, who asked that it not be published until someone fixed the grammar. Lewis had sent a sergeant's journal to Saint Louis and would send his own and others separately, "to multiply the chances of saving something." He hoped to reach the Pacific before winter and be home in a year and a half. Ten days later, Lewis and Clark and their men left the Mandan nation, familiar to a few French Canadian traders, and disappeared up the Missouri into the unknown.

To his uncontained joy, Jefferson received Lewis's letter and its list of curiosities on July 13, three months after they were sent, the first word from the expedition in over a year. Aglow with Lewis's news, he wrote to the governor of New Orleans "in the moment of my departure for Monticello." Packages "filled with very curious subjects" would come to the governor soon on their way to Washington, he wrote, and he pointed them out particularly.

As Jefferson relished Lewis's list, he examined with no joy a petition signed by laborers on the Capitol and the President's House that begged him for a raise to meet the cost of bread. He did not suggest cake, but explained to John Lenthall, clerk of the works, that the president ought to do nothing for these men that he would not do for "every work-yard in the U.S.," which he could not run personally. Workmen's appeals were "entirely out of my sphere," and Lenthall should do for this group "what your duties will permit."

* * *

Referring to the first floor, Louisa Adams had said that the President's House "*below* stairs was very handsome," but *upstairs* "were strong indications of the want of female inspection." In 1805, Jefferson started improving the second floor, converting empty shells lacking walls, floors, and ceilings to extraordinary bedchambers with beds set in alcoves and built-in cabinets and drawers, a European form unfamiliar to Americans, admired in France and installed at Monticello.

On the public first floor, the huge storage space at the eastern end of the house was finally made habitable. "As we shall move into the Mammoth room within 2 or 3 days," Jefferson told Claxton in June of 1805, two dozen stick chairs would have to furnish it. The furniture fund was small for the house, "which is very large and as yet has been very scantily accommodated . . . and necessaries must take precedence of ornaments." The necessities included a custom-made fire engine involving leather, brass cylinders, a copper air vessel, painted woodwork, fifteen bushels of coal, and a hundred and fifteen dollars and forty-two cents. Upstairs, where the public did not go, a "decent lanthern" like the ones in the servants' hall would do for the corridor, abetted by half a dozen wall lamps, lit one by one, shedding pale cones of light. "Our painter took to drinking," Jefferson wrote, went away and never returned. Now the corridor's canvas floorcloth would have to be painted at the Capitol.

Eight months later, Claxton had to tell the president there was still no word on the stick chairs, despite Claxton's urgent letters. The president of the United States seemed to carry no weight in the world of Philadelphia furniture; but a local craftsman's sideboard was progressing nicely, and his side table for the Setting Room would be convenient and "very ornamental" when it got its marble top. Jefferson asked Claxton to buy four wool-and-cotton blankets woven at an almshouse, the kind of small-scale manufacturing he liked to promote. Someone had given him samples, as people often did.

Out of sight of his critics and most of his friends, things were looking up in the president's suite in the second floor's light-filled southwest quarter, none of it notably republican. Two corniced, south-facing windows commanded his handsome bedchamber, with a lovely river view and curtains of patterned dimity, a sheer cotton fabric imported from India. A mahogany fireplace screen kept sparks off the costly Brussels carpet. A mahogany headboard five or six feet tall with a curtain-draped cornice matched the mahogany chests and tables, set off by five crimson-and-gold stick chairs, which Jefferson called "fashionable." On his walls were engravings of all three presidents, symbols of respect, continuity, and buried hatchets. Having no valet, Jefferson chose his own clothes from a remarkable rotating "machine" he installed in an oversized closet and put them back when he took them off.

Adams had partitioned the once enormous bedroom to create two smaller ones for family guests. Jefferson used the one in the corner as a dressing room, much longer than wide, with a common carpet, a mahogany table, a window looking south and two looking west, corniced and draped with dimity. No fewer than eleven of those crimson-and-gold stick chairs lined the room, to be taken downstairs when needed. A water closet sat in a cubicle with its overhead tank and chain. Rounding out the suite, a windowless passage between the bedroom and the dressing room, big enough to sleep a young Adams relative, had a fine Brussels carpet, a mahogany wardrobe and stool, and room for eight more chairs. The president took his afternoon naps on an elegant couch, curled up, perhaps, in his eiderdown coverlet of dove-gray silk, dearly bought in Philadelphia in 1793, which he took back and forth to Monticello, "rolled into a compass not bigger than a man's leg."

By the fall of 1805, the formal rooms downstairs were finished, as were six or seven bedrooms, counting the president's. Beautifully crafted chair rails, door and window frames, wainscoting, baseboards, cornices, and molded classical friezes embellished the plastered walls, painted in flat pastels. The paneled doors of burled San Domingo mahogany swung on huge cast brass hinges with matching five-pound knobs. Hidden foldaway shutters flanked the recessed windows, the lower sections closable for privacy, the upper ones for shade. The curtains in all but three rooms were cheerful Indian prints. In one of the others hung the heavy crimson damask drapes that Adams had shipped from Philadelphia. The stately curtains in the other two were not otherwise described. The Great Hall of Entrance and other heavily tread floors were protected by canvas painted green, the color Gilbert Stuart had recommended to Jefferson, mixing it on his palette. Less frequently visited rooms were adorned with costly Brussels carpets, "exceedingly elegant" in Claxton's view.

* * *

Lewis and Clark's Western treasures reached the President's House in August 1805, four months after they were sent. They would have come quicker from China. Jefferson was at Monticello, and Secretary of War Dearborn had Lemaire break the shipment open—a barrel, four crates, and two cages. In the cages were a bird like a magpie and what Clark called a burrowing squirrel, the first living things sent east from the plains, alive and remarkably well. What Clark had called "one liveing hen of the Prarie" had perished on the way, and three magpies had been killed and consumed by the survivor.

Perfectly preserved in the barrel were wonderful Indian ornaments and dress. Joseph Dougherty packed them carefully in two boxes and sent them to Monticello, one at a time on Jefferson's orders, raising the odds that at least one would survive several nights at dubious inns. Among other tokens of the West were soft, clean pelts, a set of horns of the mountain ram, and two stunning buffalo hides, meticulously dressed and "highly embellished with Indian finery." One was the work of the Gros Ventre, an Algonquin-speaking nation in a place to be called Montana. On the other, a Mandan had painted in bright colors a great battle fought in the 1790s by the Mandans, the Gros Ventre, and their allies against the Sioux and the Arikara. Augustus Foster later saw at the President's House two colorful battles on buffalo hides, "grotesque figures on horseback with shields & spears," he called them, "and where a white man is introduced with a gun they give him a cocked hat." Coaxed by Lewis and Clark, the Mandans had made peace with the Arikara, who the Mandans claimed had started the war. They had killed the Arikara like birds, the Mandans said. They were tired of killing them.

One of the crates unpacked at the President's House was full of minerals, soils, and salts, specimens of plants, and a Mandan pot. The other three were writhing with vermin that had feasted for months on the undressed skins of antelope, blacktail deer, and bear; the unclean bones of a wolf; and Indian corn, tobacco, and other plants, one of which the natives prized as a cure for the bites of rattlesnakes and mad dogs. A Mandan bow and a quiver of arrows survived the infestation, as did a tin box of insects and mice, presumably deceased.

General Dearborn took charge of preservation. The decorated buffalo robes and the barrel's other contents were damp, and Lemaire put them out to dry for a day, then sprinkled them with snuff, wrapped each piece in clean linen, and packed them in trunks and boxes. The insects were destroyed, and the damaged items aired. An experienced conservator, Jefferson had written Lemaire to expect "the skins & furs may be suffering," and asked him to have them dried, brushed, and "done up close in strong linen to keep the worm-fly out." The crates he ordered kept in his Cabinet to frustrate rats and mice, no testimonial to the rest of the house. Particular care should be taken of the little mammal and the bird, "that I may see them alive at my return." Lemaire assured him that the painted hides of the "*Boeuf Saûvage*" were in good order, beaten and left in the sun for four days and rolled with leaf tobacco in freshly made sacks. The goods had all been put in the creatively spelled "*granié d'ans le n'ouveau Stor*," but Lemaire would move them to the Cabinet if Jefferson wished. "The magpie and the kind of squirrel are very well," he wrote; "they are in the room where Monsieur receives his callers."

Monsieur returned on October 4, possibly eager for the first time to get back, having ridden half a day "in a pretty steady rain, which I thought preferable to staying at Brown's." Most of the stack of paper on his desk would keep while he enjoyed his Western prizes. On October 6, he wrote Peale that a captain of marines was on his way to Philadelphia with a box of minerals Lewis wanted the Philosophical Society to have, its members having taught him his geology. To Peale himself would go some skeletons and skins; the branching horns of what Jefferson took to be a roe deer, surprised to find it in America; what Lewis called the pelt of "a burrowing dog of the prairies," which Jefferson identified as a badger; the cannibalistic magpie; and the chirping squirrel-like animal the president called a marmot. "I am much afraid of the season of torpidity coming on him before you get him," he wrote Peale. "He is a most harmless & tame creature." Such joy the president took in these living Western migrants far from home in the care of the United States.

He packed the boxes with his own hands, happy as an elf, apparently unconcerned that it was not the Philosophical Society or Peale but the taxpayers who had bought them. For himself and the "Indian Hall" he planned for Monticello he set aside the painted buffalo hides and some of the pelts and horns. The Great Hall of Entry at the President's House would have been the better venue, as it later turned out to be. Charmed by the gentle marmot, Peale thanked the president for his gifts and promised to display them in his museum, for "everything that comes from Louisiana must be interesting to the Public."

On October 6, the same day he sent Peale the news about Western artifacts on their way to Philadelphia, Jefferson replied to a letter from the sheriff of

Fairfax County, Virginia, just across the river, who had jailed and held for a month a young black man named James Hubbard, having taken him in suspiciously good clothes with papers "that was soe bad wrote and formed" that they must be forged. "Now he Confeses he is the property of yours. . . . As large a fellow as he is if you thinke proper to Bestow Aney thinge on me more than the Law givs it will be thank full Recivd by your most Obedient and Most humble Servt, Daniel Bradley."

Hubbard had probably gotten as far as he had with information obtained from Jack Shorter or John Freeman, conveyed at Monticello, where both men enslaved at the President's House often went with Jefferson. "I will ask the favor of you to deliver him when called for," the president wrote back, and "in the mean time to keep him in jail." Bradley's bill would be paid, he wrote, and the forgery probed "to the bottom." Hubbard was brought back to Monticello. A year after Jefferson retired, he ran away again.

15

ORIENTAL LUXURY AND TASTE

Washington City had grown and improved since the last family visit, and so had the President's House. Despite miserable weather and worse roads, Jefferson persuaded Martha to make another trip in December 1805, about eight months pregnant in a coach stuffed with six young children. This was no "flying visit" but a five-month occupation, and the president insisted on paying every expense, "so that the visit may not at all affect Mr. Randolph's pecuniary arrangements." It must have affected his pride.

On January 17, 1806, a night so cold that the fire only took the edge off it, Martha gave birth to a child named James Madison Randolph, who would grow to be a gentle boy and die at twenty-eight, known throughout his life as the first child born in the President's House. No one counted infants born as slaves. With no other woman in the house, it had not occurred to anyone that Martha would need postpartum nourishment, and no servant had been put on call. Roaming the house in the night, the midwife found not a scrap of bread to soak or a scoop of meal for gruel and, beyond the public rooms, neither "cleanliness nor comfort." When the story spread, Louisa Adams blamed it on the European scarcity of female servants, as Jefferson was too deep in French habits for "the homespun domesticity of American."

The Ninth Congress of the United States had opened on December 2, 1805, the day the family arrived, and it stayed in business until April 21, 1806, prolonged by a full agenda. Jefferson called it "a squally session." In the course of that extended campaign, he hosted sixty-three dinners, up to four a week. Martha served as hostess when ladies were present and sometimes when they were not, particularly when the mix risked conflict, which her presence defused. Her eldest child Anne, a beauty at sixteen, the age for her debut, made social appearances with her mother and sometimes helped entertain.

The conflict with the Merrys still simmered, and Martha became a combatant. The weighty issue of who would be visited first struck again when Mrs. Merry sent Mrs. Randolph a note: Did she wish to be treated as the daughter of the head of state or the wife of a member of Congress? Neither, she replied with her father's advice; she would expect only the courtesies given strangers. Nothing but polite on its face, the note may bear a hint of guile. In Mrs. Merry's world, strangers were entitled to the first visit.

Whatever Mrs. Merry thought of her, Martha achieved the feat of pleasing Augustus Foster. At the New Year's Day reception, Merry had presented the poet Thomas Moore, the Merrys' friend from their transatlantic crossing, and the president had barely said a word to him, provoking Merry yet again; but Martha explained to Foster that her father had taken Moore for a boy. (Sir Walter Scott called him "a little—a very little man.") Foster thought "we probably owe some angry verses to the circumstance" but accepted Mrs. Randolph's explanation and liked her.

Martha could see her father whenever she pleased, even when he was working. When he was free he left the door open; when he was pressed he left the key in the lock as a sign that she could turn it. His grandchildren would sidle up to him while he spoke with Margaret Bayard Smith, and without breaking stride "he would quietly caress them." When they caught him outside at Monticello, the younger ones liked to challenge him to a footrace en masse. As Mrs. Smith could see, he "delighted in delighting them," and he probably raced them at the President's House. "It is only with them," he said, "that a grave man can play the fool."

On a soft Sunday evening in May, the Smiths came to tea and found him on a sofa with his daughter. One of the toddlers was standing with her arms around his neck, and the others sat on his knees as the older ones entertained. It occurred to Mrs. Smith that here was one of the most celebrated men alive, cavorting with squealing children. When the squealers were in bed, he nursed his happy mood and chatted with Martha and the Smiths about gardening, farming, different countries' crops and flowers, what thrived in various climates. "The evening passed delightfully and rapidly away" for Mrs. Smith, "and I felt quite ashamed to find it almost ten when we rose to depart. Mr. Jefferson gave me some winter melon seed from Malta. He doubts whether it will come to perfection here, on account of the early frosts."

Soon thereafter, Martha and the children left the President's House for the last time as a family. Three years later, a letter from eleven-year-old Ellen advised her grandfather that a room he designed at Monticello was the most beautiful she had ever seen, "without excepting the drawing rooms at Washington."

* * *

Hammuda Pasha, bey of Tunis, a princely vassal of the sultan of Turkey, made a handsome living out of piracy and extortion off the Barbary Coast of North Africa. On April 15, 1801, a month after Jefferson's inauguration, the "bashaw," as Americans called him, had sent a letter to Washington City that assured the new president of his high regard. As a good sign of friendship in return, he expected forty cannon, which "will not appear in the least extraordinary to you" in light of the bashaw's friendly treatment of American ships, "different from others," while he patiently awaited the gifts the Adams administration had promised. "Hoping to see that good harmony which happily subsists between us continued and remain undisturbed," the pirate prince prayed to "Almighty God to preserve you."

Jefferson had replied that the American "tokens of esteem" (promised by treaty before his time) were on their way, but the ruler of Tripoli (one of the bashaw's rival criminals) had made unacceptable demands, and the United States meant to rely on its strength, not "dishonorable condescensions," for its right to ply the seas. A squadron was on its way to the Mediterranean to protect American commerce, Jefferson wrote, under orders to respect the flags and subjects of the bashaw, whose demand for heavy arms was ignored.

In March of 1803, another letter from the bashaw had arrived in perfect French. Hammuda Pasha, "Prince of Princes of Tunis, the City Well Guarded, the Abode of Happiness," liked the gifts he had received; but "I must not hide from you that I nevertheless do not see myself treated with the same distinction and respect as your other friends." (Bigger bribes had gone from the Adams administration to Tripoli, and Hammuda had found out.) He would now be "infinitely pleased" by the gift of a thirty-six-gun frigate. The letter came through the U.S. consul at Tunis, who enclosed a coded note. Hammuda was a cunning man, William Eaton wrote, never stupid enough to think he would get such a ship. Its refusal would be a pretext to plunder American vessels, but eight hundred United States Marines could destroy his pirate navy in a surprise attack on the Abode of Happiness's harbor, which Eaton was hot to see.

On Friday, November 29, 1805, the morning after "a day of feasting in New England, that is, of thanksgiving," Senator Plumer told his diary, he made a courtesy call at the President's House and found him chatting with a Tennessee Republican congressman, an Irish-born veteran of the Revolution. The president had outdone himself in footwear—"white hose, ragged slippers with his toes out"—and his hair was unbrushed. He was telling the Tennessean "with much apparent indifference" (dry wit lost on Plumer) that a purchase of land from the Creeks had been a *fair* bargain, but we might have done better with a bribe. The Southern congressman left when some colleagues from Vermont dropped by. As Jefferson chatted with the New Englanders, Plumer noticed in his hand a penciled note of the Vermonters' names.

In midconversation, a cannon saluted in the distance as a frigate sailed into the Navy Yard. Jefferson said the ship brought an ambassador from Tunis, who would board at Stelle's Hotel at government expense, the cost to be covered by the sale of his gifts. One of the congressmen said the bashaw had showed us respect by sending an ambassador. Jefferson called it a necessity. The American squadron interdicting the shores of Tripoli had seized a Tunisian warship and its two captured vessels as they tried to run the blockade. When the bashaw threatened revenge, Commodore John Rodgers had sailed his guns into Tunis's harbor, causing the bashaw to send an ambassador to negotiate, and here the ambassador was. Plumer called bribes a humiliation, and Jefferson agreed, saying none would be paid. The conversation closed on the deadly risk of war with Bonaparte and Spain. Plumer had come to raise all of these things, more useful, he told his diary, than talk "of weather, health & crops, which usually engross the time of these ceremonial visits."

Cut off from Islamic culture by the vast Atlantic Ocean and a vast sea of ignorance, few Americans had ever seen a Moor, typically through the bars of a dungeon or the sights of a gun, still fewer a bashaw's ambassador. Louisa Adams had met an Ottoman official in Berlin. "There is something very singular," she wrote, "in their costume and appearance." The bashaw's theatrical envoy, a Turkish aristocrat in his fifties, was a big, dark, fiercely handsome man with flashing black eyes and a smile. In his hosts' clean-shaven world, his formidable gray beard, half a foot thick ear to ear, was a shock in itself. He moved like a tale from the Arabian Nights in a stunning white turban—twenty yards of cloth in the way of a Turkish crown—a magnificent scarlet jacket embellished with gold and buttoned with precious stones, and a gorgeous cloak embroidered with silver and gold. He wore neither britches nor pantaloons, a bemused American wrote, "but much cloth wound & folded on him in a loose but curious manner" over immaculate white silk hose and bright yellow shoes worked with gold.

Needless to say, the ambassador drew a crowd as he and his entourage disembarked to booming cannon and a drift of half-burnt powder. His face "bespeaks intelligence and integrity," Plumer was soon to say, before he changed his mind on the part about integrity. His name was Siddi Suliman

Mella Menni. Innocently or not, the best his hosts could do was Melli Melli. He called himself the "Ambassador Plenipotentiary from His Excellency the Bashaw of Tunis" when he wished to make an impression, "the poorest slave of God" when he needed something. Some classically educated men called him the ambassador from Carthage.

His long train of servants, "the African savages," an American said, seemed as exotic as he. His animated Ottoman secretary, a talented young artist only lightly exposed to English, struck Plumer as bright and cunning, the word he attached to Burr. Two tall, thin, whiskered aides from Istanbul were athletic men of "more barbarous appearance" than their master, an American woman thought, "inspiring more of dread than any other feeling," but in taverns on the Capitol Hill, they were said to be "strongly inclined to sociability" and undiluted gin. The ambassador's pipe bearer kept his four-foot pipe filled with fine tobacco, which he smoked without end. The rest of his help included a cook; a barber; a translator; three enormous, scarlet-robed African bodyguards; another eye-popping servant or two; and a good Italian band.

After a day of rest, carriages were sent to Stelle's on the Capitol Hill to bring Melli Melli and his side-whiskered Turkish aides to the president. An English expatriate named Janson thought "the pompous forms of Turkish despotism" might clash with Jefferson's clothes. In languid Eastern style, Melli Melli arrived at the President's House in no rush to get started on business. After pleasantries were exchanged, he proposed to return in a day or two, sip coffee, and smoke his pipe. No American could have been a better match for him than Jefferson. They chatted in Italian without a translator, though the ambassador's command of the language fell short of the president's standards. Only days before, Jefferson had sent Madison a note from Tripoli's deposed ruler, whose "barbarous Italian would require more consideration to be perfectly understood than I have time to bestow on it," but he showed more patience now, hoping for peace and intrigued by a chat with such a man as Melli Melli. Famously—or infamously in some quarters—Jefferson had preached respect not only for the Catholic, the Quaker, and the Jew, but also for the "Mahometan, the Hindoo," and the "infidel of every denomination," a virtue he had little chance to practice.

The Barbary pirate emissaries made a lifelong impression on his grandchildren, still in Washington at the time. Four-year-old Virginia recalled in old age the brilliantly lit room where her grandfather received them, their dazzling dress, an unexpected kiss from Melli Melli's secretary, and talk of exotic presents that excited "my childish curiosity," but she never got to see the "beautiful specimens of Oriental luxury and taste," much less keep any. "My grandfather did not allow them to be brought to the President's House" before they were displayed for sale. Her mother coveted a fabulous Eastern shawl that the Moors had meant for her, but when Mrs. Madison went to buy it, it was gone. Melli Melli brought a mare for Madison and a black Arabian stallion for Jefferson. Early on a Saturday afternoon, Plumer passed him on his way to present them. Two African servants preceded his carriage, both of them leading a horse. The stunning Arabian caught the senator's eye, but the mare seemed unremarkable. "What will the President do with them?" He made profitable use of the Arabian before it was sold. At the presidential stable, a congressman's mare was "put to" the stallion for a stud fee paid to the Treasury.

Janson thought Jefferson overindulged Melli Melli's love of ease and prestige. To keep away the crowds and the taunting boys who followed him, the ambassador was given a military guard—"preceded by music," Janson said, which might have been a droll exaggeration were it not for his Italian band—as well as a carriage and a driver. He rolled around the capital "in luxury and sloth" as he and the secretary of state negotiated without effect until Madison grew impatient, withdrew Melli Melli's guard, and put him on a budget. An admirer of attractive young women, he was known for doing them the favor of holding them close under his cloak, simply because it "possessed many *virtues* desirable to those without families." Mrs. Madison was his favorite, Mrs. Adams said, given her status as "the reigning Sultana at the Court of Mr. Jefferson." His fellow diplomat Augustus Foster found Melli Melli a bright, "conversable" man, who shared some of Foster's high-hat London friends and enriched "our Corps Diplomatique," especially since Britain was at war with France and Spain, which barred the British diplomat from fellowship with their ministers.

At the height of the buzz he stirred, Jefferson issued eight invitations to dine with Melli Melli and his two lieutenants. For exotica alone, no ticket could have been more prized, and John Quincy Adams made the list. Nearly all of the president's family who were old enough to come without risking an embarrassing remark would be there. The billets of invitation did not mention the Muslim holy season of Ramadan, during which, Adams knew, "the Turks fast while the sun is above the horizon," but the usual 3:30 dinner hour was dropped, and the billets were specific: "Dinner will be on the table precisely at sunset." The sun went down at 4:49 with American stomachs growling, a respectful accommodation to the ambassador.

Adams was not impressed by the respect he showed in return. Melli Melli and his aides came half an hour late, having had to wait for sundown to come down from the Capitol Hill, which Jefferson had overlooked. The ambassador saluted the president and his hungry guests, and "proceeded to retire and smoke his pipe." With dinner more than ready, Jefferson asked him to smoke it on the spot, which he did, and took from a gold-and-diamond box a pinch of costly snuff scented with the oil of rose petals, very agreeable to some Americans. His secretary peddled it about town at fifty cents a vial. When the party went in to dinner, Adams watched Melli Melli dig in. Apparently unafraid of the risk of pork or wine folded into a sauce, he "freely partook of the dishes on the table without enquiring into the cookery."

The company was carefully chosen. Martha and her auburn-haired daughter Anne were the only females, perhaps in deference to Islamic sensibilities. A former chargé d'affaires at Tunis played the interpreter. Adams, the only Federalist, contributed a bipartisan touch and a famous name. The inimitable John Randolph of Roanoke added oddity and wit. ("I have been a skeptic," he would later tell a friend, "a professed scoffer, glorying in my infidelity and vain of the ingenuity with which I could defend it. Prayer never crossed my mind but in scorn.") Senator Samuel Smith of Maryland was a powerful friend of Jefferson's and the secretary of the navy's brother, which may have signaled strength to a pirate's ambassador. Pennsylvania's senator George Logan and Congressman Joseph Nicholson of Maryland were Jefferson's close friends, Senator Samuel Latham Mitchill of New York a fellow philosopher. Far from taken with Melli Melli, Mitchill soon said on the Senate floor that the government should not have given "this half-savage the dignified title of ambassador." He deserved no more deference than an Indian chief.

Melli Melli sat on the president's right and reported that a visiting delegation of Cherokees had paid him a diplomatic courtesy call. Having taken a good look, he suspected their ancestors came from Yemen, and asked them which prophet was their messenger of God—Abraham, Jesus, or Mohamed. None of these, they said. The Great Spirit consulted no one and communed with them unaided. Melli Melli's reply had not been welcoming, or so he told the president: "You are all vile Heretics!" Pressing the point, he asked how Jefferson could prove the Indians' descent from Adam. Many members of Congress feared that Jefferson did not believe in anyone's descent from Adam, and his reply got around the Capitol Hill. "It is difficult," he said.

When Martha and Anne retired to the Oval Room, as ladies did, Melli Melli followed them in with his ponderous pipe, and his secretaries stayed with the men to enjoy a glass of wine, which Adams thought "they did not venture to do in his presence." The senator must not have been looking when the president's grandson Jeff, placed between the secretaries, followed orders to keep their silver goblets full, which he found himself doing repeatedly when their master turned his head. The expatriot Charles Janson later claimed they would drink nearly as much hard liquor "as a London coal heaver would of porter," which they proved at the bar of Stelle's Hotel.

The dinner did Melli Melli no good. After Madison convinced him that the United States would consider restitution for the bashaw's seized ships but not a cent for tribute, the ambassador's plea turned personal. If his mission succeeded to his master's satisfaction, praise would go only to God. If he came back defeated, the bashaw's displeasure "might operate against me individually, to an extent which no adequate idea can be formed by the inhabitants of this country." (Among other memorable means, the bashaw could express his disappointment by having one's feet beaten off to the ankle and leaving him to die.) Madison sympathized but was not moved.

* * *

Early in December of 1805, as tensions with Britain stretched thin, Senator Plumer was glad to see Jefferson's annual message stronger and more warlike than any he had sent before. Something about his position felt "more noble, liberal & just than any he ever before avowed."

On December 22, Augustus Foster watched a second band of stunning Plains Indians sent back by Lewis and Clark ride down the Pennsylvania Avenue in diverse regalia, two dozen men and boys of ten Western tribes on white men's saddles, cheering the end of their journey with a "song of joy and triumph" and rattles of hollow gourd. By horse, stage, and water, they had traveled as much as 1,800 miles, the most distant people yet to come east, and they raised such a cry as they passed the President's House, Foster wrote, that the sound seemed to echo through Washington City. Two groups of men kept their distance from one another, for the Osage, led by their chief the Orator, were at war with the Sauk, whose moccasins were shaped so tightly to their feet that they seemed to be barefoot. Their French Canadian interpreters and American guides rode just ahead of the Indians. As if to impress his mother with Barbary and tribal envoys in town at the same time, Foster told her "I am here in the midst of Africans and savages."

The Orator wore a white man's coat, his left eye circled with green and white paint. The rest of his face was bright red. The head of his impressive tomahawk, a blade on one side and a pipe on the other, was a product of the North West Company, a Canadian fur trading enterprise. Two young warriors followed him closely, their faces painted red, their ears green, naked to the waist in winter with blankets around their middles and deerskin pants and moccasins. Some of the others had painted or streaked their heads and faces in black. One handsome boy of about sixteen wore a crest of red feathers and a broad streak of light green paint. Foster thought he looked terrific.

Most of the twenty-one chiefs of the Pawnee, Little Osage, Kansas, Iowa, Pottawatomie, Oto, Missouri, Sauk, Fox, and Sioux nations were "strangers to us," General Wilkinson had written from Saint Louis, but some had fought Americans, and some had fought each other from time immemorial. Now their chiefs had been coaxed into a monthlong trek to be awed with American might and filled with the wisdom of peace. Falling in with the common view, Plumer was impressed by the Osage, whom he found to be a quiet, polite people, an opinion not shared by their neighbors.

Fascinated by the Western Indians, Augustus Foster, of all people, recognized them as gentlemen, and had them to dinner. Their behavior in his home surely matched how they acted in Jefferson's. They would not touch a fork or spoon until they saw what he did with his, "particularly observant not to commit the slightest impropriety." The President's House must have awed them, but they never gave it away, knowing that awe was the point. Taken to the Navy Yard, an Osage chief inspected its warships indifferently before the Americans had him pull a cannon's lanyard without warning him what would happen. The weapon bucked and roared, and the chief never twitched. Jefferson told a friend that for all the marvels he had shown his Western visitors at his table over the years, expecting shock, he had only seen it once. Astonished by ice at a hot July dinner, a chief took a piece in his hand, flinched at finding it cold, and passed it to his startled peers for an animated discussion. Speaking through the interpreter, the chief said unabashedly they had heard of the wonders in the east and thought they were lies, but nothing so shocking as this. Perhaps they had no fear of being thought to be cowed by ice.

Based on observation, Augustus Foster thought Jefferson was as fond of the Indians as if they *were* his children, out of charity, the diplomat surmised, and "because they were savages," men of nature in a drawing room. He paid their chiefs far more deference than the puffed up Europeans, "which annoyed not a little Mr. Merry." Purely out of duty, Merry came with Foster to the New Year's Day reception of 1806, which had grown far beyond its beginnings. Followed by a crowd on a springlike day down the Pennsylvania Avenue, the Indians came in paint, with tomahawks on their belts and "all the splendor of savage royalty," in the words of Mrs. Smith. On a horse with a gilded saddle led by two African slaves, Melli Melli arrived like Aladdin, gorgeous in a great white turban, scarlet coat, purple cloak, and silk slippers, all worked with gold, trailed by turbaned aides and American gawkers.

CHAPTER 15

In the Great Hall of Entrance, the Marine Band played in their scarlet uniforms, much improved in September by the absorption of fifteen Sicilian musicians, arrived from North Africa on the USS *Constitution*, a superb band of music recruited by the marine commandant Lt. Col. William Ward Burrows, which Jefferson was said to have suggested. Accustomed to a Barbary prince's palace, the ensemble's Italian maestro had found himself in "a desert" composed of two or three taverns and a few scattered "cottages or log huts, called the City of Washington, the metropolis of the United States of America." Now they played, said Mrs. Smith, for "ambassadors and ministers of state, colliers and tinkers, and the Lord knows what," a distasteful mix, she thought, black and white in Sunday clothes, "fifty or sixty somebodies at most," the rest of the sort "no one sees on other occasions." Perched in every alcove were tables of wine and punch, delicate cakes, ice creams, and oranges, and a jelly enjoyed with a spoon. The crowd of common folk spilled into the Mammoth Room and up the steps of the new grand staircase, parting for their betters. At the following year's event, Jefferson would hire constables to manage the crowd.

The Indians were at ease in the midst of it all. Mrs. Smith had expected discomfort in these graceful "sons of the forest." Instead "they stood in a kind of dignified and majestic stillness." As Merry and Foster arrived, the chiefs were entering the Oval Room with their guides, and Jefferson was bowing them in, looking respectable in his plain black suit. Foster called it "his gala dress." He bowed to Merry and Foster too, asked Merry how he did, and walked right past him to the end of the room where the Indians had gone, "wholly taken up with his natives." Merry told Foster he would not be treated so, and they headed for the door. On their way out, Merry told Jefferson's friend Senator Logan why they were leaving, knowing he would pass it on. If it cost the president sleep, he made no record of it.

On January 4, Jefferson addressed the chiefs at the President's House with Dearborn at his side. In a message sent back to Washington, Lewis and Clark had assessed their tribes. The Kansas, they said, were "dissolute, lawless banditti," the Pawnee hospitable to whites, the Little Osage in "continual warfare with their neighbors," the Missouri near extinction, their Sauk and Fox enemies having reduced them to fewer than three hundred souls. Now the native envoys to Thomas Jefferson wore their chief coats with upright crests of hair or black, flowing tresses dressed with foxtails or feathers, according to their tribes. Their ornaments included brooches of carved bone, shell, or polished wood; Jefferson peace medals; the decorated bills of birds; silver nose rings like coins, heart shaped or round; jingling bells acquired in trade and sewn like buttons to their clothes. One had rubbed his face with powdered ore of cinnabar. Others colored half their features black or red or streaked with daubs of green. Some wore no paint at all. There were several great men like the Sauk chief Jumping Fish, attended by youths like the Pawnee warrior the Wolf. Some were tall old men, a Kentucky newspaper had said when they passed through Frankfort, "and the dignity of their manners is truly philosophic and impressive. It is said there are several orators among them."

Jefferson gave the address he had given other chiefs and would give again to more, with minor variations. Two interpreters translated, one in the Siouan tongue, the other in the Algonquin. His genuine warmth was plain, and the cautionary undercurrent too. He thanked them for risking the journey to "this side of our island" and the Great Spirit for his protection en route. "My children, we are strong," he said, as if they could not see. "We are numerous as the stars in the heavens, and we are all gun men. Yet we live in peace with all nations." He hoped they would visit the cities on "the edge of the great water" and see "how many friends and brothers they had where the sun was rising," and be guided safely home to tell their people what they saw.

To deliver their reply they had chosen their most respected man, the principal chief of the Little Osage, a band of hardly more than a thousand men, women, and children encamped along a river in a land to be known as Kansas. Their chief was called the Wind. The Wind rose and spoke through Paul Chouteau, half-Québécois, half-Osage, reputed to be the only English-speaking man fluent in their Siouan dialect. "Lofty," a reporter called the sound of it, "and not inharmonious." A Canadian said it was "sung, so to speak," slowly and deliberately, which gave each word "a great force of expression," and the Wind began to speak to Jefferson and Dearborn in the spirit of the day. "My grandfather and my father," he said. "It is with an open heart that we receive your hands," welcomed to this "Grand Lodge of prosperity" and "numbered among your most cherished children." Their delegation had rejected "the crowing of bad birds" who had warned them not to come here and be killed. Their interpreters had told them "our fathers were good and would pity us," and wished to know their new red children, "and we see that you are as worthy of pity as we."

White flatterers came to their fathers making promises they would break, said the Wind, "and your children suffer." He believed his fathers meant well, "but look sharp," he told the president, for the whites took too much fur for too few goods. His children had seen the beloved man of the president's household and "heard the words you put in his mouth," that their fathers wished to meet them. "Here we are," he said, happy to see and hear their brethren of the rising sun. But "fathers, meditate on what you say. You tell us your children on this side of the Mississippi hear your word. You are mistaken." His people were glad that the

French, the Spanish, and the English were gone, but the beloved man was gone too, far away, and could do them no more justice.

"You say you are as numerous as the stars in the skies," the Wind went on. So much the better, for then they would punish the red men who killed their red children and tell their white children who thought "truth will not reach your ears" to keep their fathers' word. The Wind said his people were powerful too, but did not wish to fight. "Shut the mouth of your children who speak war," he said, stop the arms of those who raise the tomahawk over our heads, and "then we will confess that we have good fathers" and tell the people so. The chiefs would speak the truth to the people, said the Wind, for "you know that the truth must come out of the mouth of a father."

* * *

Many delegations of half-assimilated Eastern tribes passed through the President's House with far less fanfare than the Westerners drew, though troops of boys followed them in the streets. Chickasaws arrived from the Deep South on January 12, many in old cocked hats and one in a Spanish officer's tunic, green faced with white. Cherokees in white men's dress reminded Foster of the people of the South of France. More than just attracting curiosity, which they did, Indians were feared, which made them thrilling. When Louisa Adams and her sister found themselves alone with a group of Cherokees who came to their door and insisted on hearing the fortepiano, the sisters obliged, concealed their fear, and gave them ribbons, beads, and feathers from their own wardrobes, relieved to see them go.

In 1806, General Wilkinson sent east from Saint Louis an Arikara chief with his own escorting officer, an interpreter, and a letter that called him a great man. Lewis had persuaded him to come against the will of his people, a long-haired nation also known as the Ree, who valued him too highly to risk, a warrior, a linguist, a cartographer, and a well-traveled source of information. "He is certainly a <u>learned</u> savage," Wilkinson wrote, conversant in eleven languages and a master of "dumb communication," the only form of speech at the annual council of the dozen or more tribes he knew. So ingrained were his sign language skills he was "more indebted to his fingers than his tongue." So valuable could he be as "an instrument of humanity" and a voice of U.S. policy that Wilkinson recommended his return as soon as possible "by a military escort loaded with presents."

His name was Too Né. Proud in his blue chief's coat, an imposing old man with light hazel eyes and rings in his ears, the sign language master brought to

Jefferson, carefully packed in a pouch, a recommendation from Lewis and Clark and a map. Senator Mitchill judged such maps "a most impressive proof of the proficiency" of these "children of nature." Too Né liked to show on his map the place where he had met Louis and Clark, his country's location, the Missouri River, the domains of many tribes—including the Arapaho in a land of red earth, tinted red on his map, and the distant Apache—the lands of "a nation of whites, with blue and gray eyes and light colored hair," the route he had taken east, and the President's House, beside which he had drawn a sword, a gun, ammunition, and tobacco, suggesting the gifts he expected. Jefferson spoke of him for days and honored him at "an Indian dinner." He was known for ending his descriptions of the West with the sign for truth, drawing a finger from his heart to his mouth "thence straight to the auditor or spectator." To call out a lie, "the line comes crooked from any part of the abdomen & on issuing from the lips, splits, diverges & crosses in every direction."

Hoping to trace an ancestral connection to Europe, the president was fascinated by Indian languages. He had lately told Senator Pickering he had identified about a hundred, but when some of Pickering's friends dined with him later, the senator wrote, "that number was materially reduced." Pickering was convinced that one of Jefferson's ungodly goals was to find vast numbers of such languages, "calculate how many ages must elapse" to account for them, and insist from the results that the scriptural chronology of creation was wrong.

The sign language master's visit to the capital overlapped with the arrival of a New Yorker named William Dunlap, a painter, playwright, and theatrical producer. Dunlap saw little that made him proud, though the Capitol was a sight on its field of rubble and scattered blocks of stone, "towering like some antique ruin & wanting nothing but some colossal columns with their heads at their feet to remind one of Rome or Persepolis." Two days after a snowstorm, the frogs had "already commenced their town meetings" in the heart of the metropolis, though their orators were not fully tuned up.

But Dunlap was impressed when he dropped in uninvited at "the magnificent house of the president," surrounded by clustered homes, an unfinished church, and a partly built house, and was warmly received. "Yes," he told his wife, "I have seen, touched & heard the great man. A fresh sheet of paper must be devoted to him, and all he said and all he did," starting with the shock of finding him "*en dishabille* and slippered" with his hand out in welcome. Jefferson's effortless banter started with the early spring. He too had heard the frogs, and logged their debut. He spoke of French gardening and the more tasteful English kind, which led him to painters like his guest, which led him to "an extraordinary man" from the West, two hundred miles beyond the lands of any tribe yet encountered, adept at many languages and "possessing the art of speaking by signs, of which we have often heard but never before seen an example."

Dunlap had arrived a Jefferson skeptic and went away enthralled. He had begun to copy Gilbert Stuart's new portrait of the president, "so that my poor head is full of Jefferson." Having said that Stuart's portrait of him was the best, Jefferson paid Stuart $100 for it and hung it in the President's House.

* * *

After Melli Melli told Secretary of the Navy Smith he was surprised that a country so fine as the United States would cross an ocean to make war on Tunis, he was scheduled to tour the great cities, to show him what he was up against, the tactic practiced on Indians. By the spring of 1806, Secretary of War Dearborn had found him out as an "avaricious, cunning, swindling man" to be sent on his way "as soon as may be convenient," all the novelty having worn off. But bearing the diplomat no grudge, Jefferson wrote to the bashaw and tried to keep Melli Melli's feet attached to his ankles. He had received the ambassador with great respect, he wrote, and Melli Melli had served his master well; but the bashaw should know "we calculate neither expense nor danger" in defending the freedom of the seas. The taking of his ship was lawful; but the war with Tripoli being over, a better ship would bring the bashaw's ambassador home with other respectful gifts and "my prayers that God will have you, great and good friend, in his holy keeping." No mention was made of tribute, and none was paid.

Pleased with the president's position on bribery, Senator Plumer was softening on him. The more closely he studied Jefferson, he admitted to himself, the more highly he judged his integrity. "I am really inclined to think I have done him injustice." General Washington, his fellow Virginian, had made him secretary of state "with a full & perfect knowledge of him," which spoke very well of the man; but Jefferson knew little of human nature, sophisticate though he was. Trained in intrigue at Versailles, a man of science with "much knowledge of books—of insects—of shells," of whatever charms a virtuoso, "he knows not the human heart." This modest country lawyer from Epping, New Hampshire, thought Thomas Jefferson was naïve, "an infidel in religion—but in every thing else credulous to a fault!" There was too much cunning in him and not enough resolve, but his errors "partake more of credulity than of wickedness."

Flawed as he knew him to be through personal observation, would Plumer have come to like and respect him had he never been to his home, seen his toes poking out of his slippers, watched him dish out his coq au vin and pour his Veuve Clicquot, enjoyed his amusing company, heard him share his stirring memories and tell his improbable tales and confess the shocking price of Hungarian wine?

Plumer pondered his naïveté around the Ides of March 1806, when Aaron Burr threatened Jefferson in the President's House. Having lost the vice presidency he deserved some high office, Burr said; on the one hand he had earned it by helping make Jefferson president; on the other he could do him much harm, but preferred to be "on different ground." Jefferson had been warned that Burr was hatching treason but misread him as threatening some exposé. He replied that he had never done a thing he feared to see "fully laid open," that Burr held no office, despite his talents, because the public had no confidence in him. Almost unimaginably, Jefferson had him back within a month, and not just to any dinner but a star-studded sitting of his cabinet, Turreau, and Melli Melli.

On Wednesday morning, April 2, 1806, Plumer spoke with Jefferson for over an hour, having come to the President's House not for form but to vet the national interest, which they did alone, a first in their five-year acquaintance. Plumer had heard that a bargain had been struck with the bashaw of Tunis on dishonorable terms, which Jefferson assured him was false. The bashaw's captured ships would be returned, but no bribe would be paid, and the Senate should postpone its review of the treaty. There was much talk of character at this meeting, the character of emperors and kings, of bashaws and their emissaries. Plumer had changed his mind on Jefferson for the better and Melli Melli for the worse: "that half savage, half brute" should not have been given the respect an ambassador was due. Unavoidable, Jefferson said. To keep peace with the Barbary princes, "the irregular conduct of their ministers" must pass unnoticed.

They discussed Louisiana and the great powers. The prospect of peace with Britain was high, Jefferson said, and Bonaparte, "an astonishing man," meant to make a federation of kings with their emperor at its head, but he had no quarrel with us, and "our peace he will not disturb." Plumer disagreed at times, but plainly relished his treatment as a friend and fellow patriot in the President's House, flattered by his attention. "He appeared pleased with my visiting him."

John Quincy Adams told Plumer the next day that Madison had pressed him to ratify the Tunisian treaty immediately. Plumer said Jefferson had just told him it should be postponed. How could these things be reconciled? They could not, Adams said. There was no placing confidence in these men.

In the spring of 1806, Jefferson's presidency was turning sour. In no position to wage war in a war-torn world, he led a small navy, next to no standing army, a fiercely divided country with one side tilting toward England, the other toward France, and a people who considered taxes un-American. His foreign policy was anchored, in part, on the notion that "the good men of the world form a nation of their own, and when promoting the well-being of others never ask of what country they are." The other part rested, as his predecessors' had, on keeping the country's head down and avoiding wars with the great powers until it could win one. Referring to France and Britain, Jefferson understood that "the Mammoth cannot swim, nor the Leviathan move on dry land, and if we will keep out of their way, they cannot get at us."

Yet he knew he must "correct the dangerous error that we are a people whom no injuries can provoke to war." Escalating impressments of American seamen and British and French contempt for U.S. neutrality in the Napoleonic Wars provoked him to call for a Non-Importation Act barring key British goods, which Congress promptly passed. On April 25, a British ship fired a warning shot off New York Harbor that killed an American sailor. Turreau informed Paris that Jefferson was sick with worry "and has grown ten years older." Appalled by the thought of a slide toward another English war, Pickering wrote a friend that whatever Thomas Jefferson "might have been in better times," he had done more as president to "corrupt and debase" his country "than any other cause since the Revolution." America's safety from Napoleon was inseparable from Britain's. "Once more then I say (what in the lapse of more than thirty years I have not said), God save the King!"

16

IT WAS A GOOD LESSON FOR THEM

In July of 1806, having told a friend who had sent him tulip bulbs that "the misfortune of my present situation" included "not a foot of ground enclosed" at the President's House, Jefferson left for home and planted them at Monticello. He did not bring his enslaved apprentice cook, Edy Fossett, whose husband, Joe Fossett was there, or James, their three-year-old son. Virginia law did not recognize slave marriages, but Jefferson did.

As a ten-year-old boy, Joe Fossett, a Hemings on his mother's side, had been one of many enslaved child laborers in Jefferson's nailhouse who cut nails from iron bars with hammers in a hot, smoky space from dawn until dusk. He spent most of the rest of his time fetching wood and water, making fires, and waiting at table. Having proved himself an able nail maker, he was chosen at sixteen for the blacksmith's trade. Jefferson's overseer knew his skills: "a very fine workman" he was, "could do anything it was necessary to do with steel or iron."

On the last day of July 1806, Jefferson wrote a nervous note at Monticello and handed it to John Perry, his head carpenter, to take to Joseph Dougherty in Washington. Skipping his usual pleasantries, he went straight to a command to keep his embarrassment secret: "In the first place, say not a word on this subject but to Mr. Perry, who delivers this letter to you." Perry had come "in pursuit of a young mulatto man, called Joe, 26 years of age, who ran away from here" two nights ago. Inexperienced at explaining himself to servants, the master of Monticello explained himself now in shame. Joe had fled "without the least word of difference with anybody & indeed having never in his life received a blow from any one." He seemed to have taken the road to Washington, and he "may possibly trump up some story to be taken care of at the President's House til he can make up his mind which way to go; or perhaps he will make himself known to Edy only, as he was formerly connected with her."

Joe was "formerly" connected to Edy because she was in Washington City at the pleasure of the president. Joe went to her now out of love, anxiety, or both, perhaps after John Freeman or Jack Shorter told him something disconcerting at Monticello. Edy was in her late teens and permitted to socialize in Washington City's black community. She and her husband may not have seen each other for several years.

Jefferson's note to Dougherty, "relying on your exertions," instructed him to search for Joe with "all possible diligence" and bring others to help take him if he was found, "as he is strong & resolute." He was all of that for sure, a blacksmith in his prime determined to reach his wife and child. After he was taken, Jefferson wrote, Joe should be "delivered" to Mr. Perry, who would lodge himself near the President's House and "keep within doors himself, least he should be seen by the runaway," who knew him.

Dougherty reported to Jefferson the day Perry arrived. He had set out immediately to find "your boy," he wrote, based on Perry's description of his clothes and the marks on his body, and returned empty handed, but "got wind" of him and took him without resistance "in the President's Yard, going from the President's House." Whether he had reached his wife and child Dougherty did not say. Perry had him jailed overnight and brought him back to Monticello. Edy stayed in Washington with their son. Two days later, Jefferson's maître d' Étienne Lemaire made a typically kind remark in a letter to the president and added a rare request. "The poor unhappy mulatto" did not resist his capture Lemaire wrote, and "he well deserves a pardon for that." In Jefferson's eyes, Joe had committed a forgivable crime of passion when he went to his wife and child. In the following year, he put him in charge of the blacksmith shop, which local farmers patronized, and paid him a sixth of the profits for any work he chose to do after hours.

On September 25, Jefferson wrote Lemaire from Monticello and advised him to buy winter vegetables for the President's House, followed by two terse sentences: "We have bad news for Edy. Her sister Patty died a few days ago of a dropsy." He added no condolences. He did say John Freeman had been feverish for six days. "Should he recover even quickly, he will be too weak to return with me." Jefferson brought Freeman back and forth to Monticello because he was useful. He had no need for Edy there, and Edy stayed in Washington, instead of enjoying the two months with her family that he enjoyed with his. She would have no chance to nurse her sister or say goodbye. Lemaire surely broke the news gently.

Always pained by his own family partings, Jefferson would later advise Dougherty, who was coping with a troubled marriage, that strains between husbands and wives never matched the suffering that their separation caused. Not long after leaving Monticello in October, he wrote morosely to Martha. He had recently kept the Fossetts apart and seemed unaware of the irony: "Having been so long in the midst of a family, the lonesomeness of this place is more intolerable than I ever found it. My daily rides are too sickening for want of some interest in the scenes I pass over; and indeed I look over the two ensuing years as the most tedious of my life." In October, Isaac Coles started a second stint as his secretary, Burwell having launched a successful run for Congress. Coles would stay on through the end of Jefferson's presidency.

Edith Fossett was joined that fall by her enslaved eighteen-year-old sister-in-law, Frances Gillette Hern, called Fanny, also sent up from Monticello to learn the art of French cuisine. Edy and Fanny were nearly the same age. Perhaps they were friends. With Edy's help and company, the transition would have been easier for Fanny than it had been for Edy and Ursula before her, dropped friendless one by one into an alien world. Fanny's enslaved husband, David Hern, had earned Jefferson's trust as his wagoner, often working far from home. Now he brought his own young wife to Washington. After two nights and one day with her at the President's House, he drove himself back alone. He was twenty-two. She was eighteen.

Unlike Edy and Joe Fossett, Fanny and Davy Hern saw each other in Washington a few days and nights several times a year when Davy carted goods back and forth to Monticello. On one of his trips to the President's House, he and Fanny quarreled furiously, and Jefferson's overseer never forgot the consequences. "Davy was jealous of his wife," Edmund Bacon recalled decades later, "and I reckon with good reason," for Fanny saw her husband only rarely. Intolerant of disharmony anywhere, especially in his home, Jefferson summoned Bacon to take Davy and Fanny to Alexandria to be sold and probably separated. Unlike some local slave trader, Bacon could be counted on to keep the transaction quiet. In the residence of the president of the United States, he recalled, Davy and Fanny "wept, and begged, and made good promises" and eventually "begged the old gentleman out of it. But it was a good lesson for them."

* * *

On October 26, 1806, Jefferson read "with unspeakable joy" a report from Meriwether Lewis that he and his men were safe in Saint Louis and on their way back to Washington with a Mandan chief. His fears, the president replied, "had begun to be felt awfully," and the Mandan should be told "I have already opened my arms to receive him." Two months later, Lewis reached Washington after three and a half years at risk. Clark had gone to friends in Virginia. Encamped by the Pacific almost exactly a year earlier, Lewis had dreamed of telling tales of his adventures at Jefferson's table on New Year's Day 1807, "when in the bosom of our friends we hope to participate in the mirth and hilarity of the day." Now he was free to live it, and presumably did.

Lewis had brought the Mandan chief Coyote, his ten-year-old son, his French Canadian interpreter, and the interpreter's family. Generous to their friends and fearsome to their enemies, the Mandans wore their hair "thrown back from the forehead," taking "no small pains to arrange it," and had traded with the French since the 1730s. The Quebecois called Coyote *Le Grand Blanc*, for his light skin and European features, common among the Mandans, who had welcomed Lewis and Clark 1,500 miles from home and helped them survive the winter. Passing through again on their way home, the explorers had convinced Coyote to come with them. Osages led by a French Canadian fur trader had reached Washington a few days earlier, and Jefferson had a celebratory dinner on a windy evening in January, seating Mandans, Osage, and Quebecois together.

The celebrations of Lewis's heroism were as extravagant as they should have been, and he stayed at the President's House through the winter, regaling riveted dignitaries with his tales. To excite national pride and interest in the West and pursue the Enlightenment ideal of a manor house improving its community, Jefferson made the Great Hall of Entrance a museum of Indian costumes, weapons, and ornaments, and pelts, crops, and antlers, all of it collected by Lewis and Clark and Zebulon Pike, mounted on the walls and displayed on tables. It did not melt Senator Pickering's heart. "Our chief magistrate seems to be absorbed in what might amuse a minute philosopher," Pickering told his wife, "but which is a reproach to one who holds the reins of an empire."

Whether Jefferson led an empire or not, the reins no longer enticed him. On January 13, he told John Dickinson, a sometime ally and sometime rival in the days of the Revolution, he was tired of his office and could do no more good with it than many others who wanted it. "To myself personally it brings nothing but unceasing drudgery and daily loss of friends." He had warned the country in November that persons he did not name were plotting a private attack on Spain's American dominions. Now it was publicly known they were led by Aaron Burr, whose plans for a personal empire were said to include parts of the United States. The sensational Burr conspiracy stole attention from Lewis and Clark's return and shadowed much of the rest of Jefferson's presidency. His power, nonetheless, had never been so full, alarming even a Republican from

Vermont who told a Federalist colleague that if Jefferson asked them to do it, Congress would repeal the gospels.

* * *

Anthony Merry had taken his last leave of Jefferson on November 3, 1806, recalled by a new pro-American government, purportedly based on ill health that did not exist and "other circumstances" that did, including his hostility to the president. His successor, Lord David Montague Erskine, was happy to be called Mr. Erskine. Jefferson's rapport with Merry had been doomed at first sight. In Erskine he found a friend. Just thirty years old, educated at Winchester, then at Trinity College, Cambridge, Erskine was a liberal Whig, sympathetic to Jefferson's philosophy and comfortable with his style. Trinity had been turning out proper English snobs since 1546, Winchester since 1382, but Erskine, born in 1776 to a celebrated Scottish barrister, a champion of civil rights who had defended Tom Paine and was now lord chancellor in the new Whig government, was not among them. Erskine was tall and gangly with a face scarred by childhood acne (which Gilbert Stuart's portrait did not conceal), an affable, unpretentious young man as confident in society as Merry was not.

Augustus Foster stayed on as Erskine's secretary and did not quite know what to make of him. Having been to America before, Erskine had seen in its people an obsessive pursuit of wealth and contempt for British manners and was not amused. As if to prove his point, Frances Few met him at dinner, and "some of the twirls & twitches of English manners" put her off, though she liked him just the same. But Erskine was cut more like Jefferson than Merry. He "is everything you please, in a way," Foster wrote, but "never in my life did I know a man of so little vanity, or with less concern for dignity of behavior. He would have gone in boots to visit the President but for me, and cares nothing about driving up constantly to his house or palace (which it may be called for its size) in a dirty hack without a servant." Americans held the post of British minister in high esteem, Foster wrote, "but when it is frisked and jerked about upon the shoulders of a hail fellow well met sort of man, I confess it gives me pain."

It gave Jefferson pleasure. Here was a British envoy he liked and could talk to freely. His secretary Isaac Coles liked him too. After Coles paid Erskine a courtesy call on the day after Merry presented him, Erskine called on Coles two days later at the President's House, launching a full-blown friendship. Merry would have sooner befriended his bootmaker. After their visit, Coles walked Erskine to the door and found Lady Erskine waiting in a common hack, playing with their four-year-old son, the future Baron Erskine, whose middle name was Americus.

Coles made a startled diary entry. "What in the name of heaven will Mrs. Merry say when she hears this? How undignified. This is downright republicanism."

Lady Frances Erskine was fondly said to be the same sweet soul she had been as Fanny Cadwalader, a Philadelphia merchant's daughter. According to Catharine Mitchill, the worldly senator's wife from New York, a better bargain could not have been struck than the replacement of Mrs. Merry with Lady Erskine, "chatty and unceremonious," attractive, petite, with great black eyes strikingly painted by Gilbert Stuart, "a fine and accomplished American."

* * *

On December 27, Senator Plumer came down from the Capitol Hill to dine with Jefferson as a friend as much as a Federalist. A regular now, Plumer told his diary he made a habit of saying little in the Oval Room before the party moved to the table, dessert had been served, "and we have drank a glass or two." From this he recoiled as soon as he wrote it. "I do not mean that the president is under the influence of wine, for he is very temperate." Plumer sat next to him more often than not, was "placed" there he said, *pêle-mêle* trumped by wooing. As most of the evenings progressed, the guests "in little parties eagerly talking" exercised their rights to free speech, "and even two glasses of wine oft times renders a temperate man communicative."

Having had his glass or two, Jefferson confided in his friend what he knew of the Burr conspiracy, who was in it, against it, foreign or domestic, an astonishingly loose-lipped rundown of the perilous ins and outs of a threat to the republic itself, some of it accurate, some not. The president was astonished by the newspaper accounts, he said. Maybe one in a hundred paragraphs were true. "And he darkly intimated" that the law should impose some restraint on them. Plumer reminded him of the Constitution, and Jefferson conceded the point. Before they were done, and it must have been an hour by the scope of it, they had talked about Bonaparte, the expense of the Revolution, the wisdom of buying the Floridas, and more.

Having often been Jefferson's guest, the farm boy from Epping, New Hampshire, was a bit of a connoisseur. This evening the president's table was "well furnished" with a fine dinner and a surplus of desserts, "but his wine, except Madeira & Hermitage, not good." He always made his company easy nonetheless, Plumer wrote, and put them in a good mood. His hearing was fading at sixty-three under the eighteen-foot ceiling in the clink and clatter of dozens of pieces of glassware, plate, and cutlery; overlapping conversations; loud bursts of laughter; and requests to pass the salt. He bent his head to listen several times and asked Plumer what he had said. "Age has some effect upon him."

In January of 1807, a new Republican senator named Henry Clay moved into Plumer's boardinghouse with a Republican uncle in Congress and broke its Federalist monopoly. All of twenty-nine, the Kentuckian was a year shy of the minimum age for a Senate seat, a constitutional breach he would later wink away as a juvenile indiscretion. He paid a call at the President's House, where Jefferson convinced him that Burr, his former client, was a traitor. Jefferson had Clay come to dinner three times, once with the Connecticut poet Joel Barlow and the inventor Robert Fulton, who hoped to try a commercial steamboat on the Hudson River if such a thing could be done.

Clay was "a man of pleasure," Plumer sniffed, talented though he was, a man "very fond of amusements," a gambler more than a reader, and a ladies' man to boot, a man who went out most nights and "declaims more than he reasons." Yet Plumer welcomed Republicans to Frost and Quinn's just as much he wished for ecumenical dining at the President's House, for the more men associated together the better they thought of each other. At a Republican colleague's funeral, he lamented that only two other Federalists came, and was driven to the edge of profanity: "Cursed be the spirit of the party!"

Stopping by the President's House one January morning, Plumer found him alone and asked for news from the West, which got them talking about Burr until men with appointments came. Plumer said he would return when the president was at leisure, which Jefferson urged him to do. A few weeks later the president admitted his Federalist friend to the sanctity of his Cabinet and showed him the fragment of his library that he kept in Washington City. The bound and lettered newspapers contained some useful things, he said, unreliable "vehicles of slander and falsehood" though they generally were. Given its loyalty to him, it was no surprise that he thought the *Intelligencer*, "Smith's paper" he called it, was most often correct, but it too could err.

When the moment seemed right, Plumer blurted out "with great freedom" that he planned to write a history of the United States, to take years to do it, to preserve what was daily passing away, and make his politics disappear in neutrality. Jefferson's demeanor changed as Plumer spoke. Sometimes he seemed uneasy, even embarrassed, and sometimes pleased, looking alternately at the senator and the floor. Plumer requested his help, which he said he was eager to give. With scant interruption, he had served his country since the Revolution, he said, and had kept a letterpress, and his letters would enlighten key events. He gave Plumer leave to see State Department documents on any closed matters, suggested other sources, and promised to recruit Madison. His duties took all his time, he said, but he could help in two years, for he would not seek reelection. And this he told a Federalist.

Plumer liked what he heard but not what he saw. He was not entirely sure, but he thought he had upset his friend. There was something uncomfortable there, something like disapproval he was anxious to conceal. Plumer confided Jefferson's surprise and shifting moods to Senator Adams, to whom they made perfect sense. The president could not love history, Adams said. There were elements of his life and character he did not want posterity to see, and Mr. Madison was much the same. "He will suffer in history."

Two weeks later, word reached the President's House that Aaron Burr had been captured in the Mississippi Territory and charged with treason.

* * *

Several members of Congress were accused of making death threats a parliamentary maneuver. Duels were illegal and slipping out of favor; Dr. Rush called them private murders; but the custom was still admired in certain circles, especially in the South. In June of 1806, Jefferson had helped dissuade his son-in-law Thomas Randolph from challenging his explosively eccentric kinsman John Randolph of Roanoke. Cousin John had recently turned on the president and discussed it over dinner with a colleague named Alston. Randolph having poured himself a glass of wine and thrown it in Alston's face, "Alston sent a decanter at his head in return, and these and similar missiles continued to fly to and fro, until there was much destruction of glassware." For John Randolph, violence was a lifetime hobby. In a duel over college debating society politics, he had shot a fellow student in the buttocks. They were reconciled on the spot, presumably standing up. A fellow Virginia congressman called the gentleman from Bizarre as sensitive to criticism as "a man without a skin." On the floor of the House, a colleague from New Jersey called him "a maniac in his straight-jacket," just broken out of his cell.

After Cousin John made a remark that Cousin Thomas took personally, Thomas accused John on the floor of the House of being "leaky" with secrets and threatening duels for political ends. Thomas was not afraid, he said, of "powder, ball, pistol, and steel"; but when John sent a friend to tell him the remark had not been meant for him, Thomas returned to the floor and apologized, which can only have embarrassed his father-in-law. Though they lived in the same house, Jefferson put in writing his anxieties about the Randolphs' bad blood. Terrified of its risks, he wrote Thomas "with an aching heart" that duels were for "striplings of fashion," and "the thinking part of society" condemned them. Thomas had a wife and seven children. His adversary had "a single life of no value to himself or others." Would Thomas take the risk of breaking Martha's heart, condemning her to a lifetime of misery, and costing his children their father? No duel materialized.

Jefferson was close to his other son-in-law, whose loss of Maria drew them closer. Eppes and his three-year-old son Francis continued to live in the President's House when Congress was in session, living links to Maria that could not have pleased Jefferson more. But Eppes was intemperate too. He *did* invite John Randolph to a duel, which mutual friends averted, and came close to challenging Josiah Quincy, who talked his way out without backing down. None of this helped the president. In February 1806, Eppes declared on the House floor that France "demanded" a certain U.S. policy, which incited Senator Pickering to send Jefferson a note. "This sentiment, sir, publicly expressed by your son-in-law, living under your roof, and in your daily conversation" would be "traced up to you as its source." Senator Plumer dined with Jefferson that evening. He seemed "absent" and "in low spirits."

In the winter of 1807, sickness, snow, and single-digit temperatures hit Washington hard, and a rift opened up between Thomas Randolph and Eppes. Their father-in-law had avoided any hint of favor, or tried, but Randolph's dark moods and tepid political appetites contrasted poorly with Eppes's joie de vivre and his vibrant congressional career. Many years later, Ellen Randolph said her father was jealous of Eppes; and their conflicting interests in a division of Jefferson's property put still more strain on the ropes. On Monday, February 16, Jefferson noticed a gloom about Randolph and a tension between his sons-in-law and ignored it; but his instincts were tripped, and Randolph's mood made the president uneasy. Senator Adams dined with him that evening at a table full of Federalists and found him less than cheerful, but the dour Bostonian may have put him in a mischievous mood, as Adams often did. Jefferson launched a sample of "his customary startling stories," Adams wrote that night, including a tale about pears sewn up in bags before he left for France that candied themselves while he was gone.

On a cold, rainy morning two days later, with the "wind very violent from the south," Randolph left the president a note. In a dark fit of pique, triggered by some trivial invitation that Jefferson had offered to Eppes but not him, he had moved out of the President's House and into Frost and Quinn's on the Capitol Hill. It was clear, he wrote like an eight-year-old child, that his father-in-law liked Eppes better.

Jefferson wrote a reply on the spot and asked his former secretary William Burwell, Randolph's friend and fellow congressman, to deliver it. "My very dear sir," it began. "Your letter received this morning has given me a pang under which I am overwhelmed." That anything he had said or done could produce such a thing "I cannot conceive." He had seen Randolph's tension with Eppes, he wrote, but had not guessed its cause. He had worried that Maria's loss might make *Eppes* doubt his affections but had never feared for Randolph's. "I well recollect the invitation which dropped from me to Mr. Eppes the other day in your presence. It was unpremeditated. I felt my error the moment I had uttered it, but it could not be recalled." Maria had loved Eppes, and he had thought the attachment too sacred to give offense. (Was Randolph duly shamed?) He felt more for Randolph than any other man he had known, he said. Any doubt must have come from his failure to show it plainly or "too much sensibility in yourself" (as close as he came to a rebuke). Their estrangement would be a great loss, but a separation from Martha and the children was "a calamity against which I could not bear up."

A friend would deliver the letter, he wrote, conveying face-to-face still more affection and regard. "Your return to the house would indeed be a consolation to me. I leave it to be decided by your own feelings and inclinations." Letter in hand, Burwell sat down with Randolph, who insisted his love and respect for his father-in-law were too deep to damage. He had left "to prevent the possibility of such a thing." What could that have meant? A risk of confrontation with Eppes? Something worse?

Still lost in darkness, Randolph wrote to Jefferson the next day, suspecting that someone had denounced him for joining the Federalists on votes in which Eppes had stayed loyal. "I have been guilty of an error," Jefferson replied. Loving Randolph as "a son (for I protest I know no difference)," he had taken it for granted that he knew. As far as Randolph's allegiance was concerned, "constant proofs" made disloyalty impossible. On his honor, Jefferson wrote, "no mortal" had ever presumed to tell him anything else. Perhaps some enemy had told Randolph other lies. This time something took. With the sky still bright on a windy afternoon, Randolph came to the President's House and dined with Black Hoof, a famously fierce Shawnee turned reluctant accommodationist, and eight other chiefs from Ohio. The Navy Yard's band entertained. Burwell was there. Eppes was not.

After dinner, Randolph went back to his boardinghouse, where Burwell worked on him and kept at it in the morning. The dinner had changed nothing. So frightening was Randolph's talk that Burwell told Jefferson he would keep him in sight every moment. "I am certain, from a promise I have exacted and received, no step will be taken without my previous knowledge, & under that condition I do not fear consequences." Dark talk indeed.

Unaware of any of this, Senator Plumer, Randolph's fellow boarder at Frost and Quinn's, got to know and like him. The Virginian dined alone in his room, a bashful man, Plumer thought, but pleasant nonetheless, "a man of study—much devoted to books." His choice to leave the President's House to chew his mutton alone in a monk's cell at Frost and Quinn's was noticed on the Capitol Hill, but something else puzzled Plumer: "One thing appeared singular. Mr. Randolph is not a military man—yet he has a pair of pistols & sword laying on the mantle piece on his chamber at his house."

Rumors began to run around the Capitol Hill. Some said a quarrel with his father-in-law had pushed Randolph out, but Plumer was sure it could not be so, "for he speaks of the President with great cordiality—visits him often & dined at his house with him on Saturday." A clash with Eppes seemed unlikely too. The simple explanation was the sheer convenience of living near the Capitol, "but this is conjecture." The president's secretary, Isaac Coles, came up to see the prodigal son-in-law. Did it help throw gossip off the scent?

On Monday, February 23, a raw cold day, Randolph came down with chills after riding with Jefferson to Main's garden nursery without a greatcoat. The fever came and went for days until it put him in danger. A team of secretaries past and present—Lewis, Burwell, and Coles—took nursing turns at Frost and Quinn's. A few days later, informed by Joseph Dougherty that Randolph's fever had not broken, Jefferson tried coaxing again: "I would certainly not urge any thing that would be strongly repugnant to your feelings, but I wish, my dear Sir, you could consent to return to your former room, here," where comfort and care could be had. Joseph would bring the carriage. Wrapped in his father-in-law's fur cloak, "you would be as if in your bed." He himself had caught a cold, and because the day was "tempestuous," he could not come to visit, but "your return will make me extremely happy." Randolph stayed put but decided not to seek reelection, almost surely advised by the president, who knew his son-in-law's demons.

Randolph sent Jefferson a message through Burwell. He would have come home today, Burwell wrote, but his fever and miserable weather made tomorrow seem better. It was crucial that he return "to your house. His disease has originated in the state of his mind, & will be much relieved by tender attentions from yourself."

On March 2, 1807, its last full day in session, Congress banned the importation of slaves at Jefferson's initiative, effective January 1, 1808, the earliest date the Constitution allowed. It was hardly noticed. Jefferson wrote to Martha about Randolph's health that day and said not a word about the modest antislavery milestone. In a *stream* of letters to her, he stepped as lightly as he honestly could around her husband's health, saying nothing about his darkness. Randolph was "considerably reduced and weakened," and could not travel home before he was ready. Coles hardly left him. Captain Lewis and Dr. Jones never did. More than once, Coles sat up with him all night. Dougherty was with him constantly, for Randolph was attached to him. The family owed infinite obligations to Burwell, which were not explicitly described.

There was much talk of fear around Randolph. Plumer was afraid "his sickness will terminate fatally. I think he has much to fear from his physicians." Burwell feared Jefferson's reaction to Randolph's remark that "he was indifferent to live," and "impressed with shame for having left you—but if he lives he will make amends to you & his family by his increased love for both.—I have quieted his mind." No one could be more attentive to Randolph than the president, Plumer wrote, or show more anxiety for him, but Plumer now feared the sons-in-law had quarreled, for Eppes never came to his sickbed. In fact, Eppes rode home to Virginia.

Plumer had decided to go home for good. On March 4, the day after the Senate adjourned, ending his Washington career, he came to the President's House to take his final leave. Jefferson was with his friend Senator Giles and received the New Englander "very cordially." They talked about Burr and a treaty with Britain sent back by Monroe that said not a word about impressment. Jefferson had just declared he would not submit it to the Senate. He "bid me a very polite farewell," Plumer wrote, "Mr. Giles a very affectionate one." The president, so it seemed, had made a friend but not a convert.

A few days later, Jefferson sent Martha good news and stretched it: "I have the happiness to inform you that Mr. Randolph is entirely well." He had come back to the President's House, and Dr. Jones had moved into Eppes's empty room to be near Randolph round the clock, an odd thing to do for an entirely well man. Jefferson marked his son-in-law's progress literally step by step. On March 11, he took five or six hundred steps around the circular room upstairs, managed twelve hundred the next day, and risked a ride in the chariot on day three. Jefferson shared Plumer's concerns about what he had to fear from his doctors: "The quantity of blood taken from him occasions him to recover strength slowly." The president was ill himself, he wrote, and Lewis and Coles too, "so that we are but a collection of invalids."

On Friday the thirteenth, another storm blasted the capital, and a run of disabling headaches hit the president, a chronic affliction brought on by stress, this time by the Randolph ordeal, the unacceptable treaty, and Burr's pending trial for treason. The migraines were not as bad as they might be, he wrote Martha, but "they hold me very long," striking him in the morning and gripping him until dark. Coles went to Georgetown for medicine, but Jefferson found "Neither Camomel nor bark have as yet made the least impression" on his pain. "Indeed we have quite a hospital, one half below and above stairs being sick." Lemaire was dangerously ill, and Freeman was recovering from a broken jaw of unstated origin.

On March 21 Jefferson wrote Monroe excoriating the treaty. Britain had "screwed every article as far as it would bear," and his headache left him "scarcely command enough of my mind to know what I write." Over time, his fits of torment diminished from nine-hour ordeals to five. He could only lie helpless in a dark room until they passed, unable to eat, work, or even think in pure suffering. "I write while a fit is coming on," he told Martha on the twenty-third, "and therefore must conclude with my kisses to you all." On the twenty-sixth the fit lasted just two hours, and the next day it was gone.

On April 3, Jefferson gave Randolph a check and asked him to hold it until the fourth, when his salary would be deposited (living payday to payday as he was) and "not to consider it a loan at all." Years later, Ellen thought her mother's gentle healing and her grandfather's kindness coaxed her father and her uncle back to peace if not love, until the wound reopened.

17

CHAINED TO A WRITING TABLE

With the building season about to begin, Latrobe drew up on paper in March of 1807 what he and Jefferson had been working out for years, a plan to give the mansion a gracious, parklike setting, an appealing combination of the bucolic and the urbane. The spoil from old digs would be shoveled into carts and hauled away. Uneven ground would be graded. Jefferson's word was "smoothed." Bluestone paths and gravel carriage drives would be laid down in a harmonious blend of curves and straight lines. An eight-foot wall of neatly dressed stone would enclose the house and its park along the course of the split rail fence, which would mercifully come down.

Jefferson approved the plan and left for his spring sabbatical, but as absentee homeowners do, he returned to maddening results and fired off a letter to Latrobe. The smoothing had begun in the southwest corner, exactly where it "would cost the most and show the least" and precisely contrary to what he said he had "recommended to Mr. Lenthall (and I thought I had mentioned to you)." He had surely done more than mention and recommend, and he reassigned the laborers to the southeast quarter on the spot. With $15,000 budgeted for the year, Jefferson planned to finish the wings and grade, manure, and plant the grounds, starting in the southeast, "where a little money will smooth a great surface." He and Latrobe would defer the "immensity" of smoothing in the southwest, where clay had been dug for bricks, and spend whatever might be left to start on the rest of their list. The president assumed the wall could not be finished before he was, "whether a little more or less of it be done," and he knew he would never see what Latrobe called necessities, including a kitchen garden, for which the torn up grounds were unfit.

In the following month, landscaping was the least of his worries. On June 25, 1807, an overcast day almost cold enough for a fire, two federal officials came to the President's House with news of an act of war. Near the mouth of Chesapeake Bay, the British warship *Leopard* had attacked the USS *Chesapeake*, killed three men and wounded seventeen, taken off and hanged a British deserter, and impressed three seamen. Jefferson could not recall such an outraged national response since Lexington and Concord, "and even that did not produce such unanimity." It took a week for the cabinet to assemble and endorse a proclamation banning all British ships from U.S. waters. The traditionally relaxed July Fourth reception at the President's House became a patriotic rally fueled by an immense crowd, which "respectable" Federalists, the *Intelligencer* said, made a point of joining. Holding out an olive branch, Jefferson had Erskine and Foster to dinner on July 13 to soothe and be soothed by friends like the Madisons and the former ambassador to Britain, Rufus King, and his wife.

Gently chiding Ellen, Jefferson complained that she had sent him no letters since May, "but perhaps there is one on the road for me. Hope is so much pleasanter than despair." On the same day, he wrote a merchant friend in Marseilles. The macaroni, Parmesan cheese, and choice Turkish raisins he had ordered had come through safely, but a certain vineyard's wines would no longer do. They had been "what we call soft or silky & what I believe you express by the terms *doux, et liquoreux*," but now they were "dry and hard" and "will not be drank here." His retirement was nearly two years off, but combined with what he had on hand, he could manage the rest of the way with a hundred bottles of the finest Hermitage wine, another hundred of Vin rouge de Nice, abundant anchovies, capers, artichokes, almonds, candied fruits, and dried plums, a dozen pots of Dijon *moutarde de Mailly*, and other costly delights. He would retire after forty years of service to his countrymen "poorer than when I entered it," he wrote, but with "nothing to reproach them with. They have always allowed me as much as I thought I deserved myself, but I have believed it my duty to spend, for their credit, whatever they allowed me and something more." With a head "well silvered by eight grandchildren," he looked forward to his farms, books, and family, though "I have one daughter only remaining alive."

With war on the near horizon, he left for his summer retreat in August, proving his point that nothing would keep him in Washington during the bilious months, but his choice of Augustus Foster as a guest at Monticello was no coincidence. The work on the president's grounds went on in his absence, a risk he had to take with his time running out, and Latrobe kept him posted by mail, "tormented by the quarriers" who reneged on shipping stone, a persistent breach of contract protested without effect, due to lack of competition. Surprises emerged, of course, as drawings bumped into the earth. Latrobe reported his progress to the president at a level of detail that respected his expertise and received precise replies that guided and annoyed him.

While Latrobe worked on the grounds, the wall, and the wings, Lenthall attacked the interior. A disoriented letter had once made Jefferson wonder if his clerk of the works was "always in a state of temperance," but his doubts had been dispelled. Repairs were more urgent than improvements. The visible timbers supporting the floors and walls had decayed, and ceiling cracks betrayed the hidden ones. Incredibly, the President's House had been framed with green wood, and rain had soaked through when the roof was replaced. The ceiling in the Mammoth Room was sagging again, its floor was not much sounder, and the water closets were failing. But when Jefferson returned in October, the wooden Venetian blinds in two big windows pleased him with their craftsmanship as much as their looks. "They are beautiful and convenient," he wrote, "the slats move on two pivots, as mine do, and are made to lie close when shut into the jamb that they may occupy less thickness."

As the wings and the wall took shape, so did a triple-arched gate of stone-trimmed brick that Jefferson and Latrobe had conceived together, twenty-five feet high and sixty-six feet long at the point where the Pennsylvania Avenue ran "straight as a gun barrel" from the grounds' southeast corner to the Capitol. The avenue's gravel carriage road ran through the center arch, flanked by two pedestrian entrances, all with iron picket gates. Hacks, gigs, and coaches would pass through the gate and curve around a stand of trees and flowering shrubs until the house popped into view. For the private southeast grounds, a garden of vegetables, flowers, and ornamental plants was planned, screened from the sovereign people. For the public north lawn, a straight gravel drive to the door was drawn on paper. Curving flagstone paths would wind through groves of trees. The driveways were built in Jefferson's time, some of the landscaping was finished, and Latrobe's great arch would stand for half a century. The rest was left to future tenants.

No time remained to break ground on other ideas. Latrobe thought the Great Hall of Entrance and the cross hall it opened into made the house "all mouth." He would have broken it up with alcoves, pillars, and passages. The kitchen facing the sunken areaway beneath the front door he described with his native subtlety: "Darkness is synonymous with filth, with underdone and overdone and burnt pastry, and with broken china, and casseroles covered with verdigris." Green scum. Noise was an irritant too. "Oh the clatter of knives and skewers and dishes that assailed me out of the den of a kitchen going in to dine with the President." If not for the aproned servants rinsing pots in the areaway and the aromas that rose to greet you from "the rattling of irons, you might have supposed yourself listening to the tortures in the dungeons of the inquisition." Latrobe would have moved the kitchen to the southwest corner of the walkout basement, exposed to light and air. The Cabinet, directly above it, would become the dining room, with dumbwaiters moving food up and dirty dishes down. The existing kitchen would become a wine cellar, and the president's office would move upstairs. The State Dining Room was big enough to divide in two, creating a bedchamber with one of Jefferson's space-saving alcove beds and built-in cabinets and drawers, and a dressing room with a water closet. All of it made sense, and none of it was done, but for moving the office upstairs years later.

* * *

Martha's husband had given up his seat in the House, but to Jefferson's great joy, when Maria's widower returned with Congress in October, he brought their son Francis Wayles Eppes, now six years old, back to live in the President's House and enrolled him in a day school. With the grounds improved to the point of safety, the president was glad that Francis could play "in the neighborhood of the house." Maria's son, he later told Eppes, "will ever be to me one of the dearest objects of life."

On October 27, he sent Congress his annual message, and his enslaved apprentice cook Edith Fossett gave birth to a daughter in the servants' quarters. Meaningfully or not, she named the girl Maria. Was Francis brought downstairs to admire her? He was thrilled, no doubt, by the pair of grizzly bear cubs shipped by Zebulon Pike from the Arkansas River, who arrived about the same time Francis did, "too dangerous and troublesome for me to keep," Jefferson wrote his granddaughter Anne, but he put them on display for a while, another advertisement for the West. Perfectly tame and gentle for now, having been fed in Pike's camp of explorers almost from birth, they knew "no benefactor but man" and lived in a ten-foot-square cage on the circle before the north entrance, where they played, entertained the president's guests, and were happy, though "one is much crosser than the other." When the weather turned cold they were shipped up to Peale for his museum.

On November 3, John Quincy Adams came to dinner with other members of Congress. Whether he admired the bears or not, all but one of his fellow guests was a Republican. He may have even smiled a time or two, for the president's banter with the scholarly Senator Mitchill amused him: "There was, as usual, a dissertation upon wines; not very edifying," and Jefferson's remark that the

Epicurean philosophy came nearest to the truth of any ancient creed was merely worth noting, but Adams watched and listened to Dr. Mitchill like a boy sitting cross-legged at his feet. The doctor spoke "of chemistry, of geography, and of natural philosophy; of oils, grasses, beasts, birds, petrifactions, and incrustations," of Zebulon Pike and Baron Humboldt, Meriwether Lewis and the poet Joel Barlow, "and a long train of et cetera—for the Doctor knows a little of every thing, and is communicative of what he knows." It "makes me delight in his company." At a different dinner party, Frances Few found Senator Mitchill self-absorbed: "'I did this' & 'I do that,' he says"; but Adams put up with the vanity for love of the erudition, and Jefferson's confession impressed him too. Fond as he was of agriculture, the president said, he knew nothing about it, and the man who best combined it with other sciences was Mr. Madison, "the best farmer in the world." Adams gave it all an ecstatic New Englander's review: "On the whole, it was one of the agreeable dinners I have had at Mr. Jefferson's."

He was back three weeks later with Louisa, her English mother, and her sisters. Jefferson may have thought the Anglo-American women would pair well with the British minister, Mr. Erskine, his pretty American wife, and his secretary Augustus Foster. It did not work out that way. Jefferson sat between Mrs. Erskine and Mrs. Adams, who resented his focal point. "Being occupied with Mrs. Erskine, he said but little to me," she wrote. He did not win her back when he taught her to make the most of a canvasback duck. The raw carcass on his plate, he said, was "the perfection of eating." All told, Louisa found nothing much to please her, and the president was again "very sparing of his fuel. We returned home early." Jefferson lent Foster his copy of *Corinne*, Madame de Staël's controversial new French novel, perhaps the first to feature a woman of letters.

On November 23, Jefferson told Martha there was little out-of-town company that fall and just nine congressional wives. "A caucus of malcontent members," about twenty renegade Republicans led by John Randolph, a man "egotistic to the point of madness," Henry Adams would later say, was doing mischief but not much harm. The president was tired of contention nonetheless, being cast as an object of hate, "chained to a writing table," longing for home and family. He would soon assure Martha, who still worried about its cost, what a relief their Washington visit had been from his "comfortless solitude," meaning solitude from his loved ones, "for of others I have more than enough."

Increasingly joyless in his presidency, he made two mistakes in the last month of 1807, the worst of which crippled it. On December 10, with fifteen months left in his term, he declared he would not serve another, surrendering some of his power before it was due. On the eighteenth, he called for an embargo on all foreign trade, to avoid being drawn into the European war through both sides' depredations on American shipping. Outnumbered and outgunned, it was crucial, he thought, to buy time to prepare for a life-threatening war or let it pass. Congress enacted the Embargo Act immediately, keeping all American ships out of foreign ports and vice versa, which devastated New England, New York, and other shipping hubs, damaged the rest of the economy, and poisoned Anglo-American relations. John Quincy Adams supported it, stunning his Massachusetts constituents.

As the embargo inflamed his enemies and some of his friends, Jefferson endured an abscessed tooth and the fever and swollen face that went with it. "For 4 or 5 days I suffered much," he wrote, and after the pain subsided the swelling did not. As he chatted with powerful men at the New Year's Day reception of 1808, a chance to defend the embargo he had feared he might have to miss, he drew sympathy for the "knot as big as a pigeon's egg" on his jaw if not for his destruction of commerce. He did not tell the crowd that the ban on the African slave trade became effective that day, nor did any major newspaper. Every state but South Carolina had banned it already.

The rock-hard lump on his jaw shrank grudgingly for weeks. On January 16, lump and all, he received a special envoy from the king, an instant Federalist darling named George Henry Rose, a thirty-six-year-old, Cambridge-educated member of Parliament dispatched to defuse the crisis. An interesting, unexceptional man, Louisa Adams thought, Rose projected what Louisa's grandson Henry later called a "slightly patronizing courteousness," a polite condescension "impressive to Americans of that day, who rarely felt at ease in the presence of an Englishman," a sort of "benevolent superiority." Jefferson knew the type and felt perfectly at ease in the Englishman's presence, spotting neither benevolence nor superiority but careful to show respect, still smarting from his clash with the Merrys. In the tradition of Augustus Foster, Rose advised his Foreign Office that Congress included "one tailor, one weaver, six or seven tavern-keepers, four notorious swindlers, one butcher, one grazier, one curer of hams, and several schoolmasters and Baptist preachers." Two months of talks yielded nothing but a stony farewell at the President's House.

Jefferson's jaw knotted up again in February, from riding in the cold, he thought, which kept him in the house. His letters from eleven-year-old Ellen helped him soldier on. "My dearest Grand Papa must have a bad opinion of my affection for him," she wrote, "if he can suppose that I would stand upon ceremony with him and wait for answers to my letters without considering how much he has got to do and how little in comparison I have." She apologized for "the bad writing of this letter as my pen is shocking." Here was a problem he could fix. He sent her a new steel pen to replace her shocking quill and assured her he loved the small news she sent. "With great news I am more than surfeited from other quarters." Spring had come in mid-March. "Our birds and flowers are well and send their love to yours." Ellen, in return, was grateful for her pen. "You are the only correspondent I have and therefore I can write to you very often."

Among his other correspondents was Dr. Caspar Wistar, a student of paleozoology and vice president of the American Philosophical Society, the scientific institution in Philadelphia that honored Jefferson as its president. In March of 1808, hundreds of bones of extinct animals newly dug in Kentucky were delivered to the President's House, the "horn of a colossal animal" and remains of wooly mammoths among them, including a nine-foot tusk. On the very day they arrived, Jefferson spread them out on tables, suitably enough in the Mammoth Room, and invited Dr. Wistar to come and study them "undisturbed by any mortal from morning to night, taking your breakfast & dinner with us" for a week, a pleasure he surely wished he had more time to share. Wistar arrived in July and stayed for four days. There was scarcely a more important man in Jefferson's pantheon, yet he offered him no bed and suggested he lodge at a nearby tavern and "mess with me every day." The mansion's only upstairs residents were the president himself, Coles, Eppes, and little Francis, who must have been impressed by the monsters' bones, but presentable accommodations were in short supply.

* * *

In March of 1808, an accounting made it plain that the work on the Capitol and the mansion had overrun its 1807 appropriation by a shocking $51,500. Within hours of Jefferson's report to Congress revealing and explaining the deficit and saying it had taken him by surprise, his enemies pounced on him and his architect too. Even Eppes condemned Latrobe, whose nemesis Dr. Thornton ripped him up in the *Washington Federalist*, provoking Latrobe to a libel suit. The disharmony cost Jefferson a week of migraines. On March 29, not thinking straight, he told young Ellen the pain left him just an hour a day to write. A memorandum he sent Gallatin was "a very imperfect sketch (for I am not in a condition to think attentively)." The pitiless Senator Pickering, so cordial at his table, shared reports of his suffering with a friend: "If conscience does its duty, he may never recover; unless, excited by a strong fit of remorse for his evil deeds, he should rise, and like Judas go away and hang himself."

The broken construction budget exposed his fiscal austerity policy to ridicule, and yet the Republican Congress not only filled the deficit but also authorized $14,000 of new money for the grounds, with a war against a great power looming. Having less than eleven months left to spend it, Jefferson gave Latrobe strict instructions. The wall would be finished first, then a stone arch and steps would replace the wooden bridge to the front door, then the grounds would be further planted, and maybe the wall could be capped and its gates and a gatekeeper's lodge built, "closing one thing at a time," leaving nothing half-done for his successor. The mere possibility of a dollar over budget was out of the question, he wrote, scolding Latrobe like a child and compounding his mortification with a copy to the superintendent of Washington City: "The lesson of last year has been a serious one. It has done you great injury, and has been much felt by myself." It contradicted the very "principles of our government" to force public works on Congress beyond what they thought the nation could afford.

Later that month, Latrobe sent the president a full account of his drawing board, priced to the penny, and blamed everyone but himself for the debacle. The "<u>undeniable facts</u>" should have made him quit long ago, he wrote, and Jefferson had thrown all the blame on him, though none of it was his. He could have cleared himself by producing the president's imprudent orders, and the Federalists would have loved him for it, but he was an honorable man.

Jefferson's reply took a patient father's tone. He had never faced a stiffer challenge, he wrote, than to inculpate Latrobe as little as possible while sparing himself false blame. He had even told some congressmen that if *they* had ever gone 15 or 20 percent over budget on a building project, they had done well. Latrobe had not been fair in implying Mr. Eppes spoke for him. It was common to suppose Mr. Eppes and Mr. Randolph did, but they respected themselves too much "to take opinions from me." The consequence was a monastic silence between him and them on congressional affairs, and no Republicans had diverged from his positions more often than they. He closed with gentle thanks for a chance to explain himself. If everyone who heard false rumors were equally just, he could save himself and them from grievances never expressed.

More important news came from Massachusetts. On June 28, coaxed toward republicanism since 1802, John Quincy Adams resigned his Senate seat, having drifted ever further from the Federalists, confident that his country's interests were poorly served by theirs and more worthy of his loyalty. Had he not resigned and jumped parties he would have been pushed, despised by Timothy Pickering and other Massachusetts Federalists and welcomed by Jefferson.

The president returned from Monticello in June and wrote Ellen on July 5, already talking about when "I shall leave this place" for the bilious months. In

Latrobe's aspirational rendering of the President's House from the east. ***Library of Congress***

a week of temperatures in the high nineties, two men had died after drinking cold water. Far from savoring the holiday tied to his name, "I thank heaven that the 4th of July is over. It is always a day of great fatigue to me, and of some embarrassments from improper intrusions and some from unintended exclusions." But the job still had its pleasures, like a chat in the President's House with a New York entrepreneur named John Jacob Astor, "a most, excellent man" who led an exciting new company starting up in commerce with the Western Indians. A master of the fur trade, Mr. Astor expected to raise an astonishing million dollars of capital, and Jefferson told him his enterprise was vital to peace with the Indians.

In August, Latrobe drew up the new stone arch and steps to the north entrance that would soon replace the wooden ramp. His beautiful rendering of the projected east view of the house, drawn either then or later, included two pillared porticos, front and back. The steps to the front door and the north portico's adjoining foundation would be built before the weather turned cold. The budget put the porticos out of reach, but the north portico's base would assure its future construction and give the bland north front a commanding three-dimensional presence combining strength, classic beauty, and republican simplicity, not to mention keeping people dry as they got in and out of their carriages. Jefferson drew the south portico over Hoban's rendering of the south elevation, which would one day give it a stately look and shade the oval rooms from the sun, but the rotten south-facing balcony was a higher priority.

CHAPTER 17

Choosing the heat of the summer of 1808 to fail, the wooden sewer that ran along the road in front of the house collapsed and left the route impassible, to put it mildly. Lacking the budgeted funds, Latrobe convinced the city's superintendent, Thomas Monroe, to rebuild it "in solid work," dipping into the municipal till. But for its stone capping, the wall was finished that summer. "Jefferson's wall" it would be called throughout its seventy-year life.

When Jefferson returned from Monticello in October, he brought his sixteen-year-old grandson Jeff for a two-week stay at the President's House on his way to Philadelphia to be schooled by his grandfather's friends. Charles Willson Peale's letter to Jefferson welcoming the boy to his home may have made the president smile. "I have only one fear to overcome," Peale wrote, "the discipline of my house may be too rigid for a Virginian." His door was locked at ten, except in special circumstances, "an indulgence rarely given," and persons accustomed to wine at dinner would miss it until time rid them of the habit. On his grandson's arrival at the President's House, Jefferson had him open his trunks and lay out their contents in his room. "He examined my wardrobe as my mother would have done," Jeff recalled decades later, made a list of what else the boy would need, took him shopping, sent him to the president's tailor, and filled his purse.

The entitled Frances Few came to dinner on October 11. The dark stone parapet rising around the mansion looked familiar to her, "very like the wall belonging to the State Prison, but it is not finished and may be improved upon." The house she found well furnished but not up to many a Manhattan merchant's home. A servant showed Miss Few and her companion to the Oval Room, where Isaac Coles received them, a pleasant, genteel young man, she thought, but Jefferson fell short of the mark. Well mannered he was, admirably superior to ceremony and show, a good-humored man with a laugh, but distinguished "only by the shabbiness of his dress."

18

THE HERMIT OF MONTICELLO

In December of 1808, beginning his last congressional "campaign" with his power slipping away in his final months in office, his enthusiasm gone, and an escalating risk of a second war with Britain threatening everything he had built, literally and figuratively, Jefferson was beset by physical pain, mental exhaustion, and a belated realization that his retirement would be "loaded with serious debts."

There was pain in the servants' hall too, where several children were suffering from the whooping cough and terrifying their parents. When Jefferson was told, he recalled that Mrs. Smith had a recipe for a cure and asked her to share it, for "two or three children in the family" needed it. It did not help Fanny and Davy Hern's enslaved infant. The sounds of childish death in the President's House began with the frantic cries of a baby gasping for breath and became an incessant cough that blackened its face until its strength was gone. Lemaire wrote in his daybook a quiet record of the construction manager's kindness. "Peter Lenox built the little coffin for Fanny's infant child." Jefferson sent his overseer at Monticello, Edmund Bacon, a list of debts to pay: "Be so good," he added, "as to inform Davy his child died of the whooping cough on the 4th day after he left this. I tender you my good wishes. Th. Jefferson." Ten days later, Bacon told the president that Davy had asked "to come to see his wife at Christmas. He being such a good fellow I hate to deny him, and probably you have some thing for him to bring a cart for." Davy was given a ten-day leave in the Servants' Hall, a chance for him and Fanny to grieve.

On November 9, the genial British minister had come to the President's House alarmed about talk that a war on Britain was about to be declared.

If he were an American, Erskine said, he would let his merchant shipping "go out and take its chance" or declare war on all the great powers at once, producing no "rancorous" conflict at all and a quick and easy peace, an odd idea at best. Jefferson replied that for years he had wanted nothing more than peace with Britain, for "as long as she was our friend, no enemy could hurt." But now there were three alternatives—embargo, war, or submission—"and no American would look a moment at the last." Erskine agreed, and worked cordially with the president to avoid violence, too cordially for his superiors. Four days later, Jefferson wrote Levi Lincoln that Congress would soon decide between embargo, war, or "submission & tribute," and the last "will not want advocates." So much for no American considering it; and yet he would not lead. With four months left in his term and Madison all but sure to succeed him, he would now be "but a spectator," unwilling to make decisions whose consequences would fall on his successor.

Later that week, Dr. Bruff came by to draw pus from his abscessed tooth, followed by the pulling of the piece that was left of it, and was paid a five-dollar fee loaned to Jefferson by Lemaire. An exfoliation of the bone came next, then a six-week confinement to the house, for fear of cold weather interfering with the healing, lightened for a moment by a letter from nine-year-old Cornelia: "I hope you will excuse my bad writing, for it is the first letter I ever wrote, there are a number of faults in it, I know, but those you will excuse."

While Jefferson suffered in tooth and jaw, an angry message from the Massachusetts legislature was read in the U.S. Senate siding with Britain on the issues risking war. And then there were the sleepless nights caused by worry about money. As early as 1806, he knew he had "gotten into arrears at Washington," compelling him "to suspend every expense which is not indispensable. Otherwise I shall leave that place with burthens contracted there, which if they should fall on my private fortune, will doom me to a comfortless old age." Two years later, having thought he had gotten his spending under control based on "rough estimates in my head," he discovered he was wrong in December of 1808, three months before his retirement, and would have to sell land and borrow money to pay the debts he had run up in the President's House. In "an agony of mortification," he convinced himself that his creditors might not let him leave. The most important lesson Martha could teach the children, he wrote, was not to face ruin "after a few years of splendor above their income."

And yet he would not stop building. As he prepared to go home, a Treasury clerk recorded $42.21 received "of Th. Jefferson for glass sold to him," surplus glazing material at the President's House gingerly packed for Monticello. Careful with his wines as the end of his term approached, he had them carted south a little at a time. Yet he kept up the pace of his dinners, which he knew he could not afford, long after they could do him any personal good. Some were farewells to friends, but most of them amounted to gifts to Madison, who would benefit from them now, and the republican cause they served.

With Jefferson holed up in the President's House, the embargo was shaking the Union itself and eroding his influence in Congress, even in his own party. In the 1808 elections, Madison was elected to succeed him, but the Federalists recaptured New England and came close in New York. As anger over the embargo grew, he advised his grandson to ignore a raging zealot like an angry bull: "It is not for a man of sense to dispute the road with such an animal." In December he wrote a friend that he had lately received five Indian delegations with two more coming. He meant to impress them "profoundly" with "temperance, peace & agriculture," but would take no more controversial stands out of respect for Madison. "I am therefore chiefly an unmeddling listener to what others say."

He was sixty-five now, an impressive old age. Feeling every bit of it, he had left a sheaf of papers at Monticello, "which distresses me infinitely, the more so the forgetfulness which produces the omission." To a friend he wrote, "I am already sensible of decay in the power of walking, and find my memory not so faithful as it used to be. This may be partly owing to the incessant current of new matter flowing constantly through it; but I ascribe to years their share in it also." His jaw had healed by mid-January, but "as the term for my relief from this place approaches," he told Martha, "its drudgery becomes more nauseating & intolerable."

As the rift over the embargo widened, some of its supporters wore homespun cloth to signal their rejection of British goods, a nostalgic tactic for those who recalled the Revolution. Some Americans who hated the embargo made a point of wearing British broadcloth. John Randolph went about in the dress of an English lord. Homespun was a theme of the 1809 New Year's Day reception, but after decades of low-priced, high-quality imports, American cloth was hard to find. The president wrote Jeff that he and his cabinet meant to "exhibit" themselves in homespun on New Year's Day and asked him to find him enough in Philadelphia for a pair of knee britches. Searching every nook, Peale came up with "a walnut died brown cotton cloth worth 12 cents per yard," which Jefferson matched with a dark woolen coat manufactured in Connecticut. On the day of the reception, he wrote his son-in-law Randolph that "the monarchists of the North" were promoting the secession of everything east of the Hudson River to form a separate confederacy under British protection. Pickering was one of their leaders. For all of Jefferson's wooing, even Plumer joined in, a step he later called the blunder of his career.

The New Yorker Catharine Mitchill saw a silver lining in the embargo's devastation. It gave her friends in business the leisure to visit her. She enjoyed New Year's Day 1809 at "the Castle," she wrote, where the Great Hall of Entrance, lined with antlers and Indian finery, and several adjoining rooms were so jammed it was hard to squeeze from one into another and impossible to sit down. The Marines' "exquisite band of music" the "Italian Band," some people had begun to call it for its enhancement by the Sicilians, impressed even Frances Few, which was no small feat. Feathered Cherokees and Delawares of both sexes arrived in paint, and it struck Mrs. Mitchill that the women were not as skilled with their rouge as "our civilized ladies." Then again, "the latter paint to deceive" and the former were "not ashamed to own it."

It was Jefferson's last public event in the President's House, and he seemed to enjoy it as such, looking happy to Frances Few shaking hands with hundreds of celebrants, "all very much dressed." His homespun clothes were probably an improvement, but Miss Few compared the British minister's dress unfavorably to the band's. Erskine wore an ornate sword and his diplomatic garb. "It is not as handsome as the uniform of the Marines but something like it."

* * *

Jefferson had kept sheep at Monticello since 1794, some of them the offspring of a smuggled ram whose prized merino wool the Spanish wished to monopolize. The Barbary wars heightened his interest, as naval officers and diplomats gave him prized North African rams and ewes. The tacit exemption of sheep from his refusal of valuable gifts seemed to rest on his thought that the improvement of the herds did his country good. In the summer of 1806, he had started buying and grazing them in Washington, some on the President's Square, and Joseph Dougherty hired an old man to shepherd them. Within a year the president was breeding them. "I am now possessed of the most remarkable varieties of the race of sheep," he wrote Ellen—the Spanish, Icelandic, Barbary, and Senegal breeds—and "I mean to pay great attention to them, pro bono publico." He did not pay attention enough.

In 1807, Dougherty had told him that a rare, four-horned Shetland ram "is become very unruly" and "will make battle without offense," turning on anyone but Dougherty himself, sensing something dangerous in the Irishman but battering his aged shepherd until Dougherty had the old man protect himself with a formidable dog. The ram and his ewes remained on the public square for a year and a half nonetheless, and on February 6, 1808, he savaged a little boy. Jefferson sent the boy's father, Mr. Alexander Kerr, a note of "inexpressible concern." He had recently given orders to secure the ram, he wrote, and "this great calamity would have been prevented" if they had been followed. With "unceasing regret" and distress, he would pray for the boy's recovery. Mr. Kerr replied that day, honored by the president's concern. The wound was very dangerous, but he hoped God would "save my darling boy."

The boy soon died, and Jefferson's frequent dinner guest Ana Thornton, Dr. Thornton's wife, made a note in her diary: "a fine little boy killed by the Ram the president has." People must have talked, and Jefferson was distraught, but the ram remained at large or was soon untied almost literally at his door. Not quite a year later, in his presidency's closing days, the animal attacked a penniless man as he passed through the President's Square. Having come to apply for a Revolutionary War veteran's pension, he was living in the poorhouse with no allowance for food and begged the president's help. Jefferson gave him five dollars, about two weeks' wages for unskilled work.

* * *

In mid-February 1809, Latrobe told Thomas Claxton he was going to lose his job in the incoming administration. Having eased his way into the Madisons' confidence, Latrobe would procure their furniture and Claxton was out, though Jefferson had commended him to Madison. Claxton closed his duties honorably. His son, "a smart boy," he told Jefferson, conducted an inventory at the house, and Lemaire counted its costly copperware, a task that Martha, skeptical of his virtue, might have put in other hands. On March 2, following precedent set in the first two presidential turnovers, Congress authorized the sale of any items "decayed, out of repair, or unfit for use," the proceeds to be combined with up to $14,000 more from the Treasury's furniture account at Madison's discretion.

As his overseer Edmund Bacon recalled years later, Jefferson had him come from Monticello to "settle up his business, and move home his goods and servants," the polite word for slaves. With only days left in office, he sent Bacon a note. Fanny Hern and Edy Fossett would replace Peter Hemings, their fellow slave, as Monticello's cooks, and one of them would have his room adjoining the kitchen. Hemings would have his choice of any of the vacant cabins, to be fitted up for him "in an entirely comfortable and decent manner." Some of Jefferson's valuables would be going back by wagon, so "would it not be well to have with you a good dog who will lie by it?"

Bacon's memory failed him when he recalled in 1862 that he had spent two weeks in Washington in 1809 instead of a few days; but he had been there before and sat at the president's table with "Congressmen, foreigners, and all sorts of people," a gentleman in his employer's eyes, if not in all of theirs, though none of them seem to have objected. Jefferson told him now that he was "perfectly tired out with company," and Bacon could see why. "He dined at four o'clock, and they generally sat and talked until night. It used to worry me to sit so long, and I finally quit when I got through eating, and went off and left them." In his last few weeks in the President's House, Jefferson wrote valedictory letters to friends. A note to Pierre Dupont de Nemours said nature had meant him for "the tranquil pursuits of science, by rendering them my supreme delight. But the enormities of the times in which I have lived have forced me to take a part in resisting them." He hoped "curiosity may lead you to visit the hermit of Monticello."

As Davy Hern and other wagoners came up from Monticello to haul Jefferson's belongings home, his enslaved servant John Freeman wrote him anxiously, again too distressed to approach him face-to-face, about his wife, Maria's former maid Melinda, and their children. Melinda and the children had been freed by a different master and were living with Freeman in the servants' hall. To serve him in retirement, the president planned to take Freeman to Monticello, valuing him as he did, and apparently expected his family to join him, until Freeman learned from Eppes that a new Virginia law exposed them to reenslavement if they returned. Freeman wrote to Jefferson like a man who faced a choice and not a command: "As you wosh me to go with you rather than dis ples you I will go and Do the best I Can," but Melinda and the family would be at risk if they joined him, and "I shall be oblige to Leave hir and the children." After eight years at the president's side, Freeman knew him well. He was giving him a chance to do the right thing and betting that he would. Jefferson could have freed him, as his family had been freed, or removed him to Monticello as the president wished. Instead he took a middle course. At Jefferson's request, Madison bought Freeman from him for the oddly precise sum of $231.81, subject to his contractual right to freedom in 1815, which kept him at the President's House, one of the best positions a black man could have in 1809, and kept his family whole. Jefferson could have done better, and he could have done much worse.

More people had come to Washington for Madison's inauguration than had ever come before and, for once, as many ladies as gentlemen, "all in full dress," Mrs. Smith observed, which gave the day "rather a gay than a solemn appearance." Madison had welcomed Jefferson to stay past his time in the President's House as he packed, and his grandson had come down from Philadelphia. When the president was told that a unit of militia was coming to escort him to the Capitol, he and Jeff rode up the Pennsylvania Avenue alone like an old man and a boy on their way to a fair. On the Capitol grounds, they picked a path through the crowd and hitched their own horses to a fence. In the recently finished chamber of the House, a gem of Latrobe and Jefferson's creation, filled from top to bottom with a beautifully dressed crowd and an aura of magnificence, Madison took his oath, and Jefferson was a former president. Leaving his grandson with friends, he turned his horse away.

Ahead of the dispersing crowd, a young man named George Washington Parke Custis, the general's adopted son and as purebred a Federalist as any man could be, was riding back down the avenue with two older, like-minded men, former officers of the Revolution, when he glanced at another rider and recognized Thomas Jefferson, "entirely alone." Custis turned in the saddle to his friends. See how soon a great man is neglected, he said, and whatever his current politics might be, they were right in 1776. The veterans asked to be introduced, and the three of them rode over and touched their hats. Compliments were exchanged, "and the small party falling into line," the High Federalist trio escorted their fellow American down the Pennsylvania Avenue to the President's House.

EPILOGUE

THE PRESIDENT'S HOUSE

A generation after Jefferson's presidency, an American blueblood was still appalled by his "abolition of all official dignity" at the President's House. Opened to all comers, the mansion had "descended, at once, to the lowest level." In 1901, a hundred years after Jefferson's inauguration, a privileged Washingtonian condemned him for advancing "the shibboleth of social equality" and replacing quiet dignity with "crude and discourteous innovations." The writer was pleased to say that when Jefferson went home, capital society swung back to class distinctions.

James and Dolley Madison did restore weekly levees at the President's House, hosted in formal dress, but they welcomed rich and poor, and meant it, even advertised in the papers. Latrobe and Mrs. Madison redid the house in exquisite Greek Revival, not uniformly approved. "Many alterations to the President's House," Ohio's senator Thomas Worthington wrote. "Mr. Jefferson's style was neat, economical and simple. Mr. Madison's more costly in furniture, etc. but I augur no good from it." Two months after Jefferson left the house, Joseph Dougherty told him he would scarcely know it. "The north front is become a wilderness of shrubry and trees," Dougherty wrote, and Mrs. Madison's decorators reminded him of fortune-tellers in Ireland "who makes their bread by going among the most ignorant class of the community, telling them to change their fire places to the other end of the house and they would be rich verry soon."

In 1814, during the War of 1812, British raiders led by Rear Admiral George Cockburn, who had captained the Merrys' voyage to America, gutted the Capitol and the President's House with fire, depriving we the people of part of Jefferson's

Burned-out shell of the President's House, 1814, and its empty surrounding countryside. ***Library of Congress***

legacy. Instead of tearing down the mansion's burned-out shell, Madison began a restoration that Monroe completed under the oversight of its designer, James Hoban, who added the porticos that Jefferson and Latrobe had envisioned. Jefferson's wings have been expanded and redone, but parts of them survive.

THOMAS JEFFERSON

Jefferson wrote Baron Humboldt on his first day out of office: "You have wisely located yourself in the focus of the science of Europe. I am held by the cords of love to my family and country, or I should certainly join you." Six days into the Madison administration he was still packing up in the President's House, distracted by "visits of leave" and "interruptions of every kind." Grateful for Jefferson's "particular notice" of him, "a highlight of my life," Claxton sent him a list of the house's government-owned furniture to give to Latrobe, now Madison's agent: "Your caution Sir, on this occasion, is necessary," Claxton wrote, "as in a few short hours, great depredations may take place."

Edmund Bacon left for Monticello ahead of his employer in a train of three wagons, two packed with crated goods, one with shrubs from Thomas Main's nursery. Edy Fossett and Fanny Hern rode home on one of the wagons. Bacon followed in a carriage. Jefferson left the President's House for the last time in his open two-wheeled gig, accompanied by Jack Shorter, and found the roads "excessive bad." Just short of sixty-six, he switched to horseback for the expedition's last three days and overtook the wagons after an eight-hour slog "through as disagreeable a snow storm as I was ever in."

In seventeen years of retirement, he founded and nurtured the University of Virginia, never saw Washington again, and never traveled far from Monticello. He had gone home, he said, with his hands clean and empty, and his perilous finances were not improved by the cost of his uninvited guests. A New England clergyman with a letter of introduction was "adhesive" for three weeks. "I have often sent a wagon-load of hay up to the stable," Bacon wrote, "and the next morning there would not be enough left to make a hen's nest. I have killed a fine beef, and it would all be eaten in a day or two." Strangers sat in Jefferson's reception hall to watch him go into dinner, or hung about the grounds. A woman punched her parasol through a window to get a better look.

Yet Jefferson took to retirement like a boy. He was constantly outdoors, and apologized that his letter writing, "as with other country farmers, is put off to a rainy day." His garden and farm "added wonderfully to my happiness," he wrote, but his debts bore down on him hard. When he wrote of his time in Washington he took pride in stopping the slide toward plutocracy. The nation faced great difficulties, "but when viewed in comparison with those of Europe, they are the joys of paradise . . . and the system of government which shall keep us afloat amidst the wreck of the world will be immortalized in history." And so, he knew, would he.

In 1812, John Adams wrote to him at Benjamin Rush's persistent urging, starting a conversation that lasted the rest of their lives: "You and I ought not to die," Adams wrote, "before we have explained ourselves to each other." At Monticello, Jefferson displayed a bust of Adams, who treasured a portrait of Jefferson. They died within hours of one another on Independence Day 1826, precisely half a century after the first great Fourth of July. Jefferson was eighty-three.

In 1863, Abraham Lincoln, Jefferson's thirteenth successor, met an Indian delegation at the White House, where a Kiowa chief named Yellow Wolf wore a Jefferson peace medal. It was given to an ancestor, he said, and his tribe prized it highly.

BENJAMIN LATROBE

Jefferson commended Latrobe to Madison, but "you will find that the reins must be held with a firmness that never relaxes." Working with Dolley Madison,

Latrobe did brilliant work furnishing and embellishing the President's House, all of which burned in 1814. A year later, he built Saint John's Church on the President's Square, at which the natives stared excessively, he wrote, because it looked nothing like a barn. Blamed for reconstruction delays as architect of the Capitol, the reins being held too loose, Latrobe resigned in 1817. He saw no alternative, he told President Monroe, consistent with self-respect. His later works include the Decatur House on the President's Square and the Baltimore Basilica. He died of yellow fever at fifty while working in New Orleans in 1820. His buildings are still discussed among the early republic's best.

JEFFERSON'S SECRETARIES

Jefferson appointed Meriwether Lewis governor of the Louisiana Territory in 1807. Headquartered in Saint Louis, something like an outpost at the edge of the Roman Empire, Lewis did a hard job well. On his way back to Washington in 1809, suffering from political and financial pressure, real and imagined disease, and the depression Jefferson had noticed in the President's House, he died of a gunshot wound, almost surely self-inflicted, at the age of thirty-five. The inventory of his effects, exotic and mundane, is tinged with the air of sadness that touches the goods of the dead.

In 1821, always loyal to old friends, Joseph Dougherty stayed up nights with Jefferson's second secretary, Congressman William Burwell, who was ill and not yet forty-one. In the end, Dougherty let Jefferson know "I have just closed the eyes of our worthy, good friend."

Lewis Harvie practiced law in Richmond, served in the legislature, and died young in Norfolk in 1807, about to sail for France for his health.

Isaac Coles stayed on as secretary to President Madison, scuffled with a Maryland congressman, and was succeeded by his brother, a fellow antislavery man. He served as an army officer in the War of 1812, returned to Jefferson's home county, and represented it in the House of Delegates for a year until he died at sixty-one in 1841.

HONORÉ JULIEN

A few days after Jefferson's retirement, Julien came to Monticello for several weeks to assess his kitchen, prepare Edy Fossett and Fanny Hern to run it, and have Jefferson order eight grated iron stew holes in three sizes, "indispensable in a kitchen." For the next twenty years, Julien ran a Washington catering service and an F Street cake and confectionery shop. His son catered James K. Polk's White House events. Over the years, Julien sent Jefferson a swiss cheese, "usually eaten grated," he explained, "on buttered slices of bread"; vegetable seeds with planting instructions; and his recipe for cream cheese, dispatched at the former president's request. As late as 1825 he sent to Monticello some canvasback ducks, a "magnificent present," Jefferson wrote him back, heightened by "the proof they brought of your kind recollection of me" and returned by a "constant and affectionate attachment to you." Julien died with a sterling reputation in 1830, aged about seventy.

ÉTIENNE LEMAIRE

A few days after his retirement, Jefferson wrote Lemaire from Monticello, confessing that words had failed him. He had meant to say goodbye with "all the sentiments of obligation I have felt myself under to you. But my heart was so full that I could utter but the single word Adieu." Lemaire's services, he wrote, had been superb, and cheerfully performed. "It would be ingratitude," Lemaire replied in French, if he failed to say the president had made them pleasant. "I take the liberty in this letter," Lemaire wrote him later, "to inform you how to make vinegar syrup."

Lemaire returned to Philadelphia and did not fare well as a maître d'. By 1814 he was a barber. In 1817, Julien informed Jefferson that "this good man" had broken down after lending $5,000 to a friend who went bankrupt. He drowned himself in the river, despite a remaining fortune of $10,000, and was found ten days later with $200 in his pockets, wealth that may have provoked Martha's suspicions about undue enrichment in the President's House. Jefferson lamented "poor Le Maire," whom he had "never suspected of gloom enough to bring himself to so tragical an end."

JOSEPH DOUGHERTY

After Jefferson retired, Dougherty procured him sheep, geese, and books in Washington City; failed in several businesses; and suffered when the British raiders consumed and destroyed his beer bottling enterprise in 1814. Rescued from "the lowest ebb" to manage the State, War, and Navy Department building, he "cowhided" a colonel named Lane "for insolence to me, without the least shadow of cause" and was fired by President Monroe, though he claimed in his defense that Colonel Lane could be provocative, having "been four times whipped with the cowhide, and twice beaten with the fists within two years."

Dougherty kept in touch with veterans of the old staff and two presidents. In 1819, after Jack Shorter's wife abandoned him for the Western country, Shorter, now freed under his former master's will, came to Dougherty as he had for sixteen years, to "set him right," so Dougherty told Madison, and "keep him from an untimely end," too dissipated to survive on his own. To Jefferson Dougherty wrote, "I succeeded in reforming him," for he "both fears & loves me—and I cannot refuse him any thing in my power." In 1823, Julien sent a box of raisins to Monticello by way of Dougherty, just as Dougherty's wife Mary, the former housemaid at the President's House, was begging through the mails for Jefferson's "generous heart" to ease their poverty, unbeknownst to her husband. Jefferson sent her twenty-five dollars, a sum he could not afford. Having befriended Margaret Bayard Smith sharing stories of "the dear old man," Dougherty died at about sixty in 1832.

JOHN FREEMAN

After John Freeman's contractual right to liberty vested in 1815, he stayed in his post at the President's House as a free man until the Madisons left it two years later, fulfilling the design of his sale between presidents. He worked as a waiter at Gadsby's Hotel and a State Department messenger, and he and his wife Melinda joined the free black antislavery movement. When he died in 1839, he left her a house on K Street not far from the president's.

THE FOSSETTS AND THE HERNS

Edy Fossett returned to Monticello in the capacity of head cook and remained so through Jefferson's death, with Fanny Hern second in command. Lemaire assured Jefferson that *idé et fanné* were "good workers, they are two good girls and I am convinced that they will give you much satisfaction." On the pivotal issue of dessert, Edy "ought to remember the way I used vanilla sparingly." Two years had passed between her husband Joe Fossett's flight to her in Washington and their reunion at Monticello. How much had she changed after seven years in the President's House? Daniel Webster praised her dinners, prepared in "half Virginian, half French style," and she and Joe had another eight children.

Jefferson's death was a calamity for most of Monticello's enslaved people. Joe Fossett was one of five slaves freed under his will, but Edy and their children were among the "130 valuable negroes" sold with most of the mansion's desirable contents to reduce the estate's debts, which the sale of the house and land would not cover. Fossett tried to get Charlottesville folk to buy his family one by one to keep them close, and succeeded with Edy and some of their children, but distant strangers took three of their daughters. A University of Virginia professor bought Davy and Fanny Hern. Jefferson left Fossett his blacksmith's tools as well as his freedom, and he set himself up in Charlottesville. By 1837, he had bought his wife, five of their children, and four grandchildren, and moved them north to Cincinnati, where the sons worked in his blacksmith shop, then switched to their mother's trade and became the city's premier caterers. The Fossetts and their freed children helped run the Underground Railroad. Nearly all of their enslaved children reached Ohio before their parents died.

THOMAS JEFFERSON RANDOLPH

Jefferson having named him the executor of his estate, his grandson Jeff never forgot his supervision of the sale of the former president's slaves, mandated by law to reduce his debts. "I had known all of them from childhood," he wrote, with "strong attachments to many. I was powerless to relieve them." They were auctioned off in lots from Monticello's back steps, leaving Jeff the painful image of "a captive village" sold into slavery in ancient times. After serving six terms in the legislature and proposing unsuccessfully a plan to apprentice and eventually emancipate children born as slaves, he was given in old age a colonel's commission in the Confederate army and stayed active in Democratic politics until he died at eighty-three in 1875.

MARTHA JEFFERSON RANDOLPH

Estranged from her husband until shortly before he died in 1828, Martha lived with her father at Monticello until his death two years earlier. Both men having died deep in debt, Martha was left penniless. "Unfortunately," she wrote, "I was educated as the heiress to a great estate," learning music and the like "when I ought to have been acquiring dexterity with my needle." As it was she moved to Boston to live with Ellen and her merchant husband, looking "back to Monticello as Eve did to Paradise." In 1829, while she lived for a while in Washington,

Mrs. Smith gave her and some of her daughters a tour of Andrew Jackson's White House. "She was very much affected," and Jackson honored her with a call "in all due form." She lived at Monticello one more summer before it was sold, and then with a succession of her children. She died at sixty-four in 1836 while living with Jeff within sight of Monticello, the place of her birth. She lies there still with her parents, her husband, and her sister.

THOMAS MANN RANDOLPH

Randolph's biographer says he played out his life on Jefferson's stage, a difficult role to play well. After Jefferson's retirement, Randolph served two terms in Virginia's House of Delegates and capped his career as its governor, supporting the empowerment of the common man and, unsuccessfully, a gradual emancipation of Virginia's slaves. He did not visit Jefferson in his final illness and died at Monticello, living separately from the family at his own insistence. The *Richmond Enquirer* gave him credit for chivalry and courage, and imagined that "had he possessed less irritability and a larger acquaintance with the volume of men and things, he would have stood foremost."

JOHN WAYLES EPPES AND FRANCIS WAYLES EPPES

In July of 1809, Randolph's jealousy of Eppes temporarily drove the latter into self-imposed exile from Monticello. Eppes stayed in Congress through March of 1815, with a one-term interregnum, served in the United States Senate for two years, and resigned in poor health. After Maria's death, before and during his second marriage, Eppes took an enslaved woman, Betsy Hemings, a niece of Sally and James Hemings, as his concubine, and apparently had children with her. He died at age fifty in 1823. Betsy Hemings's grave, with an elaborate testimonial headstone, adjoins his. His second wife was buried elsewhere.

In his twenties, Maria's only surviving child, Francis Wayles Eppes, who had lived in the President's House, bought his childhood nurse, Critta Hemings Bowles, at the auction following Jefferson's death and freed her to join her husband, a free man. Francis inherited his grandfather's second home, Poplar Forest, and lived there for a while, but sold it and moved to Florida, served as Tallahassee's mayor, and founded the future Florida State University, where his casually seated statue welcomes students to his bench today. He died in 1881.

WILLIAM PLUMER

Jefferson's gentle wooing bore late season fruit when Plumer broke publicly with the Federalists and switched his party affiliation, first returning, as a Republican, to the New Hampshire Senate, which restored him to its presidency, and then as elected governor as a member of Jefferson's party. In 1820, he cast the only electoral college vote against his fellow Republican James Monroe's reelection. Unhappy with Monroe's spending and fond of Washington's record as the only U.S. president elected unanimously, Plumer voted for his fellow defector John Quincy Adams, stiff though he had found him to be. Plumer never finished his history of the United States, but he left incisive notes and character studies. He died in 1850 on his Epping farm at the fully grown age of ninety-one.

ELIZABETH PATTERSON BONAPARTE

When word of Jerome Bonaparte's marriage reached Paris, Napoleon ordered him back alone, but he and Madame Eve sailed together, sure that she would charm the emperor. Barred from setting foot in France, she never got a chance. Virtually under arrest, Jerome saw the wisdom of accepting an annulment, a German wife, and the principality of Westphalia, and Elizabeth went home to be fashionable for years. During Madison's presidency, Catharine Mitchill watched "the pretty little duchess of Baltimore" float blithely through the President's House in a near "state of nudity" with "a fondness to be heard," immersed in "the pleasures of this life, without bestowing a thought on a future state."

THE MERRYS

Judged by his peers as a gentle, worthy, "nervous man," Anthony Merry closed his career as His Majesty's minister to Sweden, Augustus Foster serving again as his secretary. After friendlessness in London forced Merry's retirement at fifty-three in 1809, the Merrys lived the lives of country gentry on the East Anglia coast at Herringfleet Hall, Mrs. Merry's first husband's legacy, until she died in 1824, leaving a will requesting a funeral "without parade" and endowing a poor children's school. Herringfleet Hall reverted to her late husband's family, and Merry lived comfortably with a sister in Dedham, where he likely met John Constable painting landscapes. He died at seventy-nine in 1835, having earned his neighbors' respect as "a diplomat from head to foot, a ceremonious, polite, highly refined looking old gentleman" who walked about the village "with the most impenetrable face possible."

SIR AUGUSTUS JOHN FOSTER

In 1805, Augustus Foster told his mother that once he escaped from Washington he would not come back, even as the king's minister, for £10,000 a year, "and if I did, I would not take—I was going to say my wife—I would not take my sister for £20,000." Six years later, he did just that, alone and with much less pay. A lady he had been courting turned for comfort to Lord Byron and married him. Liked in America as he was, Foster was called a British opiate prescribed to ease the pain of British policy but proved to be no cure, and he left Washington for good when the Americans declared war in 1812.

After a short time in Parliament, Foster capped his career, successively, as Britain's minister to Denmark and the Kingdom of Sardinia. His stunning mother's open ménage à trois with the Duke and Duchess of Devonshire having raised his social status since his youth, he married the sister of an earl, was knighted in 1825, and was made a baronet in 1831. In a fit of fevered delirium at home at Branksea Castle, he cut his throat in 1848. He was sixty-eight years old. But for excerpts in the *Quarterly Review* of 1841, his insightful *Notes on the United States of America* first saw print more than a century after his death when the Huntington Library published them in Los Angeles in 1954, giving every irreverent historian hope for a posthumous career.

NOTES

All correspondence not otherwise cited is available on the National Archives website, www.Founders.archives.gov ("Founders"), often with annotations. As of May 2019, the ongoing, thoroughly annotated, definitive work *The Papers of Thomas Jefferson*, published by Princeton University Press, is complete through June 1804.

PROLOGUE

xiii. *cold*: Charles Willson Peale, *The Selected Papers of Charles Willson Peale and His Family*, 5 vols., ed. Lillian B. Miller (New Haven, CT: Yale University Press, 1983) ("*Peale*"), vol. 2, pt. 2, pp. 783–85.

xiii. *"no imagination"*: ed. Vere Foster, *The Two Duchesses* (London: Blackie & Son, 1898) ("*Two Duchesses*"), p. 196.

xiii. *Foster*: Augustus J. Foster, *Jeffersonian America*, ed. Richard Beale Davis (San Marino, CA: Huntington Library, 1954) ("Foster"), pp. ix–xi; Donald H. Mugridge, "Augustus Foster and His Book," *Records of the Columbia Historical Society* 53/56 (1953/1956): 327–52 ("'Foster and His Book'"), pp. 327–36.

xiii. *"unfit"*: William Plumer to T. W. Thompson, January 1, 1803, Papers of William Plumer, Library of Congress ("LOC").

xiii–xiv. Rustic Washington: Samuel Clagett Busey, *Pictures of the City of Washington in the Past* (Washington, DC: W. Ballantyne and Sons, 1898) ("Busey"), pp. 128–29; S. S. Moore and T. W. Jones, *The Traveller's Directory* (Philadelphia: printed for Mathew Carey, 1802), Plate 25; Don A. Hawkins, "The City of Washington in 1800: A New Map," *Washington History* 12 (Spring/Summer 2000): 74–77; George W. Waterston, *The L . . . Family at Washington* (Washington, DC: Davis and Force, 1822), pp. 21–22; Charles

William Janson, *The Stranger in America, 1793–1806* (London: printed for J. Cundee, 1807) ("Janson"), p. 205; Abigail Adams to Abigail Smith and Mary Cranch, November 21, 1800; John Melish, *Melish's Travels*, 2 vols. (London: George Cowie, 1818) ("Melish"), vol. 1, p. 144; Bernard Mayo, *Henry Clay* (Boston: Houghton Mifflin, 1937) ("*Henry Clay*"), p. 263.

xiii–xiv. *roads*: Janson, p. 202; Louisa Catherine Adams, *The Adams Papers: Diary and Autobiographical Writings of Louisa Catherine Adams*, 2 vols. (Cambridge, MA: Belknap Press of Harvard University Press, 2013) ("Louisa Adams"), vol. 1, p. 261; Samuel Eliot Morison, *The Life and Letters of Harrison Gray Otis*, 2 vols. (Boston: Houghton Mifflin, 1913), vol. 2, p. 170; Abigail Adams to Mary Cranch, February 7, 1801; John B. Osborne, "The Removal of the Government to Washington," *Records of the Columbia Historical Society* 3 (1900): 136–60 ("Osborne"), pp. 154–55.

xiv. *sheets* and *itch*: Typescript of Memoir of Thomas Jefferson Randolph, Albert and Shirley Small Special Collections Library, University of Virginia ("TJR Memoir") pp. 11–13.

xiv. *"a heap"*: *Two Duchesses*, p. 196.

xiv. Bucolic landscape: Busey, p. 131.

xiv–xv. *the Tiber*: www.parkviewdc.com/2011/09/08/hidden-washington-tiber-creek; John Davis, *Travels of Four Years and a Half in the United States of America* (London: R. Edwards, 1803) ("John Davis"), pp. 174–75.

xv. Merry's description: George Jackson, *Diaries and Letters of Sir George Jackson*, ed. Catherine Charlotte Jackson, 2 vols. (London: R. Bentley and Son, 1872), ("Jackson") vol. 1, pp. 212–13.

xv. Flash flood: Rosalie Stier Calvert, *Mistress of Riversdale: The Plantation Letters of Rosalie Stier Calvert*, ed. Margaret Law Callcott (Baltimore: Johns Hopkins University Press, 1991) ("Calvert"), p. 89.

xv. Foster, Talleyrand, and Washington City: "Foster and His Book," pp. 327, 335, and passim; Foster, pp. ix–xi; *Two Duchesses*, pp. 196–97.

xv–xvii. *Jefferson*: Maurizio Valsania, *Jefferson's Body: A Corporeal Biography* (Charlottesville: University of Virginia Press, 2017) ("Valsania"), pp. 2, 8–13, 36–39, 198 n. 8, 203 n. 38, 210 n. 101, and figs. 5 and 6; William Dunlap, *Diary of William Dunlap*, 2 vols. (New York: J. J. Little and Ives, 1930) ("Dunlap"), vol. 2, p. 388; Augustus John Foster, "Notes on the United States," *Quarterly Review* 68 (June and September 1841): 20–57 ("Foster's Notes"), p. 24; *Two Duchesses*, pp. 197–98; Foster, pp. 10, 12, 147; Margaret Bayard Smith, *The First Forty Years of Washington Society*, ed. Gaillard Hunt (New York: Scribner, 1906) ("*First Forty*"), p. 6; Annette Gordon-Reed and Peter S. Onuf, *"Most Blessed of the Patriarchs": Thomas Jefferson and the Empire of the Imagination* (New York: Liveright, 2016) ("*Patriarchs*"), p. 244.

xvii–xviii. *Washington City*: *Two Duchesses*, pp. 196, 203–5, 226, 228; "Foster and His Book," pp. 327, 346, 348; *National Intelligencer* ("*Intelligencer*"),

November 23, 1801, and August 9, 1802; Jefferson to John Davidson, March 30, 1806; Frederick D. Nichols and Ralph E. Griswold, *Thomas Jefferson: Landscape Architect* (Charlottesville: University Press of Virginia, 1978) ("Nichols and Griswold"), p. 72; Foster, p. 18; William Seale, *The President's House: A History*, 2 vols. (Baltimore: Johns Hopkins University Press, 2008) ("Seale"), vol. 1, p. 79; William Plumer Jr., ed., *Life of William Plumer* (Boston: Phillips, Sampson, 1857) ("*Life of Plumer*"), p. 244; *First Forty*, pp. 10–12; Louisa Adams, vol. 1, p. 204; Cynthia A. Kierner, *Martha Jefferson Randolph, Daughter of Monticello: Her Life and Times* (Chapel Hill: University of North Carolina Press, 2012) ("Kierner"), pp. 116–17.

xviii. *Capitol Hill*: Foster, p. 8; *Peale*, vol. 2, pt. 2, p. 692; Janson, p. 205; Allan C. Clark, "William Duane," *Records of the Columbia Historical Society* 9 (1906): 14–62 ("'William Duane'"), p. 29; James S. Young, *The Washington Community, 1800–1828* (New York: Harcourt, Brace, 1966) ("Young"), p. 97; Kierner, p. 121; Henry Adams, *The Life of Albert Gallatin* (Philadelphia: J. B. Lippincott, 1879) ("*Life of Gallatin*"), p. 253.

xviii. *Navy Yard*: Janson, p. 208; Young, p. 23.

xviii–xix. President's House and neighborhood: Benjamin Latrobe, *Correspondence and Miscellaneous Papers of Benjamin Henry Latrobe*, 3 vols., ed. John G. Van Horne and Lee W. Formwalt (New Haven, CT: Yale University Press, 1984) ("*Latrobe Papers*") vol. 2, p. 686; Founders: December 31, 1805, Abstract of Money Spent on the President's House in 1805; Seale, vol. 1, pp. 73–77, 90; John B. Boles, *Jefferson: Architect of Liberty* (New York: Basic Books, 2017) ("Boles"), p. 333; Foster, pp. 12–13; Michael Fazio and Patrick A. Snadon, *The Domestic Architecture of Benjamin Henry Latrobe* (Baltimore: Johns Hopkins University Press, 2006) ("Fazio and Snadon"), p. 364; Osborne, pp. 144, 149; Seale, vol. 2, pp. 73, 90; Young, p. 73; Seale in Wendell Garrett, ed., *Our Changing White House* (Boston: Northeastern University Press, 1995) ("*Changing White House*"), p. 8; Thomas Munroe to Jefferson, November 19, 1805; Helen Duprey Bullock, "A View from the Square," *Historic Preservation* 19 (July–December 1967): 53–68 ("Bullock"), p. 53.

xix. West and George Town: Seale, vol. 1, p. 65; Barnes to Jefferson, April 16, 1801; Irving Brant, *James Madison: Secretary of State, 1800–1809* (Indianapolis, IN: Bobbs-Merrill, 1953) ("Brant"), p. 42; Abigail Adams to Mary Cranch, November 21, 1800; Dunlap, vol. 2, p. 393; William Ryan and Desmond Guinness, *The White House: An Architectural History* (New York: McGraw-Hill, 1980) ("Ryan and Guinness"), fig. 89; Historic American Engineering Record, No. DC-37, "M Street Bridge"; Foster, p. 41; David B. Warden, *A Chorographical and Statistical Description of the District of Columbia* (Paris: Smith, Rue Montmorency, 1816) ("Warden"), p. 106.

xix–xx. *society*: Barbara Carson, *Ambitious Appetites: Dining, Behavior, and Patterns of Consumption in Federal Washington* (Washington, DC: American Institute of Architects Press, 1990) ("Carson"), p. 11; Jefferson to John Adams, August 30, 1787; Calvert, p. 158; Coles Diary, January 26 and 28, 1807.

xx. *Burr*: Louisa Adams, vol. 1, p. 223; Joanne B. Freeman, *Affairs of Honor: National Politics in the New Republic* (New Haven, CT: Yale University Press, 2002) ("Freeman"), p. 160.

xx. *slaves*: *Intelligencer*, April 13, 1801; Wilhelmus Bogart Bryan, *A History of the National Capital*, 2 vols. (New York: MacMillan, 1914–1916) ("Bryan"), vol. 1, p. 425; Frances Few, "The Diary of Francis Few, 1808–1809," ed. Noble E. Cunningham Jr., *Journal of Southern History* 29 (August 1963): 345–61 ("Few"), p. 353.

xx. *much else to see*: Bryan, vol. 1, p. 425; Herman R. Friis, "Baron Alexander von Humboldt's Visit to Washington, D.C., June 1 through June 13, 1804," *Records of the Columbia Historical Society of Washington, D.C.* 63 (1963): 1–35 ("Friis"), p. 24; Kierner, p. 116.

xx–xxi. *hostile parties*: Jefferson to William Giles, December 17, 1794; Jefferson to John Taylor, June 4, 1798; "Selections from the Correspondence of Judge Richard Peters of Belmont," *Pennsylvania Magazine of History and Biography* 44 (1920): 325–42 ("Peters"), pp. 331–32, 336.

xxi. *"darling model"*: Jefferson to Richard Johnson, March 10, 1808.

xxi. *"a ship"*: Foster, p. 81.

xxi–xxiii. Jefferson on slavery: Lucia Stanton, *"Those Who Labor for My Happiness": Slavery at Thomas Jefferson's Monticello* (Charlottesville: University Press of Virginia, 2012) ("Stanton"), pp. 4, 14, and passim; *Patriarchs*, passim; Thomas Jefferson, *Notes on the State of Virginia* (Boston: Lilly and Wait, 1832), pp. 171, 50, 169–70; Jefferson to John Strode, June 5, 1805; Jefferson to Henri Grégoire, February 25, 1809; Jefferson to Edward Coles, August 25, 114.

xxiii. *"eventually destroy"*: Catharine Mitchill, "Catharine Mitchill's Letters from Washington, 1806–1812," ed. Carolyn Hoover Sung, *Quarterly Journal of the Library of Congress* 34 (July 1977): 171–89 ("Catharine Mitchill"), p. 178.

xxiii. Federalists v. Republicans: William Plumer, *William Plumer's Memorandum of Proceedings on the United States Senate 1803–1807*, ed. Everett S. Brown (New York: Macmillan, 1923) ("Plumer"), pp. 348, 390; Seale, vol. 1, p. 84; Gerald H. Clarfield, *Timothy Pickering and the American Republic* (Pittsburgh, PA: University of Pittsburgh Press, 1980), p. 146; James Elliott Cabot, *A Memoir of Ralph Waldo Emerson*, 2 vols. (Boston: Houghton Mifflin, 1895), vol. 1, p. 85 n. 2; Albert J. Beveridge, *The Life of John Marshall: Conflict and Construction, 1800–1815* (Boston: Houghton Mifflin, 1919), p. 7; William Cabell Bruce, *John Randolph of Roanoke*, 2 vols. (New York: Putnam, 1922) ("Bruce"), vol. 1, p. 79; Abigail Adams to Cotton Tufts, January 15, 1801.

xiii–xxiv. *Theodore Dwight*: Henry S. Randall, *The Life of Thomas Jefferson*, 3 vols. (New York: Derby & Jackson, 1858) ("Randall"), vol. 2, p. 661.

xxiv. *brilliance*: Boles, pp. 119, 176, 211, 220, 235–36, 241, 258–59, 308, 311; Founders: Summary of Public Service, after September 2, 1800.

xxiv–xxv. Pickering, Morse, and Moore: Rufus King, *Life and Correspondence of Rufus King*, 6 vols., ed. Charles R. King (New York: Putnam, 1894–1900) ("King"), vol. 4, pp. 364–65; Henry Adams, *History of the United States*, 9 vols. (New York: Antiquarian, 1962) ("Henry Adams"), vol. 1, p. 78; *The Oxford English Dictionary*, on "philosopher"; Gaye S. Wilson, *Jefferson on Display: Attire, Etiquette, and the Art of Presentation* (Charlottesville: University of Virginia Press, 2018) ("Wilson"), pp. 107–8; Thomas Moore, *The Poetical Works of Thomas Moore* (London: Longman, Brown, Green, and Longmans, 1849), p. 122; Dumas Malone, *Thomas Jefferson and His Time*, 6 vols. (Boston: Little, Brown, 1948–1981) ("Malone"), vol. 4, p. 177.

xxv. *"suspicious"*: Jefferson to Thomas McKean, July 24, 1801.

xxv. *"federal sect"*: Jefferson to Levi Lincoln, July 11, 1801.

xxv. *"social intercourse"*: Jefferson to Thomas Lomax, February 25, 1801.

AUTHOR'S NOTE

xxvii. *White House*: Irving Brant, *James Madison: The President 1809–1812* (Indianapolis, IN: Bobbs-Merrill, 1956), pp. 32–33; Robert V. Remini, "Becoming a National Symbol: The White House in the Early Nineteenth Century," in *The White House: The First Two Hundred Years*, ed. Frank Freidel and William Pencak (Boston: Northeastern University Press, 1994) ("Remini"), p. 23; W. B. Bryan, "The Name White House," *Records of the Columbia Historical Society* 33–34 (1932): 306–8; Constance M. Green, *Washington: Village and Capital* (Princeton, NJ: Princeton University Press, 1962) ("Green"), p. 48.

CHAPTER ONE

1. *December 12*: Diary of Ana Thornton, LOC when dated herein, Anna Maria Brodeau Thornton, "Diary of Mrs. William Thornton, 1800–1863," *Records of the Columbia Historical Society* 10 (1907): 88–226 when paginated ("Thornton Diary").

1. *Conrad & McMunn's*: *First Forty*, p. 12; *Life of Gallatin*, p. 253; Seale, vol. 1, p. 87.

1. *separate bed*: *The Correspondence and Miscellanies of the Hon. John Cotton Smith*, ed. John C. Smith (New York: Harper & Brothers, 1847) ("Cotton Smith") p. 206.

1. Boardinghouses: Bryan, vol. 1, p. 574; Plumer, pp. 523–24; *Life of Gallatin*, pp. 252–55; Cotton Smith, pp. 205–6; Young, pp. 97–106.

1. *Conrad & McMunn's*: Walter Hines Page and Arthur Wilson Page, *The World's Work* (New York: Doubleday, Page, 1913), vol. 25, p. 510; DC inhabitants to Jefferson, March 21, 1801.

1–2. *Washington*: Allan C. Clark, "Daniel Rapine, the Second Mayor," *Records of the Columbia Historical Society* 25 (1923): 194–215, p. 198; Nichols and Griswold, p. 65; Young, p. 22; Allen C. Clark, "Doctor and Mrs. William Thornton," *Records of the Columbia Historical Society, Washington, D.C.* 18 (1915): 171 ("'Doctor and Mrs. Thornton'"); John H. B. Latrobe, "Mr. Latrobe's Address," *Proceedings of the Fifteenth Annual Convention of the American Institute of Architects* 13–15 (1882): 2–21, p. 18.

2. *Conrad & McMunn's*: *First Forty*, p. 12; *Life of Gallatin*, p. 253; Stewart Lillard, *Lost in the District* (Silver Spring, MD: Lulu, 2017), p. 189.

2. *"put me out"*: Seale, vol. 1, p. 85.

2. Jefferson-Burr deadlock: Edward J. Larson, *A Magnificent Catastrophe* (New York: Free Press, 2007) ("Larson"), pp. 241–70; Abigail Adams to John Quincy Adams, January 29, 1801; Jefferson to Martha, January 16, 1801; Jefferson to Thomas McKean, March 9, 1801.

2–3. *"choice"* and *returned the compliment*: Abigail Adams to Mary Cranch, May 8, 1785; Jefferson to Madison, May 25, 1788; Valsania, p. 237 n. 131.

3. *causeway*: Byron Sunderland, *A Sketch of the Life of Dr. William Gunton* (Washington, DC: Joseph L. Pearson, 1878), p. 15.

3. Jefferson's ride: Abigail Adams to Thomas Adams, February 3, 1801; Busey, pp.128–29; Thornton Diary, pp. 205–6; Fazio and Snadon, p. 366; Ryan and Guinness, p. 85; Seale, vol. 1, pp. 24, 53–55, 66–67, 78–79, 99, 108–9; Janson, pp. 203, 205; Thornton Diary, pp. 119–20, 205–6.

3. Mrs. Adams and the house: Osborne, pp. 151–52; Abigail Adams to Mary Cranch, Abigail Smith, and Cotton Tufts, November 21, 1800, and November 27, 1800; Abigail Adams to Thomas Adams, January 15, 1801; Seale, vol. 1, pp. 80–82.

3–4. *"dreadful"* and *"expected"*: Abigail Adams to Mary Cranch, February 7, 1801; Abigail Adams to Thomas Adams, February 3, 1801.

4. *her thoughts*: Ryan and Guinness, p. 93.

4. Whites in Washington: Abigail Adams to Cotton Tufts, November 28, 1800.

4. *Dougherty*: Founders: Dougherty's letters to Jefferson, passim; Jefferson to Joseph Varnum, September 19, 1811; Thomas Jefferson, *Jefferson's Memorandum Books: Accounts, with Legal Records and Miscellany, 1767–1826*, ed. James A. Bear Jr. and Lucia C. Stanton, 2 vols. (Princeton, NJ: Princeton University Press, 1997) ("*Mem. Books*"), vol. 2, pp. 1036 n. 72, 1042, 1044–45; Kevin J. Hayes, *Thomas Jefferson in His Own Time: A Biographical Chronicle of His Life Drawn from Recollections, Interviews, and Memoirs by Family, Friends, and Associates* (Iowa City: University of Iowa Press, 2012) ("*Jefferson in His Own Time*"), p. 176; Randall, vol. 2, pp. 664–65; *First Forty*, p. 313.

4. *stable*: Ryan and Guinness, p. 94; Seale, vol. 1, p. 77.

4. *Süverman*: Dougherty to Jefferson, on or before April 25, 1802.

4. *John Quincy Adams*: Abigail Adams to Thomas Adams, February 3, 1801; Founders: Diary of John Quincy Adams, March 9 and 11, 1785; John Adams to Jefferson, January 22, 1825.

5. *dying wife's request*: *Patriarchs*, p. 121.

5. *"enemy's country . . . forgotten me"*: Jefferson to Martha, January 16, 1801.

5. Martha's letter: Martha and Thomas Randolph to Jefferson, January 31, 1801.

5. *"spies . . . hard indeed"*: Jefferson to Martha, February 5, 1801.

5–6. *Martha*: Kierner, p. 8; William H. Gaines Jr., *Thomas Mann Randolph, Jefferson's Son-in-Law* (Baton Rouge: Louisiana State University Press, 1966) ("Gaines"), p. 40; Sarah Butler Wister, ed., *Worthy Women of Our First Century* (Philadelphia: Lippincott, 1877) ("Wister"), pp. 17, 24; *Jefferson in His Own Time*, p. 173; Boles, p. 150; *First Forty*, p. 34; Fawn M. Brodie, *Thomas Jefferson: An Intimate History* (New York: Norton, 1974) ("Brodie"), pp. 168–69.

6. *substitute*: *Jefferson in His Own Time*, p. 159; Gaines, pp. 78–79.

6. *Maria*: Jon Meacham, *Thomas Jefferson: The Art of Power* (New York: Random House, 2013) ("Meacham"), pp. 195, 307; Randall, vol. 3, p. 102; Malone, vol. 4, pp. 171–72; Wister, pp. 16, 23, 35–36; Sarah N. Randolph, *The Domestic Life of Thomas Jefferson* (New York: Harper, 1871) ("Randolph"), pp. 294–302; Maria to Jefferson, April 18, 1801, and January 11, 1803; Dolley Madison, *Memoirs and Letters of Dolly Madison* (Boston: Houghton, Mifflin, 1886) ("*Dolley Madison*"), p, 29; Edwin Morris Betts and James Adam Bear, eds., *The Family Letters of Thomas Jefferson* (Columbia: University of Missouri Press, 1966) ("*Family Letters*"), pp. 6–7; Boles, p. 150; Abigail Adams to Jefferson, June 26 and July 6, 1787; John Adams to Thomas Jefferson, July 10, 1787.

6. *"comfortless moments"*: Jefferson to John Eppes, January 19, 1801.

7. *he told Maria*: Jefferson to Maria, February 15, 1801.

7. *tipped* and *"experiments"*: Larson, pp. 248–69; James A. Bayard to Hamilton, January 7, 1801.

7. *old ladies*: TJR Memoir, p. 34.

7. Salary and expenses: Stanton, p. 45; *Mem. Books*, passim; Noble E. Cunningham, *The Process of Government under Jefferson* (Princeton, NJ: Princeton University Press, 1978) ("*Process*") pp. 44–45; Polkinhorn & Hall to Jefferson, March 12, 1805.

7. *"a Stuard"*: Patrick Sim to Jefferson, February 26, 1801.

7–8. Letter to Létombe: Jefferson to Létombe, February 22, 1801.

8. *Evans*: Jefferson to William Evans, February 22, 1801; Evans to Jefferson, February 23 and February 27, 1801.

8. *Hemings*: *Patriarchs*, p. 212; Thomas J. Craughwell, *Thomas Jefferson's Crème Brûlée* (Philadelphia: Quirk Books, 2012) ("*Crème Brûlée*"), pp. 3, 12–13, 76; Boles, pp. 129, 151.
8. *glad to have him back*: Jefferson to William Evans, February 22, 1801.
8–9. *Say*: Francis Say to Jefferson, February 23, 1801.

CHAPTER TWO

11. *"suitable for you"*: Adams to Jefferson, February 20, 1801.
11. *stable*: Patrick Phillips-Schrock, *The White House: An Illustrated Architectural History* (Jefferson, NC: McFarland, 2013) ("Phillips-Schrock"), p. 148; Malone, vol. 4, p. 41; Seale, vol. 1, p. 90; Margaret Brown Klapthor, "A First Lady and a New Frontier," *Historic Preservation* 15 (1963): 88–93 ("Klapthor"), p. 93.
11–12. *inauguration*: Boles, p. 277; *Patriarchs*, p. 182; British Ministers' Transcribed Letters to the Foreign Office ("British Ministers"), LOC, vol. 5/32, p. 53, no. 15; Thornton to Grenville, March 4, 1801; Samuel Clagett Busey, "The Centennial of the First Inauguration of a President at the Permanent Seat of the Government," *Records of the Columbia Historical Society* 5 (1902): 96–111, pp. 98–99; Seale, vol. 1, pp. 86–87; *First Forty*, p. 26; Boles, p. 325; Jefferson to Létombe, March 19, 1801.
12. *Marshall*: Meacham, p. 350; Marshall to Joseph Story, September 18, 1821.
12. *"decent respect"*: *Life of Plumer*, p. 240.
12. *"scattered buildings"*: John Davis, p. 185.
13. *maître d'hôtel*: Létombe to Jefferson, February 28 and March 5, 1801; Jefferson to Rapin, April 3, 1801; Jefferson to Thomas Randolph, January 10, 1801.
13. *Yrujo*: Yrujo to Jefferson, March 13, 1801.
13–14. Rapin and Julien: *Intelligencer*, March 20, 1801; Létombe to Jefferson, February 28, March 15, and March 26, 1801; Jefferson to Létombe, March 5, 19, and 31, 1801; Jefferson to Yrujo, March 24, 1801.
14. Letter to Evans: Jefferson to William Evans, March 31, 1801.
14. Damaged wrist: Valsania, p. 95; *Patriarchs*, p. 216.
14–15. Jefferson and speeches and public appearances: Valsania, p. 2; Boles, p. 27; Joseph J. Ellis, *American Sphinx: The Character of Thomas Jefferson* (New York: Knopf, 1997) ("*Sphinx*"), p. 192; *Patriarchs*, p. 194.
15. *Lewis*: Thomas C. Danisi and John C. Jackson, *Meriwether Lewis* (Amherst, NY: Prometheus Books, 2009) ("Danisi and Jackson"), passim; Jefferson to Lewis, February 23, 1801; *Peale*, vol. 2, pt. 2, p. 829 n. 3; Reuben Gold Thwaites, ed., *Original Journals of the Lewis and Clark Expedition, 1804–1806*, 7 vols. (New York: Dodd & Mead, 1904–1905) ("*Original Journals*"), vol. 1, p. xxiv; Thomas Jefferson, "Memoir of Meriwether Lewis," in *History*

of the Expedition under the Command of Lewis and Clark, by Elliott Coues, 4 vols. (New York: Francis P. Harper, 1893) ("'Memoir of Lewis'"), vol. 1, pp. xxiv–xxvii; Jefferson to Volney, February 11, 1806.

15–17. Jefferson recruits Lewis: Jefferson to Wilkinson, February 23, 1801; Jefferson to Lewis, February 23, 1801; Lewis to Jefferson, March 10, 1801.

17. Black and white servants: Stanton, p. 43; Jefferson to John Eppes, August 7, 1804; *Patriarchs*, pp. 65–71, 91–93, 122–32, 147–49, 177–80.

17–18. *Freeman*: *Mem. Books*, vol. 2, p. 1043 n. 88; Jefferson to Ropin, April 17, 1801; Stanton, pp. 43–44; Founders: Certificate of Sale and Manumission of John Freeman, July 23, 1804; Thomas Jefferson and John Freeman, people.wku.edu/andrew.mcmichael/freeman.html; author's correspondence with Lucia Stanton in March 2019.

18. *livery*: Founders: Carpenter's invoices, March 31 and July 1, 1801; Stanton, p. 43.

18. *"abominable crime"*: Founders: Jefferson's Observations on DéMeunier's Manuscript, June 22, 1789.

18. *Maher*: *Mem. Books*, vol. 2, pp. 1035 n. 69, 1036, 1040, 1042, 1045, 1054; Founders: Statement of account, July 1, 1801; Rapin to Jefferson, April 3, 1801.

18. *servants' hall*: Seale, vol. 1, pp. 76, 83–84, 97, 99.

18. Generous pay and good food: Founders: Terms for Conrad & McMunn's Boarding House, ca. November 27, 1800; Margaret Bayard Smith, "The President's House Forty Years Ago," *Rover* 3 (1844): 145–50 ("'Forty Years'"), p. 148; Jean Hanvey Hazelton, "Thomas Jefferson Gourmet," *American Heritage* 15 (October 1964): 20 and 102–5 ("'Gourmet'"), p. 105.

19. *Süverman*: Stanton, p. 44; *Mem. Books*, vol. 2, pp. 1040, 1042, 1056, 1061, 1071; Rapin to Jefferson, May 17, 1802; Jefferson to Rapin, June 3, 1802.

19. *scullion*: *Mem. Books*, vol. 2, p. 1040.

19. *Kramer*: *Mem. Books*, vol. 2, pp. 1042, 1045, 1054, 1056, 1061.

19. *Noel*: Stanton, p. 45; *Mem. Books*, vol. 2, pp. 1045, 1054, 1056, 1061, 1077, 1100.

19. *"Never allow"*: Stanton, p. 44.

19. *tailor*: John Barnes to Jefferson, March 28, 1801; Founders: Statements of Account with Thomas Carpenter, March 31 and July 1, 1801.

19–21. Jefferson as architect: Jefferson to L'Enfant, April 10, 1791; *Patriarchs*, p. 103; Boles, pp. 105, 132, 219, 267; Fiske Kimball, *Thomas Jefferson, Architect* (New York: Da Capo, 1968) ("*Thomas Jefferson, Architect*"), pp. 56–57, 68–71; Nichols and Griswold, pp. 3, 6; Jefferson to Latrobe, November 2, 1802; April 23, 1803, February 28, 1804, November 3, 1804; Jefferson to John Lenthall, July 14, 1805; *Process*, p. 316; Jefferson to James Oldham, January 19, 1805.

21. Jefferson and early Washington: Ryan and Guinness, pp. 23–24; Edward Dumbauld, "Thomas Jefferson and the City of Washington," *Records of the*

Columbia Historical Society 50 (1980): 67–80; John W. Reps, *Monumental Washington: The Planning and Development of the Capital Center* (Princeton, NJ: Princeton University Press, 1967) ("Reps"), pp. 10–15, 21, and fig. 7; Catherine Allgor, *Parlor Politics: In Which the Ladies of Washington Help Build a City and a Government* (Charlottesville: University Press of Virginia, 2000) ("*Parlor Politics*"), pp. 10–17; Seale, vol. 1, pp. 11–27, 87; Gordon S. Brown, *Incidental Architect: William Thornton and the Cultural Life of Early Washington, D.C., 1794–1828* (Athens: Ohio University Press, 2009) ("Brown").

21–22. *competition*: Phillips-Schrock, pp. 20–29; Ryan and Guinness, pp. 31–61; Seale, vol. 1, pp. 27–32, 89; Jefferson to L'Enfant, April 10, 1791; Bess Furman, *White House Profile: A Social History of the White House, Its Occupants, and Its Festivities* (Indianapolis, IN: Bobbs-Merrill, 1951) ("Furman"), p. 38.

22. *the mansion rose*: Seale, vol. 1, pp. 24–34, 70–72, 80, 88–90.

22. *"Presidoliad"*: Ryan and Guinness, p. 61; Remini, p. 18; Plumer, p. 600; Thomas A. Diggs to Jefferson, September 11, 1809.

CHAPTER THREE

23. *"simplicity and purity"*: *Intelligencer*, March 11, 1801.

23. *little to constrain him*: *Parlor Politics*, pp. 16–17.

23. *"savage enough"*: Jefferson to Geismar, September 6, 1785.

23. *two weeks* and *transform*: Seale, in *Changing White House*, p. 8; Seale, vol. 1, pp. 87–90.

23–24. *Adams* and *Washington*: Seale, vol. 1, p. 78; Washington to the Commissioners, March 3, 1793.

24. *Commissioners* and *Congress*: National Archives, Records of the Commissioners for the District of Columbia, February 23, 1801, Microcopy 371, Roll 2; *U.S. Statutes at Large*, March 3, 1801, vol. 2, pp. 121–22.

24. *Claxton*: Claxton to Jefferson, March 4, 1801; Hamilton to William Johnson, March 27, 1789.

24. Furnishings: "Thomas Jefferson's Windsor Chairs," Typescript by Fiske Kimball, Kimball Manuscripts, Box 48, "Jefferson's Furniture—General," No. 5232 UVA, Smalls Library; Marie G. Kimball, "The Original Furnishings of the White House" Parts I and II, *Antiques* 16 (June 1929): 481–86 and (July 1929): 33–37 ("'Original Furnishings'"); Abigail Adams to Abigail Smith, November 27, 1800; Klapthor, p. 90.

25. *household furnishings fund*: *Philadelphia Aurora*, March 6, 1801; *Annals of Congress*, 6th Cong., 1799–1801, pp. 1069–70.

25. *decaying*: Fazio and Snadon, p. 364.

25–26. *"true Republicanism"*: Abigail Adams to Cotton Tufts, November 28, 1800.

26–27. *Cabinet: Oxford English Dictionary*; Jefferson to Peale, November 28, 1804; Andrea Wulf, *The Invention of Nature* (New York: Knopf, 2015) ("Wulf"), p. 100; Jefferson to Martha, June 10, 1793; Jefferson to Lemaire, April 25, 1809; Peter Waddell, "A Bird That Whistles," *White House Historical Association*, www.whitehousehistory.org; Phillips-Schrock, p. C-3; Fazio and Snadon, p. 360; Seale, vol. 1, pp. 92–93; Jefferson to Lemaire, August 5, 1807; *First Forty*, pp. 70–71, 385; Edwin Thomas Martin, *Thomas Jefferson, Scientist* (New York: H. Schuman, 1952) ("Martin"), p. 86; Jefferson to John Adams, May 17, 1818; "Doctor and Mrs. Thornton," p. 201.

28. *Setting Room*: Melish, vol. 1, pp. 148–49; Jefferson to Lemaire, May 14, 1802; Malone, vol. 4, pp. 44–45.

28. *Oval Room*: Jefferson's Oval Room is not to be confused with the Oval Office, to be built in the distant future in a new west wing. National Archives, Records of the Commissioners for the District of Columbia, March 12, 1801, Microcopy 371, Roll 2; Jonathan Pliska, *A Garden for the President* (Washington, DC: White House Historical Association, 2016) ("Pliska"), p. 12; Fazio and Snadon, pp. 360, 364; Seale, vol. 1, pp. 33, 89.

28. *stairs*: Fazio and Snadon, p. 363; Claxton to Jefferson, May 18, 1801; Malone, vol. 4, p. 44.

28. *view* and *bedchamber*: Abigail Adams to Amelia Smith, November 21, 1800; Malone, vol. 4, p. 46; Phillips-Schrock, p. 37.

28. *warmth* and *cold*: Jefferson to William Dunbar, January 12, 1801; Abigail Adams to Abigail Smith, November 27, 1800; Lemaire to Jefferson, September 25, 1804; Jefferson to George Jefferson, October 23, 1806; Seale, vol. 1, p. 98; Thornton Diary, pp. 92–93.

28–29. Privies, water closets, and pots: National Archives, Records of the Commissioners for the District of Columbia: Letters sent by the Commissioners, March 12, 1801, Microcopy 371, Roll 4; Furman, p. 27; Claxton to Jefferson, June 13 and 18, 1802; Founders: Lemaire's Memorandum of Items for the President's House, May 28, 1802.

29. *porticos*: Phillips-Schrock, p. 22.

29. *Ladies' Drawing Room*: Jefferson to Martha, March 12, 1807; "Original Furnishings," p. 36.

29. *Jefferson moved in*: *Intelligencer*, March 20, 1801.

29. *"necessary"*: National Archives, Records of the Commissioners for the District of Columbia, Letters sent by the Commissioners, March 20, 1801, Microcopy 371, Roll 4; Seale, vol. 1, p. 88.

29. *bells*: Seale, vol. 1, pp. 81, 88; Jackson, pp. 212–13.

29. *his messages*: Malone, vol. 4, p. 29.

29. *East Room*: Seale, vol. 1, pp. 33, 81, 83; Claxton to Jefferson, May 18, 1801; *Mem. Books*, vol. 2, pp. 1035, 1040; "Forty Years," p. 146; "Foreword," *White House History* 17 (Winter 2006), p. 3; Catharine Mitchill, p. 181; Ryan and

Guinness, p. 124; Fazio and Snadon, p. 363; Malone, vol. 4, p. 43; William Cranch to John Adams, May 13, 1801.

29–30. Lighting: Seale, vol. 1, pp. 97–98; Claxton to Jefferson, May 18, 1801; Caldcleugh & Thomas to Jefferson, November 6, 1804; Jefferson to Charles Thomson, December 11, 1784; Abigail Adams to Abigail Smith, November 21, 1800.

30. Jefferson, Lewis, and Rapin: Jefferson to Lewis, March 31, 1801; Lewis to Jefferson, April 3, 1801; Rapin to Jefferson, April 3, 1801.

30. *carter* and *Hern*: Jefferson to Samuel Carr, May 1, 1801; *Mem. Books*, vol. 2, p. 1189 n. 65; Stanton, pp. 17, 23, 46; Jefferson to Dougherty, August 24, 1809; Jefferson to Edmund Bacon, November 21, 1806.

30. *Jefferson wrote Rapin*: Jefferson to Rapin, April 18, 1801.

31. Trips to Monticello: Jefferson to Madison, April 25, 1801; Jefferson to Levi Lincoln, April 25, 1801; Randolph, p. 289; Jefferson to John Barnes, July 20, 1805; *Mem. Books*, vol. 2, p. 1043 n. 88; Founders: Notes on Travel Distances, October 2, 1808; Jefferson to Henry Dearborn, August 26, 1805; Jefferson to Mr. Brown, January 18, 1805; Jefferson to Martha, June 3, 1802; Jefferson to Thomas Randolph, October 22, 1802; Jefferson to Madison, April 30, 1801; author's correspondence with Lucia Stanton in March 2019.

31. Cleaning and Edward's complaints: Rapin to Jefferson, April 3, 1801; Carson, pp. 94–95, 192 n. 61; Jefferson to Rapin, April 17, 1801.

32. *$19.50*: National Archives, RG 42, Entry 15, Journals, vol. 3, p. 332.

32. *Cranch*: William Cranch to Samuel Shaw, May 15, 1801, Massachusetts Historical Society, Photostats Collection, Box 43.

32. *"grand lama"*: Bryan, vol. 1, pp. 405–6.

32. *disgraced*: Brant, p. 41; Jefferson to Thomas Randolph, May 14, 1801; Jefferson to Martha, May 28, 1801; Catherine Allgor, *A Perfect Union: Dolly Madison and the Creation of the American Nation* (New York: Henry Holt, 2006) ("*A Perfect Union*"), p. 95.

32–33. Letters to daughters: Jefferson to Maria and to Martha, May 28, 1801; Jefferson to Maria, June 24, 1801.

33. Lewis and Randolph: Stephen E. Ambrose, *Undaunted Courage* (New York: Simon & Schuster, 1996) ("Ambrose"), pp. 59–60; Jefferson to Thomas Randolph, June 4, 1801.

33. *better-built town*: National Archives, Records of the Commissioners for the District of Columbia, June 9, 1801, Microcopy 371, Roll 2; Bryan, vol. 1, p. 436; *Mem. Books*, vol. 2, p. 1043 n. 90; Brown, p. 53; Jefferson to James Currie, June 23, 1805 (Dr. Bruff); *Intelligencer*, December 11, 1801, and January 4, 1802; Jefferson to Monroe, April 17, 1816.

CHAPTER FOUR

35. *executive council*: Much of the material on the executive council is in *Process*, passim.

35–36. *Madison*: Brant, pp. 35, 37, 57; Meacham, pp. 121–22; Boles, p. 110; Louisa Adams, vol. 1, p. 204; Foster's Notes, p. 44; Foster, pp. 139–40, 155; *Parlor Politics*, p. 90; Paul Jennings, *A Colored Man's Reminiscences of Mr. Madison* (Brooklyn, NY: George C. Beadle, 1865), p. 19; Few, p. 351; William W. Story, ed., *Life and Letters of Joseph Story*, 2 vols. (Boston: C. C. Little and J. Brown, 1851) ("Story"), vol. 1, p. 152; *First Forty*, pp. 28–29, 61 n. 1; Minnie Clare Yarborough, ed., *The Reminiscences of William C. Preston* (Chapel Hill: University of North Carolina Press, 1933) (*Preston*), pp. 7, 9.

36. Dolley Madison: Louisa Adams, vol. 1, pp. 204–5, 232–33; Anne H. Wharton, *Social Life in the Early Republic* (Philadelphia: J. B. Lippincott, 1903), p. 117; *First Forty*, p. 29; Few, pp. 351–52.

36. *Albert Gallatin*: Dunlap, vol. 2, p. 384; Brant, p. 57; Jefferson to Thomas Randolph, May 14, 1801; Louisa Adams, vol. 1, p. 199; Story, 152.

37. Hannah Gallatin: *A Perfect Union*, p. 58; *First Forty*, p. 27; Louisa Adams, vol. 1, pp. 199–200, 207; Meacham, pp. 361–62.

37. The Dearborns: Malone, vol. 4, p. 58; William P. Cutler and Julia P. Cutler, *Life, Journals and Correspondence of Manasseh Cutler, LL.D.*, 2 vols. (Cincinnati: Robert Clarke, 1888) ("Cutler"), p. 96; Louisa Adams, vol. 1, pp. 206, 220; Jefferson to John Strode, August 26, 1805.

37–38. *Levi Lincoln*: Louisa Adams, vol. 1, pp. 206–7; Cutler, vol. 2, p. 96; *Life of Gallatin*, p. 276; James Henry Lea, *The Ancestry of Abraham Lincoln* (Boston: Houghton Mifflin, 1909), p. 136.

38. The Smiths: Jefferson to Gouverneur Morris, May 8, 1801; *Process*, pp. 13–14; Plumer, p. 343; Louisa Adams, vol. 1, p. 206; Few, pp. 348, 352.

38–41. The administration and its processes: *Process*, passim; Jefferson to Thomas Randolph, May 14, 1801; Malone, vol. 4, pp. 61–63 n. 23; *Sphinx*, 188; Founders: Circular Letter from Jefferson, November 6, 1801; Jefferson to Gallatin, November 10, 1801; Young, pp. 28–31, 232; *Sphinx*, pp. 189, 193–95; Jefferson to Thomas Randolph, November 16, 1801; Jefferson to Destutt de Tracy, January 26, 1811; "Forty Years," p. 145; Jefferson to Gallatin, November 20, 1806, and July 10, 1807; Madison to Monroe, December 26, 1803; Coles Diary, March 17, April 3, and July 4, 1807; *The Complete Anas of Thomas Jefferson, 1791–1809*, ed. Franklin B. Sawvel (New York: Round Table, 1903) ("*Anas*"), pp. 213–73; Jefferson to John Breckinridge, March 21, 1806; Jefferson to Walter Jones, March 5, 1810; Jefferson to William Short, June 12, 1807; *Parlor Politics*, p. 30; Jefferson to William Duane, March 22, 1806; J. Q. Adams to Abigail Adams, April 23–May 16, 1817; Massachusetts Historical Society, Adams Papers, reel 437; Brant, p. 56.

41–42. Cabinet editors: Jefferson to Madison, November 22, 1805; Malone, vol. 5, p. 198; Brant, pp. 57–58; Albert Gallatin, *Writings of Albert Gallatin*, 3 vols., ed. Henry Adams (Philadelphia: J. B. Lippincott, 1879), vol. 1, pp. 62–68, 104, 106, 215, 227; Levi Lincoln to Jefferson, October 10, 1803; Robert Smith to Jefferson, November 27, 1805.

42. Invented words: *The Oxford English Dictionary.*

42. *impossibility*: Jefferson to Thomas Cooper, April 17, 1801.

42. *furniture*: Marie G. Kimball, "Thomas Jefferson's French Furniture," *Antiques* 15 (February 1929): 123–28, p. 124.

42. Claxton and Rapin: Thomas Claxton to Jefferson, May 18, 1801.

CHAPTER FIVE

43. *letter of contrition*: Jefferson to Moustier, May 17, 1788.

43. *"great machine"*: Jefferson to Walter Jones, March 31, 1801.

43–44. *Washington*: Joseph Ellis, *His Excellency George Washington* (New York: Knopf, 2004), pp. 184–85; Martin Van Buren, *Insights into the Origin and Cause of Political Parties of the United States* (New York: Hurd and Houghton, 1867).

44. *"idolatry"*: Wilson, p. 83.

44. *poorly served*: Valsania, p. 212 n. 115.

44. *sycophants*: Jefferson to Madison, June 9, 1793.

44. *Hamilton*: *Patriarchs*, pp. 173, 186–92; Hamilton to Washington, May 5, 1789.

44. *"itching for crowns"*: Jefferson to Thomas Paine, June 19, 1792.

44. Jefferson and Macon: Nathaniel Macon to Jefferson, April 20 and 23, 1801; Jefferson to Macon, May 14, 1801.

45. *Washington's birthday*: Jefferson to Madison, February 15, 1798; Gail Weesner and Henry Lee, *Boston Common* (Charleston, SC: Arcadia, 2005), p. 21.

45. Jefferson's birthday: Thornton Diary, February 22, 1804; Margaret Bayard Smith, *A Winter in Washington; or, Memoirs of the Seymour Family*, 2 vols. (New York: E. Bliss and E. White, 1824) ("*Winter in Washington*"), a novel in which Smith is understood to have lightly dramatized facts, vol. 1, p. 11; Jefferson to Lincoln, August 30, 1803; Robert M. S. McDonald, *Confounding Father: Thomas Jefferson's Image in His Own Time* (Charlottesville: University of Virginia Press, 2016) ("McDonald"), p. 131.

45–46. *manners*: TJR Memoir, pp. 8–10; Jefferson to Dolley Madison, July 6, 1805; Jefferson to Martha, June 18, 1802; Henry Adams, vol. 1, p. 133; J. Hamilton Moore, *The Young Gentleman and Lady's Monitor and English Teacher's Assistant* (New York: Evert Duyckinck, 1813) ("J. Hamilton Moore"), p. 180; Jefferson to Livingston, April 30, 1800.

46. *dress*: Wilson, pp. 11, 26–27, 105; Valsania, p. 37, fig. 2, and pp. 48–50, 181, 210 n. 101.

46. *letters*: See Jefferson's endorsements on his mail in Founders, passim; Susannah Febvrier to Jefferson, January 8, 1805; Samuel Harrison to Jefferson, May 15, 1805; Mary Glenholmes to Jefferson, March 11, 1801.

46. *"Etiquette!"*: Robert R. Davis Jr., "Pell-Mell: Jeffersonian Etiquette and Protocol," *Historian* 43 (August 1981): 509–29 ("Davis"), p. 510.

46. relaxed *protocol*: Madison to Monroe, January 19, 1804.

46. Handshakes: Davis, p. 511; Valsania, pp. 24, 202 n. 36; Journal of Augustus Foster ("Foster Journal"), vol. 2, LOC, December 6, 1804.

46–47. Washington's dinner: William Maclay, *Journal of William Maclay* (New York: D. Appleton, 1890) ("Maclay"), p. 138.

48. Adams's vanity: Founders: Letter from Alexander Hamilton concerning the Public Conduct and Character of John Adams, October 24, 1800; Maclay, p. 7; "William Duane," p. 31.

48. *William Duane*: "William Duane," p. 31.

48. *no state dinners*: Jefferson to William Short, January 23, 1804.

48. *levees*: Wilson, p. 98; www.mountvernon.org, "Levees"; Richard Côté, *Strength and Honor: The Life of Dolley Madison* (Mount Pleasant, SC: Corinthian Books, 2004) ("Côté"), pp. 210–12.

48–50. *open door*: Jefferson to Philippe Reibelt, December 31, 1804; "Forty Years," pp. 150; *First Forty*, pp. 397, 405; Randall, vol. 2, p. 667 n.; Côté, p. 216; Foster, pp. 106–7; John Quincy Adams, *Memoirs of John Quincy Adams*, 12 vols., ed. Charles Francis Adams (Philadelphia: J. B. Lippincott, 1874) ("*JQA Memoirs*"), vol. 1, p. 314; Jefferson to Lafayette, April 11, 1787; *Anas*, p. 222; Robert Smith to Jefferson, November 28, 1803; Thomas Moore to Jefferson, January 22, 1807; Nancy Ray to Jefferson, January 31, 1807; Melish, vol. 1, pp. 148–49; David Ramsay to Jefferson, May 19, 1805; Malone, vol. 4, p. 181; Monroe to Jefferson, September 28, 1803; Lafayette to Jefferson, June 4, 1805; William Hamilton to Jefferson, October 30, 1805; John Symmes to Jefferson, September 5, 1806; Jefferson to Zachariah Poulson, April 24, 1806.

50–51. *gentlemen of science*: Jefferson to William Roscoe, July 1, 1806; Jefferson to Robert Patterson, January 10, 1805; Jefferson to Paul Pillsbury, October 18, 1806.

51. *"refrigerator"*: *Mem. Books*, vol. 2, p. 1132 n. 4.

51. *Thornton*: Charles O. Paullin, "Early British Diplomats in Washington," *Records of the Columbia Historical Society* 44–45 (1942–1943): 241–67, p. 244; Davis, p. 518; William Henry Masterson, *Tories and Democrats: British Diplomats in Pre-Jacksonian America* (College Station: Texas A&M University Press, 1985) ("Masterson"), pp. 53–56, 60; Jefferson to Thornton, November 5, 1802.

51–52. Thornton's reports: British Ministers, vol. 5/32, nos. 2, 4, 17, and 58, March 1, 1802, July 3, 1802, and vol. 5/35, no. 9.

52. *Kosciuszko*: Jefferson to Kosciuszko, April 2, 1802.

53. *Aurora*: Malone, vol. 4, pp. 499–500.

53. *"frivolities"*: Adams to Rush, December 25, 1811.

53. Jefferson's routine: Jefferson to Thomas Randolph, November 16, 1801, James Madison, December 29, 1801, William Thornton, February 14, 1802, and James Maury, June 16, 1815; *Process*, pp. 35–41.

54–55. Horseback, no carriage: Thomas Jefferson, *Thomas Jefferson's Farm Book*, ed. Edwin Morris Betts (Charlottesville, VA: Thomas Jefferson's Memorial Foundation, 1953) ("*Farm Book*"), pp. 99–100; Jefferson to James Madison, June 9, 1793, John Eppes, January 1, 1802 and May 27, 1805, Martha, June 18, 1802, Thomas Randolph, November 16, 1801, James Madison, December 29, 1801, William Thornton, February 14, 1802, Abiel Holmes, December 7, 1804, Anne Randolph, December 8, 1806, and William Short, April 10, 1824; *Jefferson in His Own Time*, pp. 165, 170; *Process*, pp. 35–41; Valsania, pp. 12–16; *Patriarchs*, p. 46; McDonald, p. 131; Thornton Diary, p. 208; Plumer, p. 550; Samuel Taggart, "Letters of Samuel Taggart," *Proceedings of the American Antiquarian Society*, New Series 33 (April 11–October 17, 1923): Part One: 113–226 ("Taggart"), p. 125; Wilson, pp. 105–6, 165; Gouverneur Morris to Hamilton, March 11, 1802 n. 3; "Forty Years," p. 149; Randolph, p. 421; Foster, pp. 8–9; *First Forty*, p. 393; Thomas Main to Jefferson, June 27 and February 24, 1806, and March 10, 1807; *Intelligencer*, November 24, 1802.

55. *mockingbird*: "Forty Years," p. 146; Jefferson to Lemaire, April 25, 1809.

55–56. *Independence Day*: Wilson, p. 120; Thornton Diary, pp. 187 and 191; Ryan and Guinness, pp. 126–27; Remini, p. 19; "Forty Years," p. 150; Founders: Editorial Note: Conference with Little Turtle, pp. 4–5, and Inventory of President's House, February 19, 1809; *First Forty*, pp. 14, 30–31, 398–99; Plumer, p. 361; Seale, vol. 1, pp. 106–7; Ryan and Guinness, pp. 126–27; Damon Lee Fowler, ed., *Dining at Monticello: In Good Taste and Abundance* (Charlottesville, VA: Thomas Jefferson Foundation, 2005, dist. by University of North Carolina Press) ("Fowler"), p. 13; Klapthor, pp. 91, 93; Brown, p. 61; "Fourth of July Celebrations at the White House in the 19th Century" and "The First Fourth of July Celebration at the President's House," www.whitehousehistory.org; *Intelligencer*, July 7, 1802.

CHAPTER SIX

57. *bowel disorder*: Benjamin Rush, *Letters of Benjamin Rush*, ed. L. H. Butterfield, 2 vols. (Princeton, NJ: Princeton University Press, 1951) ("*Rush Letters*"), vol. 2, pp. 56–59, 863; Valsania, pp. 92–93.

57. *Men of science*: Warden, pp. 16–18, 21.

57. *lethal*: Thornton Diary, pp. 186, 192–94; Louisa Adams, vol. 1, p. 194; Stanley Lane-Pool, *Life of the Right Hon. Stratford Canning, Viscount Stratford de Redcliffe*, 2 vols. (London: Longmans Green, 1888) ("Lane-Pool"), pp. 319–21; Jefferson to Gouverneur Morris, May 8, 1801, Madison, July 25, 1805, and Gallatin, September 18, 1801; Melish, vol. 1, p. 203.

58. *"executive recesses"*: *Process*, pp. 45–46; Jefferson to Gallatin, September 18, 1801, John Harvie, April 15, 1805, Joseph Dougherty, May 19, 1806, and John Barnes, August 1, 1807; John Barnes to Jefferson, August 20, 1802; Boles, p. 335; Foster, p. 144.

58. Medical care: Founders: Gantt's invoice to Jefferson, March 2, 1802; Parrott to Jefferson, March 14, 1801 n.; Jefferson to Waterhouse, June 26, 1801; John Barnes to Jefferson, September 28, 1802.

58–59. Rapin leaves, Lemaire recruited: Jefferson to Rapin, August 14, 1801, and October 11, 1801; Létombe to Jefferson, June 16, July 11, August 1 and 5, 1801; Jefferson to Létombe, July 15 and 29, 1801; Rapin to Jefferson, August 10, 1801; Stanton, p. 49; Fazio and Snadon, p. 374.

59–60. *Lemaire*: "Gourmet," pp. 21, 103; "Forty Years," p. 148; Stanton, pp. 42, 44–45, 49–51; *Crème Brûlée*, p. 156; Marie Kimball, *Thomas Jefferson's Cook Book* (Charlottesville: University Press of Virginia, 1976) ("*Cook Book*"), p. 10; John Hailman, *Thomas Jefferson on Wine* (Jackson: University Press of Mississippi, 2006) ("Hailman"), pp. 26, 290; *Mem. Books*, vol. 2. pp. 1053 n. 18; Jefferson to Lemaire, August 11, 1803, July 29 and September 25, 1804, July 28, 1808, and March 16, 1809; Lemaire to Jefferson, August 6, 1803, and September 17, 1804; *Jefferson in His Own Time*, p. 176; John Barnes to Jefferson, September 21, 1802; Seale, vol. 1, p. 96; Donald Jackson, ed., *Letters of the Lewis and Clark Expedition, with Related Documents, 1783–1854* (Urbana: University of Illinois Free Press, 1962) ("*L&C Letters*"), p. 254 n.; Jefferson to Maria, January 18, 1803.

61. *fence*: Jefferson to Létombe, July 29, 1801; Randall, vol. 3, p. 118; Suzanne Turner, "The Landscape of the President's House: Garden of Democracy," in *Changing White House*, ed. Wendell Garrett (Boston: Northeastern University Press, 1995), pp. 161–81; National Archives, Records of the Commissioners for the District of Columbia, Letter from the Commissioners to Richard Forrest, Esq., July 29, 1801, Microcopy 371, Roll 4: Records of the Commissioners; Pliska, pp. 11–12; Thomas Froncek, ed., *An Illustrated History of the City of Washington* (New York: Knopf, 1977), p. 85.

61. *demolition*: Remini, p. 22; National Archives, RG 42, Entry 16, Contract File, April 10, 1807.

61. *interior work*: Rapin to Jefferson, August 10, 1801; Claxton to Jefferson, August 27, 1801.

61–62. *Oval Room*: Phillips-Schrock, p. 99.

62. *anxious notes*: National Archives, Records of the Commissioners for the District of Columbia, Letters sent by the Commissioners, September 21 and 22, 1801, Microcopy 371, Roll 4.

62. *disarray*: National Archives, Records of the Commissioners for the District of Columbia, Letters sent by the Commissioners, letter to Lovering & Dyer, November 19, 1801, Microcopy 371, Roll 2; Abby G. Baker, "The Erection of the White House," *Records of the Columbia Historical Society* 16 (1913): 120–49, pp. 146–47.

62. *Hemings*: Jefferson to William Evans, November 1, 1801; Henry Wiencek, *Master of the Mountain: Thomas Jefferson and His Slaves* (New York: Farrar, Straus and Giroux, 2012) ("Wiencek"), p. 183; Jefferson to Thomas Randolph, December 4, 1801.

62. *considerate note*: Jefferson to Rapin, October 11, 1801.

63. *"grates"*: Claxton to Jefferson, October 19, 1801; Jefferson to Claxton, October 22, 1801.

63. *Intelligencer*: *Intelligencer*, November 25, 1801.

63–64. Improvements and auction: Nichols and Griswold, p. 64; Bryan, vol. 1, pp. 418–19 n. 2; National Archives, Records of the Commissioners for the District of Columbia, November 12, 1801, and May 6, 1802, Microcopy 371, Roll 2; Ryan and Guinness, p. 94.

64. *Dougherty*: Jefferson to Samuel H. Smith, August 15, 1813; *Mem. Books*, vol. 2, p. 1036 n. 72; Stanton, p. 42; Founders: Thomas Jefferson's Circular to Certain Republican Senators, September 19, 1811; *First Forty*, pp. 313–14.

64. *Thermo Lamps*: *Intelligencer*, April 18, 1802; *Mem. Books*, vol. 2, p. 1071 n. 61; Benjamin Henfrey to Jefferson, December 19, 1801.

64. *Betsy Süverman*: Dougherty to Jefferson, on or before April 25, 1802.

64. *nearly blind*: Rapin to Jefferson, May 7, 1802.

65. *"honest man"*: Stanton, p. 48; Jefferson to William Meriwether, August 21, 1810.

65. Kramer, Maher, and Fitzjames: Maher to Jefferson, October 9, 1801; Dougherty to Jefferson, May 11, 1802; *Mem. Books*, vol. 2, pp. 1054–55; Lemaire to Jefferson, May 10 and 24, 1802; Jefferson to Lemaire, May 14 and 20, 1802.

65–66. *Duval*: Lemaire to Jefferson, May 24, 1802.

66. *silver lining*: Jefferson to Rapin, June 3, 1802.

66. Süvermans' pay and support: Jefferson to Rapin, June 3, 1802; *Mem. Books*, vol. 2, pp. 1040, 1042, 1044, 1053, 1077, 1101; John Tyler to Jefferson, October 3, 1801.

66. *"charity"*: *Mem. Books*, passim.

66–67. *Shorter*: Dougherty to Jefferson, March 14, 1803.

67. *Houseman*: John Houseman to Jefferson, May 18, 1803; *Mem. Books*, vol. 2, p. 1100; Stanton, p. 44.

67. *"malcontents"*: Thomas Munroe to Jefferson, July 3, 12, and 14, 1804; Jefferson to Munroe, July 14, 1804.

67. *"FOR SALE"*: *Intelligencer*, May 24, 1802.

67–68. Ursula and the Grangers: Stanton, pp. 6–7, 44, 189–91; Boles, pp. 43, 96; Freeman to Jefferson, March 2, 1809; Stanton, p. 53; *Mem. Books*, vol. 2, pp. 1057, 1061, 1077, 1080 n. 79, 1091 n. 9.

68. Correspondence with Maria and Martha: Jefferson to Maria, October 26, 1801; Maria to Jefferson, November 6, 1801; Martha to Jefferson, November 10 and 18, 1801.

68. *Lucy*: Valsania, p. 187.

CHAPTER SEVEN

69. *spectacles*: Jefferson to John McAllister, November 12 and 19 and December 6, 1806; Jefferson to Peale, March 29, 1807.

69. *office seekers*: Young, p. 25; James Neale to Jefferson, August 26, 1806; George Meade to Jefferson, March 19, 1801; Jefferson to Larkin Smith, November 26, 1804; Jefferson to John Dickinson, January 13, 1807.

69. *every word*: George M. Curtis III, "Sphinx without a Riddle: Joseph Ellis and the Art of Jefferson Biography," *Indiana Magazine of History* 95 (June 1999): 178–201 ("Curtis"); *Process*, p. 35; Silvio A. Bedini, *Jefferson and Science* (Raleigh: University of North Carolina Press, 2002) ("Bedini"), p. 4; see Jefferson to Lewis, February 23, 1801; March 31, 1801; Lewis to Jefferson, March 10, 1801, April 5, 1801.

70. *spelling*: Jefferson to John Quincy Adams, Samuel Mitchill, and Joseph Nicholson, December 6, 1805.

70–71. Writing tools and volume: Jefferson to Joseph Nicholson, Joseph Nicholson Papers, vol. 2, LOC; Founders: Statement of Account with William Duane, July 7, 1803, November 27, 1804, and February 15, 1806; Jefferson to Lemaire, August 5, 1807; Jefferson to Peale, August 19, 1804, and April 9, 1805; *Mem. Books*, vol. 2, pp. 1222 n. 68, 1119; *Peale*, vol. 2, pt. 1, pp. 639–41; Randolph, p. 320.

70–71. Copy presses: Bedini, pp. 10, 17–21; Jefferson to Madison, September 1, 1785; Claxton to Jefferson, May 28, 1801.

71. Filing: Jefferson to Madison, December 29, 1801; *Process*, pp. 36, 87; *Sphinx*, p. 192; Bedini, pp. 1–4, 17–18; Jefferson to Benjamin Barton, November 21, 1805; Plumer, p. 469; *Jefferson in His Own Time*, p. 162; Coles Diary, March 14, 15, 16, 18, and 26, 1807; Meacham, p. 165.

71. *his image*: *Sphinx*, p. 192.

71. *"absolutely equal"*: Jefferson to Monroe, May 29, 1801.

71. *116 letters*: *Sphinx*, pp. 185, 335 n. 27.
71. *Samuel Adams*: Jefferson to Samuel Adams, March 29, 1801.
71–72. *Gerry*: Jefferson to Elbridge Gerry, March 29, 1801.
72. *George III*: Jefferson to George III, November 23, 1802, April 18, 1803, May 12, 1806, and March 1, 1808.
72. *"So constant"*: Jefferson to Phillip Mazzei, July 18, 1804.
72. *Anne*: Anne to Jefferson, February 22, 1805.
72–73. *scientific gentlemen*: Jefferson to George Taylor, August 16, 1806; Jacob Bouldin to Jefferson, July 15, 1802; Jefferson to Bouldin, July 20, 1802; Cutler, vol. 2, p. 153; *Peale*, vol. 2, pt. 1, p. 349 n. 2; Jefferson to Charles Buxton, July 13, 1805; William Lambert to Jefferson, December 15, 1804; Jefferson to Lambert, December 22, 1804, and January 17, 1805; Jefferson to J. Philippe Reibelt, April 30, 1805; Jefferson to Andrew Ellicott, October 25, 1805; James McLean to Jefferson, September 30, 1802; Jefferson to McLean, October 25, 1802.
73. *postage-free*: Jefferson to Philippe Reibelt, January 9, 1805.
73. *two thousand*: *Process*, p. 35.
73. *endorsed*: Founders, passim.
73. *entrepreneurs*: John May to Jefferson, October 20, 1805; John Somarsall to Jefferson, December 7, 1805.
73–74. *charity*: Emilia Jervis to Jefferson, November 4, 1804; Louisa Keets to Jefferson, July 16, 1806; Thomas Jones to Jefferson, June 1, 1805; Nathaniel Ingraham to Jefferson, April 28, 1803; Jefferson to Joseph Stanton Jr., February 17 and March 28, 1806.
74. *"Scoundrel"*: "A Republican" to Jefferson, May 17, 1803.
74. *advice*: "An Observer" to Jefferson, April 10, 1803; Jefferson to Dearborn, June 26, 1801.
74. *a laugh*: William Jefferson to Jefferson, July 11, 1806.
74. *Unbalanced*: Archibald McAllister to Jefferson, January 7, 1805; George Odenheimer to Jefferson, July 12, 1806; Samuel Henley to Jefferson, August 18, 1803.
74. *Threats*: William Herring to Jefferson, November 20, 1804; "A Friend to the Constitution" to Jefferson, December 6, 1804; John O'Neill to Jefferson, February 11, 1806.
74. *Presents*: Noah Webster to Jefferson, February 20, 1806; Jefferson to Webster, February 25, 1806; Jefferson to Samuel Hawkins, November 30, 1808.

CHAPTER EIGHT

75. *inaugural address*: *Sphinx*, p. 192; Founders: First Inaugural Address, March 4, 1801.

75. *gift of conversation*: Meacham, p. 236; *Patriarchs*, pp. 254–60; *Crème Brûlée*, p. 115; Valsania, pp. 17–20.

75. Evening entertainments: *Winter in Washington*, vol. 1, p. 189; Louisa Adams, vol. 1, p. 219; David M. R. Culbreth, *The University of Virginia: Memories of Her Student-Life and Professors* (New York: Neale, 1908) ("Culbreth"), p. 29; *First Forty*, p. 55; *Jefferson in His Own Time*, p. 160; Jefferson to Madison, August 13, 1801.

76. *"pic nic"*: John Davis, p. 176.

76. *costs*: *Cook Book*, p. 21 and passim, *Mem. Books*, vol. 2, pp. 1053–55; Jefferson to Dabney Carr, May 25, 1807; Jefferson to Littleton Tazewell, March 13, 1807; *Process*, pp. 44–45; Jefferson to George Jefferson, December 24, 1808.

76. *Julien*: "Forty Years," p. 148.

76–77. *ingredients*: "Gourmet," pp. 21, 102; Fowler, p. 5; *Crème Brûlée*, p. 11; Thornton Diary, passim; *Jefferson in His Own Time*, p. 176; Barnes to Jefferson, March 6, 1805; Fowler, p. 16; Seale, vol. 1, p. 100; *Intelligencer*, December 23, 1801; Foster, pp. 8, 19, 20; Catharine Mitchill, p. 185; Young, p. 72; British Ministers, vol. 5/32, no. 15; Thornton to Grenville, March 4, 1801; Jefferson to Adam Lindsay, December 27, 1801.

77. Meals: *Latrobe Papers*, vol. 2, p. 396; Seale, vol. 1, p. 102; *Cook Book*, pp. 30–35; "Gourmet," pp. 21, 103; Coles Diary, March 31, April 1–3, and June 6 and 9, 1807; Marie G. Kimball, "The Epicure of the White House," *Virginia Quarterly Review* 9 (January 1933): 71–81 (""Epicure""), p. 73.

77. *"very choice"*: *Jefferson in His Own Time*, p. 170.

77–78. Foods and supplies: Jefferson to Lemaire, April 24, 1807; *Cook Book*, pp. 7–9, 13–14, 30; Jefferson to William Drayton, July 30, 1787; "Gourmet," p. 103 and passim; *Crème Brûlée*, pp. 116, 137, and passim; Fowler, p. 3 and passim.

78. *sesame seed oil*: Jefferson to Anne, March 22, 1808.

78. *Virginia fare*: Lane-Pool, p. 298; Coles Diary, April 3, 1807; Jefferson to George Jefferson, May 3, 1801; George Jefferson to Jefferson, May 9, 1805, and April 4, 1806.

78. *"clock"*: *Crème Brûlée*, p. 150.

78–79. *kitchen*: Seale, vol. 1, pp. 60, 77, 83–84, 99–100; Fazio and Snadon, p. 373; Peale to Jefferson, March 30, 1805; Founders: Anonymous chart of 1804 expenses, December 31, 1804; *Crème Brûlée*, pp. 75, 147; Fowler, p. 1; "Gourmet," p. 104; Claxton to Jefferson, February 17, 1809; Jefferson to Henry Foxall, March 24, 1809.

79–81. Jefferson and wine: Hailman, pp. 264–75; Jefferson to Fulwar Skipwith, July 11, 1804; Jefferson to Thomas Newton, July 12, 1802; Boles, pp. 160, 162; "Epicure," p. 78; *Cook Book*, pp. 1–2; "Wines," www.monticello.org; Founders: Memorandum on Wine after 23 April, 1788; Jefferson to Thomas Appleton, March 30, 1807; James M. Gabler, *Passions: The Wines and Travels of Thomas Jefferson* (Baltimore: Bacchus, 1995) ("*Passions*"); Lawrence R. de

Treville, ed., *Jefferson and Wine* (The Plains, VA: Vinifera Wine Growers Association, 1976).

80. *whiskey*: Henry Adams, vol. 1, p. 47.

80. *"cyder"*: *Mem. Books*, vol. 2, p. 1065 n. 43.

80. *"disguised in drink"*: Jefferson to Rush, January 16, 1811.

80. *tariffs*: Jefferson to Gallatin, June 1, 1807; Hailman, pp. 317–18.

80. *Kentucky wines*: Jefferson to John Brown, February 23, 1805.

81. *banknotes* and *"holy writ"*: Jefferson to Thomas Newton, March 9, 1801; Jefferson to Ralph Izard, September 26, 1785; Jefferson to John Page, January 24, 1799; Jefferson to Phillip Mazzei, July 18, 1804.

81. Varieties and quantities of wine: Hailman, pp. 266, 269–270, 275, 277, 308; *Mem. Books*, vol. 2, pp. 1115–17; Thornton Diary, March 3, 1806; *Crème Brûlée*, p. 147.

81–82. Temperance and toasts: Jefferson to Charles Bellini, September 30, 1785; Plumer, p. 123.

82. *"Health Law"*: Hailman, p. 293.

82. *Family Dining Room*: Jefferson to Peter Lenox, August 22, 1805; "Original Furnishings," p. 486; Klapthor, p. 91; *Cook Book*, p. 17; Seale, vol. 1, pp. 101–2; Jefferson to Claxton, May 26 and June 1, 1805; Jefferson to Claxton, June 18, 1802.

82. *screens*: Jefferson to Claxton, June 13, 1802; Jefferson to Peter Lenox, July 20, 1806; Jefferson to Latrobe, July 18, 1806.

82–83. *floorcloths* and *fortepiano*: Claxton to Jefferson, June 13, 1802; Jefferson to Claxton, June 18, 1802.

83. *tables* and *linen*: *First Forty*, p. 391; "Gourmet," p. 103; *Mem. Books*, vol. 2, pp. 1100, 1118; Rosanna McKinna to Jefferson, July 13, 1805.

83. *State Dining room*: *Mem. Books*, vol. 2, p. 1081 n. 47; *First Forty*, p. 387; *Passions*, p. 199; Fowler, p. 13; Stuart D. Hobbs, "The Adena Dumbwaiters: A Glimpse into Jefferson's Executive Mansion?" *White House History* 17 (Winter 2006): 45–49 ("Hobbs"), passim.

83–84. *Tatham*: Jefferson to Dearborn, August 31, 1807; William Tatham to Jefferson, May 22, 1805; "William Tatham," www.monticello.org.

84. *adjournment* and *practice*: *Winter in Washington*, vol. 2, p. 188; Jefferson to John Glendy, March 3, 1805; Masterson, p. 80; "Forty Years," pp. 146–47; Randall, vol. 4, p. 94.

84. *"slovenly"*: Ambrose, p. 63.

84. Informal dinners: "Forty Years," pp. 146–47; *First Forty*, pp. 28–29, 391–92.

84. *invitations*: Malone, vol. 4, pp. 376–77; Kierner, p. 114; Fowler, p. 189 n. 8; Jefferson to John Steele, July 1, 1802; Jefferson to the Smiths, April 23, 1803; Jefferson to Joseph Nicholson, April 24, 1805.

85. *Hacks*: Jefferson to William Short, October 8, 1802; *Peale*, vol. 2, pt. 2, p. 691.

85. Hostesses: Seale, vol. 1, p. 102; Hailman, p. 271; Louisa Adams, vol. 1, p. 219; Jefferson to the Madisons and Anna Payne, May 27, 1801; Jefferson to Gallatin, June 3, 1801.

85–87. Protocol and service: Stanton, pp. 50–51; Plumer, p. 213; Madison to Monroe, January 19, 1804; Merry Ellen Scofield, "The Fatigues of His Table: The Politics of Presidential Dining during the Jefferson Administration," *Journal of the Early Republic* 26 (Fall 2006): 449–69 ("Scofield"), p. 453 n. 4; *A Perfect Union*, pp. 89, 430 n. 7; *First Forty*, pp. 387–88; Seale, vol. 1, p. 104; Hailman, pp. 291–98; "Dumbwaiters," www.monticello.org; "Forty Years," p. 147; Fowler, pp. 13–14.

87–89. Jefferson as conversationalist: "Forty Years," p. 147; Foster's Notes, p. 44; Foster, pp. 155–56; Samuel L. Mitchill, "Dr. Mitchill's Letters from Washington: 1801–1813," *Harper's New Monthly Magazine* 58 (April 1879): 740–55 ("'Mitchill's Letters'"), p. 744; Pickering to Dr. George Logan, January 15, 1805, Massachusetts Historical Society, Pickering Papers, reel 15; Culbreth, p. 26; *First Forty*, pp. 6–8, 65; Jefferson to his grandchildren, March 7, 1802; *Henry Clay*, pp. 232–33, 241–42; Jefferson to Thomas Paine, February 21, 1806; Alfred Steinberg, *The First Ten: The Founding Presidents and Their Administrations* (New York: Doubleday, 1967), p. 103; *Patriarchs*, pp. 82–83; Louisa Adams, vol. 1, p. 216; Brodie, p. 146–47; Joseph J. Ellis, *American Creation* (New York: Knopf, 2007), p. 120; Hailman, p. 15; *Jefferson in His Own Time*, pp. 92–97.

CHAPTER NINE

91. *"the Oven"*: Founders: Jefferson to Claxton, October 26, 1802, and Editor's note.

91. *campaigns* and *"interims"*: E.g., Jefferson to Martha, October 7, 1804; Malone, vol. 5, p. 18; Cotton Smith, pp. 207–8; Furman, p. 27; Macon to Jefferson, April 20, 1801.

91–92. *state of the Union*: Cotton Smith, pp. 207–8; Furman, p. 27; Macon to Jefferson, April 20, 1801; *Sphinx*, pp. 192–93; British Ministers, vol. 5/32, no. 55.

92. *Irving*: Washington Irving, *Life of George Washington*, 5 vols. (Leipzig, Germany: B. Tauchnitz, 1856–1859), vol. 5, p. 41.

92. *salary* and *privileges*: Young, pp. 215–17, 282 n. 41, 288 n. 6; Jefferson to William Short, March 28, 1786; Thornton Diary, April 3, 1803; *First Forty*, p. 65.

92. *third person*: Jefferson to Dolley Madison, July 6, 1805.

92. *"this place"*: E.g., Jefferson to Kezia Norris, October 20, 1801.

93. Time pressures: Jefferson to Thomas Randolph, November 16, 1801; Jefferson to John Eppes, January 1, 1802; Jefferson to Gallatin, October 24, 1807; Jefferson to Nathaniel Macon, March 22, 1806.

93. Letters to Martha: Jefferson to Martha, February 5, 1801, and October 7, 1804.

93. *frustration*: Jefferson to Madison, June 9, 1793.

93. *"promiscuously"*: "Forty Years," p. 147.

94. Mrs. Adams at dinner: Abigail Adams to Thomas Adams, ca. January 1801.

94. *palpitations*: Catharine Mitchill, p. 175.

94. *public accommodation*: Louisa Adams, vol. 1, p. 231.

95. *etiquette forbade*: Young, pp. 72, 158–59.

95. *invited its members*: *Mem. Books*, vol. 2, p. 1055 n. 22; Charles T. Cullen, "Jefferson's White House Dinner Guests," *White House History* 17 (Winter 2006): 25–43 ("Cullen"), passim; James Fenner to Jefferson and Jefferson to James Fenner, February 14, 1807.

95. *no alternative*: Foster's Notes, pp. 23 and 29; Foster, pp. 8–9, 37, 60, 68, 86; *Two Duchesses*, p. 240; "The Early American Presidents," *Harper's New Monthly Magazine* 68 (December 1883–May 1884): 548–60, p. 555; A. I. Mudd, "Early Theatres in Washington City," *Records of the Columbia Historical Society of Washington, D.C.* 5 (1902): 64–86, p. 68; Coles Diary, December 22, 1806; *Intelligencer*, September 10, 1802.

95. *"unfashioned persons"*: Foster's Notes, p. 23; *Latrobe Papers*, vol. 1, p. 257.

96. Snubs and regrets: Cutler, vol. 2, p. 152; Scofield, pp. 454, 458, 465; Edmund Quincy, *Life of Josiah Quincy* (Boston: Ticknor and Fields, 1868) ("Quincy"), p. 88; Linda K. Kerber, *Federalists in Dissent: Imagery and Ideology in Jeffersonian America* (Ithaca, NY: Cornell University Press, 1970), p. 23.

96. *explained* and *explanation*: David R. Williams to Jefferson, January 29, 1806; Jefferson to Williams, January 31, 1806.

96. *silenced*: Meacham, p. 362.

96–97. *French cuisine*: *Cook Book*, p. 1; Plumer, p. 390; Catharine Mitchill, p. 175.

97. American diet and manners: TJR Memoir, p. 14; Carson, pp. 30–45, 111; Lane-Pool, pp. 315, 317.

97. *first time*: *Parlor Politics*, pp. 68–75; Cullen, passim.

97. *Bayard*: "James Asheton Bayard Letters, 1802–1814," *Bulletin of the New York Public Library* 4 (July 1900): 227–48, pp. 229–30.

97–98. *scant exposure to gentility*: Carson, pp. 69, 83–85; Valsania, pp. 24–25, 34–35; J. Hamilton Moore, pp. 183–86; Foster's Notes, pp. 23 and 27–29; Few, p. 355; Malcolm Lester, *Anthony Merry Redivivus: A Reappraisal of the British Minister to the United States, 1803–06* (Charlottesville: University Press of Virginia, 1978) ("Lester"), p. 79; *Life of Plumer*, p. 245; *First Forty*, pp. 52–53; Bernard Mayo, "A Peppercorn for Mr. Jefferson," *Virginia Quarterly Review* 19 (Spring 1943): 222–35 ("Mayo"), p. 231; *Preston*, p. 7.

98–99. *regional menu of manners*: *Preston*, p. 7; Foster's Notes, pp. 28 and 36; Foster, pp. 55–57, 85, 87, 107, 153; Henry Adams, vol. 1, pp. 48–55; *Two Duchesses*, pp. 197, 275; Louisa Adams, vol. 1, p. 268; McDonald, p. 126; Hobbs, p. 45; Henry Nimrod, *The Fudge Family in Washington* (Baltimore: Joseph Robinson, 1820), pp. 16, 41–43.

99. *Randolph*: David Johnson, *John Randolph of Roanoke* (Baton Rouge: LSU Press, 2012); Foster's Notes, pp. 28–29.

99. *mammoths*: Mayo, p. 225; Jefferson to Michael Fry and Nathan Coleman and to John Beckley, October 22, 1801.

100. *Morris*: Morris to Hamilton, March 11, 1802.

100–102. Cutler and Jefferson: Charles G. Dawes, Biographical Introduction to the Cutler Papers, Northwestern University; Cutler, vol. 2, pp. 51–52, 64, 66, 71–72, 94–97, 119, 132–33, 155; Cutler to Jefferson, February 11, 1802.

CHAPTER TEN

103–4. New Year's Day reception: "Mitchill's Letters," p. 743; Jefferson to William Short, January 23, 1804; Anne H. Wharton, *Salons Colonial and Republican* (Philadelphia: J. B. Lippincott, 1900) ("*Salons*"), pp. 194–95; Plumer, p. 345; Louisa Adams, vol. 1, pp. 207, 218, 265; *First Forty*, pp. 397–403; *Port Folio*, 1802, vol. 2, p. 16; Wilson, p. 140; Mayo, p. 225; Charles Augustus Goodrich, *The Family Tourist* (Philadelphia: J. W. Bradley, 1848), p. 367.

104–5. Leland and the cheese: Founders: Editorial Note: Presentation of the "Mammoth Cheese," and sources cited therein; Cutler, vol. 2, pp. 54, 66; Cotton Smith, pp. 59–60; C. A. Browne, "Elder John Leland and the Mammoth Cheshire Cheese," *Agricultural History* 18 (October 1944): 145–53; "Mitchill's Letters," p. 744; L. H. Butterfield, "Elder John Leland, Jeffersonian Itinerant," *Proceedings of the American Antiquarian Society* 62 (April 1952): 155–242; *Sphinx*, p. 256; Malone, vol. 4, pp. 107–8; John Bach McMaster, *A History of the People of the United States*, 5 vols. (New York: D. Appleton, 1885), pp. 604–6; Mayo, p. 222; Jefferson to Thomas Randolph, January 1, 1802; *Mem. Books*, vol. 2, pp. 1062 n. 33, 1069 n. 55; *Life of Gallatin*, p. 304; Green, p. 47.

105–6. *pilgrimage*: Cutler, vol. 2, pp. 55–56; Cotton Smith, pp. 59–61.

106. Ursula Granger and child: *Mem. Books*, vol. 2, p. 1069; Wiencek, pp. 166–67; Jefferson to Martha, June 18, 1802; Lemaire to Jefferson, August 17, 1802.

106–7. Edith Fossett and child: Stanton, p. 44; *Mem. Books*, vol. 2, p. 1091 n. 9; Jefferson to Edmund Bacon, October 6, 1806, and to Martha, January 27, 1803; "Meet Edith and Fanny" and "Edith Fossett," www.monticello.org; Lucia Stanton, "A Well Ordered Household: Domestic Servants in Jefferson's White

House," *White House History* 17 (Winter 2006): 4–23 ("'Well Ordered'"), pp. 9, 21 n. 35; Wiencek, p. 168.

107. Family visit plans: Maria to Jefferson, April 18, 1801; Jefferson to Maria, March 3 and June 3, 1802; Jefferson to Martha, June 18, 1802; Kierner, p. 115; Wister, p. 33; Malone, vol. 4, p. 173; *First Forty*, p. 393.

107. Sally Hemings: Kierner, p. 119.

107–8. Family visit plans renewed: Jefferson to Martha and Maria, October 7 and 18 and November 2, 1802; Martha to Jefferson, October 29 and November 9, 1802; Maria to Jefferson, November 5, 1802; Kierner, p. 115; Wister, p. 27; Malone, vol. 4, p. 170.

108. The family arrives: Founders: Statement of Account with Meriwether Lewis, November 21, 1802; *Mem. Books*, vol. 2, p. 239; Wister, pp. 35–36; Stanton, p. 44; *Intelligencer*, November 26, 1802; "William Duane," p. 32.

108. *behaved so well*: *First Forty*, p. 70.

108. *"unsafe"*: Maria to Jefferson, January 11, 1803; Stanton, p. 44.

107–8. Washington growing: *Intelligencer*, November 26, 1802; "William Duane," p. 32.

109. *woke the capital*: Kierner, p. 115; Wister, pp. 35–36.

109. *"tolerably handsome"* and *New Year's Day*: Cutler, vol. 2, pp. 113–16.

109–10. Martha, Ellen, Maria, and Anne: *Crème Brûlée*, pp. 40, 140, 150; *First Forty*, pp. 34–35, 404; Louisa Adams, vol. 1, p. 216; Wister, p. 41.

110. *chariot*: Malone, vol. 4, p. 172; Furman, p. 43; TJR Memoir, p. 30; Jefferson to Enoch Edwards, March 30, 1801.

110. *bonding* and *violin*: Malone, vol. 4, p. 174; Wister, p. 36; TJR Memoir, p. 2.

110–12. Plumer's background: *Life of Plumer*, pp. 4–5, 7, 12–31, 35, 37, 53–60, 82–86, 112–13, 235, 241; Plumer, pp. 523, 541.

112. *"even chance"*: Jefferson to William Short, May 19, 1807.

113. Plumer, Jefferson, and Paine: *Life of Plumer*, pp. 242–43.

113. Paine: Brodie, p. 361; King, vol. 4, p. 182; *Sphinx*, pp. 216, 339 n. 86; "Mitchill's Letters," pp. 745–46; Cutler, vol. 2, pp. 114, 118–19; Jefferson to Thomas McKean, July 24, 1801.

113. *first presidential dinner*: *Life of Plumer*, pp. 245–46.

114. Plumer's letters: *Life of Plumer*, pp. 248, 256–57.

114. The family leaves: Martha to Jefferson, January 11, 1803; Kierner, p. 120; Thornton Diary, January 4, 1803; *Mem. Books*, vol. 2, p. 1090; Maria to Jefferson, January 11, 1803; Jefferson to Martha, January 27, 1803; Malone, vol. 4, p. 173.

114–15. *Thomas Mann Randolph Jr.*: Jefferson to Angelica Church, November 27, 1793; Randall, vol. 1, p. 558; Foster, p. 153; Gaines, pp. 40–41, 50–53, 66–67, 78–79; Wister, pp. 24, 47, 48; Kierner, pp. 118, 133, 135; Meacham, pp. 9–10, 233–34; Boles, pp. 208–9, 263–64, 424; Brodie, pp. 379, 394; TJR

Memoir, p. 4; Malone, vol. 4, p. 612; Ellen Randolph Coolidge to "Sarah," January 6, 1876, Papers of the Randolph Family of Edgehill, Albert & Shirley ("Randolph Papers") Special Collections Library, University of Virginia, MSS 1397, Box 11; Thomas Randolph to Jefferson, October 29, 1802.

116. *John Wayles Eppes*: TJR Memoir, p. 2; Jefferson to Maria, June 14, 1797; Wister, p. 26; *Jefferson in His Own Time*, pp. 172–73; Boles, pp. 263–64; Kierner, p. 135; Randall, vol. 2, p. 664; *Mem. Books*, vol. 2, pp. 1038, 1154; *Farm Book*, p. 102.

116. Jefferson and his sons-in-law: Scofield, p. 454 n. 6; Jefferson to Martha, June 18, 1802; Kierner, p. 135.

CHAPTER ELEVEN

117–18. Beginnings of Lewis and Clark's expedition: Founders: Meriwether Lewis: Estimated Costs, January 18, 1803; Jefferson to Benjamin Barton, February 27, 1803, Benjamin Rush and Caspar Wistar, February 28, 1803, and Robert Patterson, March 2, 1803; *L&C Letters*, p. 57; British Ministers, vol. 5/38, no. 15; Danisi and Jackson, pp. 64–65.

118. *"courage"*: Ambrose, p. 27.

118. *"depressions"*: Jefferson to Paul Allen, August 18, 1813.

118. *Harvie*: Jefferson to Harvie, February 28, 1803; Brodie, p. 366; Harvie to Jefferson, before March 12, 1803.

118. Thornton chat: British Ministers, vol. 5/38, no. 25.

118–19. Preparations to go west: Friis, p. 2; Jefferson to William Dunbar, May 25, 1805; *L&C Letters*, pp. 61–66, 100, 107; Jefferson to Lewis, July 4 and 11, 1803; Meacham, p. 387; *First Forty*, pp. 38–39.

119. Letters on route: Malone, vol. 5, pp. 182–83, 188; Boles, p. 383.

119–20. *Latrobe*: Ryan and Guinness, p. 97; John H. B. Latrobe, *The Capitol and Washington at the Beginning of the Present Century* (Baltimore: W. K. Boyle, 1881) ("*Present Century*"), p. 11; Fazio and Snadon, p. 359; Seale, vol. 1, p. 108; *Latrobe Papers*, vol. 1, p. 219.

120–21. Latrobe at dinner: *Latrobe Papers*, vol. 1, p. 232; Talbot Hamlin, *Benjamin Henry Latrobe* (New York: Oxford University Press, 1955), pp. 576–77; Letter from Benjamin Latrobe to Mary Latrobe, November 30, 1802, "Dining with Jefferson: Art, Science and Ribaldry," archives.dickinson.edu.

122. Latrobe and Thornton and Hoban: John H. B. Latrobe, "Construction of the Public Buildings in Washington," *Maryland Historical Magazine* 4 (1909): 221–28 ("'Construction'"), pp. 222–26; Henry Adams, vol. 1, pp. 111–12; Paul F. Norton, "Jefferson, the Making of an Architect," in *Jefferson and the Arts: An Extended View*, ed. William Howard Adams (Washington, DC:

National Gallery of Art, 1976) ("Norton"), p. 214; Seale, vol. 1, pp. 112–13; *Latrobe Papers*, vol. 2, pp. 600, 604–5, 607 n. 22.

122. Latrobe's barbs: Fazio and Snadon, p. 359; "Construction," p. 223; *Latrobe Papers*, vol. 1, pp. 463–64, 466.

123. Latrobe and Jefferson's vision and priorities: *Patriarchs*, p. 238; Jefferson to Thomas Munroe, August 4, 1804, and September 12, 1806; Ryan and Guinness, p. 97; Fazio and Snadon, pp. 359–60.

123–24. *"tooth and nail"*: Travis McDonald, "The East and West Wings of the White House: History in Architecture and Building," *White House History* 29 (Summer 2011): 44–87 ("'Wings'"), n. 53; Jefferson to Latrobe, October 5, 1804, September 8, 1805, and April 22, 1807; Paul F. Norton, "Thomas Jefferson and the Planning of the National Capitol," in *Jefferson and the Arts: An Extended View* (Washington, DC: National Gallery of Art, 1976), pp. 212–25; Phillips-Schrock, pp. 33–34.

124. Repairs and improvements: Fazio and Snadon, p. 363; S. K. Padover, *Thomas Jefferson and the National Capital, 1783–1818* (Washington, DC: Government Printing Office, 1946) ("Padover"), pp. 348–50; Ryan and Guinness, pp. 97–98; Norton, p. 211; Jefferson to Latrobe, April 23, 1803.

124. *"instantly"*: Jefferson to Thomas Munroe, April 26, 1805.

124. *Pennsylvania Avenue*: Thomas Munroe to Jefferson, March 14, 1803; Bryan, vol. 1, pp. 456–59; Ryan and Guinness, p. 97; Reps, p. 29; *Latrobe Papers*, vol. 1, p. 257; Benjamin Latrobe, *The Journal of Latrobe* (New York: D. Appleton, 1905) ("*Latrobe Journal*"), p. 134; *Peale*, vol. 2, pt. 2, p. 692; *Thomas Jefferson, Architect*, p. 63; *Present Century*, p. 25.

124. *staircase*: Seale, vol. 1, p. 115; Fazio and Snadon, p. 363.

125. *icehouse*: Cutler, vol. 2, p. 153.

125–27. *polygraph*: Bedini, pp. 18, 60–78, 90, 99, 125, 136–38; *Latrobe Papers*, vol. 1, pp. 435–36, 474–75; e.g., *Peale*, vol. 2, pt. 1, pp. 435–36, 475–79, 595, 647, and vol. 2, pt. 2, 850; e.g., Jefferson to Peale, August 19, 1804, April 5, June 9, July 12, October 6, and November 13, 1805, January 1 and 23, and June 19 and 27, 1806, January 15, 1809; Peale to Jefferson, October 2, 1807; Jefferson to Edward Preble, July 6, 1805; Jefferson to James Bowdoin, July 10, 1806.

127. *Stylograph*: Jefferson to Peale, October 5, 1807, and January 15, 1809; Bedini, pp. 154–58; *Mem. Books*, vol. 2, p. 1158 n. 81.

127–28. *John Quincy Adams*: *JQA Memoirs*, vol. 1, p. 264; Brodie, 354–55; Malone, vol. 4, p. 139; Plumer, p. 643.

128. Mr. and Mrs. Adams at dinner: *JQA Memoirs*, vol. 1, p. 272; Henry Adams, *The Education of Henry Adams* (Boston: Houghton Mifflin, 1918), p. 16; Louisa Adams, vol. 1, pp. 201, 265; Plumer, p. 636.

CHAPTER TWELVE

129. Thornton's advice: British Ministers, vol. 5/35, p. 35, vol. 5/38, March 1, 1803, vol. 5/32, pp. 179–80; Lester, p. 19.

129. *Anthony Merry*: Lester, pp. 4, 20; Davis, p. 517; *First Forty*, p. 46; Masterson, p. 73.

130. *Atlantic crossing*: Herbert G. Eldridge, "Anacreon Moore and America," *PMLA* 83 (March 1969): 54–62 ("Eldridge"), p. 55; Thomas Moore, *Memoirs, Journal, and Correspondence of Thomas Moore*, 35 vols., ed. Lord John Russell (London: Longman, Brown, Green, and Longmans, 1853) ("Moore"), vol. 1, pp. 137–38; Masterson, p. 74.

130. *Elizabeth Merry*: *First Forty*, p. 46; Louisa Adams, pp. 200, 221, 233; Lester, pp. 22–23, 44, 46–47, 81; Davis, p. 517; *Parlor Politics*, pp. 35, 43–45.

130. *Rufus King*: King, vol. 4, p. 327.

130. From Norfolk to Washington and accommodations: Lester, pp. 18, 32; Eldridge, p. 55; Moore. vol. 1, pp. 139, 141, vol. 8, pp. 50–51.

130–32. Merry's presentation to Jefferson: Davis, pp. 518–19; Joel Larus, "Growing Pains of the New Republic: III, Pell-Mell along the Potomac," *William and Mary Quarterly* 17, no. 3 (July 1960): 349–57 ("Larus"), pp. 351–54; Jefferson to Moustier, May 17, 1788; Henry Adams, vol. 2, pp. 365–67; *Two Duchesses*, pp. 197–99; Cutler, vol. 2, pp. 92–93; Foster Journal, vol. 2, December 30, 1804; King, vol. 4, p. 340; Malone, vol. 4, pp. 384–85; Quincy, pp. 92–93; Lester, pp. 31–33; Taggart, p. 125; Lane-Pool, p. 316.

132. Jefferson's intent: Jefferson to William Short, March 28, 1796; Boles, p. 156; Meacham, p. 194; British Ministers, vol. 5/32, nos. 15 and 55; Foster, pp. 53–54; Côté, pp. 216–17; Davis, p. 518; Henry Adams, vol. 2, pp. 365–77.

132. *first social calls*: Davis, pp. 509–29; Foster, pp. 21, 52, 54.

132–41. *the Merry imbroglio*: Plumer, p. 345; Louisa Adams, pp. 200, 207, 209–10, 221, 233; Madison to Monroe, December 26, 1803, January 19 and February 16, 1804; *Peale*, vol. 2, pt. 2, pp. 690–91; Madison to Rufus King, December 18, 1803; Founders: Notes on Diplomatic Etiquette in England, December 22, 1803; Côté, p. 219; *A Perfect Union*, pp. 79–101; *Dolley Madison*, p. 49; *Parlor Politics*, p. 37; Henry Adams, vol. 2, pp. 360–88; Beckles Willson, *Friendly Relations* (Boston: Little, Brown, 1933) ("Willson"), pp. 41–49; Jackson, pp. 212–13; Foster's Notes, pp. 26–27; Foster, pp. 49–52 and 55; Lester, pp. 29–47; Larus, pp. 352–57; *Two Duchesses*, p. 226; Jefferson to Madison, January 30, 1787; Malone, vol. 4, pp. 168, 173, 387–92; *JQA Memoirs*, vol. 1, pp. 280–81; Davis, pp. 521–29; Founders: Canons of Official Etiquette and accompanying Editorial Note; Malone, vol. 4; Calvert, pp. 70, 72; Jefferson to Elizabeth Merry and she to him, December 26, 1803;

Cutler, vol. 2, pp. 152, 163–64; Jefferson to Monroe, January 8, 1804; Peters, pp. 331–32; King, vol. 4, pp. 332–33, 341; Founders: Notes on Diplomatic Etiquette in England, December 22, 1803; Few, p. 351; Monroe to Madison, March 3, 1804; "Documents," *American Historical Review* 33, no. 4 (July 1928): 832–35, p. 834 n. 5; Jefferson to Martha and to William Short, January 23, 1804; Madison to Merry, February 9, 1804; Founders: Response to the Washington Federalist, February 13, 1804; Quincy, p. 93.

138. *entertaining slip*: *Parlor Politics*, p. 39.

CHAPTER THIRTEEN

143–44. *Madame Bonaparte* and *"Madame Eve"*: Calvert, pp. 34, 62; *Two Duchesses*, p. 206; Charlene M. Boyer Lewis, *Elizabeth Patterson Bonaparte: An American Aristocrat in the Early Republic* (Philadelphia: University of Pennsylvania Press, 2012) ("*Elizabeth Patterson Bonaparte*"), passim; *First Forty*, pp. 46–47; *Salons*, p. 204; Merrill D. Peterson, *Thomas Jefferson and the New Nation: A Biography* (New York: Oxford University Press, 1970), pp. 732–33; Côté, p. 161; *Latrobe Papers*, vol. 1, pp. 434–35; Thornton Diary, February 14, 1805; Louisa Adams, p. 213; Malone, vol. 4, p. 384; Boles, pp. 372–73; Lester, p. 38.

145. *Harvie*: Burwell, p. 105.

145. Maria's death: Jefferson to Martha, March 8, 1804; Randolph, p. 300.

145. *Freeman* and *Colbert*: Stanton, p. 47; Eppes to Jefferson, July 16, 1804; Jefferson to Eppes, August 7, 1804; Founders: Certificate of Sale and Manumission of John Freeman, July 23, 1804.

146–49. *Humboldt*: Friis, pp. 1–13, 18, 22–34; Burwell, pp. 114–15 n. 34; Paul Hawken, *Drawdown* (New York: Penguin, 2017), p. 24; Humboldt to Madison, May 24 and June 27, 1804; Bedini, p. 79; Vincent Gray to Madison, May 8, 1804; "Forty Years," p. 149; Wulf, pp. 101–7; Jefferson to William Lambert, December 22, 1804; Thornton Diary, June 5, 1804; Founders: List of Newspapers, January 1, 1805; Jefferson to Levi Lincoln, March 11, 1809; Meacham, p. 405; McDonald, pp. 128–29; *Mem. Books*, vol. 2, p. 1122–23 n. 79; Jefferson to Elbridge Gerry, March 29, 1801; *Peale*, vol. 2, pt. 2, pp. 690–700.

CHAPTER FOURTEEN

151–55. *Indians*: Gallatin to Jefferson, July 12, 1804, and February 12, 1805; Jefferson to W. C. C. Claiborne, April 27, 1806; Jefferson to Reibelt, January 10, 1806; *L&C Letters*, p. 199; Founders: Instructions for Meriwether Lewis, June

20, 1803; *Intelligencer*, December 15, 1802; Herman J. Viola, *Diplomats in Buckskins: A History of Indian Delegations in Washington City* (Washington, DC: Smithsonian Institution Press, 1981) ("Viola"), pp. 43, 69, 141, 173–74; Founders: Address of Little Turtle, January 4, 1802, Editorial Note: Conference with Little Turtle, Jefferson to Owl and Others, January 8, 1803; John C. Ewers, "'Chiefs from the Missouri and Mississippi' and Peale's Silhouettes of 1806," *Smithsonian Journal of History* 1 (1966): 1–26 ("Ewers"), passim; *Mem. Books*, vol. 2, p. 1132 n. 2; Jefferson to Robert Smith, July 13, 1804; Valsania, p. 135; Jefferson to White Hairs and Notes on Reply of White Hairs, July 16, 1804; Jefferson from White Hairs, September 20, 1806; Malone, vol. 4, p. 202 n. 1.

155. *"fragment of a journal"*: *Port Folio*, August 18, 1804, p. 262.

155–57. Burr, Plumer, and Jefferson: Plumer, pp. 193–95, 203–4, 213, 352, 407; *Life of Plumer*, pp. 329–30; "P. C." to Jefferson, November 18, 1805; Foster, p. 105; Bryan, vol. 1, p. 610.

157. *Turreau*: Plumer, p. 636; Henry Adams, vol. 3, p. 205.

157–58. Adams at dinner: Cullen, pp. 30, 40; *JQA Memoirs*, vol. 1, p. 316.

158–59. Taggart and Pickering at dinner: Taggart, pp. 113, 140–41; Peters, pp. 336–38; Louisa Adams, p. 210; Plumer, p. 221; Pickering to Jefferson, December 3, 1804.

158–59. Invitations: Plumer, pp. 211–12.

159. Plumer at dinner: Plumer, p. 212; *Life of Plumer*, pp. 326–27.

159. *written to Martha*: Jefferson to Martha, December 3, 1804.

159. *"amuses us . . . immense debt we owe"*: Plumer, p. 192.

159. *Federalists were spent*: *Sphinx*, p. 227; Jefferson to William Heath, December 13, 1804.

160. *"habitable"*: Latrobe to Jefferson, November 17, 1804.

160–63. The wings: Latrobe to Jefferson, April 22, May 5 and 11, and December 22, 1805; Latrobe to Jefferson, May 5, 1805; Fowler, p. 21; Phillips-Schrock, pp. 33–35; Fazio and Snadon, pp. 364–65, 371; "Wings," passim; Remini, p. 22; Seale, vol. 1, pp. 109–12; *Latrobe Papers*, vol. 2, pp. 66 n. 1, 686–87; Ryan and Guinness, p. 98; Latrobe to John Lenthall, May 11, 1805; Jefferson to Peter Lenox, July 20, 1806.

163. *Burr*: Louisa Adams, p. 223. Mrs. Adams's memoir, written long after the fact, conflates some events or dates them out of order, including her introduction to Burr. She recalled being introduced to Burr in March of 1805 (see Louisa Adams, p. 223) but had dined with him at the President's House on January 11. See *JQA Memoirs*, vol. 2, p. 330; *Anas*, pp. 224–28; Lester, pp. 105–6; Malone, vol. 5, pp. 234–35; Plumer, p. 436.

163. *painfully cold*: *Peale*, vol. 2, pt. 2, p. 785.

163. *zero in Paris*: *JQA Memoirs*, vol. 2, p. 330; Malone, vol. 4, p. 375.

163. *Mrs. Adams*: Louisa Adams, p. 205.

163. *"smoothing iron"*: Plumer, p. 383.

164–65. The Peales: *Peale*, vol. 2, pt. 2, pp. 794–95.

164. Jefferson and cold: Jefferson to Constantin Volney, February 8, 1805.

164–65. *Francis*: Jefferson to Martha, January 21, 1805; Ellen to Jefferson, March 18, 1808.

165. *wolf-skin cloak*: Charles Henry Hart, "The Life Portraits of Thomas Jefferson," *McClure's Magazine* 11 (May 1898): 47–55, pp. 54–55; Margaret Bayard Smith, "The Fur Cloak, A Reminiscence," in *The Token and Atlantic Souvenir: A Christmas and New Year's Present*, ed. S. G. Goodrich (Boston: Gray and Bowen, 1833), pp. 342–50; Wilson, pp. 148–53; Jefferson to Peale, January 23, 1806.

165. Burwell and Coles: Burwell to Jefferson, January 18, 1805; Jefferson to Burwell, January 28, 1805, Tadeusz Kosciusko, February 25, 1809, and Pierre DuPont De Nemours, March 2, 1809; Wiencek, p. 235; *Family Letters*, p. 265 n. 3.

165. *Washington's birthday*: Plumer, p. 299.

165. *new blade*: Jefferson to John Strode, March 11, 1805; "Moldboard Plow," www.monticello.org.

165–66. Inauguration: Foster, p. 15; "Foster and His Book," p. 344; *Two Duchesses*, pp. 229–30; *JQA Memoirs*, vol. 1, p. 373; Mary Cable, *The Avenue of the Presidents* (Boston: Houghton Mifflin, 1969), pp. 28–29; *Dolley Madison*, p. 53.

166. *Ellen*: Jefferson to Ellen Randolph, March 4, 1805.

166. *Lewis*: *Original Journals*, vol. 1, p. 215; Lewis to Jefferson, April 7, 1805; *L&C Letters*, pp. 331–42; "Memoir of Lewis," p. xxxvi.

167. *to the governor*: Malone, vol. 5, pp. 188 n. 34, 189; Jefferson to William Claiborne, July 14, 1805; *L&C Letters*, pp. 232–33, 252.

167. *laborers*: Jefferson to John Lenthall, July 14, 1805.

167. *"female inspection"*: Louisa Adams, vol. 1, p. 219.

167. Mammoth Room, fire engine, lighting, and painter: Jefferson to Claxton, June 9, 1805, and Philippe Reibelt, July 10, 1805; Benjamin King to Jefferson, July 8, 1805.

167. *Claxton*: Claxton to Jefferson, February 8, 1806; Jefferson to Claxton, March 2, 1806.

168. Bedroom suite: Phillips-Schrock, p. 33; Claxton to Jefferson, August 27, 1801; "Original Furnishings," p. 485; "Forty Years," p. 146; McMaster, p. 605; Ryan and Guinness, p. 124; Dougherty to Jefferson, March 19, 1809, Jefferson to Dougherty, March 24, 1809.

168–69. *By the fall of 1805*: Jefferson to Peter Lenox, August 22, 1805; Seale, vol. 1, p. 89; Ryan and Guinness, pp. 121, 124; Jefferson to James Dinsmore, June 8, 1805; Claxton to Jefferson, May 22, 1805.

169–170. *Lewis and Clark's Western treasures*: *L&C Letters*, pp. 253–56; Foster Diary, vol. 2, p. 17; Jefferson to Lemaire, August 17, 1805; Lemaire to Jefferson, August 12 and 20, 1805.

170. *Monsieur returned*: Jefferson to Martha, October 13, 1805; Jefferson to Philippe Reibelt, October 12, 1805.

170. Gifts to Peale: Jefferson to Peale, October 6, 9, and 21, 1805; Peale to Jefferson, October 22 and November 3, 1805; *L&C Letters*, pp. 260–64, 267; *Mem. Books*, vol. 2, p. 1168 n. 5; James McNeill to Jefferson, August 12, 1805.

171. *Hubbard*: Daniel Bradley to Jefferson, September 7 and October 6, 1805; Jefferson to Bradley, October 6, 1805; Stanton, p. 150; Wiencek, pp. 144–45; author's correspondence with Lucia Stanton in March 2019.

CHAPTER FIFTEEN

173–75. *family visit*: Kierner, pp. 127–28, 131–32, 146; Jefferson to Martha, November 7, 1805; *JQA Memoirs*, vol. 1, p. 386; "James Madison Randolph," www.monticello.org; Wiencek, p. 168; Boles, p. 396; Louisa Adams, vol. 1, p. 232; Wister, pp. 40, 48–49; *First Forty*, pp. 49–50, 76, 404–5; Stanton, p. 28; Foster, pp. 10–11.

173. *"squally session"*: Jefferson to Elizabeth Trist, April 27, 1806.

175. Hammuda and Jefferson: Hammuda Pasha to Jefferson, April 15, 1801, and September 8, 1802; Jefferson to Hammuda Pasha, September 9, 1801.

175–76. Plumer's call on Jefferson: Plumer, pp. 333–36; Louisa Adams, vol. 1, p. 267 n. 303; Janson, p. 2.

176. *"very singular"*: Louisa Adams, vol. 1, p. 231.

176–80 and 186. *Melli Melli*: Melli Melli to Madison, February 11, 1806; Jefferson to James Cathcart, June 21, 1806; Bedini, p. 134; Melli Melli to Jefferson, July 26, 1806; Plumer, pp. 344, 351, 358–59, 364–65; 382, 384, 469, 473; Louisa Adams, vol. 1, pp. 229–30; *JQA Memoirs*, vol. 1, p. 378; Janson, pp. 143, 216–18; Brant, pp. 306–7; Louis B. Wright and Julia H. Macleod, "Mellimelli: A Problem for President Jefferson in North African Diplomacy," *Virginia Quarterly Review* 20 (Autumn 1944): 555–65, passim; Dunlap, vol. 2, pp. 383–84; *Winter in Washington*, vol. 1, pp. 36–38, 50; Catharine Mitchill, p. 174; Melli Melli to Madison, January 12, 1806; Furman, p. 37; Foster, pp. 32–33, 39, 47, 259; Jefferson to Madison, November 22, 1805; Laura Carter Holloway, *The Ladies of the White House* (New York: United States Publishing Company, 1870), pp. 149–50; Brant, pp. 306–8; Jefferson to John Quincy Adams, Samuel Mitchill, and Joseph Nicholson, December 6, 1805; www.timeanddate.com; Cullen, pp. 41–42; Bruce, vol. 1., p. 30; TJR Memoir, pp. 31, 34.

180. *Early in December of 1805*: Plumer, pp. 339, 342.

180. *Plains Indians*: Foster, pp. 29–34, 42, 256; *Two Duchesses*, p. 257; *Original Journals*, vol. 6, pp. 82–120; Ewers, p. 7–9; *L&C Letters*, pp. 189, 265–66; Plumer, p. 382.

181. Silverware, awe and intimidation, New Year's Day: Foster, pp. 35–36, 41, 43, 46; *Two Duchesses*, p. 258; *First Forty*, pp. 402–3.

181. *his children* and Merry and Foster: Foster, pp. 22, 27.

181–82. *New Year's Day reception*: *Mem. Books*, vol. 2, p. 1196 n. 90; *Winter in Washington*, vol. 1, pp. 19–44; *First Forty*, pp. 400–403; Foster's Notes, p. 26; Foster, pp. 22–23, 52.

182. Sicilian band: Helen Cripe, *Thomas Jefferson and Music* (Chapel Hill: University of North Carolina Press, 2009), p. 30.

183–84. Jefferson and the Wind: Dunlap, vol. 2, p. 388; Founders: Jefferson's Address to Chiefs, February 27, 1808; *History of the Expedition of Captains Lewis and Clark* 1804–5–6, 2 vols. (Chicago: A. G. McClurg, 1903), vol. 1, p. 61; Foster, p. 23; *Two Duchesses*, p. 257; Augustus John Foster, "Foster and 'The Wild Natives of the Woods,' 1805–1807," ed. Dorothy Wollon and Margaret Kinard, *William and Mary Quarterly* 9 (April 1952): 191–214, figs. 1–8; King, vol. 4, p. 109; *Original Journals*, vol. 6, pp. 82–120; www.lewis-clark.org, "Osage Indians"; *L&C Letters*, vol. 10, pp. 284–89, 306–7; Ewers, pp. 2–9, 11, 14–17, 21; Founders: Chiefs of Nations to Jefferson, January 4, 1806.

184. Chickasaws and Cherokees: Foster, p. 40; *Two Duchesses*, p. 258, Louisa Adams, vol. 1, p. 231.

184–85. *sign language master*: Christopher Steinke, "'Here Is My Country': Too Né's Map of Lewis and Clark in the Great Plains," *William and Mary Quarterly* 71 (October 2014): 589–610, pp. 599, 601, and passim; *L&C Letters*, pp. 272–74; Foster Diary, vol. 2, p. 17; Viola, p. 169; Jefferson to John Breckinridge, March 5, 1806; Dunlap, vol. 2, pp. 389–92.

185. *Indian languages*: Valsania, p. 230 n. 82; King, vol. 4, pp. 502–3; Jefferson to John Sibley, May 27, 1805; Jefferson to Levett Harris, April 18, 1806.

185–86. *Dunlap*: Dunlap, vol. 2, pp. 386–93.

186. *Stuart's new portrait*: *Mem. Books*, vol. 2, p. 1156 n. 74

186. *After Melli Melli . . . none was paid*: Plumer, pp. 344, 473; Jefferson to the Bey of Tunis, June 28, 1806.

186. Plumer on naïveté: Plumer, pp. 453–55.

187. *Burr*: *Anas*, pp. 237–40; Founders: Notes on Aaron Burr, April 15, 1806; Cullen, p. 33, April 9, 1806 dinner.

187–88. Plumer's conversations with Jefferson and Adams: Plumer, pp. 465–72.

188. *foreign policy*: Jefferson to Robert Moore, March 11, 1805; Masterson, p. 97; Jefferson to Walter Jones, March 5, 1810, and Madison, September 18, 1805.

188. *"ten years older"*: Henry Adams, vol. 3, p. 206.

188. *Pickering*: Peters, pp. 336–38.

CHAPTER SIXTEEN

189. *tulip bulbs*: Jefferson to Bernard McMahon, July 15, 1806.

189–90. Fossett and his flight: Wiencek, pp. 168–69; Stanton, pp. 9, 12, 17, 187–89, 309 n. 58; Founders: Thomas Jefferson's Notes on Joseph Fossett's Account for Plating Saddle Trees, November 18, 1811; Jefferson to Edmund Bacon, May 13, 1807; *Mem. Books*, vol. 2, p. 1185; Jefferson to Dougherty, July 31, 1806; *Farm Book*, pp. 22–23; Dougherty to Jefferson, August 3, 1806; Lemaire to Jefferson, August 5, 1806; "Joseph Fossett," www.monticello.org.

191. Jefferson's letters to Dougherty, Lemaire, and Martha: Jefferson to Dougherty, September 6, 1807; Jefferson to Lemaire, September 25, 1806; see "Well Ordered," p. 12 and Wiencek, p. 168; Jefferson to Martha, October 20, 1806.

191. *Coles*: Coles Diary; *Mem. Books*, vol. 2, p. 1147 n. 45.

191. Frances Hern and David Hern: "David Hern," www.monticello.org; *Mem. Books*, vol. 2, pp. 1189 n. 65, 1193; Stanton, pp. 17, 44–46; Wiencek, p. 168.

191. *"unspeakable joy"*: Lewis to Jefferson, September 23, 1806; Jefferson to Lewis, October 26, 1806; Boles, p. 399; Malone, vol. 5, p. xxvii.

192. *"bosom of our friends"*: Ambrose, pp. 320, 417, 420.

192. Mandans, Osage, and Quebecois: Charles de Wolf Brownell, *The Indian Races of America* (Boston: Dayton and Wentworth, 1855), pp. 442–45; *Original Journals*, vol. 6, pp. 89–90 and vol. 7, pp. 349–50; Plumer, p. 554; Coles Diary, December 28, 1806.

192. Lewis through the winter: Ambrose, pp. 322–23; Boles, p. 400.

192. *museum*: "President Thomas Jefferson's White House Museum," www.whitehousehistory.org; Kierner, pp. 148–49.

192. *Pickering*: Charles W. Upham, *The Life of Timothy Pickering*, 4 vols. (Boston: Little, Brown, 1874), vol. 4, p. 104.

192. *Dickinson*: Jefferson to John Dickinson, January 13, 1807.

192. *Burr conspiracy*: Founders: Jefferson's Proclamation, November 27, 1806; Malone, vol. 5, pp. 197–99.

193. *repeal the gospels*: Plumer, p. 527.

193. Merry's exit: Lester, pp. 115–18.

193. *Erskine*: Quincy, p. 132; Coles Diary, November 3, 1806; Jefferson to David Erskine, December 1, 1807; Few, pp. 355, 357; Story, p. 161; Masterson, pp. 98–104, 109; Foster Papers, letter to his mother, November 1–3, 1807; Plumer, pp. 564, 635.

193–94. Coles and Erskine: Coles Diary, November 6 and December 25, 1806, January 29, February 17 and 27, March 21, April 2 and 6, and July 14, 1808.

194. *Lady Frances Erskine*: Coles Diary, November 6, 1806; Catharine Mitchill, p. 179; *Salons*, p. 196; Few, p. 355.

194–96. Jefferson and Plumer: Plumer, pp. 34, 460, 544–47, 561–62, 570, 600–608; *Henry Clay*, pp. 265–66; Cullen, p. 34.

196. Dueling: *Rush Letters*, vol. 2, p. 885; Plumer, pp. 269–76, 305; Taggart, p. 203; Cutler, vol. 2, p. 121; Freeman, pp. 168–71.

196. *Randolph of Roanoke*: *Two Duchesses*, pp. 197, 275; Edgar P. Richardson, ed., *Gilbert Stuart: Portraitist of the Young Republic 1755–1828* (Washington, DC and Providence, RI: National Gallery of Art and Rhode Island School of Design, 1967), p. 39; Bruce, vol. 1, pp. 36, 125, 256–57, 362.

196–97. Randolph v. Randolph: Plumer, pp. 490–91; Jefferson to Randolph, June 23, 1806; Jefferson to James Ogilvie, June 23, 1806.

196–97. Eppes, Jefferson, and Randolph: Jefferson to Martha, October 7, 1804; Plumer, pp. 270–73, 276, 436; Quincy, pp. 166–73; Catharine Mitchill, p. 179; Pickering to Jefferson, February 24, 1806.

197–201. Randolph's breakdown: Plumer, pp. 102–3, 242–43, 623, 642; Ellen to Henry Randall, July 31, 1856, Randolph Papers; Gaines, pp. 54–67; Jefferson to Randolph, February 18, 19, and 28 and April 3, 1807; *JQA Memoirs*, vol. 1, pp. 457–58; Coles Diary, February 16, 19, and 22, 1807; William Burwell to Jefferson, February 18, 20, and 28 and March 3, 1807; Malone, vol. 5, p. xxviii; Jefferson to Martha, March 2, 1807.

200. Plumer's farewell: Donald R. Hickey, "The Monroe-Pinkney Treaty of 1806: A Reappraisal," *William and Mary Quarterly* 44 (January 1987): 65–88, pp. 66–67; Plumer, p. 642.

200–201. *"invalids"* and recovery: Jefferson to Martha, March 2, 6, 9, 12, 13, 16, 20, and 23 and April 3 and 5, 1807; Coles Diary, March 1807, passim; Scofield, p. 454 n. 6; Valsania, p. 94; Brodie, p. 396; Jefferson to Monroe, March 21, 1807; Jefferson to Randolph, April 3, 1807; Kierner, p. 135; Eppes to Jefferson, July 10, 1809.

CHAPTER SEVENTEEN

203. Landscaping: *Changing White House*, p. 164; Fazio and Snadon, p. 365; *Latrobe Papers*, vol. 2, pp. 394, 686–87; Seale, vol. 1, pp. 110–11; Jefferson to Latrobe, May 22, 1807; Pliska, p. 15.

204. War clouds: Coles Diary, June 25 and July 2 and 4, 1807; Jefferson to du Pont de Nemours, July 14, 1807; Esther Singleton, *The Story of the White House*, 2 vols. (New York: S. S. McClure, 1907), vol. 1, p. 52; Meacham, p. 426; Cullen, p. 34.

204. *chiding Ellen*: Jefferson to Ellen, June 29, 1807.

204. *merchant friend in Marseilles*: Jefferson to Stephen Cathalan, June 29, 1807.

204–5. Work on the house and grounds: *Latrobe Papers*, vol. 2, pp. 461–63; Jefferson to Latrobe, April 3, 1805, and August 18, 1807; Jefferson to Madison, March 30, 1809; Jefferson to James Dinsmore, October 4, 1807; Phillips-Schrock, pp. 22, 36; Pliska, p. 15; *Jefferson in His Own Time*, p. 176; Fazio and Snadon, p. 367, 369, 372, 381–83; Seale, vol. 1, pp. 49, 107–9, 113, 118; Ryan and Guinness, pp. 99, 106.

205–6. Latrobe's plans: Fazio and Snadon, pp. 371–75; Ryan and Guinness, pp. 106–7; Seale, vol. 1, pp. 115–16.

206. *Francis*: Jefferson to Eppes, May 24, 1806, and May 28, 1807; Jefferson to Ellen, January 12, 1808; Randolph, pp. 313–14; *Mem. Books*, vol. 2, p. 1215 n. 41.

206. Maria Fossett's birth: Malone, vol. 5, p. xxviii; Wiencek, p. 168.

206. Bears: Jefferson to Anne, November 1, 1807; Jefferson to Peale, November 5, 1807, January 6 and February 6, 1808; Seale, vol. 1, pp. 94–95.

206–7. Adams at dinner twice: *JQA Memoirs*, vol. 1, pp. 472–73; Few, p. 356; Louisa Adams, vol. 1, p. 264; Foster to his mother, December 4, 1807, Foster Papers, vol. 3.

207. Jefferson to Martha: Jefferson to Martha, November 23, 1807; Henry Adams, vol. 2, p. 151.

208. Tooth and jaw: Jefferson to Martha, December 29, 1807; January 5 and 7 and February 10, 1808; *Mem Books*, vol. 1, p. 1217 n. 47; Jefferson to Ellen, December 6 and 8, 1807 and February 23, 1808; *JQA Memoirs*, vol. 1, p. 498; Louisa Adams, vol. 1, p. 265; *Intelligencer*, January 4, 1808; Malone, vol. 5, p. 541.

208. *Rose*: Burwell, p. 129 n. 83; Louisa Adams, vol. 1, p. 266; Henry Adams, vol. 4, pp. 182–83.

208–9. Correspondence with Ellen: Jefferson to Ellen, March 14 and 29, 1808; Ellen to Jefferson, March 18 and April 1, 1808.

209. *bones*: Jefferson to Caspar Wistar, December 19, 1807, March 8 and 20 and April 24, 1808; Martin, pp. 113–15; Cullen, p. 36.

209–10. The deficit and its aftermath: Malone, vol. 5, pp. xxix, 537–39; *Mem. Books*, vol. 1, p. liii; Jefferson to Ellen and Cornelia, March 29 and April 3, 1808; Jefferson to Gallatin, March 30, 1808; Edward Hake Phillips, "Timothy Pickering's Portrait of Thomas Jefferson," *Essex Institute Historical Collections* 94 (October 1958): 309–27, p. 317; Jefferson to Latrobe, April 26 and June 2, 1808; Latrobe to Jefferson, May 23, 1808.

210–11. Letter to Ellen: Jefferson to Ellen, July 5, 1808.

211. *Astor*: Jefferson to John Jacob Astor, July 17, 1808.

211–12. Porticos, balcony, sewer, and wall: *Latrobe Papers*, vol. 2, pp. 622–24, 627 n. 2, 658–59; Malone, vol. 5, p. 531; Padover, pp. 445–46, 451; Jefferson to Latrobe, September 8, 1808; Fazio and Snadon, p. 384; Seale, vol. 1, pp. 115–16.

212. *Jeff*: Peale to Jefferson, August 30, 1807; Jefferson to Martha, October 18, 1808; *Mem. Books*, vol. 2, p. 1233 n. 95; *Peale*, vol. 2, pt. 2, pp. 1027–29; TJR Memoir, p. 32; Randall, vol. 3, p. 231.

212. *Francis Few*: Few, pp. 349–50.

CHAPTER EIGHTEEN

213. *"serious debts"*: Jefferson to Martha Randolph, January 5, 1808.

213. *whooping cough*: Wiencek, p. 168; Stanton, p. 46; Jefferson to Margaret Smith, November 2, 1808; Eppes to Jefferson, November 6, 1801; Maria to Jefferson, November 6, 1801; Jefferson to Edmund Bacon, November 7, 1808; Bacon to Jefferson, November 17, 1808; author's correspondence with Lucia Stanton in March 2019.

213–14. Erskine and Lincoln: Founders: Notes on Conversation with David M. Erskine, November 9, 1808; Jefferson to Levi Lincoln, November 13, 1808.

214. *Dr. Bruff*: *Mem. Books*, vol. 2, p. 1235 n. 5; Jefferson to Martha, December 6, 1808, January 10, 1809; Jefferson to Ellen, December 20, 1808.

214. *Cornelia*: Cornelia to Jefferson, December 19, 1808.

214. *debts*: Jefferson to John Eppes, May 24, 1806, George Jefferson, December 24, 1808, and Martha, January 5 and February 27, 1808; Jefferson to Abraham Venable, January 23, 1809.

214. *"glass"*: National Archives, RG 42, Entry 15, Journals, vol. 4.

214–15. Wines and dinners: Cullen, pp. 36–37; Hailman, pp. 318–19.

214–15. Fading power: Malone, vol. 5, pp. 622–25, 643–49; *Mem. Books*, vol. 1, p. liii; Jefferson to Thomas Jefferson Randolph, November 24, 1808, and George Logan, December 27, 1808.

215. *old age*: Jefferson to Charles Thomson, December 25, 1808; Jefferson to Martha, January 10, 1809.

215. *homespun*: Jefferson to Abraham Bishop, December 8, 1808; Jefferson to Thomas Jefferson Randolph, December 19, 1808; TJR Memoir, pp. 38, 40; Wilson, pp. 193–94.

215. *secession*: Jefferson to Thomas Mann Randolph, January 2, 1809.

215–16. *New Year's Day*: Catharine Mitchill, p. 176; Few, pp. 356–57; Jefferson to Thomas Jefferson Randolph, December 19, 1808; *Mem. Books*, vol. 2, p. 1237 n. 11; Malone, vol. 5, p. 629.

216–17. Sheep and rams: *Mem. Books*, vol. 2, pp. 1194 n. 81, 1220 n. 60; *Farm Book*, pp. 111–12; Jefferson to Lemaire, August 29, 1807; James Barry to Jefferson, June 6, 1807; Jefferson to Ellen, June 29, 1807; Dougherty to Jefferson, August 31 and September 17, 1807; Thornton Diary, February 24, 1808; Jefferson to Alexander Kerr and Kerr to him, February 7, 1808; William Keough to Jefferson, February 15, 1809; "Sheep," www.monticello.org.

217. *Claxton*: Claxton to Jefferson, February 16 and 17 and March 10, 1809; Jefferson to Claxton, February 19, 1809; Founders: Inventory of President's House, February 19, 1809.

217. *authorized the sale*: *Latrobe Papers*, vol. 2, p. 706.

217. *"settle up"*: *Farm Book*, pp. 27–28.

217–18. *Bacon*: *Jefferson in His Own Time*, pp. 175–76.

218. *valedictory letters*: Jefferson to David Warden, February 25, 1809, and Dupont de Nemours, March 2, 1809.

218. *Freeman*: Founders: Enclosure: Deed of John Freeman's Indenture to James Madison, April 19, 1809; Freeman to Jefferson, March 2, 1809; Stanton, p. 53.

218–19. *Madison's inauguration*: *First Forty*, pp. 58–59; Randolph, pp. 323–24; John Quincy Adams, *Writings of John Quincy Adams*, ed. Worthington Chauncey Ford (New York: Macmillan, 1914), p. 289; *JQA Memoirs*, vol. 1, p. 544.

219. *Custis*: Bullock, p. 56.

EPILOGUE

221–22. *the President's House*: William Sullivan, *Familiar Letters on Public Characters and Public Events* (Boston: Russell, Odiorne, and Metcalf, 1834), pp. 157–58; Busey, pp. 102–4; Catherine Allgor, "Dolley Madison Creates the White House," in *The White House: Actors and Observers*, ed. William Seale (Boston: Northeastern University Press, 2002), pp. 26–27; Phillips-Schrock, pp. 38, C-2-3; Dougherty to Jefferson, May 15, 1809; Hobbs, p. 49; Moore, vol. 1, p. 137; Ryan and Guinness, p. 121; Steve Vogel, *Through the Perilous Fight: Six Weeks That Saved the Nation* (New York: Random House, 2013), pp. 180–81, 230, 387–88, 399.

222–23. *Jefferson*: Jefferson to Humboldt, March 6, 1809, William Short, March 8, 1809, John Barnes, April 27, 1809, and Walter Jones, March 5, 1810; Claxton to Jefferson, March 10, 1809; *Jefferson in His Own Time*, pp. 176, 178; Randolph, pp. 397–432; Lester J. Cappon, ed., *The Adams-Jefferson Letters* (Chapel Hill: University of North Carolina Press, 1959), p. 43 and passim; Viola, p. 102.

223–24. *Latrobe*: Jefferson to Madison, March 30, 1809; Phillips-Schrock, pp. 38, C-2–C-3; Fazio and Snadon, p. 384; *Latrobe Papers*, vol. 3, p. 700; *Latrobe Journal*, pp. 150–51.

224. *Secretaries*: Ambrose, pp. 425–484; *L&C Letters*, pp. 470–72, 476–78; Coles to Jefferson, March 13, 1809; Brant, p. 31; Lewis Harvie to Jefferson, January 19, 1803; Dougherty to Jefferson, February 13 and 16, 1821.

224–25. *Julien*: Julien to Jefferson, January 1, 1810, July 2, 1812, and October 14, 1818; Jefferson to Julien, April 25, 1809, January 8, 1810, December 25, 1817, September 11 and October 6, 1818, and January 14 and 27, 1825; Jefferson to Henry Foxhall, March 24, 1809; Dougherty to Jefferson, December 18, 1823; Stanton, p. 53.

225. *Lemaire*: Jefferson to Lemaire, March 16 and April 25, 1809; Lemaire to Jefferson, May 10, 1802, and March 22 and May 25, 1809; Julien to Jefferson, November 7, 1817; Jefferson to Julien, December 25, 1817.

225–26. *Dougherty*: Dougherty to Madison, February 4, 1819; Dougherty to Jefferson, March 14, 1803 (on Shorter), February 10, 1819, and December 13, 1823; Dougherty to Thomas Randolph, July 20, 1819; Mary Dougherty to Jefferson, October 25 and December 7, 1823, and January 27, 1824; Stanton, pp. 54–55.

226. *Freeman*: Stanton, pp. 54–55.

226–27. *The Fossetts and the Herns*: "Edith Hern Fossett," www.monticello.org; Lemaire to Jefferson, May 6, 1809; Stanton, pp. 3, 9–10, 13, 15, 17–20, 24, 47, 53, 188–90, 309 n. 58; "Joseph Fossett," www.monticello.org; Founders: Jefferson's Notes on Joseph Fossett's Account for Plating Saddle Trees, November 18, 1811.

227. *Thomas Jefferson Randolph*: TJR Memoir, pp. 21–23; Founders: Thomas Jefferson Randolph to Jefferson, ca. February 26, 1802, Editor's note.

227–28. *Martha Jefferson Randolph*: Kierner, pp. 208–72; Wister, pp. 51–70; *First Forty*, pp. 307–9.

228. *Thomas Mann Randolph*: Gaines, pp. 67–188.

228. *John Wayles Eppes and Francis Wayles Eppes*: Eppes to Jefferson, July 10, 1809; "John Wayles Eppes" and "Francis Wayles Eppes," www.monticello.org.

229. *Plumer*: *Life of Plumer*, pp. 377–543; Lynn Warren Turner, *William Plumer of New Hampshire, 1759–1850* (Chapel Hill: University of North Carolina Press, 1962), p. 150.

229. *Elizabeth Patterson Bonaparte*: *Elizabeth Patterson Bonaparte*, pp. 37–47; Catharine Mitchill, p. 184.

229–30. *The Merrys*: Lester, pp. 118ff; Masterson, p. 96.

230. *Foster*: *Two Duchesses*, p. 240; Foster, pp. xi–xiii; *Oxford Dictionary of National Biography*.

SELECTED BIBLIOGRAPHY

PRIMARY SOURCES

Manuscript Collections

Albert and Shirley Small Special Collections Library, University of Virginia: Fiske Kimball Manuscripts; Papers of the Randolph Family of Edgehill; Memoir of Thomas Jefferson Randolph.

American Antiquarian Society: *National Intelligencer* and other newspapers.

Library of Congress: British Ministers to the USA Writing to the Foreign Office, Transcriptions; Diary of Isaac Coles; Papers of Anna Marie Thornton; Papers of Augustus Foster; Papers of William Plumer; various correspondence.

Massachusetts Historical Society: Adams Family Papers, Papers of Thomas Jefferson, Papers of Timothy Pickering; Photostats Collection.

National Archives: Records of the Commissioners for the District of Columbia.

Books

Adams, John Quincy. *The Diary of John Quincy Adams*. Edited by D. G. Allen et al. 2 vols. Cambridge, MA: Belknap, 1981.

———. *Memoirs of John Quincy Adams: Comprising Portions of His Diary from 1795 to 1848*. Edited by Charles Francis Adams. 12 vols. Philadelphia: J. B. Lippincott, 1874.

Adams, Louisa Catherine. *The Adams Papers: Diary and Autobiographical Writings of Louisa Catherine Adams*. 2 vols. Cambridge, MA: Belknap Press of Harvard University Press, 2013.

Cutler, William P., and Julia P. *Life, Journals and Correspondence of Manasseh Cutler, LL.D.* 2 vols. Cincinnati, OH: Robert Clarke, 1888.

Davis, John. *Travels of Four Years and a Half in the United States of America*. London: R. Edwards, 1803.

Dunlap, William. *Diary of William Dunlap*. 2 vols. New York: J. J. Little and Ives, 1930.

Foster, Augustus J. *Jeffersonian America*. Edited by Richard Beale Davis. San Marino, CA: Huntington Library, 1954.

Foster, Vere. *The Two Duchesses*. London: Blackie & Son, 1898.

Gallatin, Albert. *Writings of Albert Gallatin*. 3 vols. Edited by Henry Adams. Philadelphia: J. B. Lippincott, 1879.

Hayes, Kevin J. *Thomas Jefferson in His Own Time: A Biographical Chronicle of His Life Drawn from Recollections, Interviews, and Memoirs by Family, Friends, and Associates*. Iowa City: University of Iowa Press, 2012.

Jackson, Donald, ed. *Letters of the Lewis and Clark Expedition, with Related Documents, 1783–1854*. Urbana: University of Illinois Free Press, 1962.

Janson, Charles William. *The Stranger in America, 1793–1806*. London: printed for J. Cundee, 1807.

Jefferson, Thomas. *Jefferson's Memorandum Books: Accounts, with Legal Records and Miscellany, 1767–1826*. Edited by James A. Bear Jr. and Lucia C. Stanton. 2 vols. Princeton, NJ: Princeton University Press, 1997.

——. The Papers of Thomas Jefferson. 2nd ser. Princeton, NJ: Princeton University Press, 1950–2016.

——. *Thomas Jefferson's Architectural Drawings*. Edited by Frederick D. Nichols. Boston: Massachusetts Historical Society; Charlottesville: Thomas Jefferson Memorial Foundation and University of Virginia Press, 1961.

——. *Thomas Jefferson's Farm Book*. Edited by Edwin Morris Betts. Charlottesville, VA: Thomas Jefferson's Memorial Foundation, 1953.

Kimball, Fiske. *Thomas Jefferson, Architect: Original Designs in the Collection of Thomas Jefferson Coolidge, Jr.* New York: Da Capo, 1968, originally published in 1916.

Latrobe, Benjamin. *Correspondence and Miscellaneous Papers of Benjamin Henry Latrobe*. 3 vols. Edited by John G. Van Horne and Lee W. Formwalt. New Haven, CT: Yale University Press, 1984.

——. *The Journal of Latrobe*. New York: D. Appleton, 1905.

Madison, James. *The Writings of James Madison*. 9 vols. Edited by Gaillard Hunt. New York: Putnam, 1900–1910.

McLaughlin, Jack, ed. *To His Excellency Thomas Jefferson: Letters to a President*. New York: Norton, 1991.

Moore, S. S., and T. W. Jones. *The Traveller's Directory, or A Pocket Companion, Showing the Course of the Main Roads from Philadelphia to Washington*. Philadelphia: printed for Matthew Carey, 1802.

Peale, Charles Willson. *The Selected Papers of Charles Willson Peale and His Family*. 5 vols. Edited by Lillian B. Miller. New Haven, CT: Yale University Press, 1983.

Plumer, William. *William Plumer's Memorandum of Proceedings on the United States Senate 1803–1807*. Edited by Everett S. Brown. New York: Macmillan, 1923.

Plumer, William, Jr., ed. *Life of William Plumer*. Boston: Phillips, Sampson, 1857.

Randolph, Sarah N. *The Domestic Life of Thomas Jefferson*. New York: Harper, 1871.

Smith, Margaret Bayard. *The First Forty Years of Washington Society in the Family Letters of Margaret Bayard Smith.* Edited by Gaillard Hunt. New York: Scribner, 1906.

———. *A Winter in Washington; or, Memoirs of the Seymour Family*. 2 vols. New York: E. Bliss and E. White, 1824.

Thwaites, Reuben Gold, ed. *Original Journals of the Lewis and Clark Expedition, 1804–1806*. 7 vols. New York: Dodd, Mead, 1904–1905.

Warden, David. B. *A Chorographical and Statistical Description of the District of Columbia*. Paris: Smith, Rue Montmorency, 1816.

Articles and Chapters of Books

Burwell, William A. "'Strict Truth': The Narrative of William Armistead Burwell." Edited by Gerald W. Gawalt. *Virginia Magazine of History and Biography* 101 (January 1993): 103–32.

Few, Frances. "The Diary of Francis Few, 1808–1809." Edited by Noble E. Cunningham Jr. *Journal of Southern History* 29 (August 1963): 345–61.

Foster, Augustus John. "Foster and 'The Wild Natives of the Woods,' 1805–1807." Edited by Dorothy Wollon and Margaret Kinard. *William and Mary Quarterly* 9 (April 1952): 191–214.

———. "Notes on the United States." *Quarterly Review* 68 (June and September 1841): 20–57.

Jefferson, Thomas. "Memoir of Meriwether Lewis." In *History of the Expedition under the Command of Lewis and Clark*, by Elliott Coues. 4 vols. New York: Francis P. Harper, 1893.

Klapthor, Margaret Brown. "A First Lady and a New Frontier." *Historic Preservation* 15 (1963): 88–93.

Latrobe, John H. B. "Construction of the Public Buildings in Washington." *Maryland Historical Magazine* 4 (1909): 221–28.

Mitchill, Catharine. "Catharine Mitchill's Letters from Washington, 1806–1812." Edited by Carolyn Hoover Sung. *Quarterly Journal of the Library of Congress* 34 (July 1977): 171–89.

Mitchill, Samuel L. "Dr. Mitchill's Letters from Washington: 1801–1813." *Harper's New Monthly Magazine* 58 (April 1879): 740–55.

Mugridge, Donald H. "Augustus Foster and His Book." *Records of the Columbia Historical Society* 53/56 (1953/1956): 327–52.

Smith, Margaret Bayard. "The President's House Forty Years Ago." *Rover* 3 (1844): 145–50.

Taggart, Samuel. "Letters of Samuel Taggart." *Proceedings of the American Antiquarian Society*, New Series 33 (April 11–October 17, 1923): Part One, 113–226.

Thornton, Anna Maria Brodeau. "Diary of Mrs. William Thornton, 1800–1863." *Records of the Columbia Historical Society* 10 (1907): 88–226.

SECONDARY SOURCES

Books

Adams, Henry. *History of the United States of America during the Administrations of Thomas Jefferson and James Madison.* 9 vols. New York: Antiquarian, 1962.

Allgor, Catherine. *Parlor Politics: In Which the Ladies of Washington Help Build a City and a Government.* Charlottesville: University Press of Virginia, 2000.

——. *A Perfect Union: Dolly Madison and the Creation of the American Nation.* New York: Henry Holt, 2006.

Ambrose, Stephen E. *Undaunted Courage.* New York: Simon & Schuster, 1996.

Bedini, Silvio A. *Jefferson and Science.* Raleigh: University of North Carolina Press, 2002.

——. *Thomas Jefferson and His Copying Machines.* Charlottesville: University Press of Virginia, 1984.

Boles, John B. *Jefferson: Architect of Liberty.* New York: Basic Books, 2017.

Brant, Irving. *James Madison: Secretary of State, 1800–1809.* Indianapolis, IN: Bobbs-Merrill, 1953.

Brown, Gordon S. *Incidental Architect: William Thornton and the Cultural Life of Early Washington, D.C., 1794–1828.* Athens: Ohio University Press, 2009.

Bryan, Wilhelmus Bogart. *A History of the National Capital.* 2 vols. New York: MacMillan, 1914–1916.

Busey, Samuel Clagett. *Pictures of the City of Washington in the Past.* Washington, DC: W. Ballantyne and Sons, 1898.

Carson, Barbara. *Ambitious Appetites: Dining, Behavior, and Patterns of Consumption in Federal Washington.* Washington, DC: American Institute of Architects Press, 1990.

Côté, Richard. *Strength and Honor: The Life of Dolley Madison.* Mount Pleasant, SC: Corinthian Books, 2004.

Craughwell, Thomas J. *Thomas Jefferson's Crème Brûlée.* Philadelphia: Quirk Books, 2012.

Cunningham, Noble E. *The Process of Government under Jefferson.* Princeton, NJ: Princeton University Press, 1978.

Danisi, Thomas C., and John C. Jackson. *Meriwether Lewis.* Amherst, NY: Prometheus Books, 2009.

Fazio, Michael, and Patrick A. Snadon. *The Domestic Architecture of Benjamin Henry Latrobe.* Baltimore: Johns Hopkins University Press, 2006.

Fowler, Damon Lee, ed. *Dining at Monticello: In Good Taste and Abundance.* Charlottesville, VA: Thomas Jefferson Foundation, 2005. Distributed by University of North Carolina Press.

Gabler, James M. *Passions: The Wines and Travels of Thomas Jefferson*. Baltimore: Bacchus, 1995.

Gaines, William H., Jr. *Thomas Mann Randolph, Jefferson's Son-in-Law*. Baton Rouge: Louisiana State University Press, 1966.

Gordon-Reed, Annette, and Peter S. Onuf. *"Most Blessed of the Patriarchs": Thomas Jefferson and the Empire of the Imagination*. New York: Liveright, 2016.

Hailman, John. *Thomas Jefferson on Wine*. Jackson: University Press of Mississippi, 2006.

Hamlin, Talbot. *Benjamin Henry Latrobe*. New York: Oxford University Press, 1955.

Harbaugh, Marjorie Warvelle. *The First Forty Years of Washington, D.C. Architecture*. Houston: Danzmark Productions, 2013.

Kierner, Cynthia A. *Martha Jefferson Randolph, Daughter of Monticello: Her Life and Times*. Chapel Hill: University of North Carolina Press, 2012.

Kimball, Fiske. *Life Portraits of Jefferson and Their Replicas*. Philadelphia: American Philosophical Society, 1944.

———. *Thomas Jefferson, Architect*. New York: Da Capo, 1968, reprint of the 1916 edition.

Kimball, Marie. *Thomas Jefferson's Cook Book*. Charlottesville: University Press of Virginia, 1976.

Larson, Edward J. *A Magnificent Catastrophe*. New York: Free Press, 2007.

Lester, Malcolm. *Anthony Merry Redivivus: A Reappraisal of the British Minister to the United States, 1803–06*. Charlottesville: University Press of Virginia, 1978.

Malone, Dumas. *Jefferson and His Time*. 6 vols. Boston: Little, Brown, 1948–1981.

Martin, Edwin Thomas. *Thomas Jefferson, Scientist*. New York: H. Schuman, 1952.

Masterson, William Henry. *Tories and Democrats: British Diplomats in Pre-Jacksonian America*. College Station: Texas A&M University Press, 1985.

Meacham, Jon. *Thomas Jefferson: The Art of Power*. New York: Random House, 2013.

Miller, John C. *The Wolf by the Ears: Thomas Jefferson and Slavery*. Charlottesville: University Press of Virginia, 1991.

Nichols, Frederick D., and Ralph E. Griswold. *Thomas Jefferson: Landscape Architect*. Charlottesville: University Press of Virginia, 1978.

Padover, S. K. *Thomas Jefferson and the National Capital, 1783–1818*. Washington, DC: Government Printing Office, 1946.

Phillips-Schrock, Patrick. *The White House: An Illustrated Architectural History*. Jefferson, NC: McFarland, 2013.

Pliska, Jonathan. *A Garden for the President*. Washington, DC: White House Historical Association, 2016.

Randall, Henry S. *The Life of Thomas Jefferson*. 3 vols. New York: Derby & Jackson, 1858.

Ryan, William, and Desmond Guinness. *The White House: An Architectural History*. New York: McGraw-Hill, 1980.

Seale, William. *The President's House: A History*. 2 vols. Baltimore: Johns Hopkins University Press, 2008.

Singleton, Esther. *The Story of the White House*. 2 vols. New York: S. S. McClure, 1907.

Stanton, Lucia. *"Those Who Labor for My Happiness": Slavery at Thomas Jefferson's Monticello*. Charlottesville: University Press of Virginia, 2012.

Valsania, Maurizio. *Jefferson's Body: A Corporeal Biography*. Charlottesville: The University of Virginia Press, 2017.

Viola, Herman J. *Diplomats in Buckskins: A History of Indian Delegations in Washington City*. Washington, DC: Smithsonian Institution Press, 1981.

Wharton, Anne H. *Salons Colonial and Republican*. Philadelphia: J. B. Lippincott, 1900.

——. *Social Life in the Early Republic*. Philadelphia: J. B. Lippincott, 1903.

Wiencek, Henry. *Master of the Mountain: Thomas Jefferson and His Slaves*. New York: Farrar, Straus and Giroux, 2012.

Wilson, Gaye S. *Jefferson on Display: Attire, Etiquette, and the Art of Presentation*. Charlottesville: University of Virginia Press, 2018.

Wister, Sarah Butler, ed. *Worthy Women of Our First Century*. Philadelphia: Lippincott, 1877.

Young, James S. *The Washington Community, 1800–1828*. New York: Harcourt, Brace, 1966.

Articles and Chapters of Books

Abrams, Rochonne. "Meriwether Lewis: Two Years with Jefferson, the Mentor." *Missouri Historical Society Bulletin* 36 (October 1979): 3–18.

Baumgarten, Linda. "Jefferson's Clothing." *Antiques* 144 (July 1999): 100–105.

Boorstin, Daniel J. "Roles of the President's House." In *The White House: The First Two Hundred Years*, edited by Frank Freidel and William Pencak, 3–15. Boston: Northeastern University Press, 1994.

Browne, C. A. "Elder John Leland and the Mammoth Cheshire Cheese." *Agricultural History* 18 (October 1944): 145–53.

Busey, Samuel Clagett. "The Centennial of the First Inauguration of a President at the Permanent Seat of the Government." *Records of the Columbia Historical Society* 5 (1902): 96–111.

Butterfield, L. H. "Elder John Leland, Jeffersonian Itinerant." *Proceedings of the American Antiquarian Society* 62 (April 1952): 155–242.

Casper, Gerhard. "A Young Man from 'Ultima Thule' Visits Jefferson: Alexander von Humboldt in Philadelphia and Washington." *Proceedings of the American Philosophical Society* 155 (September 2011): 247–62.

Catanzariti, John. "Thomas Jefferson, Correspondent." *Proceedings of the Massachusetts Historical Society* 102 (1990): 1–20.

Cullen, Charles T. "Jefferson's White House Dinner Guests." *White House History* 17 (Winter 2006): 25–43.

Davis, Robert R., Jr. "Pell-Mell: Jeffersonian Etiquette and Protocol." *Historian* 43 (August 1981): 509–29.

Dumbauld, Edward. "Thomas Jefferson and the City of Washington." *Records of the Columbia Historical Society* 50 (1980): 67–80.

Ewers, John C. "'Chiefs from the Missouri and Mississippi' and Peale's Silhouettes of 1806." *Smithsonian Journal of History* 1 (1966): 1–26.

Fazio, Michael, and Patrick Snadon. "Benjamin Latrobe and Thomas Jefferson Redesign the President's House." *White House History* 8 (Fall 2000): 36–53.

Friis, Herman R. "Baron Alexander von Humboldt's Visit to Washington, D.C., June 1 through June 13, 1804." *Records of the Columbia Historical Society of Washington, D.C.* 63 (1963): 1–35.

Grigg, Milton L. "Thomas Jefferson and the Development of the National Capital." *Records of the Columbia Historical Society* 42 (1953/1956): 81–100.

Hawkins, Don A. "The City of Washington in 1800: A New Map." *Washington History* 12 (Spring/Summer 2000): 74–77.

Hazelton, Jean Hanvey. "Thomas Jefferson Gourmet." *American Heritage* 15 (October 1964): 20 and 102–5.

"John Wayles Eppes." *Dictionary of American Biography* 6 (1928–1936): 170–71.

Kimball, Marie G. "The Epicure of the White House." *Virginia Quarterly Review* 9 (January 1933): 71–81.

———. "The Original Furnishings of the White House." Parts I and II, *Antiques* 16 (June 1929): 481–86 and (July 1929): 33–37.

———. "Thomas Jefferson's French Furniture." *Antiques* 15 (February 1929): 123–28.

Larus, Joel. "Growing Pains of the New Republic: III, Pell Mell along the Potomac." *William and Mary Quarterly* 17, no. 3 (July 1960): 349–57.

Lockwood, Luke. "The St. Memin Indian Portraits." *New York Historical Society Quarterly Bulletin* 12 (1928): 3–26.

Mayo, Bernard. "A Peppercorn for Mr. Jefferson." *Virginia Quarterly Review* 19 (Spring 1943): 222–35.

McDonald, Travis. "The East and West Wings of the White House: History in Architecture and Building." *White House History* 29 (Summer 2011): 44–87.

Miles, Ellen. "Saint Mémin's Portraits of American Indians, 1804–1807." *American Art Journal* 20 (1988): 2–33.

Mount, Charles Merrill. "Gilbert Stuart in Washington." *Columbia Historical Society Records* 48 (1971–1973): 81–128.

Norton, Paul F. "Jefferson, the Making of an Architect." In *Jefferson and the Arts: An Extended View*, edited by William Howard Adams. Washington, DC: National Gallery of Art, 1976.

Paullin, Charles O. "Early British Diplomats in Washington." *Records of the Columbia Historical Society* 44–45 (1942–1943): 241–67.

Phillips, Edward Hake. "Timothy Pickering's Portrait of Thomas Jefferson." *Essex Institute Historical Collections* 94 (October 1958): 309–27.

Sassaman, Richard. "The Original 'Big Cheese.'" *American History Illustrated* 23 (January 1989): 34–35.

Scofield, Merry Ellen. "The Fatigues of His Table: The Politics of Presidential Dining during the Jefferson Administration." *Journal of the Early Republic* 26 (Fall 2006): 449–69.

Stanton, Lucia. "Nourishing the Congress: Hospitality in the President's House." In *Dining at Monticello: In Good Taste and Abundance*, edited by Damon Lee Fowler, pp. 11–18. Charlottesville, VA: Thomas Jefferson Foundation, 2005.

——. "A Well Ordered Household: Domestic Servants in Jefferson's White House." *White House History* 17 (Winter 2006): 4–23.

——. "Wine and Food at the White House, the Presidential Table." In *Jefferson and Wine*, edited by Lawrence R. de Treville. The Plains, VA: Vinifera Wine Growers Association, 1976.

Steinke, Christopher. "'Here Is My Country': Too Né's Map of Lewis and Clark in the Great Plains." *William and Mary Quarterly* 71 (October 2014): 589–610.

"Thomas Jefferson's White House." *White House History* 17 (Winter 2006).

Tinkcom, Margaret Bailey. "Caviar on the Potomac: Sir Augustus John Foster's 'Notes on the United States,' 1804–1812." *William and Mary Quarterly* 8 (January 1951): 68–107.

Wright, Louis B., and Julia H. Macleod. "Mellimelli: A Problem for President Jefferson in North African Diplomacy." *Virginia Quarterly Review* 20 (Autumn 1944): 555–65.

INTERNET SITES

Arnebeck, Bob. "The Seat of Empire: A History of Washington, 1790–1861." www.bobarnebeck.com.

The Founders Online. http://founders.archives.gov/.

The Library of Congress's collection of Jefferson's papers: http://memory.loc.gov/ammem/collections/jefferson_papers/.

Thomas Jefferson Encyclopedia, Thomas Jefferson Foundation. www.monticello.org/site/research-and-collections (e. g., "Dinner Etiquette")

INDEX

Page references for figures are italicized.

ABOUT THE AUTHOR

James B. Conroy, a trial lawyer in Boston for more than thirty-five years, is the author of *Our One Common Country: Abraham Lincoln and the Hampton Roads Peace Conference of 1865* (Lyons Press, 2014), a finalist for the prestigious Gilder Lehrman Lincoln Prize, and *Lincoln's White House: The People's House in Wartime* (Rowman & Littlefield, 2017), which won the Lincoln Prize and the Abraham Lincoln Institute's Annual Book Award. A former Naval reservist, Conroy served on Capitol Hill in Washington, D.C., as a House and Senate aide in the 1970s and early 1980s, and earned his JD degree from the Georgetown University Law Center in 1982. He and his wife, Lynn, are the parents of two accomplished grown children, the parents-in-law of an NBC News journalist, and the grandparents of two young boys and a girl.

Conroy is an elected fellow of the Massachusetts Historical Society and a member of the Boston Bar Association. He lives in Hingham, Massachusetts, on Boston's South Shore, where he serves as a member of the Hingham Historical Commission, has coached youth baseball and basketball teams, and has chaired the Town's Advisory Committee, which advises the Hingham Town Meeting, an exercise in direct democracy through which the Town has governed itself since 1635.

Learn more about the author at his website, www.jamesbconroy.com.